"Totus Tuus"

Preparation for Total Consecration to Jesus through Mary for Families™
All done in union with St. Joseph

according to St. Louis de Montfort,
with daily meditations by Pope John Paul II

Compiled and partially written by Jerome F. Coniker, Co-founder with his wife Gwen of the Apostolate for Family Consecration, Consultor of the Pontifical Council for the Family, and Director of the Bloomingdale branch of the St. Louis de Montfort Association of Mary, Queen of All Hearts

APOSTOLATE FOR FAMILY CONSECRATION®
Founded in 1975

Resource #323-115, Second Edition

*For the daily schedule of readings,
see pages 10-13.*

Dedicated to my beloved wife,
Gwen Cecelia Coniker
(September 27, 1939 – June 15, 2002)

Wife, mother of 13, grandmother of 64 and counting,
co-foundress of the Apostolate for Family
Consecration, Catholic Familyland, and
Familyland Television Network.

She truly gave her life for family consecration
to Jesus, through Mary, in union with St. Joseph,
in the spirit of our beloved Holy Father,
Pope John Paul II, whom she loved so dearly.

(For more information about Gwen, see Appendix D.)

Apostolate For
FAMILY
Consecration®

Founded in 1975

Families helping families get to Heaven through:

- Familyland® Television Network
- International Familyland® Centers
- Lay Evangelization Teams™
- Consecration in Truth® multimedia programs
  for families, parishes and schools

Nihil Obstat: Msgr. Josefino Ramirez
　　　　　　　Vicar General

Imprimatur: His Excellency Gaudencio B. Rosales, D.D.
　　　　　　　Archbishop of Manila
　　　　　　　January 10, 2006

© 2005, 2006 Apostolate for Family Consecration®, Inc.
3375 County Road 36, Bloomingdale, OH 43910-7903 USA
(740) 765-5500   Fax: (740) 765-5561   usa@familyland.org
www.familyland.org

In the Philippines: St. Joseph Center, P.O. Box 0026, Las Piñas City
(632) 871-4440   Fax: (632) 875-3506   asia@familyland.org

Published 2005. Second Edition 2006. Second Printing.
Printed in the United States of America and the Philippines.

Unless otherwise indicated, Scripture quotations are from the Revised Standard Version of the Bible, © 1946, 1952, 1971 by the Division of Christian Education of the National Council of the Churches of Christ in the USA. Used by permission.

Excerpts from papal documents and pictures of Pope John Paul II printed with permission of L'Osservatore Romano. Illustrations by Charles Jaskiewicz and taken from *The Apostolate's Family Catechism*, ©1993, 1994, 2005 Apostolate for Family Consecration, Inc. Picture on page 162 printed with permission of the Apostleship of Prayer. *Preparation for Total Consecration* excerpts ©1993, *True Devotion to Mary* adapted by Eddie Doherty, ©1994, *Secret of Mary* by St. Louis de Montfort, and *Catechism on True Devotion to Mary* by Rev. Ralph Beiting printed by permission of Montfort Publications, Bay Shore, New York. (Emphasis added by publisher).

Library of Congress Control Number: 2006920056
ISBN 13: 978-0-932406-59-0
ISBN 10: 0-932406-59-9

Totus Tuus

Mater Ecclesiae

The front cover is a mosaic on the outside facade of St. Peter's Basilica in Vatican City. It is the only image of our Blessed Mother on the outside of the Basilica and was commissioned personally by Pope John Paul II.

This mosaic publicly proclaims Pope John Paul II's spirituality, which is also depicted on his coat of arms — *Totus Tuus Mater Ecclesiae* (Totally Yours, Mother of the Church).

At night the image is lit up, along with the great dome. While facing St. Peter's, this picture is on the right side of the second level above the narrow section of the Master of Papal Protocol's office.

One picture says a thousand words. This picture is certainly John Paul's plea to the world to come to Jesus in the most perfect way, the way He chose to come to us, and that is through His Most Immaculate Mother.

The Apostolate for Family Consecration was founded in 1975 by Jerry and Gwen Coniker. The Conikers were one of twenty couples in the world appointed as members of the Pope's Pontifical Council for the Family. Shortly after Gwen's death on June 15, 2002, Jerry was appointed by Pope John Paul II to be one of six consultors for the above council. See Appendix B for more information about the vision and mission outreach ministries of the Apostolate for Family Consecration, which includes Catholic Familyland, International St. Joseph Media and Training Centers, Lay Ecclesial Teams of volunteers, Familyland Television Network, Consecration in Truth Catechetics (which unites the family with the parish), Be Not Afraid Family Hours, Peace of Heart Forums (which provide continuous adult formation), and podcasting. All these outreach ministries utilize the vast video library of over 15,000 programs that feature more than 500 leading authorities of the Faith. Roman Curia Cardinal Francis Arinze has produced over 1800 of these programs over a nineteen year period.

Please note: Through this meditation book, we pray for all those who are doing apostolic work to draw others closer to the Lord (referred to as "members of the apostolate" in our prayers). We also pray for everyone who participates in any of our devotional or formation programs. We particularly ask you to pray for the Holy Souls of your loved ones and others in Purgatory, since those of us in the Church Militant on earth are the only ones who can help them through our indulgences. (See #9, #45a and #45b in Appendix A.)

Jerry and Gwen Coniker greeting the Holy Father during the Jubilee of Families in 2000. The Conikers, along with their children and grandchildren, were invited to be one of the presenting families during this celebration. The theme was "Children: Springtime of Hope for Family and Society."

Catholic Familyland, U.S.A.
950 acres set apart for families

International Media and Training Centers of the Apostolate for Family Consecration:

United States and Canada
Catholic Familyland, 3375 County Road 36
Bloomingdale, OH 43910
(740) 765-5500 or 1-800-77-FAMILY   Fax: (740) 765-5561
usa@familyland.org

Asia
St. Joseph Media and Training Center
P.O. Box 0026, Las Piñas City, PHILIPPINES
(632) 871-4440 Fax: (632) 875-3506 asia@familyland.org

Latin America
St. Joseph Media and Training Center
Municipio de Atlautla, Estado de Mexico, C.P. 56970, MEXICO
52-59-7976-7093 Fax: 52-59-7976-3316 latinoamerica@familyland.org

Africa
St. Joseph Media and Training Center
Archbishop's House, Holy Trinity Cathedral
Mission Road, Box 411, Onitsha, Anambra State NIGERIA
234-46-413292 Fax: 234-46-413913 africa@familyland.org

Europe
www.familylandeurope.com   europe@familyland.org

www.familyland.org

Queen
of all hearts

MONTFORT MISSIONARIES

Jerome F. Coniker, President
Apostolate for Family Consecration
Bloomingdale, OH 43910 USA

June 24, 2005

Dear Jerry,

We just want to thank you for compiling and editing your new book entitled *"Preparation for Total Consecration to Jesus through Mary for Families" according to St. Louis De Montfort with meditations by Pope John Paul II.*

This 33-day preparation resource with the Act of Consecration made on the 34th day is excellent and follows the traditions of St. Louis De Montfort's Consecration. Pope John Paul II had made De Montfort's consecration himself and this consecration was reflected in his motto "Totus Tuus".

Your Scripture selections, along with examination of conscience exercises and the different prayers for each day are a beautiful way to systematically present to families your family consecration spirituality and the basic teachings of our faith.

I agree that the idea of extending another 6 days onto the program utilizing two presentations of Cardinal Arinze's on DVD entitled "Living Your Consecration" is an excellent way to reinforce the message in a practical way for family life.

I know that Cardinal Luigi Ciappi helped you develop your consecration summary prayer: "All for the Sacred and Eucharistic Heart of Jesus, all through the Sorrowful and Immaculate Heart of Mary, all in union with St. Joseph." This "All for" prayer is truly a prayer of the total giving of oneself to Jesus through Mary in union with St. Joseph. Cardinal Ciappi's support of the Family Apostolate and his willingness to be your theological advisor while he was still the papal theologian was a great blessing in your founding years.

I am so pleased that you gave a copy of this book to His Holiness Pope John Paul II last November at the Pontifical Council for the Family meeting with him. Also, I am happy to learn that you gave a copy to Cardinal Ratzinger (now Pope Benedict XVI) when you were awarded the privilege of attending his private Mass last November. It was indeed providential that your paths crossed in this way prior to his being elected the new Pontiff of the Roman Catholic Church.

May God and His heavenly mother continue to bless your efforts to promote Total Consecration for families throughout the world. Yours in the Hearts of Jesus and Mary,

Fr. Roger Charest

Fr. Roger Charest, De Montfort Fathers

Optional Resources to Enhance your Preparation for Total Consecration

This *Preparation for Total Consecration* book can be used in conjunction with the resources listed below. These presentations may be viewed by yourself or with others.

40-Day Preparation for Total Consecration on DVD or CD (Resource #155-186DK or CK, 235 minutes)

These eight presentations, featuring Francis Cardinal Arinze, Fr. Frederick Miller, and Montfort Father Roger Charest, will guide you in your spiritual journey of entrusting your life to Jesus through Mary, as Pope John Paul II did.

See page 503 in Appendix B for more information. You may also download these presentations for free at www.familyland.org; click on "Family Consecration" or "Protect your Family."

Recommended viewing schedule:

Week 1: "The Key To Understanding the Marian Consecration of St. Louis de Montfort" with Fr. Miller (38 min.)

Week 2: "Spirit of the World" with Fr. Miller (22 min.), and "Merit, Grace and the Slavery of Love" with Fr. Charest (24 min.)

Week 3: "Knowledge of Self" with Fr. Miller (24 min.)

Week 4: "Knowledge of Mary" with Fr. Miller (25 min.)

Week 5: "Knowledge of Jesus and the Total Consecration Prayer" with Fr. Miller (27 min.)

Week 6: "Reparation, Consecration and Mission" with Cardinal Arinze (37 min.), and "Some Responsibilities of the Lay Faithful in the Present Moment" with Cardinal Arinze (47 min.)

See Appendix B for more resources.

CONTENTS

*All for the Sacred and Eucharistic Heart of Jesus,
all through the Sorrowful and Immaculate Heart of Mary,
all in union with St. Joseph.*

*This Total Consecration can bring down the Eucharistic
graces of God's Merciful Love and peace, which was
promised at Fatima by Our Lady. This "era of peace"
will be granted to the world when enough people are
consecrated to Jesus through her Immaculate Heart
and are consecrated in the Truth (John 17).*

Introduction

1.   You are about to enter upon the most powerful spiritual adventure for you and your family in your pilgrimage of faith on earth. That adventure is following Pope John Paul II on the journey to union with God through Total Consecration to Jesus through Mary, in union with St. Joseph.

Early in his life, Pope John Paul II made his Total Consecration to Jesus through Mary according to the formula of St. Louis de Montfort (*Totus tuus*) . This union with Jesus through His Mother had been the guiding force for his priesthood, episcopate and papacy, which gave him the strength and wisdom to have led the universal Church into the Third Christian Millennium of hope. Pope John Paul II is an inspiration to us all at this crossroads in history, and we believe his teachings will go on until the end of time.

Two dimensions of consecration

2.   The first dimension of Pope John Paul's consecration is *Totus Tuus* (translated "Totally Yours" from Latin), giving everything to Jesus through Mary. Cardinal Mario Luigi Ciappi, the Pope's former teacher and personal theologian, wrote to me on August 24, 1989:

> *"... when we give all our merits to Mary, she multiplies them by her own incalculable merits. This puts into motion positive spiritual forces to repair the damage due to sin and can significantly change the course of history, if enough make this commitment."* (Cf. *Catechism of the Catholic Church*, par. 1475 and 1477.)

The second dimension of Pope John Paul's consecration is *Consecrate them in Truth*. It is summarized in the Gospel of John, Chapter 17, when Our Lord said:*

> *"Father...eternal life is this: to know you... I have glorified you on earth and finished the work that you gave*

---

*Jerusalem Bible, ©1966 by Darton Longman & Todd, Ltd., and Doubleday and Co., Inc., used by permission.

me to do... I am not asking you to remove them from the world but to protect them from the evil one... Consecrate them in the truth; your word is truth... that they may be one as we are one... that the love with which you loved me may be in them and so that I may be in them."

The importance of consecration

3. Consecration is a way of life that will protect you and your family in these perilous times. It will help you become totally docile to Mary, who is one spirit with her Son, becoming her "consecrated slave," or as we say in the Apostolate for Family Consecration, her "consecrated spiritual child," whom she molds into the image and likeness of her Son.

Pope John Paul II explains this devotion in his book *Crossing the Threshold of Hope:*

"*Totus Tuus.* This phrase is not only an expression of piety, or simply an expression of devotion. It is more. During the Second World War, while I was employed as a factory worker, I came to be attracted to Marian devotion. At first, it had seemed to me that I should distance myself a bit from the Marian devotion of my childhood, in order to focus more on Christ.

"Thanks to Saint Louis of Montfort, I came to understand that *true devotion to the Mother of God is actually Christocentric, indeed, it is very profoundly rooted in the Mystery of the Blessed Trinity,* and the mysteries of the Incarnation and Redemption.

"And so, I rediscovered Marian piety, this time with a deeper understanding. This mature form of devotion to the Mother of God has stayed with me over the years, bearing fruit in the encyclicals *Redemptoris Mater* and *Mulieris Dignitatem.*"

Pope John Paul II went on to say:

"In regard to Marian devotion, each of us must understand that such devotion not only addresses a need of the heart, a sentimental inclination, but that it also corresponds to the objective truth about the Mother of God. Mary is the new Eve, placed by God in close relation to Christ, the new Adam, beginning with the Annunciation, through the night of His birth in Bethlehem, through the wedding feast at Cana of Galilee, through the Cross at Calvary, and up to the gift of the Holy Spirit at Pentecost. The Mother of Christ the Redeemer is the Mother of the Church."

The Apostolate for Family Consecration was founded to help individuals, families, parishes and members of various Church movements to make this consecration and to assist them in faithfully living it. This is done through continuous formation in the truth, using our vast audio and video resources (see Appendix B) that are available through our Familyland Television Network, podcasts, and website (go to the "Family Consecration" section of www.familyland.org). These resources can help all charisms achieve their destinies.

This book has been prepared to make it easy for you and your family to make your Total Consecration to Jesus through Mary, *Totus Tuus*, while being consecrated in Truth. The excerpts from Pope John Paul II's major documents present both dimensions of this consecration (*Totus Tuus* and "Consecrate them in Truth").

Pope John Paul II was the prophet for our times and for the "Fatima Formula for Divine Mercy"—which we believe is the era of peace (civilization of love) that Our Lady promised at Fatima. We are confident that this era of peace will be granted once enough people make and sacrificially live this consecration.

It is important to note that Pope John Paul II died at 9:30 p.m. on April 3, 2005, on First Saturday, which is a Fatima devotion day that the Pope observed throughout his pontificate. Since the Holy Father passed away on Saturday night, the Church was liturgically celebrating Divine Mercy Sunday—which is the first Sunday after Easter and which the Holy Father declared as a world-wide feast in 2000, when he canonized St. Faustina.

It is also important to note that on April 28, 2005, the feast of St. Louis de Montfort, the Vicar General of Rome and Cardinal Martins, the Prefect for the Congregation for the Causes of the Saints, asked Pope Benedict XVI to open the Pope's cause for beatification and to waive the usual five-year moratorium. Pope Benedict XVI approved this recommendation and made it public on May 13, 2005, the feast day of Our Lady of Fatima. In 1981, Pope John Paul II had been shot and miraculously saved on this same feast day.

Pope John Paul II agreed with Andre Malraux when he said that "the twenty-first century would be the century of religion or it would not be at all" (*Crossing the Threshold of Hope*, p. 229). It is up to us, and this consecration is the key to the "threshold of hope".

Preparation for Total Consecration

4.   This preparation for Total Consecration book is based on St. Louis de Montfort's 33-day formula. This formula consists of twelve Preliminary Days, in which the soul endeavors to rid itself of the "spirit of the world" (insofar as this spirit opposes the Spirit of Jesus Christ), followed by three weeks of prayer and meditation during which time the soul strives to acquire a better knowledge of self (first week), of Mary

(second week), and of Jesus Christ (third week). On the 34th day, the Act of Total Consecration is made, followed by six additional days of prayer and reflection on living that consecration in union with St. Joseph—for a total of 40 days of prayer.

Why 40 Days?

5.   In the Bible and in the Tradition of the Church, "40 days" has a symbolic and spiritual meaning, for example:

•   There were 40 days and nights of flooding in Noah's time (cf. Gen 7:4).

•   Moses fasted for 40 days and nights before receiving the Ten Commandments, on two different occasions (cf. Exodus 24:18 and 34:28).

•   When Elijah flees from the fury of Queen Jezebel, he walks for 40 days and nights on the strength given him by two hearth cakes and two jugs of water, which had been given to him by an angel (cf. 1 Kings 19:8).

•   Jonah warns the people of Nineveh that God will destroy their city in 40 days, during which time the people repented and begged God's mercy by prayer and fasting (cf. Jonah 3:4).

•   Jesus fasts for 40 days and nights in the desert before beginning His public ministry (cf. Matthew 4:2).

•   There are 40 days of Lent, during which time we repent of and make reparation for our sins by self-denial, prayer and fasting.

•   Many parishes have special Forty Hours Eucharistic devotions some time during the year.

•   Jesus appears to His Apostles and disciples for 40 days after His Resurrection and before His Ascension into Heaven (cf. Acts 1:3).

Because of the spiritual symbolism of 40 days, we felt the inspiration to extend the traditional 33-day

6

preparation for Total Consecration to include six additional days after the Consecration Day (the 34th Day) in order to deepen our understanding of living out our Total Consecration in our daily lives. As former papal theologian Cardinal Ciappi said, "Consecration is not just a prayer or a devotion but a commitment to a way of life which must be nourished through continuous formation in the eternal truths of our Faith."

How to use this book*

6. It is recommended that you block out a period of time each day to read and prayerfully reflect on the meditations selected for the particular day of the preparation period. Pray and talk to God, His Mother, and St. Joseph about what you are reading. Invite the Holy Spirit to guide you, so that you don't rush through the readings and prayers.

The objective is not necessarily to completely read all the meditations for each day, but to set aside some time every day for reflective reading of the daily meditations. You can always go back to them later after you have completed your consecration. In fact, you are encouraged to regularly reflect on these readings even after you have made your consecration.

Try not to become scrupulous; if you aren't able to finish the daily readings on some of the days, it doesn't mean that you cannot make the consecration or that you need to start over again. Just keep proceeding and do your best; Our Lady understands.

A chart has been provided with various preparation schedules from which to choose so that your Consecration Day (34th day) will fall on a special feast day of Our Lord, Our Lady or St. Louis de Montfort.

---

* You may also want to use the corresponding programs on DVD and CD that feature Cardinal Francis Arinze, Fr. Frederick Miller, and de Montfort Father Roger Charest. See page ix.

Select one of the following dates on which to begin your preparation:

	Begin	Consecration Day (34th Day)
I.	Feb. 20	The Annunciation, March 25*
II.	Mar. 26	St. Louis de Montfort's feast day, Apr. 28
III.	Apr. 10	Our Lady of Fatima, May 13
IV.	Apr. 28	The Visitation, May 31
V.	July 13	The Assumption, August 15
VI.	July 20	Queenship of Mary, August 22
VII.	Aug. 6	Birthday of Our Lady, September 8
VIII.	Aug. 13	Our Lady of Sorrows, September 15
IX.	Sept. 4	Our Lady of the Rosary, October 7
X.	Nov. 5	Immaculate Conception, December 8
XI.	Nov. 29	Mary, Mother of God, January 1
XII.	Dec. 31	Presentation of the Child Jesus, Feb. 2
XIII.	Jan. 9	Our Lady of Lourdes, Feb. 11
XIV.	Ash Wed.	Make your consecration on the 34th day of Lent and renew on Good Friday

Use the **"Daily Reading Schedule" on pages 10–13** to keep track of your daily readings. For example, if you choose to begin your preparation on July 13, use the column marked "V" on the "Reading Schedule", and your Consecration Day (34th day) would fall on the feast of the Assumption (August 15).

Protect your family

7. We hope that you will adopt the daily family Rosary as a powerful way to sanctify and protect your family.

We suggest that you share the readings in this

---

* Note: **It is recommended that you renew your consecration every year** on March 25, the Solemnity of the Annunciation and the Incarnation of Jesus, which is the primary feast day for True Devotion to Mary. You would then **begin your preparation on February 20**, the Memorial of Blesseds Jacinta and Francisco, two of the seers of Our Lady of Fatima, and end your 40 days of prayer and meditation on March 31.

book with your entire family, possibly at dinner time. Just as a child is baptized and brought into the Church, so children can be consecrated and brought into this powerful relationship of Total Consecration (also see #50b.1 in Appendix A for a prayer to consecrate children at Baptism). As parents, it is our obligation to help our children develop a relationship with God. Children can make the consecration also. It will be up to them to make faith-filled choices to continue living this Total Consecration as they grow older.

God will never interfere with our free will. He will never force us to love Him. As parents, we want to give everything we can to our children so that they, in turn, can make the right decisions. So we encourage you to enter into this consecration as a family.

Some Lay Ecclesial Teams (see pages 534–537) and their families gather together to read and reflect on each day's meditation, prayer and spiritual exercise. Prayer groups and other associations or movements may do this as well. Our website also has the daily readings on audio.

You may be interested in using our other multimedia formation and devotional materials that will further consecrate your family in the truth and draw you more deeply into your relationship with Our Lord. These resources are explained in Appendix B, and on our website at www.familyland.org, under the "Family Consecration" ["Protect Your Family"] section. Many of the resources may be downloaded or viewed on-line. We particularly recommend *The Apostolate's Family Catechism*, which is one of the most faith and love-filled resources developed for families.

How to consecrate your entire family

8. When praying the Rosary together as a family, you may choose to read aloud small portions of the reflections in this book before each decade. You could alternate by day between reading the reflection by Pope John Paul II and the reflection by St. Louis de Montfort. At the end of the Rosary, you could then

pray one of the recommended prayers or do one of the spiritual exercises for that particular day. Be careful, though, not to let it go on too long or you can "stretch" your children too far.

This technique is a good way for your entire family to prepare to make the consecration. If you think it is too much for your younger children, they would not need to participate in all of the reflections or say all of the prayers in order to make their consecration.

Our Vision and Mission

Daily Reading Schedule

Part 1 : Spirit of the world (12 Preliminary Days)

DAY	I	II	III	IV	V	VI	VII	VIII	IX	X	XI	XII	XIII	XIV
							SCHEDULE CHOICES							
1st	Feb. 20	Mar. 26	Apr. 10	Apr. 28	July 13	July 20	Aug. 6	Aug. 13	Sept. 4	Nov. 5	Nov. 29	Dec. 31	Jan. 9	Ash Wed.
2nd	Feb. 21	Mar. 27	Apr. 11	Apr. 29	July 14	July 21	Aug. 7	Aug. 14	Sept. 5	Nov. 6	Nov. 30	Jan. 1	Jan. 10	Thurs.
3rd	Feb. 22	Mar. 28	Apr. 12	Apr. 30	July 15	July 22	Aug. 8	Aug. 15	Sept. 6	Nov. 7	Dec. 1	Jan. 2	Jan. 11	Friday
4th	Feb. 23	Mar. 29	Apr. 13	May 1	July 16	July 23	Aug. 9	Aug. 16	Sept. 7	Nov. 8	Dec. 2	Jan. 3	Jan. 12	Saturday
5th	Feb. 24	Mar. 30	Apr. 14	May 2	july 17	July 24	Aug. 10	Aug. 17	Sept. 8	Nov. 9	Dec. 3	Jan. 4	Jan. 13	1st Sun.
6th	Feb. 25	Mar. 31	Apr. 15	May 3	July 18	July 25	Aug. 11	Aug. 18	Sept. 9	Nov. 10	Dec. 4	Jan. 5	Jan. 14	1st Mon.
7th	Feb. 26	Apr. 1	Apr. 16	May 4	July 19	July 26	Aug. 12	Aug. 19	Sept. 10	Nov. 11	Dec. 5	Jan. 6	Jan. 15	1st Tues.
8th	Feb. 27	Apr. 2	Apr. 17	May 5	July 20	July 27	Aug. 13	Aug. 20	Sept. 11	Nov. 12	Dec. 6	Jan. 7	Jan. 16	1st Wed.
9th	Feb. 28	Apr. 3	Apr. 18	May 6	July 21	July 28	Aug. 14	Aug. 21	Sept. 12	Nov. 13	Dec. 7	Jan. 8	Jan. 17	1st Thurs.
10th	Mar. 1	Apr. 4	Apr. 19	May 7	July 22	July 29	Aug. 15	Aug. 22	Sept. 13	Nov. 14	Dec. 8	Jan. 9	Jan. 18	1st Fri.
11th	Mar. 2	Apr. 5	Apr. 20	May 8	July 23	July 30	Aug. 16	Aug. 23	Sept. 14	Nov. 15	Dec. 9	Jan. 10	Jan. 19	1st Sat.
12th	Mar. 3	Apr. 6	Apr. 21	May 9	July 24	July 31	Aug. 17	Aug. 24	Sept. 15	Nov. 16	Dec. 10	Jan. 11	Jan. 20	2nd Sun.

Note: For the **optional** Brown Scapular and Miraculous Medal ceremonies for those who have not been enrolled, see #26 and #41c in Appendix A. We recommend that the conferral of the Brown Scapular of Our Lady of Mount Carmel take place on the 34th day and the conferral of the Miraculous Medal on the 40th day. If the celebrant is not available on one of these days, the ceremonies may be combined on the same day or may be scheduled at another time. You would need to obtain ahead of time Brown Scapulars and Miraculous Medals on a chain or ribbon for each participant. See page 515 for Miraculous Medal and Brown Scapular resources.

Part 2 : Knowledge of Self (Days 13–19)

SCHEDULE CHOICES

DAY	I	II	III	IV	V	VI	VII	VIII	IX	X	XI	XII	XIII	XIV
13th	Mar. 4	Apr. 7	Apr. 22	May 10	July 25	Aug. 1	Aug. 18	Aug. 25	Sept. 16	Nov. 17	Dec. 11	Jan. 12	Jan. 21	2nd Mon.
14th	Mar. 5	Apr. 8	Apr. 23	May 11	July 26	Aug. 2	Aug. 19	Aug. 26	Sept. 17	Nov. 18	Dec. 12	Jan. 13	Jan. 22	2nd Tues.
15th	Mar. 6	Apr. 9	Apr. 24	May 12	July 27	Aug. 3	Aug. 20	Aug. 27	Sept. 18	Nov. 19	Dec. 13	Jan. 14	Jan. 23	2nd Wed.
16th	Mar. 7	Apr. 10	Apr. 25	May 13	July 28	Aug. 4	Aug. 21	Aug. 28	Sept. 19	Nov. 20	Dec. 14	Jan. 15	Jan. 24	2nd Thurs
17th	Mar. 8	Apr. 11	Apr. 26	May 14	July 29	Aug. 5	Aug. 22	Aug. 29	Sept. 20	Nov. 21	Dec. 15	Jan. 16	Jan. 25	2nd Fri.
18th	Mar. 9	Apr. 12	Apr. 27	May 15	July 30	Aug. 6	Aug. 23	Aug. 30	Sept. 21	Nov. 22	Dec. 16	Jan. 17	Jan. 26	2nd Sat.
19th	Mar. 10	Apr. 13	Apr. 28	May 16	July 31	Aug. 7	Aug. 24	Aug. 31	Sept. 22	Nov. 23	Dec. 17	Jan. 18	Jan. 27	3rd Sun.

Part 3 : Knowledge of Our Lady (Days 20–26)

SCHEDULE CHOICES

DAY	I	II	III	IV	V	VI	VII	VIII	IX	X	XI	XII	XIII	XIV
20th	Mar. 11	Apr. 14	Apr. 29	May 17	Aug. 1	Aug. 8	Aug. 25	Sept. 1	Sept. 23	Nov. 24	Dec. 18	Jan. 19	Jan. 28	3rd Mon.
21st	Mar. 12	Apr. 15	Apr. 30	May 18	Aug. 2	Aug. 9	Aug. 26	Sept. 2	Sept. 24	Nov. 25	Dec. 19	Jan. 20	Jan. 29	3rd Tues.
22nd	Mar. 13	Apr. 16	May 1	May 19	Aug. 3	Aug. 10	Aug. 27	Sept. 3	Sept. 25	Nov. 26	Dec. 20	Jan. 21	Jan. 30	3rd Wed.
23rd	Mar. 14	Apr. 17	May 2	May 20	Aug. 4	Aug. 11	Aug. 28	Sept. 4	Sept. 26	Nov. 27	Dec. 21	Jan. 22	Jan. 31	3rd Thurs
24th	Mar. 15	Apr. 18	May 3	May 21	Aug. 5	Aug. 12	Aug. 29	Sept. 5	Sept. 27	Nov. 28	Dec. 22	Jan. 23	Feb. 1	3rd Fri.
25th	Mar. 16	Apr. 19	May 4	May 22	Aug. 6	Aug. 13	Aug. 30	Sept. 6	Sept. 28	Nov. 29	Dec. 23	Jan. 24	Feb. 2	3rd Sat.
26th	Mar. 17	Apr. 20	May 5	May 23	Aug. 7	Aug. 14	Aug. 31	Sept. 7	Sept. 29	Nov. 30	Dec. 24	Jan. 25	Feb. 3	4th Sun.

Part 4 : Knowledge of Jesus Christ (Days 27–33)

DAY	I	II	III	IV	V	VI	VII	VIII	IX	X	XI	XII	XIII	XIV
						SCHEDULE CHOICES								
27th	Mar. 18	Apr. 21	May 6	May 24	Aug. 8	Aug. 15	Sept. 1	Sept. 8	Sept. 30	Dec. 1	Dec. 25	Jan. 26	Feb. 4	4th Mon.
28th	Mar. 19	Apr. 22	May 7	May 25	Aug. 9	Aug. 16	Sept. 2	Sept. 9	Oct. 1	Dec. 2	Dec. 26	Jan. 27	Feb. 5	4th Tues.
29th	Mar. 20	Apr. 23	May 8	May 26	Aug. 10	Aug. 17	Sept. 3	Sept. 10	Oct. 2	Dec. 3	Dec. 27	Jan. 28	Feb. 6	4th Wed.
30th	Mar. 21	Apr. 24	May 9	May 27	Aug. 11	Aug. 18	Sept. 4	Sept. 11	Oct. 3	Dec. 4	Dec. 28	Jan. 29	Feb. 7	4th Thurs
31st	Mar. 22	Apr. 25	May 10	May 28	Aug. 12	Aug. 19	Sept. 5	Sept. 12	Oct. 4	Dec. 5	Dec. 29	Jan. 30	Feb. 8	4th Fri.
32nd	Mar. 23	Apr. 26	May 11	May 29	Aug. 13	Aug. 20	Sept. 6	Sept. 13	Oct. 5	Dec. 6	Dec. 30	Jan. 31	Feb. 9	4th Sat.
33rd	Mar. 24	Apr. 27	May 12	May 30	Aug. 14	Aug. 21	Sept. 7	Sept. 14	Oct. 6	Dec. 7	Dec. 31	Feb. 1	Feb. 10	5th Sun.

Part 5: Consecration Day (Day 34)

DAY	I	II	III	IV	V	VI	VII	VIII	IX	X	XI	XII	XIII	XIV
						SCHEDULE CHOICES								
34th	Mar. 25	Apr. 28	May 13	May 31	Aug. 15	Aug. 22	Sept. 8	Sept. 15	Oct. 7	Dec. 8	Jan. 1	Feb. 2	Feb. 11	5th Mon.*

Follow the instructions on Day 34 (page 163) for making your consecration, joining the St. Louis de Montfort's Association of Mary, Queen of All Hearts, and becoming a Holy Family Cooperator.

* If you are following Schedule XIII (Lenten Season), make your consecration on Day 34 as explained on page 163. Since your consecration falls on the 34th day of Lent, which is not a feast day, renew your consecration on Good Friday by praying prayer #49b on page 332. Thus, you will be renewing your consecration to Jesus with and through Mary at the foot of the Cross.

Part 6: Reparation and Consecration (Days 35–37)

DAY						SCHEDULE CHOICES								
	I	II	III	IV	V	VI	VII	VIII	IX	X	XI	XII	XIII	XIV
35th	Mar. 26	Apr. 29	May 14	June 1	Aug. 16	Aug. 23	Sept. 9	Sept. 16	Oct. 8	Dec. 9	Jan. 2	Feb. 3	Feb. 12	5th Tues.
36th	Mar. 27	Apr. 30	May 15	June 2	Aug. 17	Aug. 24	Sept. 10	Sept. 17	Oct. 9	Dec. 10	Jan. 3	Feb. 4	Feb. 13	5th Wed.
37th	Mar. 28	May 1	May 16	June 3	Aug. 18	Aug. 25	Sept. 11	Sept. 18	Oct. 10	Dec. 11	Jan. 4	Feb. 5	Feb. 14	5th Thurs

Part 7: The Responsibility of the Present Moment (Days 38–40)

DAY						SCHEDULE CHOICES								
	I	II	III	IV	V	VI	VII	VIII	IX	X	XI	XII	XIII	XIV
38th	Mar. 29	May 2	May 17	June 4	Aug. 19	Aug. 26	Sept. 12	Sept. 19	Oct. 11	Dec. 12	Jan. 5	Feb. 6	Feb. 15	5th Fri.
39th	Mar. 30	May 3	May 18	June 5	Aug. 20	Aug. 27	Sept. 13	Sept. 20	Oct. 12	Dec. 13	Jan. 6	Feb. 7	Feb. 16	5th Sat.
40th	Mar. 31	May 4	May 19	June 6	Aug. 21	Aug. 28	Sept. 14	Sept. 21	Oct. 13	Dec. 14	Jan. 7	Feb. 8	Feb. 17	Palm Sun.

Also see #26 and #41c in Appendix A for optional ceremonies for the Brown Scapular and Miraculous Medal. Please note that your participation in the Brown Scapular and Miraculous Medal enrollment ceremonies and watching the videos is optional and would not have to be done to make your Act of Total Consecration. These sacramentals assist you in understanding and living your consecration but are not essential.

Please refer to pages 501–533 for information on multimedia resources that are available to aid your continuous formation in the Truth.

Part 1: Spirit of the World
(Twelve Preliminary Days)

Ask the Holy Spirit for the grace to break with every-thing that displeases God and to become a person for others in imitation of the Holy Family.

As disciples of Christ we must struggle against the world, the flesh and the devil. The world has a very strong attraction. Our Lord tells us in Matthew 6:19-21:

"Do not lay up for yourselves treasures on earth, where moth and rust consume and where thieves break in and steal, but lay up for yourselves treasures in heaven, where neither moth nor rust consumes and where thieves do not break in and steal. For where your treasure is, there will your heart be also."

You can easily test yourself to see where your heart is by examining your small talk and conversations—are they constantly going to money, sports, or other things that are not drawing you into God's presence?

There is nothing wrong with money, sports, or the appreciation of nice things and the beauty of the world, but if these possess us so that we do not develop an interior life and a relationship with God, then they are working against us.

Our Lord goes on to say in Matthew 6:31-34:

"Therefore do not be anxious, saying, 'What shall we eat?' or 'What shall we drink?' or 'What shall we wear?' For the Gentiles seek all these things; and your heavenly Father knows that you need them all. But seek first his kingdom and his righteousness, and all these things shall be yours as well. Therefore do not be anxious about tomorrow, for tomorrow will be anxious for itself. Let the day's own trouble be sufficient for the day."

This is why we encourage people to live each moment for the Lord. When you wake up in the morning, God has a plan for you, and the devil also has distractions planned for your day. Will you walk with the Lord in His Divine Providence and be alert to His promptings so that you

can be in the world but not of the world? (cf. John 8:23-24,
John 15:18-19, John 17:6-26) Will your "eyes of faith" be
open as you walk through the world so that you might
perceive God's gentle signs telling you what to do, what
to say, and how to act? This is called living the "grace and
responsibility of the present moment."

Morning Offering:
"Lord, how much You love me and suffered for me!
Please help me today to love until it hurts. All for!"

Before beginning a new activity, such as answering the
phone, answering the door, starting a new project, or
responding to a child or someone who is speaking to you,
simply say to yourself, "All for." By this is meant: "Lord,
give me the grace to discern and to do Your Will in each
present moment, to do Your will now...All for the Sacred
and Eucharistic Heart of Jesus, all through the Sorrowful
and Immaculate Heart of Mary, all in union with St.
Joseph. This represents the practical application of living
the spirituality of Total Consecration.

The work we carry out is not to be "of the world," but
is meant to transform the world into God's Kingdom
upon earth (cf. John 17). Therefore, we need to constantly
combat the strong temptations that continually seduce us
with the capital sins of greed, lust, laziness, envy, anger,
gluttony and pride, along with our tendency to be totally
immersed in material things rather than the things of
God.

First Day
Spirit of the World

Come Holy Spirit, please awaken us to all you have in mind for us during these days of renewal and help us to let go of all sin, of the "spirit of the world," and of all else that leads to sin so that we can truly live this Total Consecration to Jesus through Mary in union with St. Joseph.

Reconciliatio et Paenitentia (Reconciliation and Penance), by Pope John Paul II

15. In the description of the "first sin," the rupture with Yahweh simultaneously breaks the bond of friendship that had united the human family. Thus the subsequent pages of Genesis show us the man and the woman as it were pointing an accusing finger at each other. Later we have the brother hating his brother and finally taking his life.

According to the Babel story, the result of sin is the shattering of the human family, already begun with the first sin and now reaching its most extreme form on the social level.

No one wishing to investigate the mystery of sin can ignore this link between cause and effect. As a rupture with God, sin is an act of disobedience by a creature who rejects, at least implicitly, the very one from whom he came and who sustains him in life. It is therefore a suicidal act. Since by sinning man refuses to submit to God, his internal balance is also destroyed and it is precisely within himself that contradictions and conflicts arise.

Wounded in this way, man almost inevitably causes damage to the fabric of his relationship with others and with the created world. This is an objective law and an objective reality, verified in so many ways in the human psyche and in the spiritual life as well as in society, where it is easy to see the signs and effects of internal disorder.

The mystery of sin is composed of this twofold wound which the sinner opens in himself and in his relationship with his neighbor. Therefore one can speak of personal and social sin: From one point of view, every sin is personal; from another point of view, every sin is social insofar as and because it also has social repercussions.

True Devotion to Mary
by St. Louis de Montfort, Chapter I

Through the Immaculate Virgin Mary, Jesus Christ came into the world. Through her He will reign over the world.

Mary lived in obscurity during most of her life. Her humility was so great that she desired to hide, not only from all other creatures, but even from herself, so that only God should know her. She asked Him to conceal her, and to make her poor and humble. God delighted to hide her; in her conception, in her birth, in her mysteries, in her resurrection and assumption.

Her own parents did not know her. And the angels asked "Who is she?" The Most High, though He revealed something of her perfection to the angels, kept infinitely more from them.

God the Father willed she should work no miracle—at least no striking one—in her life. Yet He had given her the power to work tremendous miracles.

God the Son was content she should speak but a few words. Yet He had endowed her with His wisdom.

And God the Holy Spirit arranged that His apostles and evangelists should say little about her—no more than enough to make Christ known. Yet she was His beloved spouse.

Mary is God's masterpiece whose full splendor He has reserved for Himself.

You are the light of the world. A city set on a hill cannot be hid. Nor do men light a lamp and put it under a bushel, but on a stand, and it gives light to all in the house. Let your light so shine before men, that they may see your good works and give glory to your Father who is in heaven. — Matthew 5:14-16

Now review the *Five Steps to Confession* (#53m) and pray *The Morning Offering* (#2a) in Appendix A. If you haven't already done so, read "Part I: Spirit of the World" on pages 15–16. Pray 1 decade of the Rosary (#6a-9), preferably with your family, sometime during the day. If you already pray the daily family Rosary, you do not need to pray this decade.

Second Day
Spirit of the World
Come Holy Spirit, please awaken us to all you have in mind for us during these days of renewal and help us to let go of all sin, of the "spirit of the world," and of all else that leads to sin so that we can truly live this Total Consecration to Jesus through Mary in union with St. Joseph.

Reconciliatio et Paenitentia (Reconciliation and Penance), by Pope John Paul II

16. Sin, in the proper sense, is always a personal act, since it is an act of freedom on the part of an individual person and not properly of a group or community. This individual may be conditioned, incited and influenced by numerous and powerful external factors. He may also be subjected to tendencies, defects and habits linked with his personal condition. In not a few cases such external and internal factors may attenuate, to a greater or lesser degree, the person's freedom and therefore his responsibility and guilt. But it is a truth of faith, also confirmed by our experience and reason, that the human person is free!

This truth cannot be disregarded in order to place the blame for individuals' sins on external factors such as structures, systems or other people. Above all, this would be to deny the person's dignity and freedom, which are manifested—even though in a negative and disastrous way—also in this responsibility for sin committed. Hence there is nothing so personal and untransferable in each individual as merit for virtue or responsibility for sin.

As a personal act, sin has its first and most important consequences in the sinner himself: that is, in his relationship with God, who is the very foundation of human life; and also in his spirit, weakening his will and clouding his intellect.

To speak of social sin means in the first place to recognize that, by virtue of human solidarity which is as mysterious and intangible as it is real and concrete, *each individual's sin in some way affects others.* This is the other aspect of that solidarity which on the religious level is developed in the profound and magnificent mystery of the *communion of saints,* thanks to which it has been possible to say that "every soul that rises above itself, raises up the world."

To this law of ascent there unfortunately corresponds the law of descent. Consequently one can speak of a *communion of sin, whereby a soul that lowers itself through sin drags down with itself the church and, in some way, the whole world.* In other words, there is no sin, not even the most intimate and secret one, the most strictly individual one, that exclusively concerns the person committing it.

With greater or lesser violence, with greater or lesser harm, every sin has repercussions on the entire ecclesial body and the whole human family. According to this first meaning of the term, every sin can undoubtedly be considered as social sin.

True Devotion to Mary
by St. Louis de Montfort, Chapter I

She is the admirable Mother of the divine Son, Who took delight in humbling and hiding her to favor her sweet humility. He called her "woman," as though she were a stranger; yet she was dearer to Him than all men and angels.

She is the sealed fountain, the faithful spouse of the Holy Spirit. She is the sanctuary, the resting place of the Trinity. God dwells in her more wonderfully, more divinely, than anywhere else in the universe, including the regions occupied by the angelic hosts. And no creature, however pure, is admitted to that sanctuary except through a great privilege.

With all the saints I say that our Mother Mary is the paradise on earth where the new Adam took flesh, through the operation of the Holy Spirit, that He might work there wonders beyond all understanding. She is the great, the divine world of God where lie beauties and treasures one cannot imagine. She is the magnificence of God!

What grand and secret things God has worked in her. Even she must admit it. "He that is mighty has done great things to me." The world does not know these wonders. It is unworthy of knowing them. It is incapable of understanding them.

The saints have said many beautiful things about Mary, the holy city of God; and never were they more eloquent than when they spoke of her. Yet they realized that the heights of her merits could not be glimpsed; for they reach up to the throne of God. They knew that the width of her charity could not be measured, since it is broader than the earth.

They knew that the depths of her humility—and of all her other virtues and graces—could never be fathomed.

O height beyond our understanding! O width beyond all words! O greatness beyond all measures! O depth beyond all human thought or comprehension!

You, therefore, must be perfect, as your heavenly Father is perfect. — Matthew 5:48

Now review part of *Scripture's Four C's* (#53a) and pray the *Veni Creator* (#46) in Appendix A. If you haven't already done so, read the "Introduction" on pages 1–9. Pray 1 decade of the Rosary (#6a-9), preferably with your family, sometime during the day. If you already pray the daily family Rosary, you do not need to pray this decade.

Third Day
Spirit of the World

Come Holy Spirit, please awaken us to all you have in mind for us
during these days of renewal and help us to let go of all sin, of the "spirit
of the world," and of all else that leads to sin so that we can truly live
this Total Consecration to Jesus through Mary in union with St. Joseph.

Veritatis Splendor (Splendor of Truth)
by Pope John Paul II

118. No human sin can erase the mercy of God, or prevent him from unleashing all his triumphant power, if we
only call upon him. Indeed, sin itself makes even more
radiant the love of the Father who, in order to ransom a
slave, sacrificed his Son: his mercy towards us is
Redemption.

This mercy reaches its fullness in the gift of the Spirit
who bestows new life and demands that it be lived. No
matter how many and great the obstacles put in his way
by human frailty and sin, the Spirit, who renews the face
of the earth (cf. Ps 104:30), makes possible the miracle of
the perfect accomplishment of the good. This renewal,
which gives the ability to do what is good, noble, beautiful, pleasing to God and in conformity with his will, is in
some way the flowering of the gift of mercy, which offers
liberation from the slavery of evil and gives the strength
to sin no more. Through the gift of new life, Jesus makes

us sharers in his love and leads us to the Father in the Spirit.

119. Such is the consoling certainty of Christian faith, the source of its profound humanity and extraordinary simplicity. At times, in the discussions about new and complex moral problems, it can seem that Christian morality is in itself too demanding, difficult to understand and almost impossible to practice. This is untrue, since Christian morality consists, in the simplicity of the Gospel, in following Jesus Christ, in abandoning oneself to him, in letting oneself be transformed by his grace and renewed by his mercy, gifts which come to us in the living communion of his Church.

Saint Augustine reminds us that "he who would live has a place to live, and has everything needed to live. Let him draw near, let him believe, let him become part of the body, that he may have life. Let him not shrink from the unity of the members". By the light of the Holy Spirit, the living essence of Christian morality can be understood by everyone, even the least learned, but particularly those who are able to preserve an "undivided heart" (Ps 86:11).

On the other hand, this evangelical simplicity does not exempt one from facing reality in its complexity; rather it can lead to a more genuine understanding of reality, inasmuch as following Christ will gradually bring out the distinctive character of authentic Christian morality, while providing the vital energy needed to carry it out. It is the task of the Church's Magisterium to see that the dynamic process of following Christ develops in an organic manner, without the falsification or obscuring of its moral demands, with all their consequences. The one who loves Christ keeps his commandments (cf. Jn 14:15).

True Devotion to Mary
by St. Louis de Montfort, Chapter VIII

As all our perfection consists in being conformed, united, and consecrated to Jesus, the most perfect devotion is, naturally, that which conforms, unites, and consecrates us most perfectly to Him.

And, as Mary is, among all creatures, the one most conformed to Jesus, it follows that devotion to her is the one that best consecrates and conforms a soul to her Son. Therefore, the more a soul is consecrated to Mary, the more it is consecrated to Jesus.

This is why perfect consecration to Jesus is nothing less than perfect consecration to Mary—which is the devotion I preach and teach—or, let us say, the perfect renewal of the vows and promises of Baptism.

This devotion consists in giving oneself entirely to Our Lady, so that we may belong entirely to Jesus through her. We must give her our body, with all its senses and members; our soul, with all its faculties; our goods or riches and all we shall acquire; and all our inner assets, such as merits, virtues, and the good works we have done or may do.

We must give all we have, in the order of nature and the order of grace; and all that may come to us even in the order of glory. We must reserve nothing, be it a penny, a hair, or the least good deed. And we must do this for eternity, without expecting or claiming any other reward than the honor of belonging to Jesus through and in Mary.

Do not be conformed to this world but be transformed by the renewal of your mind, that you may prove what is the will of God, what is good and acceptable and perfect" (living the grace of the present moment — "All for"). — Romans 12:2-4

Now review part of *The Seven Capital Virtues and Seven Capital Sins* (#53b) in Appendix A. Pray 1 decade of the Rosary (#6a-9), preferably with your family, sometime during the day. If you already pray the daily family Rosary, you do not need to pray this decade. Optional: reflect on the "Introduction" to *Catechism on True Devotion to Mary* (#51b).

Fourth Day
Spirit of the World

Come Holy Spirit, please awaken us to all you have in mind for us during these days of renewal and help us to let go of all sin, of the "spirit of the world," and of all else that leads to sin so that we can truly live this Total Consecration to Jesus through Mary in union with St. Joseph.

Christifidelis Laici (On the Vocation and the Mission of the Lay Faithful in the Church and in the World) by Pope John Paul II

20. One and the same Spirit is always the dynamic principle of diversity and unity in the Church. Once again we read in the Constitution *Lumen Gentium,* "In order that we might be unceasingly renewed in him (cf. Eph 4:23), he has shared with us his Spirit who, existing as one and the same being in the head and in the members, gives life to, unifies and moves the whole body. This he does in such a way that his work could be compared by the Fathers to the function which the soul as the principle of life fulfills in the human body."

And in another particularly significant text which is helpful in understanding not only the organic nature proper to ecclesial communion but also its aspect of growth toward perfect communion, the Council writes: "The Spirit dwells in the Church and in the hearts of the Faithful, as in a temple (cf. 1 Cor 3:16; 6:19). In them he prays and bears witness that they are adopted sons (cf. Gal 4:6; Rom 8:15-16, 26).

Guiding the Church in the way of all truth (cf. Jn 16:13) and unifying her in communion and in the works of service, he bestows upon her varied hierarchical and charismatic gifts and adorns her with the fruits of his grace (cf. Eph 4:11-12; 1 Cor 12:4; Gal 5:22). By the power of the Gospel he makes the Church grow, perpetually renews her, and leads her to perfect union with her Spouse. The Spirit and the Bride both say to the Lord Jesus, 'Come!' (cf. Rev 22:17)".

Church communion then is a gift, a great gift of the Holy Spirit, to be gratefully accepted by the lay faithful, and at the same time to be lived with a deep sense of responsibility. This is concretely realized through their participation in the life and mission of the Church, to whose service the lay faithful put their varied and complementary ministries and charisms.

A member of the lay faithful "can never remain in isolation from the community, but must live in a continual interaction with others, with a lively sense of fellowship, rejoicing in an equal dignity and common commitment to bring to fruition the immense treasure that each has inherited.

The Spirit of the Lord gives a vast variety of charisms, inviting people to assume different ministries and forms of service and reminding them, as he reminds all people in their relationship in the Church, that what distinguishes persons is not an increase in dignity, but a special and complementary capacity for service.

...Thus, the charisms, the ministries, the different forms of service exercised by the lay faithful exist in communion and on behalf of communion. They are treasures that complement one another for the good of all and are under the wise guidance of their Pastors" (Pope John Paul II, homily, October 30, 1987).

True Devotion to Mary
by St. Louis de Montfort, Chapter II

In the natural order, a child is born of a father and a mother. It is the same in the supernatural and spiritual generation. There is a Father—God. And there is a mother—Mary.

All the true children, the chosen ones of heaven, have God for their Father, and Mary for their mother. Whoever does not have Mary for his mother does not have God for his Father.

This is why the wicked, and the heretics and others who hate or despise or are indifferent toward Our Lady, do not have God for their Father. If they had Mary for their mother they would love and honor her, as good and true children naturally love and honor the mothers who gave them life.

... God the Son wants to be formed, and to take flesh—so to say—in the members of His Mystical Body, every day, by His dear Mother. He says to her, "Take Israel for your inheritance." That is the same as saying, "God, My Father, has given Me all nations for My inheritance, and all men, the good and the bad.

Some I will lead with a rod of gold; the others with a rod of iron. To some I will be a Father and an Advocate. The others I will justly punish. I will be the Judge of all. But you, dear Mother, will inherit and possess only the chosen ones, represented by Israel. As their mother, you will give them birth; you will feed them; you will bring them up. And as their sovereign, you will lead, govern, and protect them.

"This man and that man is born in her," the Holy Spirit sings in the 86th Psalm of David. According to some of the early Fathers of the Church, the first man born in Mary is the God-Man Jesus; the second is a mere man, the adopted child of God and Mary. Since Christ, the Head of mankind, was born in her, the chosen ones who are members of this Head, must necessarily be born in her, too.

A mother does not give birth to the head without the members, nor to the members without the head; otherwise she would, in the natural order, bring forth a monster. In the same way, in the order of grace, the Head and the members are born of the same mother. If a member of the Mystical Body of Christ—a chosen one—

were born of any other mother except Mary, who gave birth to the Head, he would be neither a chosen one nor a member of Jesus Christ. He would, in the order of grace, be a monster.

Moreover, Christ is the fruit of Mary still—as heaven and earth continually avow. "And blessed is the fruit of thy womb, Jesus." It is therefore a fact that Christ is as truly the fruit and the work of Mary, for each particular man who possesses Him, as He is for the world in general.

Consequently if any of the faithful has Christ formed in him, he may say boldly: "Many thanks to Mary! What I have is hers; and without her it should not be mine." St Paul's words, "I am in labor until Christ be formed in you," may be applied much more truly to her. ("I give birth every day to the children of God, until Jesus Christ, my Son, be formed in them in the fullness of His age.")

St. Augustine surpasses himself—and me—when he says that all the chosen ones are hidden in the womb of the Blessed Virgin, during this life, to be made into the image of the Son of God. There the good mother keeps them, nourishes them, cherishes them, and makes them grow until she bears them into glory after death—which is really their birthday, as the Church calls the death of the just.

O mystery of grace little known to the chosen ones, and totally unknown to the reprobates!

When we were children, we were slaves to the elemental spirits of the universe. But when the time had fully come, God sent forth his Son, born of woman, born under the law, to redeem those who were under the law, so that we might receive adoption as sons. And because you are sons, God has sent the Spirit of his Son into our hearts, crying, "Abba! Father!" So through God you are no longer a slave but a son, and if a son then an heir.
— Galatians 4:3-7

Now review *The Spiritual Works of Mercy* (#53c) and pray the *Prayer for the Divine Communion of Love* (#17a) in Appendix A. Pray 1 decade of the Rosary (#6a-9), preferably with your family, sometime during the day. If you already pray the daily family Rosary, you do not need to pray this decade. Optional: reflect on sections 1–7 of *Catechism on True Devotion to Mary* (#51b).

Fifth Day
Spirit of the World

Come Holy Spirit, please awaken us to all you have in mind for us during these days of renewal and help us to let go of all sin, of the "spirit of the world," and of all else that leads to sin so that we can truly live this Total Consecration to Jesus through Mary in union with St. Joseph.

Christifidelis Laici (On the Vocation and the Mission of the Lay Faithful in the Church and in the World) by Pope John Paul II

56. ...the Synod Fathers have commented, "The Holy Spirit stirs up other forms of self-giving to which people who remain fully in the lay state devote themselves".

We can conclude by reading a beautiful passage taken from Saint Francis de Sales, who promoted lay spirituality so well. In speaking of "devotion", that is, Christian perfection or "life according to the Spirit", he presents in a simple yet insightful way the vocation of all Christians to holiness while emphasizing the specific form with which individual Christians fulfill it: "In creation God commanded the plants to bring forth their fruits, each one after its kind.

"So does he command all Christians, who are the living plants of his Church, to bring forth the fruits of devotion, each according to his character and vocation. Devotion must be exercised in different ways by the gentleman, the workman, the servant, the prince, the widow, the maid and the married woman. Not only this, but the practice of devotion must also be adapted to the strength, the employment, and the duties of each one in particular.

"…It is an error, or rather a heresy, to try to banish the devout life from the regiment of soldiers, the shop of the mechanic, the court of princes, or the home of married folk. It is true, Philothea, that a purely contemplative, monastic and religious devotion cannot be exercised in such ways of life. But besides these three kinds of devotion, there are several others adapted to bring to perfection those who live in the secular state".

Along the same line the Second Vatican Council states: "This lay spirituality should take its particular character from the circumstances of one's state in life (married and family life, celibacy, widowhood), from one's state of health and from one's professional and social activity. All should not cease to develop earnestly the qualities and talents bestowed on them in accord with these conditions of life and should make use of the gifts which they have received from the Holy Spirit"(*Decree on the Apostolate of Lay People*, 4).

What has been said about the spiritual vocation can also be said— and to a certain degree with greater reason— of the infinite number of ways through which all members of the Church are employed as laborers in the vineyard of the Lord, building up the Mystical Body of Christ. Indeed as a person with a truly unique lifestory, each is called by name, to make a special contribution to the coming of the Kingdom of God. No talent, no matter how small, is to be hidden or left unused (cf. Mt 25:24-27).

In this regard the apostle Peter gives us a stern warning: "As each has received a gift, employ it for one another, as good stewards of God's varied grace" (1 Pt 4:10).

True Devotion to Mary
by St. Louis de Montfort, Chapter XIV

If Mary, the tree of life, is well tended in your soul, she will bear her fruit in due time. And this fruit is Jesus.

So many seek Jesus, one way or another. But though they try hard they do not find Him. They have labored much in their quest, but gained, perhaps, only a glimpse of Him.

Walk in Mary's immaculate way. Take the divine practice I teach. And you will find Him. Night or day, you will seek Him in a holy place, and you will see Him clearly.

There is no night in Mary, since there has never been any sin in her, not even the least shadow. She is a holy place. She is the holy of holies, where saints are formed and molded. Note, I pray you, that I say the saints are molded in her.

There is much difference between making a statue with hammer and chisel, hewing it out of wood or stone, and the method of casting in a mold. In the first method the sculptor has much toil. He spends much time, and he may make many blunders. In the second, he works swiftly, without much effort, and without the possibility of marring what he molds.

St. Augustine calls Our Lady "the mold of God." He who is cast into this mold is soon molded into Jesus Christ; and Jesus Christ is molded in him. At little cost, in little time, he will become God! Has he not been cast into the very mold that formed God?

It seems to me I might compare some directors of souls to those sculptors who trust to their own art, ingenuity, or skill. These are the directors wishing to form Christ in themselves or others, but not through true devotion.

They strike the hard stone with an infinite number of blows, or dig industriously into some tough block of wood, in an attempt to make an image of Jesus. Frequently they fail to give the image the true look of Jesus. Ignorance or inexperience may be the cause of this. Or a clumsy handling of tools may spoil the whole work—and make all their labor vain.

But those who adopt this secret of grace, this true devotion, this slavery to Jesus in Mary, may rightly be compared to those who use a mold.

Having found the beautiful mold of Mary, where Christ was so naturally and divinely formed, these artists do not need to trust to their own skill or artistry. They trust to the merits of the mold. They throw themselves into it, with those they wish to shape. They lose themselves in it.

They lose themselves in Mary to become true images of her Son!

A beautiful and real simile. But who will understand it? I hope you will.

But remember this. Only what is melted may be cast in a mold. You must melt the old Adam in you to become the new Adam in Mary.

Now there are varieties of gifts, but the same Spirit; and there are varieties of service, but the same Lord; and there are varieties of working, but it is the same God who inspires them all in every one. To each is given the manifestation of the Spirit for the common good. — 1 Corinthians 12:4-7

Now read the *Summary of Norms for Gaining Indulgences for the Holy Souls in Purgatory* (#45a) and *The Corporal Works of Mercy* (#53d) in Appendix A. Pray 1 decade of the Rosary (#6a-9), preferably with your family, sometime during the day. If you already pray the daily family Rosary, you do not need to pray this decade. Optional: reflect on sections 8–13 of *Catechism on True Devotion to Mary* (#51b).

Sixth Day
Spirit of the World

*Come Holy Spirit, please awaken us to all you have in mind for us
during these days of renewal and help us to let go of all sin, of the "spirit
of the world," and of all else that leads to sin so that we can truly live
this Total Consecration to Jesus through Mary in union with St. Joseph.*

Dives in Misericordia (On the Mercy of God) by Pope John Paul II

13. It is precisely because sin exists in the world, which
"God so loved...that he gave his only Son," that God, who
"is love," cannot reveal Himself otherwise than as mercy.
This corresponds not only to the most profound truth of
that love which God is, but also to the whole interior
truth of man and of the world which is man's temporary
homeland.

Mercy in itself, as a perfection of the infinite God, is
also infinite. Also infinite therefore and inexhaustible is
the Father's readiness to receive the prodigal children
who return to His home. Infinite are the readiness and
power of forgiveness which flow continually from the
marvelous value of the sacrifice of the Son. No human sin
can prevail over this power or even limit it. On the part
of man only a lack of good will can limit it, a lack of readi-

ness to be converted and to repent, in other words persistence in obstinacy, opposing grace and truth, especially in the face of the witness of the cross and resurrection of Christ.

Therefore, the Church professes and proclaims conversion. Conversion to God always consists in discovering His mercy, that is, in discovering that love which is patient and kind as only the Creator and Father can be; the love to which the "God and Father of our Lord Jesus Christ" is faithful to the uttermost consequences in the history of His covenant with man; even to the cross and to the death and resurrection of the Son. Conversion to God is always the fruit of the" rediscovery of this Father, who is rich in mercy.

Authentic knowledge of the God of mercy, the God of tender love, is a constant and inexhaustible source of conversion, not only as a momentary interior act but also as a permanent attitude, as a state of mind. Those who come to know God in this way, who "see" Him in this way, can live only in a state of being continually converted to Him.

They live, therefore, *in statu conversionis*; and it is this state of conversion which marks out the most profound element of the pilgrimage of every man and woman on earth *in statu viatoris*. It is obvious that the Church professes the mercy of God, revealed in the crucified and risen Christ, not only by the word of her teaching but above all through the deepest pulsation of the life of the whole People of God. By means of this testimony of life, the Church fulfills the mission proper to the People of God, the mission which is a sharing in and, in a sense, a continuation of the messianic mission of Christ Himself.

True Devotion to Mary
by St. Louis de Montfort, Chapter XV

Since time does not permit me to explain here the splendor of the mystery of Jesus living and reigning in Mary, or of the Incarnation of the Word, I will content myself with remarking that this is the first mystery of Jesus, the most hidden, the highest, the most unknown.

It is in this mystery that Jesus, in the womb of Mary, chose all the elect! It is for this reason the saints sometimes refer to the Virgin womb as the "chamber of the secrets of God."

It is in this mystery that Jesus worked all the mysteries of His life. He worked them by accepting them. Therefore this mystery is a summary of all mysteries, and contains the will and the grace of them all.

And this mystery is the throne of the mercy, of the liberality, and of the glory of God. It is the throne of His mercy toward us because one cannot see Jesus, nor speak to Him, nor come near Him, except through the mediation of Mary. Jesus, Who always listens to His Mother, always grants, through her, His grace and His mercy to us sinners.

"Let us come boldly, then, before the throne of grace" (Heb. 4:16).

It is the throne of His liberality toward Mary because, while this new Adam dwelt here, in His earthly paradise, He secretly worked so many wonders that neither men nor angels could count them. Neither could men or angels understand them. This is why the saints call Mary "the magnificence of God"—as if God showed His magnificence only in Mary. "Here, as nowhere else, our Lord reigns in majesty" (Is. 33:21).

It is the throne of His glory for His Father, because it is in Mary that Jesus perfectly soothed His Father, irritated against mankind. It is in Mary He perfectly restored the glory that sin had stolen from Him. It is in Mary that, by sacrificing His will, He gave more glory to His Father than had been rendered by all the sacrifices made under the Old Law. It is in Mary that He offered His Father the first infinite glory given Him by man.

Since then we have a great high priest who has passed through the heavens, Jesus, the Son of God, let us hold fast our confession. For we have not a high priest who is unable to sympathize with our weaknesses, but one who in every respect has been tempted as we are, yet without sinning. Let us then with confidence draw near to the throne of grace, that we may receive mercy and find grace to help in time of need. — Hebrews 4:14-16

Now read the *Additional Grants for Indulgences* (#45b) and review part of *The Precepts of the Church* (#53e) in Appendix A. Pray 1 decade of the Rosary (#6a-9), preferably with your family, sometime during the day. If you already pray the daily family Rosary, you do not need to pray this decade. Optional: reflect on sections 14–17 of *Catechism on True Devotion to Mary* (#51b).

Seventh Day
Spirit of the World

Come Holy Spirit, please awaken us to all you have in mind for us during these days of renewal and help us to let go of all sin, of the "spirit of the world," and of all else that leads to sin so that we can truly live this Total Consecration to Jesus through Mary in union with St. Joseph.

Sollicitudo rei socialis (On Social Concern)
by Pope John Paul II

28. Side-by-side with the miseries of underdevelopment, themselves unacceptable, we find ourselves up against a form of superdevelopment, equally inadmissible, because like the former it is contrary to what is good and to true happiness. This superdevelopment, which consists in an excessive availability of every kind of material goods for the benefit of certain social groups, easily makes people slaves of "possession" and of immediate gratification, with no other horizon than the multiplication or continual replacement of the things already owned with others still better.

This is the so-called civilization of "consumption" or "consumerism," which involves so much "throwing-away" and "waste." An object already owned but now superseded by something better is discarded, with no thought of its possible lasting value in itself, nor of some other human being who is poorer.

All of us experience firsthand the sad effects of this blind submission to pure consumerism: in the first place a crass materialism, and at the same time a radical dissatisfaction, because one quickly learns — unless one is shielded from the flood of publicity and the ceaseless and tempting offers of products — that the more one possesses the more one wants, while deeper aspirations remain unsatisfied and perhaps even stifled.

The Encyclical of Pope Paul VI pointed out the difference, so often emphasized today, between "having" and "being," which had been expressed earlier in precise words by the Second Vatican Council. To "have" objects and goods does not in itself perfect the human subject,

unless it contributes to the maturing and enrichment of
that subject's "being," that is to say unless it contributes
to the realization of the human vocation as such.

Of course, the difference between "being" and "having,"
the danger inherent in a mere multiplication or replacement of things possessed compared to the value of
"being," need not turn into a contradiction. One of the
greatest injustices in the contemporary world consists
precisely in this: that the ones who possess much are rel-
atively few and those who possess almost nothing are
many. It is the injustice of the poor distribution of the
goods and services originally intended for all.

This then is the picture: there are some people — the
few who possess much — who do not really succeed in
"being" because, through a reversal of the hierarchy of
values, they are hindered by the cult of "having"; and
there are others — the many who have little or nothing
— who do not succeed in realizing their basic human
vocation because they are deprived of essential goods.

The evil does not consist in "having" as such, but in
possessing without regard for the quality and the ordered
hierarchy of the goods one has. Quality and hierarchy
arise from the subordination of goods and their availability to man's "being" and his true vocation.

This shows that although development has a necessary economic dimension, since it must supply the

greatest possible number of the world's inhabitants with an availability of goods essential for them "to be," it is not limited to that dimension. If it is limited to this, then it turns against those whom it is meant to benefit.

The characteristics of full development, one which is "more human" and able to sustain itself at the level of the true vocation of men and women without denying economic requirements, were described by Paul VI (cf. *Populorum Progressio*, nn. 20-21).

True Devotion to Mary
by St. Louis de Montfort, Chapter I

Every day, throughout the world, in the highest heavens, and in the lowest pits of hell, all things proclaim and preach the wonders of the Virgin-Mother.

The nine choirs of angels, the people on earth—even the devils themselves—have to call her Blessed. So great is the power of truth.

The angels in heaven, according to St. Bonaventure, never stop calling to her, "Holy, holy, holy Mary, Virgin Mother of God!" A million times a day they give her the angelic greeting, "Hail Mary!" They prostrate themselves before her. They beg her to honor them with her commands. St. Michael, the prince of the heavenly court, is the most eager to pay her homage, St. Augustine says, and to run her errands.

The whole earth is filled with her glory. Cities, provinces, dioceses, and great nations are placed, by Christians, under her care and protection. Cathedrals are dedicated to God in her name. There is no church without an altar in her honor. There is no district or country without some miraculous image of her; without some place in which she heals all kinds of ills, in which she distributes all sorts of blessings.

There are countless organizations that honor her. There are many religious orders sharing her name and her motherly love. Religious men and women constantly sing her praises and proclaim her mercies. Little children just learning the Hail Mary praise and love her. Even the most hardened sinners have some spark of confidence in her.

And yet, with the saints, we must truthfully confess that "There is never enough about Mary." We have not given her enough praise, glory, honor, love, or service. She deserves much more honor from us, greater admiration, better service, and far more love.

Earth vies with heaven to glorify her. Yet we must say with the Holy Spirit, "All the glory of the King's daughter is within." The glory given her by angels and men is as nothing compared to that which she receives from her Maker. This glory the little creatures do not know. Who can penetrate the secret of secrets of the King?

The eye has not seen, the ear has not heard, nor has the heart of man known the beauty, the treasures, and the wonders of Mary. She is the miracle of miracles of grace, of nature, and of glory. She is the worthy Mother of God.

But, as it is written, "What no eye has seen, nor ear heard, nor the heart of man conceived, what God has prepared for those who love him," God has revealed to us through the Spirit. For the Spirit searches everything, even the depths of God. For what person knows a man's thoughts except the spirit of the man which is in him? So also no one comprehends the thoughts of God except the Spirit of God. Now we have received not the spirit of the world, but the Spirit which is from God, that we might understand the gifts bestowed on us by God. — 1 Corinthians 2:9-12

Now pray the *St. Joseph Prayer* (#2f) in Appendix A. Pray 1 decade of the Rosary (#6a-9), preferably with your family, sometime during the day. If you already pray the daily family Rosary, you do not need to pray this decade. Optional: reflect on sections 18–22 of *Catechism on True Devotion to Mary* (#51b).

Eighth Day
Spirit of the World

*Come Holy Spirit, please awaken us to all you have in mind for us
during these days of renewal and help us to let go of all sin, of the "spirit
of the world," and of all else that leads to sin so that we can truly live
this Total Consecration to Jesus through Mary in union with St. Joseph.*

Dives in Misericordia (On the Mercy of God)
by Pope John Paul II

11. Thus, in our world the feeling of being under threat
is increasing. There is an increase of that existential fear
connected especially, as I said in the encyclical *Redemptor
hominis*, with the prospect of a conflict that in view of
today's atomic stockpiles could mean the partial self-
destruction of humanity. But the threat does not merely
concern what human beings can do to human beings
through the means provided by military technology; it
also concerns many other dangers produced by a materialistic society which — in spite of "humanistic"
declarations — accepts the primacy of things over persons. Contemporary man, therefore, fears that by the use
of the means invented by this type of society, individuals
and the environment, communities, societies and nations
can fall victim to the abuse of power by other individuals,
environments and societies.

The history of our century offers many examples of
this. In spite of all the declarations on the rights of man
in his integral dimension, that is to say in his bodily and
spiritual existence, we cannot say that these examples
belong only to the past.

*Man rightly fears falling victim to an oppression that
will deprive him of his interior freedom, of the possibility
of expressing the truth of which he is convinced, of the
faith that he professes, of the ability to obey the voice of
conscience that tells him the right path to follow.*

*The technical means at the disposal of modern society
conceal within themselves not only the possibility of self-
destruction through military conflict, but also the
possibility of a "peaceful" subjugation of individuals, of*

environments, of entire societies and of nations, that for one reason or another might prove inconvenient for those who possess the necessary means and are ready to use them without scruple. An instance is the continued existence of torture, systematically used by authority as a means of domination and political oppression and practiced by subordinates with impunity.

Together with awareness of the biological threat, therefore, there is a growing awareness of yet another threat, even more destructive of what is essentially human, what is intimately bound up with the dignity of the person and his or her right to truth and freedom.

All this is happening against the background of the gigantic remorse caused by the fact that, side by side with wealthy and surfeited people and societies, living in plenty and ruled by consumerism and pleasure, the same human family contains individuals and groups that are suffering from hunger.

There are babies dying of hunger under their mothers' eyes. In various parts of the world, in various socio-economic systems, there exist entire areas of poverty, shortage and underdevelopment. This fact is universally known. The state of inequality between individuals and between nations not only still exists; it is increasing.

It still happens that side by side with those who are wealthy and living in plenty there exist those who are living in want, suffering misery and often actually dying of hunger; and their number reaches tens, even hundreds of millions. This is why moral uneasiness is destined to become even more acute. It is obvious that a fundamental defect, or rather a series of defects, indeed a defective machinery is at the root of contemporary economics and materialistic civilization, which does not allow the human family to break free from such radically unjust situations.

This picture of today's world in which there is so much evil both physical and moral, so as to make of it a world entangled in contradictions and tensions, and at the same time full of threats to human freedom, conscience and religion — this picture explains the uneasiness felt by contemporary man. This uneasiness is experienced not only by those who are disadvantaged or oppressed, but also by those who possess the privileges of wealth, progress and power.

And, although there is no lack of people trying to understand the causes of this uneasiness, or trying to react against it with the temporary means offered by technology, wealth or power, still in the very depth of the human spirit this uneasiness is stronger than all temporary means. This uneasiness concerns — as the analyses of the Second Vatican Council rightly pointed out — the fundamental problems of all human existence. It is linked with the very sense of man's existence in the world, and is an uneasiness for the future of man and all humanity; it demands decisive solutions, which now seem to be forcing themselves upon the human race.

Novo Millennio Ineunte (At the Beginning of the New Millennium), by Pope John Paul II

15. Now we must look ahead, we must "put out into the deep", trusting in Christ's words: *Duc in altum!* What we have done this year cannot justify a sense of complacency, and still less should it lead us to relax our commitment. On the contrary, the experiences we have had should inspire in us new energy, and impel us to invest in concrete initiatives the enthusiasm which we have felt.

Jesus himself warns us: "No one who puts his hand to the plough and looks back is fit for the kingdom of God" (Lk 9:62). In the cause of the Kingdom there is no time for looking back, even less for settling into laziness. Much awaits us, and for this reason we must set about drawing up an effective post-Jubilee pastoral plan.

Ours is a time of continual movement which often leads to restlessness, with the risk of "doing for the sake of doing". We must resist this temptation by trying "to be" before trying "to do". In this regard we should recall how Jesus reproved Martha: "You are anxious and troubled about many things; one thing is needful" (Lk 10:41-42).

True Devotion to Mary
by St. Louis de Montfort, Chapter II

God, made man, found His freedom by imprisoning Himself in her womb! He revealed His power by allowing Himself to be carried by a little girl! He found His glory, and that of His Father, by hiding it from all earthly creatures, Mary excepted.

He glorified His independence and His majesty by willing to depend upon her at His conception, at His birth, at His presentation in the Temple, and in His hidden years. He willed she should be present at His death, so that He might make but one same sacrifice with her, and with her consent be immolated to the Eternal Father — as Isaac was offered as a sacrifice, with Abraham's consent — to the will of God.

She nursed Him, fed Him, attended Him, brought Him up. And she sacrificed Him for us! O wonderful and awesome dependence of Almighty God!

Although in the Gospels the Holy Spirit has revealed but few of the marvelous things the Incarnate Wisdom accomplished during His hidden life, He could not keep this dependence secret. He let it be known so that we might see its infinite value.

Jesus gave more glory to His Father by submitting to His Mother for thirty years than He would have given Him by working the greatest miracles and converting the whole world!

What great glory we give God when, to please Him and to imitate Jesus, our supreme Model, we too submit to Mary!

Christ willed to begin His miracles by Mary. He sanctified John the Baptist in the womb of Elizabeth through the words of Mary. No sooner had she spoken than the unborn babe was made holy.

This is the first miracle of grace, and the greatest He performed. At the wedding in Cana He listened to Mary's humble prayer, and changed water into wine. This is the first miracle of nature Jesus worked.

He began to work miracles through Mary. He continues to work them through her. And He will go on working them through her until the end of time.

Do you not believe that I am in the Father and the Father in me? The words that I say to you I do not speak on my own authority; but the Father who dwells in me does his works. Believe me that I am in the Father and the Father in me; or else believe me for the sake of the works themselves. "Truly, truly, I say to you, he who believes in me will also do the works that I do; and greater works than these will he do, because I go to the Father. Whatever you ask in my name, I will do it, that the Father may be glorified in the Son; if you ask anything in my name, I will do it. — John 14:10-14

Now review part of *The Eight Beatitudes* (#53g) and pray *The Magnificat* (#2) in Appendix A. Pray 2 decades of the Rosary (#6a-9), preferably with your family, sometime during the day. If you already pray the daily family Rosary, you do not need to pray these 2 decades. Optional: reflect on sections 23–27 of *Catechism on True Devotion to Mary* (#51b).

Ninth Day
Spirit of the World

Come Holy Spirit, please awaken us to all you have in mind for us during these days of renewal and help us to let go of all sin, of the "spirit of the world," and of all else that leads to sin so that we can truly live this Total Consecration to Jesus through Mary in union with St. Joseph.

Sollicitudo rei socialis (On Social Concern)
by Pope John Paul II

38. For Christians, as for all who recognize the precise theological meaning of the word "sin," a change of behavior or mentality or mode of existence is called "conversion," to use the language of the Rihle (cf. Mk 13:3, 5, Is 30:15).

This conversion specifically entails a relationship to God, to the sin committed, to its consequences and hence to one's neighbor, either an individual or a community. It is God, in "whose hands are the hearts of the powerful" and the hearts of all, who according his own promise and by the power of his Spirit can transform "hearts of stone" into "hearts of flesh" (cf. Ezek 36:26).

On the path toward the desired conversion, toward the overcoming of the moral obstacles to development, it is already possible to point to the positive and moral value of the growing awareness of interdependence among individuals and nations.

The fact that men and women in various parts of the world feel personally affected by the injustices and violations of human rights committed in distant countries, countries which perhaps they will never visit, is a further sign of a reality transformed into awareness, thus acquiring a moral connotation.

It is above all a question of interdependence, sensed as a system determining relationships in the contemporary world, in its economic, cultural, political and religious elements, and accepted as a moral category. When interdependence becomes recognized in this way, the correlative response as a moral and social attitude, as a "virtue," is solidarity.

This then is not a feeling of vague compassion or shallow distress at the misfortunes of so many people, both near and far. On the contrary, it is a firm and persevering determination to commit oneself to the common good; that is to say to the good of all and of each individual, because we are all really responsible for all. This determination is based on the solid conviction that what is hindering full development is that desire for profit and that thirst for power already mentioned.

These attitudes and "structures of sin" are only conquered — presupposing the help of divine grace — by a diametrically opposed attitude: a commitment to the good of one's neighbor with the readiness, in the gospel sense, to "lose oneself" for the sake of the other instead of exploiting him, and to "serve him" instead of oppressing him for one's own advantage (cf. Mt 10:40-42; 20:25; Mk 10:42-45; Lk 22:25-27).

39. The exercise of solidarity within each society is valid when its members recognize one another as persons. Those who are more influential, because they have a greater share of goods and common services, should feel responsible for the weaker and be ready to share with them all they possess.

Those who are weaker, for their part, in the same spirit of solidarity, should not adopt a purely passive attitude or one that is destructive of the social fabric, but, while claiming their legitimate rights, should do what they can for the good of all. The intermediate groups, in their turn, should not selfishly insist on their particular interests, but respect the interests of others.

49. ...in order that the Catholic faithful may look more and more to Mary, who goes before us on the pilgrimage of faith and with maternal care intercedes for us before her Son, our Redeemer. I wish to entrust to her and to her intercession this difficult moment of the modern world, and the efforts that are being made and will be made, often with great suffering, in order to contribute to the true development of peoples proposed and proclaimed by my predecessor Paul VI.

In keeping with Christian piety through the ages, we present to the Blessed Virgin difficult individual situations, so that she may place them before her Son, asking that he alleviate and change them.

But we also present to her social situations and the international crisis itself, in their worrying aspects of poverty, unemployment, shortage of food, the arms race, contempt for human rights, and situations or dangers of conflict, partial or total. In a filial spirit we wish to place all this before her "eyes of mercy," repeating once more with faith and hope the ancient antiphon: "Holy Mother of God, despise not our petitions in our necessities, but deliver us always from all dangers, O glorious and blessed Virgin."

Mary most holy, our Mother and Queen, is the one who turns to her Son and says: "They have no more wine" (Jn 2:3). She is also the one who praises God the Father, because "he has put down the mighty from their thrones and exalted those of low degree; he has filled the hungry with good things, and the rich he has sent empty away" (Lk 1:52-53). Her maternal concern extends to the personal and social aspects of people's life on earth.

True Devotion to Mary
by St. Louis de Montfort, Chapter XIV

Mary, wonder of God! You cannot help but work wonders in the souls who agree to lose themselves in you!

Because by this practice, a soul regards its own thoughts and actions as nothing and relies entirely on the dispositions of Mary—even to speak to her Son—it reaches deeper into the virtue of humility than it would relying on itself. *It takes pleasure in this reliance on Mary, not in its own inclinations.* Hence it glorifies God in a higher degree. The deeper one's humility, the higher the glory to God. Only the little ones, the humble of heart, truly glorify Him.

Our Lady, because of her great love for us, is eager to receive the gift of our actions. With her immaculate hands she offers them to Jesus, Who is, assuredly, more glorified in this way than He would be if the gift were offered with our own guilty hands.

You never think about Mary without her thinking, in your stead, about God, her Father, Son, and Spouse. You never praise or honor her, without her praising and honoring God with you. Mary is entirely relative to God. I would even term her the relation to God, for she exists only in relation to Him. She might even be called an echo of the Most High; for she keeps repeating "God... God...God!" If you say "Mary," she says "God." When Elizabeth praised her, on the occasion of the Visitation, Mary intoned her Magnificat..."My soul does magnify the Lord and my spirit has rejoiced in God, my Savior."

What Mary did then she does today. When we praise her, love her, honor her, give anything to her, mention her name with love, God is praised, God is loved, God is honored, we give to God through her and in her.

🌿 *Then the King will say to those at his right hand, "Come, O blessed of my Father, inherit the kingdom prepared for you from the foundation of the world; for I was hungry and you gave me food, I was thirsty and you gave me drink, I was a stranger and you welcomed me, I was naked and you clothed me, I was sick and you visited me, I was in prison and you came to me. ...Truly, I say to you, as you did it to one of the least of these my brethren, you did it to me. — Matthew 25:34-40*

Now review part of *The Examination of Conscience in Light of the Ten Commandments* (#53h1) and pray the *Prayer to Blind Satan* (#48b) in Appendix A. Pray 2 decades of the Rosary (#6a-9), preferably with your family, sometime during the day. If you already pray the daily family Rosary, you do not need to pray these 2 decades. Optional: reflect on sections 28–32 of *Catechism on True Devotion to Mary* (#51b).

Tenth Day
Spirit of the World

Come Holy Spirit, please awaken us to all you have in mind for us during these days of renewal and help us to let go of all sin, of the "spirit of the world," and of all else that leads to sin so that we can truly live this Total Consecration to Jesus through Mary in union with St. Joseph.

Novo Millennio Ineunte (At the Beginning of the New Millennium), by Pope John Paul II

32. This training in holiness calls for a Christian life distinguished above all in the art of prayer... But we well know that prayer cannot be taken for granted. We have to learn to pray: as it were learning this art ever anew from the lips of the Divine Master himself, like the first disciples:

"Lord, teach us to pray!" (Lk 11:1). Prayer develops that conversation with Christ which makes us his intimate friends: "Abide in me and I in you" (Jn 15:4). This reciprocity is the very substance and soul of the Christian life, and the condition of all true pastoral life. Wrought in us by the Holy Spirit, this reciprocity opens us, through Christ and in Christ, to contemplation of the Father's face.

Learning this Trinitarian shape of Christian prayer and living it fully, above all in the liturgy, the summit and source of the Church's life, but also in personal experience, is the secret of a truly vital Christianity, which has no reason to fear the future, because it returns continually to the sources and finds in them new life.

Dominum et Vivificantem (The Holy Spirit in the Life of the Church), by Pope John Paul II

66. In the midst of the problems, disappointments and hopes, desertions and returns of these times of ours, the Church remains faithful to the mystery of her birth. While it is an historical fact that the Church came forth from the Upper Room on the day of Pentecost, in a certain sense one can say that she has never left it. Spiritually the event of Pentecost does not belong only to the past: the Church is always in the Upper Room that she bears in her heart.

The Church perseveres in prayer, like the Apostles together with Mary, the Mother of Christ, and with those who in Jerusalem were the first seed of the Christian community and who awaited in prayer the coming of the Holy Spirit.

The Church perseveres in prayer with Mary. This union of the praying Church with the Mother of Christ has been part of the mystery of the Church from the beginning: we see her present in this mystery as she is present in the mystery of her Son.

It is the Council that says to us: "The Blessed Virgin...overshadowed by the Holy Spirit... brought forth...the Son..., he whom God placed as the first-born among many brethren (cf. Rom 8:29), namely the faithful.

In their birth and development she cooperates with a maternal love"; she is through "his singular graces and offices...intimately united with the Church.... [She] is a model of the Church" (*Lumen Gentium*, 63). "The Church, moreover, contemplating Mary's mysterious sanctity, imitating her charity, ... becomes herself a mother" and "herself is a virgin, who keeps...the fidelity she has pledged to her Spouse. Imitating the Mother of The Lord, and by the power of the Holy Spirit, she preserves with virginal purity an integral faith, a firm hope, and a sincere charity" (*Lumen Gentium*, 64).

Thus one can understand the profound reason why the Church, united with the Virgin Mother, prays unceasingly as the Bride to her divine Spouse, as the words of the Book of Revelation, quoted by the Council, attest: "The Spirit and the bride say to the Lord Jesus Christ: Come!"

The Church's prayer is this unceasing invocation, in which "the Spirit himself intercedes for us": in a certain sense, the Spirit himself utters it with the Church and in the Church. For the Spirit is given to the Church in order that through His power the whole community of the People of God, however widely scattered and diverse, may persevere in hope: that hope in which "we have been saved."

It is the eschatological hope, the hope of definitive fulfillment in God, the hope of the eternal Kingdom, that is brought about by participation in the life of the Trinity. The Holy Spirit, given to the Apostles as the Counselor, is the guardian and animator of this hope in the heart of the Church.

In the time leading up to the third Millennium after Christ, while "the Spirit and the bride say to the Lord Jesus: Come!" this prayer of theirs is filled, as always, with an eschatological significance, which is also destined to give fullness of meaning to the celebration of the great Jubilee.

It is a prayer concerned with the salvific destinies toward which the Holy Spirit by his action opens hearts throughout the history of man on earth. But at the same time this prayer is directed toward a precise moment of history which highlights the "fullness of time" marked by the year 2000. The Church wishes to prepare for this Jubilee in the Holy Spirit, just as the Virgin of Nazareth in whom the Word was made flesh was prepared by the Holy Spirit.

True Devotion to Mary
by St. Louis de Montfort, Chapter II

God the Holy Spirit is barren in God. That is, no other Divine Person proceeds from Him. He became fruitful by Mary whom He espoused. It is with her, in her, and of her, that He brought forth Christ, His Masterpiece. And it is with her, in her, and of her that He brings forth, daily, His chosen ones, the members of the Mystical Body, of which Christ is the adored Head.

Therefore the more clearly He sees Mary, His dear inseparable spouse, living in a soul, the more mightily He works to bring forth Jesus in that soul, and that soul in Jesus!

We do not mean to say that the Blessed Virgin makes the Holy Spirit fruitful. Being God, He is, equally with the Father and the Son, infinitely fruitful.

What I want to say is that the Holy Spirit deigns to use the Blessed Virgin to produce His fruits—though, absolutely speaking, He does not need to do so. He brings forth in her and through her, Jesus Christ and His members. This is a mystery of grace. Even the most learned, the most spiritual Christians do not understand it.

Likewise the Spirit helps us in our weakness; for we do not know how to pray as we ought, but the Spirit himself intercedes for us with sighs too deep for words. And he who searches the hearts of men knows what is the mind of the Spirit, because the Spirit intercedes for the saints according to the will of God. We know that in everything God works for good with those who love him, who are called according to his purpose. For those whom he foreknew he also predestined to be conformed to the image of his Son, in order that he might be the first-born among many brethren. — Romans 8:26-29

Now review part of the *Examination of Conscience in Light of the Ten Commandments* (#53h2 and #53h3) in Appendix A. Pray 2 decades of the Rosary (#6a-9), preferably with your family, sometime during the day. If you already pray the daily family Rosary, you do not need to pray these 2 decades. Optional: reflect on sections 33–36 of *Catechism on True Devotion to Mary* (#51b).

Eleventh Day
Spirit of the World

Come Holy Spirit, please awaken us to all you have in mind for us during these days of renewal and help us to let go of all sin, of the "spirit of the world," and of all else that leads to sin so that we can truly live this Total Consecration to Jesus through Mary in union with St. Joseph.

Novo Millennio Ineunte (At the Beginning of the New Millennium), by Pope John Paul II

33. Is it not one of the "signs of the times" that in today's world, despite widespread secularization, there is a widespread demand for spirituality, a demand which expresses itself in large part as a renewed need for prayer?

Other religions, which are now widely present in ancient Christian lands, offer their own responses to this need, and sometimes they do so in appealing ways. But we who have received the grace of believing in Christ, the revealer of the Father and the Saviour of the world, have a duty to show to what depths the relationship with Christ can lead.

The great mystical tradition of the Church of both East and West has much to say in this regard. It shows how prayer can progress, as a genuine dialogue of love, to the point of rendering the person wholly possessed by the divine Beloved, vibrating at the Spirit's touch, resting filially within the Father's heart.

This is the lived experience of Christ's promise: "He who loves me will be loved by my Father, and I will love him and manifest myself to him" (Jn 14:21). It is a journey totally sustained by grace, which nonetheless demands an intense spiritual commitment and is no stranger to painful purifications (the "dark night"). But it leads, in various possible ways, to the ineffable joy experienced by the mystics as "nuptial union". How can we forget here, among the many shining examples, the teachings of Saint John of the Cross and Saint Teresa of Avila?

Yes, dear brothers and sisters, our Christian communities must become genuine "schools" of prayer, where the meeting with Christ is expressed not just in imploring help but also in thanksgiving, praise, adoration, contemplation, listening and ardent devotion, until the heart truly "falls in love". Intense prayer, yes, but it does not distract us from our commitment to history: by opening our heart to the love of God it also opens it to the love of our brothers and sisters, and makes us capable of shaping history according to God's plan. [*Providence*]

Veritatis Splendor (The Splendor of the Truth)
by Pope John Paul II

120. Mary is also Mother of Mercy because it is to her that Jesus entrusts his Church and all humanity. At the foot of the Cross, when she accepts John as her son, when she asks, together with Christ, forgiveness from the Father for those who do not know what they do (cf. Lk 23:34), Mary experiences, in perfect docility to the Spirit, the richness and the universality of God's love, which opens her heart and enables it to embrace the entire human race. Thus Mary becomes Mother of each and every one of us, the Mother who obtains for us divine mercy.

Mary is the radiant sign and inviting model of the moral life. As Saint Ambrose put it, "The life of this one person can serve as a model for everyone", and while speaking specifically to virgins but within a context open to all, he affirmed: "The first stimulus to learning is the nobility of the teacher. Who can be more noble than the Mother of God? Who can be more glorious than the one chosen by Glory Itself?".

Mary lived and exercised her freedom precisely by giving herself to God and accepting God's gift within herself. Until the time of his birth, she sheltered in her womb the Son of God who became man; she raised him and enabled him to grow, and she accompanied him in that supreme act of freedom which is the complete sacrifice of

his own life. By the gift of herself, Mary entered fully into
the plan of God who gives himself to the world.

By accepting and pondering in her heart events which
she did not always understand (cf. Lk 2:19), she became
the model of all those who hear the word of God and keep
it (cf. Lk 11:28), and merited the title of "Seat of Wisdom".
This Wisdom is Jesus Christ himself, the Eternal Word of
God, who perfectly reveals and accomplishes the will of
the Father (cf.Heb 10:5-10). Mary invites everyone to
accept this Wisdom.

To us too she addresses the command she gave to the
servants at Cana in Galilee during the marriage feast:
"Do whatever he tells you" (Jn 2:5).

True Devotion to Mary
by St. Louis de Montfort, Chapter III

Throughout the ages, and especially toward the end of
the world, the greatest saints will be those most zealous
in praying to Mary, and in having her always present as a
model to imitate and as a powerful ruler to protect them.

I say this will happen especially toward the end of the
world—and this soon—because then the Most High with
His holy Mother will form great saints for Himself, saints
who will tower in holiness over other saints even as the
cedars of Lebanon tower over little bushes. This has been
revealed to a holy soul.

These great saints will be chosen to fight against the enemies of God pressing on from all sides. They will be singularly devoted to the Blessed Virgin. They will be illumined by her light.

They will be fed by her milk. They will be led by her spirit. They will be supported by her arm. They will be constantly under her protection, so that they will fight with one hand and build with the other.

With one hand they will overthrow and crush heresies, schisms, idolatries, and impieties. With the other they will erect the temple of the true Solomon, the mystical city of God—meaning the Virgin Mother, who is called both the temple of Solomon and the city of God.

By word and example, these tremendous ones will draw the world toward true devotion to Mary. This will bring them many enemies, but it will bring many victories, too. And much glory for God!

This is what was revealed to St. Vincent Ferrer, the great apostle of his age. This is what the Holy Spirit seems to have foretold in the 58th Psalm: "And they shall know that God will rule Jacob and all the ends of the earth; they shall return at evening and shall suffer hunger like dogs and shall go round about the city."

The city around which men will circle at the end of the world, to be converted and to satisfy their hunger for justice, is Mary, "the city of God."

What is man that you are mindful of him, or the son of man, that you care for him? You did make him for a little while lower than the angels, you have crowned him with glory and honor, putting everything in subjection under his feet. — Hebrews 2:6-8

Now review part of the *Examination of Conscience in Light of the Ten Commandments* (#53h4) and pray *O Jesus Living in Mary* (#50a) in Appendix A. Pray 2 decades of the Rosary (#6a-9), preferably with your family, sometime during the day. If you already pray the daily family Rosary, you do not need to pray these 2 decades. Optional: reflect on *Implementing the Sacraments of Baptism and Confirmation with Mary* (#50c).

Twelfth Day
Spirit of the World

Come Holy Spirit, please awaken us to all you have in mind for us during these days of renewal and help us to let go of all sin, of the "spirit of the world," and of all else that leads to sin so that we can truly live this Total Consecration to Jesus through Mary in union with St. Joseph.

Fides et Ratio (The Relationship Between Faith and Reason), by Pope John Paul II

107. I ask everyone to look more deeply at man, whom Christ has saved in the mystery of his love, and at the human being's unceasing search for truth and meaning. *Different philosophical systems have lured people into believing that they are their own absolute master, able to decide their own destiny and future in complete autonomy, trusting only in themselves and their own powers.*

But this can never be the grandeur of the human being, who can find fulfillment only in choosing to enter the truth, to make a home under the shade of Wisdom and dwell there. Only within this horizon of truth will people understand their freedom in its fullness and their call to know and love God as the supreme realization of their true self.

108. I turn in the end to the woman whom the prayer of the Church invokes as Seat of Wisdom, and whose life itself is a true parable illuminating the reflection contained in these pages. For between the vocation of the

Blessed Virgin and the vocation of true philosophy there is a deep harmony. Just as the Virgin was called to offer herself entirely as human being and as woman that God's Word might take flesh and come among us, so too philosophy is called to offer its rational and critical resources that theology, as the understanding of faith, may be fruitful and creative.

And just as in giving her assent to Gabriel's word, Mary lost nothing of her true humanity and freedom, so too when philosophy heeds the summons of the Gospel's truth its autonomy is in no way impaired. Indeed, it is then that philosophy sees all its enquiries rise to their highest expression. This was a truth which the holy monks of Christian antiquity understood well when they called Mary "the table at which faith sits in thought". In her they saw a lucid image of true philosophy and they were convinced of the need to *philosophari in Maria*.

May Mary, Seat of Wisdom, be a sure haven for all who devote their lives to the search for wisdom. May their journey into wisdom, sure and final goal of all true knowing, be freed of every hindrance by the intercession of the one who, in giving birth to the Truth and

treasuring it in her heart, has shared it forever with all
the world.

True Devotion to Mary
by St. Louis de Montfort, Chapter X

Scripture tells us that a man who honors his mother
is like one who stores up a treasure—meaning that he
who honors Mary, his mother, to the point of subjecting
himself to her and obeying her in all things, will soon
become very rich. He heaps up treasure daily.

There is another Scripture quotation: "my old age is in
the mercy of the womb." According to the spiritual interpretation, it is in the womb of Mary that young people
mature in light, in holiness, in experience, and in wisdom.
There, in a short time, one achieves the fullness of the age
of Jesus Christ!

The road is a perfect one by which to reach Christ and
be united to Him. Mary is the most perfect creature, the
purest and holiest. And Christ, Who came to us perfectly,
chose that road.

The Most High, the One Beyond All Understanding,
the Untouchable God, He Who Is, came down, perfectly
and divinely, to us mean little worms through the humble
Mary. And He came without losing anything of His
divinity. Therefore it is through Mary that we little ones
must, perfectly and divinely, and without fear, ascend to
Him.

God, Who cannot be held or limited, let Himself be
perfectly surrounded and contained by the little Mary;
and without losing anything of His immensity.

So we must let the little Mary perfectly contain and
form us—and this without any reserve on our part.

The Untouchable God drew near to us, united Himself
closely, perfectly, and even personally, to our humanity,
through Mary. And He did so without losing anything of
His majesty and awe.

So it is through her we must go near to Him, must perfectly, closely, and fearlessly unite ourselves to Him.

He Who Is willed to come to our nothingness and to cause that nothingness to become He Who Is. This He did perfectly, by giving and submitting Himself entirely to the young maiden, Mary; and without ceasing to be, in time, what He is from all eternity. Likewise it is through the same maiden that we, who are nothing, may become like God, through grace and glory. This, by giving ourselves to her so perfectly and completely as to remain nothing, so far as self is concerned, and to be all in her, without any fear of delusion!

Do not love the world or the things in the world. If any one loves the world, love for the Father is not in him. For all that is in the world, the lust of the flesh and the lust of the eyes and the pride of life, is not of the Father but is of the world. And the world passes away, and the lust of it; but he who does the will of God abides for ever. — 1 John 2:15-17

Now review part of the *Examination of Conscience in Light of the Ten Commandments* (#53h5) and renew your baptismal vows (#50b.2) in Appendix A. Pray 2 decades of the Rosary (#6a-9), preferably with your family, sometime during the day. If you already pray the daily family Rosary, you do not need to pray these 2 decades. Optional: pray the *Chaplet of the Immaculate Heart of Mary* (#48a).

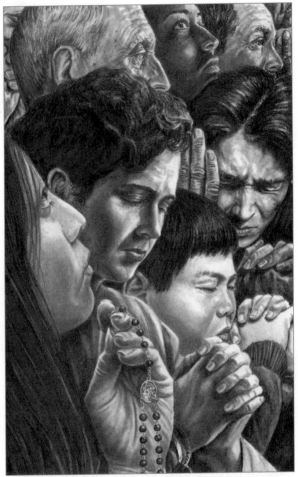

Hail Mary, full of grace; the Lord is with Thee;
blessed are thou among women
and blessed is the fruit of thy womb, Jesus.
Holy Mary, Mother of God, pray for us sinners,
now and at the hour of our death. Amen.

Part 2: Knowledge of Self
(Days 13-19)

Ask for the graces to humble yourself as a spiritual child of Mary and ask her to help you to renounce your own will and to realize that God has a plan for your life, one that is better than you could ever imagine. Whether it be in sickness or health, you just need to strive to know and accomplish God's Will. Our Lord said in Matthew 7:21, *"Not every one who says to me, 'Lord, Lord,' shall enter the kingdom of heaven, but he who does the will of my Father who is in heaven."*

Mary is the perfect model for doing God's Will. She will form you into His image and likeness if you let her. Your most precious Mother will protect you if you let go of your self-will and let her take possession of you.

Examine your conscience each day (see sections 53a, 53b and 53h in Appendix A). Try to go to Confession every two weeks or at least monthly, and follow the "Five Steps to Confession" in section 53m.

During this period, also ask St. Joseph to teach you how to live this "Total Consecration to Jesus through Mary" as he did.

Give thanks to God that you are made in His image and likeness. Realize that because of this special gift, we all have a grave obligation to bear good fruit by believing in God and producing good works of charity. Pope John Paul II was a special God-given guide and model for our modern times. Learning and living the dual dimension of his consecration is paramount: (1) offering all to Jesus through Mary in union with St. Joseph; (2) being consecrated in the truths of the Catholic Faith (i.e., catechesis of the new evangelization).

Pray for the grace to die to your selfishness and keep asking for the grace to be one spirit with Christ, for as Blessed Teresa of Calcutta said: "Everyone is called to holiness, which is achieved through God's grace and our will."

Blessed Teresa also said that the fruit of interior silence is prayer, and the fruit of prayer is faith, and the fruit of faith is love, and the fruit of love is service, and the fruit of service is peace. This was one of Gwen Coniker's favorite reflections. It brings about your union with God and neighbor and helps you find your true self in God.

Thirteenth Day
Knowledge of Self

Come Holy Spirit, please grant us true humility so that we may truly see ourselves as you see us and fully live this Total Consecration to Jesus through Mary in union with St. Joseph.

Formation in the truth of the total giving of oneself to Jesus through Mary in union of St. Joseph enables us to realize what true love is.

Redemptor Hominis (Redeemer of Man)
Pope John Paul II's first encyclical

10. Man cannot live without love. He remains a being that is incomprehensible for himself, his life is senseless, if love is not revealed to him, if he does not encounter love, if he does not experience it and make it his own, if he does not participate intimately in it.

This, as has already been said, is why Christ the Redeemer "fully reveals man to himself". If we may use the expression, this is the human dimension of the mystery of the Redemption. In this dimension man finds again the greatness, dignity and value that belong to his humanity.

In the mystery of the Redemption man becomes newly "expressed" and, in a way, is newly created. He is newly created! "There is neither Jew nor Greek, there is neither slave nor free, there is neither male nor female; for you are all one in Christ Jesus" (Gal. 3:28).

The man who wishes to understand himself thoroughly—and not just in accordance with immediate, partial, often superficial, and even illusory standards and measures of his being—he must with his unrest, uncertainty and even his weakness and sinfulness, with his life and death, draw near to Christ.

He must, so to speak, enter into him with all his own self, he must "appropriate" and assimilate the whole of the reality of the Incarnation and Redemption in order to find himself. If this profound process takes place within him, he then bears fruit not only of adoration of God but also of deep wonder at himself. How precious must man be in the eyes of the Creator, if he "gained so great a

Redeemer", and if God "gave his only Son "in order that
man "should not perish but have eternal life" (cf. Jn. 3:16).

In reality, the name for
that deep amazement at
man's worth and dignity is
the Gospel, that is to say:
the Good News. It is also
called Christianity. This
amazement determines the
Church's mission in the
world and, perhaps even
more so, "in the modern world". This amazement, which is
also a conviction and a certitude—at its deepest root it is
the certainty of faith, but in a hidden and mysterious way
it vivifies every aspect of authentic humanism—is closely
connected with Christ. It also fixes Christ's place—so to
speak, his particular right of citizenship—in the history of
man and mankind.

Unceasingly contemplating the whole of Christ's mystery, the Church knows with all the certainty of faith that
the Redemption that took place through the Cross has
definitively restored his dignity to man and given back
meaning to his life in the world, a meaning that was lost to
a considerable extent because of sin. And for that reason,
the Redemption was accomplished in the paschal mystery,
leading through the Cross and death to Resurrection.

The Church's fundamental function in every age and
particularly in ours is to direct man's gaze, to point the
awareness and experience of the whole of humanity
towards the mystery of God, to help all men to be familiar
with the profundity of the Redemption taking place in
Christ Jesus. At the same time man's deepest sphere is
involved—we mean the sphere of human hearts, consciences and events.

14. For the Church all ways lead to man

The Church cannot abandon man, for his "destiny",
that is to say his election, calling, birth and death, salvation or perdition, is so closely and unbreakably linked

with Christ. We are speaking precisely of each man on this planet, this earth that the Creator gave to the first man, saying to the man and the women: "subdue it and have dominion". Each man in all the unrepeatable reality of what he is and what he does, of his intellect and will, of his conscience and heart.

Man who in his reality has, because he is a "person", a history of his life that is his own and, most important, a history of his soul that is his own. Man who, in keeping with the openness of his spirit within and also with the many diverse needs of his body and his existence in time, writes this personal history of his through numerous bonds, contacts, situations, and social structures linking him with other men, beginning to do so from the first moment of his existence on earth, from the moment of his conception and birth.

Man in the full truth of his existence, of his personal being and also of his community and social being—in the sphere of his own family, in the sphere of society and very diverse contexts, in the sphere of his own nation or people (perhaps still only that of his clan or tribe), and in the sphere of the whole of mankind—this man is the primary route that the Church must travel in fulfilling her mission: he is the primary and fundamental way for the Church, the way traced out by Christ himself, the way that leads invariably through the mystery of the Incarnation and the Redemption.

It was precisely this man in all the truth of his life, in his conscience, in his continual inclination to sin and at the same time in his continual aspiration to truth, the good, the beautiful, justice and love that the Second Vatican Council had before its eyes when, in outlining his situation in the modern world, it always passed from the external elements of this situation to the truth within humanity: "In man himself many elements wrestle with one another.

Thus, on the one hand, as a creature he experiences his limitations in a multitude of ways. On the other, he feels himself to be boundless in his desires and summoned to a higher life. Pulled by manifold attractions, he is constantly forced to choose among them and to renounce some. Indeed, as a weak and sinful being, he often does what he would not, and fails to do what he would. Hence he suffers from internal divisions, and from these flow so many and such great discords in society" (*Gaudium et Spes*, 10).

This man is the way for the Church — a way that, in a sense, is the basis of all the other ways that the Church must walk — because man — every man without any exception whatever — has been redeemed by Christ, and because with man — with each man without any exception whatever — Christ is in a way united, even when man is unaware of it: "Christ, who died and was raised up for all, provides man" — each man and every man — "with the light and the strength to measure up to his supreme calling" (*Gaudium et Spes*, 10).

Since this man is the way for the Church, the way for her daily life and experience, for her mission and toil, the Church of today must be aware in an always new manner of man's "situation". That means that she must be aware of his possibilities, which keep returning to their proper bearings and thus revealing themselves.

She must likewise be aware of the threats to man and of all that seems to oppose the endeavor "to make human life ever more human" and make every element of this life correspond to man's true dignity — in a word, she must be aware of all that is opposed to that process.

Letter to Women, by Pope John Paul II

10. The Church sees in Mary the highest expression of the "feminine genius" and she finds in her a source of con-

stant inspiration. Mary called herself the "handmaid of the Lord" (Lk 1:38).

Through obedience to the Word of God she accepted her lofty yet not easy vocation as wife and mother in the family of Nazareth. Putting herself at God's service, she also put herself at the service of others: a service of love. Precisely through this service Mary was able to experience in her life a mysterious, but authentic "reign". It is not by chance that she is invoked as "Queen of heaven and earth".

The entire community of believers thus invokes her; many nations and peoples call upon her as their "Queen". For her, "to reign" is to serve! Her service is "to reign"!

This is the way in which authority needs to be understood, both in the family and in society and the Church. Each person's fundamental vocation is revealed in this "reigning", for each person has been created in the "image" of the One who is Lord of heaven and earth and called to be his adopted son or daughter in Christ.

Man is the only creature on earth "which God willed for its own sake", *as the Second Vatican Council teaches; it significantly adds that man "cannot fully find himself except through a sincere gift of self" (Gaudium et Spes, 24).*

The maternal "reign" of Mary consists in this. She who was, in all her being, a gift for her Son, has also become a gift for the sons and daughters of the whole human race, awakening profound trust in those who seek her guidance along the difficult paths of life on the way to their definitive and transcendent destiny.

Each one reaches this final goal by fidelity to his or her own vocation; this goal provides meaning and direction for the earthly labors of men and women alike.

True Devotion to Mary
by St. Louis de Montfort, Chapter II and III

Now, as the kingdom of Jesus Christ consists principally in the heart, or interior, of man—according to the words, "the kingdom of God is within us"—so does the kingdom of Mary. The Blessed Virgin reigns principally in the interior of man, that is to say in his soul. And in souls she and her Son are more glorified than in all visible creatures; so that, with the saints, we may call her the Queen of All Hearts!

We must conclude that Mary, being necessary to God in a necessity we call "hypothetical," as a consequence of His will, is much more necessary to men, if they would attain the goal of heaven.

We must not, therefore, confuse devotion to her with devotion to other saints. Devotion to her is far more necessary than devotion to them. It is not something superfluous. Many pious and learned men have proved, with invincible arguments, that devotion to Mary is necessary to salvation; and that, on the contrary, not to love her is a sign of depravity and doom.

That true devotion to Mary assures one of heaven is proven by prophecies and teachings in both the Old and the New Testaments, confirmed by the examples of the saints, and demonstrated by experience and reason.

Even the devil and his devotees, compelled by the power of truth, have confessed this in spite of themselves.

Of all the texts I might bring to your attention let me quote only the words of St. John Damascene: "To be devout to thee, O Blessed Virgin, is a weapon of salvation God gives to those He wants to save."

In the chronicles of St. Francis of Assisi it is related that in an ecstasy he was shown a ladder that reached into heaven. Our Blessed Mother was on the top of this ladder. And St. Francis was told that one had to go through her to enter into eternal bliss....

Since, then, devotion to Mary is essential to eternal salvation, it is ever more necessary to those called to a particular or special perfection; and I cannot see how one could acquire intimate union with Our Lord and perfect fidelity to the Holy Spirit without acquiring a very great union with Mary and a very great dependence on her.

And he said to them, "When you pray, say: 'Father, hallowed be Thy name. Thy kingdom come. Give us each day our daily bread; and forgive us our sins, for we ourselves forgive everyone who is indebted to us; and lead us not into temptation."
— Luke 11:2-4

Now read "Part 2: Knowledge of Self" on pages 65–66 and review part of *In Light of the Ten Commandments* (#53h 6&9) in Appendix A. Pray 3 decades of the Rosary (#6a-9), preferably with your family, sometime during the day. If you already pray the daily family Rosary, you do not need to pray these 3 decades.

Fourteenth Day
Knowledge of Self

*Come Holy Spirit, please grant us true humility so that we may truly
see ourselves as you see us and fully live this Total Consecration to
Jesus through Mary in union with St. Joseph.*

Veritatis Splendor (Splendor of Truth)
by Pope John Paul II

"Teacher, what good must I do to have eternal life?" (Mt
19:16)

8. The question which
the rich young man puts
to Jesus of Nazareth is
one which rises from the
depths of his heart. It is
an essential and unavoid-
able question for the life of
every man, for it is about
the moral good which
must be done, and about eternal life.

The young man senses that there is a connection
between moral good and the fulfillment of his own destiny. He is a devout Israelite, raised as it were in the
shadow of the Law of the Lord. If he asks Jesus this question, we can presume that it is not because he is ignorant
of the answer contained in the Law. It is more likely that
the attractiveness of the person of Jesus had prompted
within him new questions about moral good.

He feels the need to draw near to the One who had
begun his preaching with this new and decisive proclamation: "The time is fulfilled, and the Kingdom of God is
at hand; repent, and believe in the Gospel" (Mk 1:15).

People today need to turn to Christ once again in order
to receive from him the answer to their questions about
what is good and what is evil. Christ is the Teacher, the
Risen One who has life in himself and who is always present in his Church and in the world. It is he who opens up
to the faithful the book of the Scriptures and, by fully
revealing the Father's will, teaches the truth about moral

action. At the source and summit of the economy of salvation, as the Alpha and the Omega of human history (cf. Rev 1:8; 21:6; 22:13), Christ sheds light on man's condition and his integral vocation. Consequently, "the man who wishes to understand himself thoroughly — and not just in accordance with immediate, partial, often superficial, and even illusory standards and measures of his being — must with his unrest, uncertainty and even his weakness and sinfulness, with his life and death, draw near to Christ.

He must, so to speak, enter him with all his own self; he must 'appropriate' and assimilate the whole of the reality of the Incarnation and Redemption in order to find himself. If this profound process takes place within him, he then bears fruit not only of adoration of God but also of deeper wonder at himself" (*Redemptor hominis*, 13).

If we therefore wish to go to the heart of the Gospel's moral teaching and grasp its profound and unchanging content, we must carefully inquire into the meaning of the question asked by the rich young man in the Gospel and, even more, the meaning of Jesus' reply, allowing ourselves to be guided by him. Jesus, as a patient and sensitive teacher, answers the young man by taking him, as it were, by the hand, and leading him step by step to the full truth.

18. Those who live "by the flesh" experience God's law as a burden, and indeed as a denial or at least a restriction of their own freedom.

On the other hand, those who are impelled by love and "walk by the Spirit" (Gal 5:16), and who desire to serve others, find in God's Law the fundamental and necessary way in which to practice love as something freely chosen and freely lived out. Indeed, they feel an interior urge — a genuine "necessity" and no longer a form of coercion — not to stop at the minimum demands of the Law, but to live them in their "fullness". This is a still uncertain and fragile journey as long as we are on earth, but it is one made possible by grace, which enables us to possess the full freedom of the children of God (cf. Rom 8:21) and thus to live our moral life in a way worthy of our sublime vocation as "sons in the Son".

This vocation to perfect love is not restricted to a small group of individuals. The invitation, "go, sell your possessions and give the money to the poor", and the promise "you will have treasure in heaven", are meant for everyone, because they bring out the full meaning of the commandment of love for neighbor, just as the invitation which follows, "Come, follow me", is the new, specific form of the commandment of love of God.

Both the commandments and Jesus' invitation to the rich young man stand at the service of a single and indivisible charity, which spontaneously tends towards that perfection whose measure is God alone: "You, therefore, must be perfect, as your heavenly Father is perfect" (Mt 5:48). In the Gospel of Luke, Jesus makes even clearer the meaning of this perfection: "Be merciful, even as your Father is merciful" (Lk 6:36).

True Devotion to Mary
by St. Louis de Montfort, Chapter XI

Effects of Consecration

Another reason to recommend true devotion to us is the good it will do our neighbors. For, by it, out of our charity and through our mother, Mary, we give them the satisfactory and prayer value of all our good works, not excepting even the least good thought and the least little suffering. We agree that all we have earned and will earn in the way of spiritual riches will be used either for the conversion of sinners or the deliverance of souls in purgatory, as Our Lady wishes.

Isn't this perfect love of neighbor? Doesn't it mark the perfect disciple of Christ, whose measure is that of charity? Isn't this the means to convert sinners and to free the poor souls without endangering ourselves through any feeling of pride and without scarcely doing anything but what we are obliged to do by our state in life? We are bound to do all this anyway; but we do it better through this method.

To acknowledge the excellence of this motive one must consider how wonderful it is to convert one sinner, or to send one tortured soul to heaven out of purgatory. It is an infinite good. It is a far greater good than the creation of heaven and earth because one thus gives to a soul the possession of God!

Should we, in all our life, convert only one sinner or deliver only one poor soul, through true devotion, would that not be enough to make any really charitable person among us eagerly adopt true devotion as his own?

We must remember, I repeat again and again, that our good works, passing through the hands of Mary, take on an increase of purity, and therefore of meritorious value. [We call this the Marian Multiplier; see Cardinal Ciappi's letter of August 24, 1989, in Day 37 on page 194]. Consequently they become much more capable of relieving those in purgatory or of bringing sinners back to God. The little we give Our Lady unselfishly and with true charity becomes powerful enough to soften the anger of God and obtain His mercy.

Maybe, when a faithful slave of Mary is about to die, he learns that through true devotion he has converted several sinners, and freed several others from the purging flames! This, though he has performed only the very ordinary duties of his state in life!

What joy for him in the day of his judgment! What glory for him throughout eternity!

A new commandment I give to you, that you love one another; even as I have loved you, that you also love one another. John 13:34

Now review part of *In Light of the Ten Commandments* (#53h 7&10) and pray the *Ave Maris Stella* (#47) in Appendix A. Pray 3 decades of the Rosary (#6a-9), preferably with your family, sometime during the day. If you already pray the daily family Rosary, you do not need to pray these 3 decades. Optional: pray the *Seed Charity Prayer in the Spirit of St. Francis* (#10).

Fifteenth Day
Knowledge of Self

Come Holy Spirit, please grant us true humility so that we may truly see ourselves as you see us and fully live this Total Consecration to Jesus through Mary in union with St. Joseph.

Evangelium vitae (Gospel of Life)
by Pope John Paul II

36. Unfortunately, God's marvellous plan was marred by the appearance of sin in history. Through sin, man rebels against his Creator and ends up by worshipping creatures: "They exchanged the truth about God for a lie and worshiped and served the creature rather than the Creator" (Rom 1:25).

As a result man not only deforms the image of God in his own person, but is tempted to offenses against it in others as well, replacing relationships of communion by attitudes of distrust, indifference, hostility and even murderous hatred. When God is not acknowledged as God, the profound meaning of man is betrayed and communion between people is compromised.

In the life of man, God's image shines forth anew and is again revealed in all its fullness at the coming of the Son of God in human flesh. "Christ is the image of the invisible God" (Col 1:15), he "reflects the glory of God and bears the very stamp of his nature" (Heb 1:3). He is the perfect image of the Father.

The plan of life given to the first Adam finds at last its fulfillment in Christ. Whereas the disobedience of Adam had ruined and marred God's plan for human life and introduced death into the world *[sin brings about disorder in man and in nature], the redemptive obedience of Christ is the source of grace poured out upon the human race, opening wide to everyone the gates of the kingdom of life* (cf. Rom 5:12-21). As the Apostle Paul states: "The first man Adam became a living being; the last Adam became a life-giving spirit" (1 Cor 15:45).

All who commit themselves to following Christ are given the fullness of life: the divine image is restored, renewed and brought to perfection in them. God's plan for human beings is this, that they should "be conformed to the image of his Son" (Rom 8:29). Only thus, in the splendor of this image, can man be freed from the slavery of idolatry, rebuild lost fellowship and rediscover his true identity.

"Whoever lives and believes in me shall never die" (Jn 11:26): the gift of eternal life.

"And the dragon stood before the woman ... that he might devour her child when she brought it forth" (Rev 12:4): life menaced by the forces of evil.

104. In the Book of Revelation, the "great portent" of the "woman" (12:1) is accompanied by "another portent which appeared in heaven": "a great red dragon" (Rev 12:3), which represents Satan, the personal power of evil, as well as all the powers of evil at work in history and opposing the Church's mission.

Here too Mary sheds light on the Community of Believers. The hostility of the powers of evil is, in fact, an insidious opposition which, before affecting the disciples of Jesus, is directed against his mother. To save the life of her Son from those who fear him as a dangerous threat, Mary has to flee with Joseph and the Child into Egypt (cf. Mt 2:13-15).

Mary thus helps the Church to realize that life is always at the center of a great struggle between good and evil, between light and darkness. The dragon wishes to devour "the child brought forth" (cf. Rev 12:4), a figure of

Christ, whom Mary brought forth "in the fullness of time" (Gal 4:4) and whom the Church must unceasingly offer to people in every age.

But in a way that child is also a figure of every person, every child, especially every helpless baby whose life is threatened, because—as the Council reminds us— "by his Incarnation the Son of God has united himself in some fashion with every person". It is precisely in the "flesh" of every person that Christ continues to reveal himself and to enter into fellowship with us, so that rejection of human life, in whatever form that rejection takes, is really a rejection of Christ.

This is the fascinating but also demanding truth which Christ reveals to us and which his Church continues untiringly to proclaim: "Whoever receives one such child in my name receives me" (Mt 18:5); "Truly, I say to you, as you did it to one of the least of these my brethren, you did it to me" (Mt 25:40).

120. Mary shares our human condition, but in complete openness to the grace of God. Not having known sin, she is able to have compassion on every kind of weakness. She understands sinful man and loves him with a Mother's love. Precisely for this reason she is on the side of truth and shares the Church's burden in recalling always and to everyone the demands of morality. Nor does she permit sinful man to be deceived by those who claim to love him by justifying his sin, for she knows that the sacrifice of Christ her Son would thus be emptied of its power.

No absolution offered by beguiling doctrines, even in the areas of philosophy and theology, can make man truly happy: only the Cross and the glory of the Risen Christ can grant peace to his conscience and salvation to his life.

True Devotion to Mary
by St. Louis de Montfort, Chapter V

Now, in order to become empty of self, we must die to ourselves daily. We must disown the operations of the powers of our souls and the senses of our bodies. We must see as if we saw not, hear as if we did not hear, use the things of this world as if we did not use them. If the grain of wheat falling into the earth does not die it will not bear fruit. *If we do not die to ourselves, and if our holiest devotions do not lead us to this necessary and fruitful death, we will bear no worthwhile fruits and our devotions will be worthless.*

All our works of holiness can be soiled by self-love and self-will. In this case the greatest sacrifices we may make and the best actions we may perform will be abominations in the sight of God! And, dying, we will find ourselves without virtues, and without merits. We shall have not one spark of that pure love known to those who have died to themselves and have buried themselves with Jesus Christ in God.

We must choose, among all the devotions to Mary, the one that will most certainly lead us to this death to self. That devotion will be the best for us, the most sanctifying. We must remember that not all is gold that glitters; not all is honey that is sweet; not all is essential to our being holy that is easy to do, or that is done by the most people.

Beloved, let us love one another; for love is of God, and he who loves is born of God and knows God. He who does not love does not know God; for God is love. In this the love of God was made manifest among us, that God sent his only Son into the world, so that we might live through him. In this is love, not that we loved God but that he loved us and sent his Son to be the expiation for our sins. Beloved, if God so loved us, we also ought to love one another. — 1 John 4:7-11

Now review part of *In Light of the Ten Commandments* (#53h8) and pray the *Immaculate Conception Prayer* (#2e) in Appendix A. Pray 3 decades of the Rosary (#6a-9), preferably with your family, sometime during the day. If you already pray the daily family Rosary, you do not need to pray these 3 decades. Optional: reflect on sections 37–40 of *Catechism on True Devotion to Mary* (#51b).

Sixteenth Day
Knowledge of Self

Come Holy Spirit, please grant us true humility so that we may truly see ourselves as you see us and fully live this Total Consecration to Jesus through Mary in union with St. Joseph.

Veritatis Splendor (Splendor of Truth)
by Pope John Paul II

17. We do not know how clearly the young man in the Gospel understood the profound and challenging import of Jesus' first reply: "If you wish to enter into life, keep the commandments". But it is certain that the young man's commitment to respect all the moral demands of the commandments represents the absolutely essential ground in which the desire for perfection can take root and mature, the desire, that is, for the meaning of the commandments to be completely fulfilled in following Christ.

Jesus' conversation with the young man helps us to grasp the conditions for the moral growth of man, who has been called to perfection: the young man, having observed all the commandments, shows that he is incapable of taking the next step by himself alone. To do so requires mature human freedom ("If you wish to be perfect") and God's gift of grace ("Come, follow me").

Perfection demands that maturity in self-giving to which human freedom is called. Jesus points out to the young man that the commandments are the first and indispensable condition for having eternal life; on the other hand, for the young man to give up all he possesses and to follow the Lord is presented as an invitation: "If you wish...".

These words of Jesus reveal the particular dynamic of freedom's growth towards maturity, and at the same time they bear witness to the fundamental relationship between freedom and divine law. Human freedom and God's law are not in opposition; on the contrary, they appeal one to the other. The follower of Christ knows that his vocation is to freedom.

"You were called to freedom, brethren" (Gal 5:13), proclaims the Apostle Paul with joy and pride. But he immediately adds: "only do not use your freedom as an opportunity for the flesh, but through love be servants of one another" (ibid.).

The firmness with which the Apostle opposes those who believe that they are justified by the Law has nothing to do with man's "liberation" from precepts. On the contrary, the latter are at the service of the practice of love: "For he who loves his neighbor has fulfilled the Law.

The commandments, 'You shall not commit adultery; You shall not murder; You shall not steal; You shall not covet,' and any other commandment, are summed up in this sentence, 'You shall love your neighbor as yourself'" (Rom 13:8-9). Saint Augustine, after speaking of the observance of the commandments as being a kind of incipient, imperfect freedom, goes on to say: "Why, someone will ask, is it not yet perfect? Because 'I see in my members another law at war with the law of my reason'...

In part freedom, in part slavery: not yet complete freedom, not yet pure, not yet whole, because we are not yet in eternity. In part we retain our weakness and in part we have attained freedom. All our sins were destroyed in Baptism, but does it follow that no weakness remained after iniquity was destroyed? Had none remained, we would live without sin in this life. But who would dare to say this except someone who is proud, someone unworthy of the mercy of our deliverer?...

Therefore, since some weakness has remained in us, I dare to say that to the extent to which we serve God we are free, while to the extent that we follow the law of sin, we are still slaves".

True Devotion to Mary
by St. Louis de Montfort, Chapter III

God wants His Mother to be better known, and to be more loved and honored than she has ever been. And this will be accomplished, if the chosen ones, with the grace and light of the Holy Spirit, take up the practice I will disclose to them.

Then they will see this lovely Star of the Sea as clearly as their faith permits; and she will guide them into a safe harbor despite all perils. They will know the grandeurs of their sovereign lady. They will consecrate themselves entirely to her, as her subjects, her slaves of love. They will know the delight of her favors, her tenderness, her motherly care. And they will love her as simply as children love their mother.

They will realize how much they need her help. They will know the abundance of her mercies. They will go to her in all things as to their dear advocate. They will realize she is the shortest, safest, straightest, easiest route to Jesus; the perfect route.

They will deliver themselves to Mary, body and soul, without any reserve, that they may belong in the same manner to her Son.

Who will these followers of Mary be, these children, servants, and slaves? And what will they be?

They will be brands of fire, ministers of the Lord who scatter the fire of divine love everywhere. They will be like arrows in the hands of the mighty Mother of God, sharp arrows that will transfix her enemies.

They will be the children of Levi, well purified by the fire of great tribulations and clinging closely to God. They will carry the gold of love in their hearts, the frankincense of prayer in their minds, and the myrrh of self-denial in their bodies. They will bring to the poor and the humble everywhere the fragrance of Jesus.

Jesus said to him, "If you would be perfect, go, sell what you possess and give to the poor, and you will have treasure in heaven; and come, follow me." Matthew 19:21

Now reflect on part of *The Seven Gifts of the Holy Spirit (#53f)* and the *First Saturdays Reparation Promise (#33)* in Appendix A. Pray 3 decades of the Rosary (#6a-9), preferably with your family, sometime during the day. If you already pray the daily family Rosary, you do not need to pray these 3 decades. Optional: pray the *Go to St. Joseph Novena (#16a)*.

Seventeenth Day
Knowledge of Self

Come Holy Spirit, please grant us true humility so that we may truly see ourselves as you see us and fully live this Total Consecration to Jesus through Mary in union with St. Joseph.

Evangelium vitae (Gospel of Life)
by Pope John Paul II

25. The blood of Christ, while it reveals the grandeur of the Father's love, shows how precious man is in God's eyes and how priceless the value of his life. The Apostle Peter reminds us of this: "You know that you were ransomed from the futile ways inherited from your fathers, not with perishable things such as silver or gold, but with the precious blood of Christ, like that of a lamb without blemish or spot" (1 Pt 1:18-19).

Precisely by contemplating the precious blood of Christ, the sign of his self-giving love (cf. Jn 13:1), the believer learns to recognize and appreciate the almost divine dignity of every human being and can exclaim with ever renewed and grateful wonder: "How precious must man be in the eyes of the Creator, if he 'gained so great a Redeemer' (*Exsultet* of the Easter Vigil), and if God 'gave his only Son' in order that man 'should not perish but have eternal life' (cf. Jn 3:16)!".

Furthermore, Christ's blood reveals to man that his greatness, and therefore his vocation, consists in the sincere gift of self. Precisely because it is poured out as the gift of life, the blood of Christ is no longer a sign of death, of definitive separation from the brethren, but the instrument of a communion which is richness of life for all. Whoever in the Sacrament of the Eucharist drinks this blood and abides in Jesus (cf. Jn 6:56) is drawn into the dynamism of his love and gift of life, in order to bring to its fullness the original vocation to love which belongs to everyone (cf. Gen 1:27; 2:18-24).

35. "What is man that you are mindful of him, and the son of man that you care for him?", the Psalmist wonders (Ps 8:4). Compared to the immensity of the universe, man is very small, and yet this very contrast reveals his greatness: "You have made him little less than a god, and crown him with glory and honor" (Ps 8:5).

The glory of God shines on the face of man. In man the Creator finds his rest, as Saint Ambrose comments with a sense of awe: "The sixth day is finished and the creation of the world ends with the formation of that masterpiece which is man, who exercises dominion over all living creatures and is as it were the crown of the universe and the supreme beauty of every created being.

Truly we should maintain a reverential silence, since the Lord rested from every work he had undertaken in the world. He rested then in the depths of man, he rested in man's mind and in his thought; after all, he had created man endowed with reason, capable of imitating him, of emulating his virtue, of hungering for heavenly graces.

In these his gifts God reposes, who has said: 'Upon whom shall I rest, if not upon the one who is humble, contrite in spirit and trembles at my word?' (Is 66:1-2). I thank the Lord our God who has created so wonderful a work in which to take his rest".

True Devotion to Mary
by St. Louis de Montfort, Chapter II

God the Father gathered all the waters together and called it the sea. (The Latin word for sea is Mare.) He gathered all His graces together and called it Mary. (The Latin is Maria.) He has a treasury, a storehouse full of riches.

There He has enclosed all He holds most beautiful, striking, rare, and precious, including His own Son. This immense treasury is none but Mary. The saints called her the "treasury of God." From the fullness of this treasury all are made rich!

God the Son imparted to His Mother all the infinite merits and virtues He acquired through His life and death. He made her the treasurer of all the riches He inherited from His Father.

Through her He showers on the members of His Mystical Body all His merits, graces, and virtues. She is the mysterious channel, the gentle and generous stream, the gracious aqueduct through which His mercies flow.

God the Holy Spirit enriched His faithful spouse with gifts undreamed of. And He selected her to distribute all that is His, as she wills, when she wills, as much as she wills, to whom she wills. No heavenly gift comes to earth that does not pass through her virginal hands. This is the will of God; that whatever we receive we receive through Mary.

Thus does the Trinity enrich, elevate, and honor her who made herself poor, humble, and hidden; who reduced herself into nothingness through her profound humility.

Now in Christ Jesus you who once were far off have been brought near in the blood of Christ. For he is our peace, who has made us both one, and has broken down the dividing wall of hostility, by abolishing in his flesh the law of commandments and ordinances, that he might create in himself one new man in place of the two, so making peace, and might reconcile us both to God in one body through the cross, thereby bringing the hostility to an end. — Ephesians 2:13-16

Now review part of the *Examination of Conscience Reflections* (#53i) and pray the *Act of Consecration to St. Joseph* (#14) in Appendix A. Pray 3 decades of the Rosary (#6a-9), preferably with your family, sometime during the day. If you already pray the daily family Rosary, you do not need to pray these 3 decades. Optional: reflect on sections 41–44 of *Catechism on True Devotion to Mary* (#51b).

Eighteenth Day
Knowledge of Self

Come Holy Spirit, please grant us true humility so that we may truly see ourselves as you see us and fully live this Total Consecration to Jesus through Mary in union with St. Joseph.

Dominum et Vivificantem (On the Holy Spirit)
by Pope John Paul II

10. In his intimate life, God "is love," the essential love shared by the three divine Persons: personal love is the Holy Spirit as the Spirit of the Father and the Son. Therefore he "searches even the depths of God," as uncreated Love-Gift.

It can be said that in the Holy Spirit the intimate life of the Triune God becomes totally gift, an exchange of mutual love between the divine Persons and that through the Holy Spirit God exists in the mode of gift. It is the Holy Spirit who is the personal expression of this self-giving, of this being-love.

He is Person-Love. He is Person-Gift Here we have an inexhaustible treasure of the reality and an inexpressible deepening of the concept of person in God, which only divine Revelation makes known to us.

At the same time, the Holy Spirit, being consubstantial with the Father and the Son in divinity, is love and uncreated gift from which derives as from its source (*fons*

vivus) all giving of gifts vis-à-vis creatures (created gift): the gift of existence to all things through creation; the gift of grace to human beings through the whole economy of salvation. As the Apostle Paul writes: "God's love has been poured into our hearts through the Holy Spirit which has been given to US."

11. Christ's farewell discourse at the Last Supper stands in particular reference to this "giving" and "self-giving" of the Holy Spirit. In John's Gospel we have as it were the revelation of the most profound "logic" of the saving mystery contained in God's eternal plan, as an extension of the ineffable communion of the Father, Son and Holy Spirit. This is the divine "logic" which from the mystery of the Trinity leads to the mystery of the Redemption of the world in Jesus Christ.

The Redemption accomplished by the Son in the dimensions of the earthly history of humanity— accomplished in his "departure" through the Cross and Resurrection—is at the same time, in its entire salvific power, transmitted to the Holy Spirit: the one who "will take what is mine." The words of the text of John indicate that, according to the divine plan, Christ's "departure" is an indispensable condition for the "sending" and the coming of the Holy Spirit, but these words also say that what begins now is the new salvific self-giving of God, in the Holy Spirit.

12. It is a new beginning in relation to the first, original beginning of God's salvific self-giving, which is identified with the mystery of creation itself. Here is what we read in the very first words of the Book of Genesis: "In the beginning God created the heavens and the earth..., and the Spirit of God (*ruah Elohim*) was moving over the face of the waters."

This biblical concept of creation includes not only the call to existence of the very being of the cosmos, that is to say the giving of existence, but also the presence of the Spirit of God in creation, that is to say the beginning of God's salvific self-communication to the things he creates. This is true first of all concerning man, who has been created in the image and likeness of God: "Let us make man in our image, after our likeness." "Let us make": can one hold that the plural which the Creator uses here in speaking of himself already in some way suggests the Trinitarian mystery, the presence of the Trinity in the work of the creation of man?

The Christian reader, who already knows the revelation of this mystery, can discern a reflection of it also in these words. At any rate, the context of the Book of Genesis enables us to see in the creation of man the first beginning of God's salvific self-giving commensurate with the "image and likeness" of himself which he has granted to man.

True Devotion to Mary
by St. Louis de Montfort, Chapter III

It is Mary alone who found grace before God without the help of any other mere creature. It is through Mary alone that all those who found grace before God—after her—have found it. It is through Mary alone that future souls will find that grace. She was full of grace when the Archangel Gabriel hailed her. She was abundantly filled with grace when the Holy Spirit overshadowed her. And from day to day, from moment to moment, she has increased this double-fullness of grace.

Thus she has reached a height of grace beyond all human thought or notion. She is not only the treasurer of God's treasures, she is the only dispenser of them. She can ennoble, exalt, and enrich whom she wills. She can lead them into the narrow way to heaven. She can conduct them through the narrow door of life, in spite of all obstacles. And she can give them the throne, the scepter, and the kingly crown!

Jesus is, everywhere and always, the Son and the Fruit of Mary. Mary is, everywhere and always, the tree that bears the Fruit of Life, the true Mother that produces It.

To Mary alone God gave the keys of the cellars of divine love. To Mary alone He gave the power to enter into the most sublime and the most secret ways of perfection.

To Mary alone He gave the power to lead others along those paths. It is Mary alone who welcomes the miserable children of the faithless Eve into the earthly paradise where they may walk in all pleasure with God; where they may safely hide from their enemies; where they may delight in the fruits of the Tree of Life, and of "the tree of the knowledge of good and evil"; where they may drink all they wish of the bountiful and beautiful fountains; and where they will have no more fear of death.

And when Elizabeth heard the greeting of Mary, the babe leaped in her womb; and Elizabeth was filled with the Holy Spirit and she exclaimed with a loud cry, "Blessed are you among women, and blessed is the fruit of your womb! And why is this granted me, that the mother of my Lord should come to me?" — Luke 1:41-43

Now review part of the *Excerpt from Veritatis Splendor* (#53j) and pray the *Miraculous Medal Prayer* (#32) in Appendix A. Pray 3 decades of the Rosary (#6a-9), preferably with your family, sometime during the day. If you already pray the daily family Rosary, you do not need to pray these 3 decades. Optional: reflect on sections 45–49 of *Catechism on True Devotion to Mary* (#51b).

Nineteenth Day
Knowledge of Self

Come Holy Spirit, please grant us true humility so that we may truly see ourselves as you see us and fully live this Total Consecration to Jesus through Mary in union with St. Joseph.

Letter to Families, by Pope John Paul II

20. The history of "fairest love" begins at the Annunciation, in those wondrous words which the angel spoke to Mary, called to become the Mother of the Son of God. With Mary's "yes", the One who is "God from God and Light from Light" becomes a son of man.

Mary is his Mother, while continuing to be the Virgin who "knows not man" (cf. Lk 1:34). As Mother and Virgin, Mary becomes the Mother of Fairest Love. This truth is already revealed in the words of the Archangel Gabriel, but its full significance will gradually become clearer and more evident as Mary follows her Son in the pilgrimage of faith.

The "Mother of Fairest Love" was accepted by the one who, according to Israel's tradition, was already her earthly husband: Joseph, of the house of David. Joseph would have had the right to consider his promised bride as his wife and the mother of his children.

But God takes it upon himself to intervene in this spousal covenant: "Joseph, son of David, do not fear to take Mary as your wife, for that which is conceived in her is of the Holy Spirit" (Mt 1:20). Joseph is aware, having seen it with his own eyes, that a new life with which he has had nothing to do has been conceived in Mary.

Being a just man, and observing the Old Law, which in his situation imposed the obligation of divorce, he wishes to dissolve his marriage in a loving way (cf. Mt 1:19). The

angel of the Lord tells him that this would not be consis-
tent with his vocation; indeed it would be contrary to the
spousal love uniting him to Mary. This mutual spousal
love, to be completely "fairest love", requires that he
should take Mary and her Son into his own house in
Nazareth. Joseph obeys the divine message and does all
that he had been commanded (cf. Mt 1:24).

And so, thanks also to Joseph, the mystery of the
Incarnation and, together with it, the mystery of the Holy
Family, come to be profoundly inscribed in the spousal
love of husband and wife and, in an indirect way, in the
genealogy of every human family. What Saint Paul will
call the "great mystery" found its most lofty expression in
the Holy Family. Thus the family truly takes its place at
the very heart of the New Covenant.

It can also be said that the history of "fairest love"
began, in a certain way, with the first human couple:
Adam and Eve. The temptation to which they yielded and
the original sin which resulted did not completely deprive
them of the capacity for "fairest love".

This becomes clear when we read, for example, in the
Book of Tobit that the spouses Tobias and Sarah, in
defining the meaning of their union, appealed to their first
parents, Adam and Eve (cf. Tob 8:6). In the New Covenant,
Saint Paul also bears witness to this, speaking of Christ as

a new Adam (cf. 1 Cor 15:45). Christ does not come to condemn the first Adam and the first Eve, but to save them.

He comes to renew everything that is God's gift in man, everything in him that is eternally good and beautiful, everything that forms the basis of "fairest love". The history of "fairest love" is, in one sense, the history of man's salvation.

"Fairest love" always begins with the self-revelation of the person. At creation Eve reveals herself to Adam, just as Adam reveals himself to Eve. In the course of history newly-married couples tell each other: "We shall walk the path of life together".

The family thus begins as a union of the two and, through the Sacrament, as a new community in Christ. For love to be truly "fairest", it must be a gift of God, grafted by the Holy Spirit on to human hearts and continually nourished in them (cf.Rom 5:5). Fully conscious of this, the Church in the Sacrament of Marriage asks the Holy Spirit to visit human hearts.

If love is truly to be "fairest love", a gift of one person to another, it must come from the One who is himself a gift and the source of every gift.

Such was the case, as the Gospel recounts, with Mary and Joseph who, at the threshold of the New Covenant, renewed the experience of "fairest love" described in the Song of Solomon. Joseph thinks of Mary in the words:

"My sister, my bride" (Song 4:9). Mary, the Mother of God, conceives by the power of the Holy Spirit, who is the origin of the "fairest love", which the Gospel delicately places in the context of the "great mystery".

When we speak about "fairest love", we are also speaking about beauty: the beauty of love and the beauty of the human being who, by the power of the Holy Spirit, is capable of such love. We are speaking of the beauty of man and woman: their beauty as brother or sister, as a couple about to be married, as husband and wife.

The Gospel sheds light not only on the mystery of "fairest love", but also on the equally profound mystery of beauty, which, like love, is from God. Man and woman are from God, two persons called to become a mutual gift.

From the primordial gift of the Spirit, the "giver of life", there arises the reciprocal gift of being husband or wife, no less than that of being brother or sister.

True Devotion to Mary
by St. Louis de Montfort, Chapter XIV

The mother of fair love will rid your heart of all scruples and silly fears. She will so widen it that you may run, with the holy freedom of the children of God, along the ways of her Son's commandments. She will fill it with her treasure, pure love; so you will be governed not so much by the fear of God as by the love of Him.

She will make you see God as your Father, and you will try at all times to please Him. You will talk to Him with confidence, with the simplicity of a child. If, unfortunately, you offend Him, you will humbly beg His pardon, stretch up your hand to His, that He may grasp it again, and, without discouragement, continue walking with Him.

Our Lady will put into your heart great confidence in God and in herself. You will no longer be going to Jesus by yourself, but through her. And besides, you will be clad in her great merits; therefore you will be able to say to God, "Behold Your handmaid, Mary; be it done to me according to Your word."

Let me say again that, since you have given yourself so completely to Mary, she will give herself to you. She will give you herself in a mysterious, but real, way, so that you will be able to tell her, "I am yours"; or, with St. John, "I have received you, Mother, as my own."

You may say with St. Bonaventure, "Behold, my Lady, my salvation! I will trust in you and have no fear, because you are my strength and my praise in the Lord."

He says also, "I am yours and all I have is yours, O glorious Virgin, blessed above all. I will place you as a seal upon my heart because your love is strong as death."

While he was still speaking to the people, behold, his mother and his brethren stood outside, asking to speak to him. But he replied to the man who told him, "Who is my mother, and who is my brethren?" And stretching out his hand toward his disciples, he said, "Here are my mother and my brethren. For whoever does the will of my Father in heaven is my brother, and sister, and mother." — Matthew 12:46-50

Now review part of the *Examination of Conscience in Light of the Ten Commandments* (#53L1) in Appendix A. Then reflect on *The Holy Spirit: Secret to Sanctity and Happiness* (#46e). Pray 3 decades of the Rosary (#6a-9), preferably with your family, sometime during the day. If you already pray the daily family Rosary, you do not need to pray these 3 decades.

*O Mary conceived without sin,
pray for us who have recourse to thee.*

Part 3: Knowledge of Mary
(Days 20-26)

As you enter more deeply into this consecration according to the formula of St. Louis de Montfort (and in imitation of Pope John Paul II), you will see that the most perfect way to achieve a life of union with God is through Mary. Let me share with you what Pope John Paul II said in the "Be Not Afraid" chapter of *Crossing the Threshold of Hope*:

"In regard to Marian devotion, each of us must understand that such devotion not only addresses a need of the heart, a sentimental inclination, but that it also corresponds to the objective truth about the Mother of God.

Mary is the new Eve, placed by God in close relation to Christ, the new Adam, beginning with the Annunciation, through the night of His birth in Bethlehem, through the wedding feast at Cana of Galilee, through the Cross at Calvary, and up to the gift of the Holy Spirit at Pentecost. The Mother of Christ the Redeemer is the Mother of the Church.

"The Second Vatican Council made great strides forward with regard to both Marian doctrine and devotion. It is impossible to include here in its entirety the marvelous eighth chapter of the Dogmatic Constitution on the Church *Lumen Gentium**, but it should be done.

When I participated in the Council, I found reflected in this chapter all my earlier youthful experiences, as well as those special bonds which continue to unite me to the Mother of God in ever new ways.

"The first way—and the oldest—is tied to all the times during my childhood that I stopped before the image of Our Lady of Perpetual Help in the parish church of Wadowice. It is tied to the tradition of the Carmelite scapular, rich in meaning and symbolism, which I knew from my youth through the Carmelite convent 'on the hill' in my home town. It is also tied to the tradition of making pilgrimages...

---

* See #65c in Appendix A for the eighth chapter of *Lumen Gentium* (*The Dogmatic Constitution of the Church*).

"After my election as Pope, as I became more involved in the problems of the universal Church, I came to have a similar conviction: On this universal level, if victory comes it will be brought by Mary. Christ will conquer through her, because He wants the Church's victories now and in the future to be linked to her.

"I held this conviction even though I did not yet know very much about Fátima. I could see, however, that there was a certain continuity among La Salette, Lourdes, and Fátima—and, in the distant past, our Polish Jasna Góra.

"And thus we come to May 13, 1981, when I was wounded by gunshots fired in St. Peter's Square. At first, I did not pay attention to the fact that the assassination attempt had occurred on the exact anniversary of the day Mary appeared to the three children at Fátima in Portugal and spoke to them the words that now, at the end of this century, seem to be close to their fulfillment.

"With this event, didn't Christ perhaps say, once again, 'Be not afraid'? Didn't he repeat this Easter exhortation to the Pope, to the Church, and, indirectly, to the entire human family?

"At the end of the second millennium, we need, perhaps more than ever, the words of the Risen Christ: 'Be not afraid!' Man who, even after the fall of Communism, has not stopped being afraid and who truly has many reasons for feeling this way, needs to hear these words.

"Nations need to hear them, especially those nations that have been reborn after the fall of the Communist empire, as well as those that witnessed this event from the outside. Peoples and nations of the entire world need to hear these words.

"Their conscience needs to grow in the certainty that Someone exists who holds in His hands the destiny of this passing world; Someone who holds the keys to death and the netherworld (cf. Rev 1:18); Someone who is the Alpha and the Omega of human history (cf. Rev 22:13)—be it the individual or collective history. And this Someone is Love (cf. 1 Jn 4:8, 16)—Love that became man, Love crucified and risen, Love unceasingly present among men. It is Eucharistic Love. It is the infinite source of communion. He alone can give the ultimate assurance when He says 'Be not afraid!'

"If man accepts these demands with an attitude of faith, he will also find in the grace that God never fails to give him the necessary strength to meet those demands."

It should be noted that the Holy Father chose to close his book with the following quote, "André Malraux was certainly right when he said that the twenty-first century would be the century of religion or it would not be at all."

How we choose to follow this prophet for our time, our determination to follow the legacy of Pope John Paul II, will determine the destiny of the twenty-first century.

This consecration that you are entering into is the beginning or renewal of a life of holiness that can make an enormous difference. Consecrated souls generate the reparation for sin that Our Lady of Fatima pleaded for so that she might obtain peace for the world from her Divine Son.

This reparation offered by all those striving to live this consecration will ultimately "lift the veil" of ignorance so that others will see and want to follow God's Will.

Once we make this consecration, Mary takes all that we have, and purifies and multiplies it. This puts into the Mystical Body of Christ a tremendous spiritual power that will repair for the sins of the world and help bring about the era of peace for which we all long. Our Lady promised this at Fatima when she said that in the end her Immaculate Heart would triumph, and an era of peace would be granted to the world.

Twentieth Day
Knowledge of Mary

*Come Holy Spirit, please help us to know, understand and
see Mary as you want us to. Please teach us to fully live our
Total Consecration to Jesus through Mary in union with
St. Joseph, and thus truly live as her children.*

Veritatis Splendor (Splendor of Truth)
by Pope John Paul II

120. Mary shares our human condition, but in complete openness to the grace of God. Not having known sin,
she is able to have compassion on every kind of weakness.
She understands sinful man and loves him with a
Mother's love. Precisely for this reason she is on the side
of truth and shares the Church's burden in recalling
always and to everyone the demands of morality.

Nor does she permit sinful man to be deceived by those
who claim to love him by justifying his sin, for she knows
that the sacrifice of Christ her Son would thus be emptied of its power. No absolution offered by beguiling
doctrines, even in the areas of philosophy and theology,
can make man truly happy: only the Cross and the glory
of the Risen Christ can grant peace to his conscience and
salvation to his life.

O Mary, Mother of Mercy, watch over all people, that the Cross of Christ may not be emptied of its power, that man may not stray from the path of the good or become blind to sin, but may put his hope ever more fully in God who is "rich in mercy" (Eph 2:4). May he carry out the good works prepared by God beforehand (cf. Eph 2:10) and so live completely "for the praise of his glory" (Eph 1:12).

True Devotion to Mary
by St. Louis de Montfort, Chapter XVI

They must do all their actions *by* Mary. That is, they must obey Our Lady in all things, and act in all things by her spirit, which is the Holy Spirit of God. "Those who are led by the Spirit of God are children of God" (Rom. 8:4).

Those led by the Spirit of Mary are children of Mary, and therefore children of God, as we have shown before. And, among so many devoted to Mary, none are her true and faithful devotees but those who act by her spirit.

I said the spirit of Mary is the Spirit of God because she never acted by her own spirit but always by the Spirit of God. He made Himself master over her to such an extent that He became her own spirit. This is the reason why St. Ambrose says: "May the soul of Mary be in each one, to glorify the Lord. May the spirit of Mary be in each to rejoice in God."

How happy the soul who, after the example of St. Alphonsus Rodriguez, the Jesuit lay brother, is possessed and governed by the spirit of Mary—a spirit meek and strong, zealous and prudent, humble and courageous, pure and fruitful!

In order that the soul may allow itself to be led by this spirit of Mary, one must...

First, renounce his own spirit, his own ambitions and ideas. This he must do before he does anything else, before mental prayer, before hearing or saying Mass, before going to Communion...because the darkness of one's spirit and the malice of the will, would, if he followed his own inclinations, oppose the holy spirit of Mary. What one had in mind might appear good to him—but he could be mistaken.

> We should fast from unwholesome television...

Second, one must deliver himself to the spirit of Mary, to be moved and led the way Mary desires. One must place oneself in her possession, and leave himself there, to be used as a tool or an instrument in the hands of a worker, or a lute in the hands of a good musician.

One must abandon himself in her, like a stone that is cast into the sea. This is done simply, in a moment, by a single act of the mind, a small exertion of the will, by a few words—"I give myself to you, Mary, Mother of God, my mother."

One may not feel any happiness in this act of union. But it is none the less a real act of union. It is as real as if one were to say...God forbid..."I give myself to the devil." Although one might say this, and feel no inward [chan]ge whatsoever, he would truly belong to the devil.

Third, one must, from time to time, renew the act of offering, and the act of union.

The more frequent you do this the sooner you will become a saint. The more you repeat it the sooner you will arrive at union with Jesus, which always, necessarily, follows union with Mary—since the spirit of Mary is the Spirit of Jesus.

So then, brethren, we are debtors, not to the flesh, to live according to the flesh — for if you live according to the flesh you will die, but if by the Spirit you put to death the deeds of the body you will live. For all who are led by the Spirit of God are sons of God. For you did not receive the spirit of slavery to fall back into fear, but you have received the spirit of sonship. When we cry, "Abba! Father!" it is the Spirit himself bearing witness with our spirit that we are children of God, and if children, then heirs, heirs of God and fellow heirs with Christ, provided we suffer with him in order that we may also be glorified with him. I consider that the sufferings of this present time are not worth comparing with the glory that is to be revealed to us. — Romans 8:12-18

Now review the introduction to "Part 3: Knowledge of Mary" on pages 99–101 and part of the *Gifts of the Holy Spirit and Infused Virtues* (#53L2) in Appendix A. Pray 4 decades of the Rosary (#6a-9), preferably with your family, sometime during the day. If you already pray the daily family Rosary, you do not need to pray these 4 decades. Optional: reflect on paragraphs 42-44 of *Mother of the Redeemer* (#65b).

Twenty-First Day
Knowledge of Mary

*Come Holy Spirit, please help us to know, understand and
see Mary as you want us to. Please teach us to fully live our
Total Consecration to Jesus through Mary in union with
St. Joseph, and thus truly live as her children.*

Evangelium vitae (Gospel of Life)
by Pope John Paul II

102. At the end of this Encyclical, we naturally look again to the Lord Jesus, "the Child born for us" (cf. Is 9:6), that in him we may contemplate "the Life" which "was made manifest" (1 Jn 1:2). In the mystery of Christ's Birth the encounter of God with man takes place and the earthly journey of the Son of God begins, a journey which will culminate in the gift of his life on the Cross. By his death Christ will conquer death and become for all humanity the source of new life.

The one who accepted "Life" in the name of all and for the sake of all was Mary, the Virgin Mother; she is thus most closely and personally associated with the Gospel of life. Mary's consent at the Annunciation and her mother-hood stand at the very beginning of the mystery of life which Christ came to bestow on humanity (cf. Jn 10:10). Through her acceptance and loving care for the life of the Incarnate Word, human life has been rescued from con-demnation to final and eternal death.

For this reason, Mary, "like the Church of which she is the type, is a mother of all who are reborn to life. She is in fact the mother of the Life by which everyone lives, and when she brought it forth from herself she in some way brought to rebirth all those who were to live by that Life".

As the Church contemplates Mary's motherhood, she discovers the meaning of her own motherhood and the way in which she is called to express it. At the same time, the Church's experience of motherhood leads to a most profound understanding of Mary's experience as the incomparable model of how life should be welcomed and cared for.

"A great portent appeared in heaven, a woman clothed with the sun" (Rev 12:1): the motherhood of Mary and of the Church

103. The mutual relationship between the mystery of the Church and Mary appears clearly in the "great portent" described in the Book of Revelation: "A great portent appeared in heaven, a woman clothed with the sun, with the moon under her feet, and on her head a crown of twelve stars" (12:1).

In this sign the Church recognizes an image of her own mystery: present in history, she knows that she transcends history, inasmuch as she constitutes on earth the "seed and beginning" of the Kingdom of God. The Church sees this mystery fulfilled in complete and exemplary fashion in Mary. She is the woman of glory in whom God's plan could be carried out with supreme perfection.

The "woman clothed with the sun"—the Book of Revelation tells us—"was with child" (12:2). The Church is fully aware that she bears within herself the Saviour of the world, Christ the Lord. She is aware that she is called to offer Christ to the world, giving men and women new birth into God's own life. But the Church cannot forget that her mission was made possible by the motherhood of Mary, who conceived and bore the One who is "God from God", "true God from true God".

Mary is truly the Mother of God, the Theotokos, in whose motherhood the vocation to motherhood bestowed by God on every woman is raised to its highest level. Thus Mary becomes the model of the Church, called to be the "new Eve", the mother of believers, the mother of the "living" (cf. Gen 3:20).

The Church's spiritual motherhood is only achieved— the Church knows this too—through the pangs and "the labor" of childbirth (cf. Rev 12:2), that is to say, in constant tension with the forces of evil which still roam the world and affect human hearts, offering resistance to Christ: "In him was life, and the life was the light of men. The light shines in the darkness, and the darkness has not overcome it" (Jn 1:4-5).

Like the Church, Mary too had to live her motherhood amid suffering: "This child is set ... for a sign that is spoken against — and a sword will pierce through your own soul also — that thoughts out of many hearts may be revealed" (Lk 2:34-35).

The words which Simeon addresses to Mary at the very beginning of the Saviour's earthly life sum up and prefigure the rejection of Jesus, and with him of Mary, a rejection which will reach its culmination on Calvary. "Standing by the cross of Jesus" (Jn 19:25), Mary shares in the gift which the Son makes of himself: she offers Jesus, gives him over, and begets him to the end for our sake. The "yes" spoken on the day of the Annunciation reaches full maturity on the day of the Cross, when the time comes for Mary to receive and beget as her children all those who become disciples, pouring out upon them the saving love of her Son: "When Jesus saw his mother, and the disciple whom he loved standing near, he said to his mother, 'Woman, behold, your son!'" (Jn 19:26).

"And the dragon stood before the woman ... that he might devour her child when she brought it forth" (Rev 12:4): life menaced by the forces of evil.

Secret of Mary, by St. Louis de Montfort, Parts I and III

Therefore, if we would go up to Him and be united with Him, we must use the same means He used to come down to us, to be made man and to impart His graces to us. That means is a true devotion to our Blessed Lady...

There are several true devotions to Our Lady: here I do not speak of those that are false.

The first consists in fulfilling our Christian duties, avoiding mortal sin, acting more out of love than fear, praying to Our Lady now and then, honoring her as the Mother of God, yet without having any special devotion to her.

The second consists in entertaining for Our Lady more perfect feelings of esteem and love, of confidence and veneration. It leads us to join the Confraternities of the Holy Rosary and of the Scapular, to recite the five decades or the fifteen decades of the Rosary, to honor Mary's images and altars, to publish her praises and to enroll ourselves in her sodalities.

This devotion is good, holy, and praiseworthy if we keep ourselves free from sin; but it is not so perfect as the next, nor so efficient in severing our souls from creatures or in detaching us from ourselves, in order to be united with Jesus Christ.

The third devotion to Our Lady, known and practiced by very few persons, is the one I am now about to disclose to you, predestinate soul...

Chosen soul, this devotion consists in surrendering oneself in the manner of a slave to Mary, and to Jesus through her, and then performing all our actions with Mary, in Mary, through Mary, and for Mary.

We should choose a special feast day on which to give ourselves. Then willingly and lovingly and under no constraint, we consecrate and sacrifice to her unreservedly our body and soul. We give to her our material possessions, such as house, family, income, and even the inner possessions of our soul, namely, our merits, graces, virtues, and atonements.

If you love me, you will keep my commandments. And I will pray the Father, and he will give you another Counselor, to be with you for ever, even the Spirit of truth, whom the world cannot receive, because it neither sees him nor knows him; you know him, for he dwells with you, and will be in you. — John 14:15-17

Now review part of the *Gifts of the Holy Spirit and Infused Virtues* (#53L3) in Appendix A. Pray 4 decades of the Rosary (#6a-9), preferably with your family, sometime during the day. If you already pray the daily family Rosary, you do not need to pray these 4 decades. Optional: reflect on paragraphs 45-46 of *Mother of the Redeemer* (#65b).

Twenty-Second Day
Knowledge of Mary

Come Holy Spirit, please help us to know, understand and see Mary as you want us to. Please teach us to fully live our Total Consecration to Jesus through Mary in union with St. Joseph, and thus truly live as her children.

Redemptoris Mater (Mother of the Redeemer) by Pope John Paul II

13. As the Council teaches, "'The obedience of faith' (Rom. 16:26; cf. Rom. 1:5; 2 Cor. 10:5-6) must be given to God who reveals, an obedience by which man entrusts his whole self freely to God." This description of faith found perfect realization in Mary. The "decisive" moment was the Annunciation, and the very words of Elizabeth: "And blessed is she who believed" refer primarily to that very moment.

 Indeed, at the Annunciation Mary entrusted herself to God completely, with the "full submission of intellect and will," manifesting "the obedience of faith" to him who spoke to her through his messenger. She responded, therefore, with all her human and feminine "I," and this response of faith included both perfect cooperation with "the grace of God that precedes and assists" and perfect openness to the action of the Holy Spirit, who "constantly brings faith to completion by his gifts."

The word of the living God, announced to Mary by the angel, referred to her: "And behold, you will conceive in your womb and bear a son" (Lk. 1:31). By accepting this announcement, Mary was to become the "Mother of the Lord," and the divine mystery of the Incarnation was to be accomplished in her: "The Father of mercies willed that the consent of the predestined Mother should precede the Incarnation" (*Lumen Gentium*, 56).

And Mary gives this consent, after she has heard everything the messenger has to say. She says: "Behold, I am the handmaid of the Lord; let it be to me according to your word" (Lk. 1:38). This fiat of Mary— "let it be to me"—was decisive, on the human level, for the accomplishment of the divine mystery.

There is a complete harmony with the words of the Son, who, according to the Letter to the Hebrews, says to the Father as he comes into the world: "Sacrifices and offering you have not desired, but a body you have prepared for me.... Lo, I have come to do your will, O God" (Heb. 10:5-7).

The mystery of the Incarnation was accomplished when Mary uttered her fiat: "Let it be to me according to your word," which made possible, as far as it depended upon her in the divine plan, the granting of her Son's desire.

Mary uttered this fiat in faith. In faith she entrusted herself to God without reserve and "devoted herself totally as the handmaid of the Lord to the person and work of her Son."

And as the Fathers of the Church teach—she conceived this Son in her mind before she conceived him in her womb: precisely in faith! Rightly therefore does Elizabeth praise Mary: "And blessed is she who believed that there would be a fulfillment of what was spoken to her from the Lord." These words have already been fulfilled: Mary of Nazareth presents herself at the threshold of Elizabeth and Zechariah's house as the Mother of the Son of God. This is Elizabeth's joyful discovery: "The mother of my Lord comes to me"!

True Devotion to Mary
by St. Louis de Montfort, Chapter VII

True devotion is interior because it springs from the heart and mind. It wells up out of the esteem one has for the Virgin Mother, the high ideas he has formed concerning her splendors, and the love he bears her.

It is tender, and as trustful as a child is toward his mother. It prompts one to seek her in all his needs of body and spirit, and to ask her help in all things, everywhere and always. It beseeches her to banish his doubts, correct his errors, and keep him on the right path. It implores her protection against temptations. It begs for her strength in moments of weakness. It cries to her to lift her child up when he has fallen.

It impels one to rush to her for encouragement when despair confronts him; and to be freed from scruples and consoled in pain and woe. It inspires one to hasten to her in all spiritual weathers, and that without the least fear of annoying her or displeasing her Son, God.

It is holy because it induces us to imitate Mary's virtues and to avoid sin. It speeds one toward acquiring something of her profound humility, her lively faith, her blind obedience, her continual self-denial, her constant prayer, her divine purity, her flaming charity, her heroic patience, her angelic sweetness, and her supernatural wisdom—the ten principal virtues of Our Lady.

It is constant, for it urges one to maintain his devotion and never abandon it. It strengthens one in goodness; it furnishes him with enough courage to fight the fashions and opinions of the world, the flesh in its passions and agonies, and the devil and his temptations.

A true lover of Mary is not a changeling. He is not glum, not scrupulous, nor afraid. Oh, he sometimes falls. He sometimes is less ardent than at other times. But if he falls, he gets up again and stretches out his hand to his mother. And if he loses the taste and the "feeling" he has known, he is not at all affected thereby; for he lives on his faith in Jesus and Mary and not on the feelings of his body.

True devotion is disinterested, for it impels us to seek God alone, in His Mother, and not to seek ourselves. A true lover does not serve his beloved in a spirit of profit or gain, either for body or soul.

He serves Mary because she is most worthy of being served; and because she is, at once, the Mother, the daughter, and the holy spouse of God. God alone is the reason. God in Mary. The true lover does not love her because she is good to him or because he expects some good from her.

He loves her because she is so superbly lovable. He serves her faithfully, in dryness and boredom as in sweetness and fervor. He loves her as much at Calvary as at Cana.

How pleasing, how precious, to Mary and to God, is such a soul! And how rare!

It shall not be so among you; but whoever would be great among you must be your servant, and whoever would be first among you must be your slave; even as the Son of man came not to be served but to serve, and to give his life as a ransom for many.
— *Matthew 20:26-28*

Now pray the *Prayer to Mary* (#48) and review part of the *Gifts of the Holy Spirit and Infused Virtues* (#53L4) in Appendix A. Pray 4 decades of the Rosary (#6a-9), preferably with your family, sometime during the day. If you already pray the daily family Rosary, you do not need to pray these 4 decades. Optional: reflect on paragraphs 47-48 of *Mother of the Redeemer* (#65b).

Twenty-Third Day
Knowledge of Mary

Come Holy Spirit, please help us to know, understand and see Mary as you want us to. Please teach us to fully live our Total Consecration to Jesus through Mary in union with St. Joseph, and thus truly live as her children.

Ecclesia de Eucharistia (On the Eucharist in Its Relationship to the Church), by Pope John Paul II

53. If we wish to rediscover in all its richness the profound relationship between the Church and the Eucharist, we cannot neglect Mary, Mother and model of the Church. In my Apostolic Letter *Rosarium Virginis Mariae*, I pointed to the Blessed Virgin Mary as our teacher in contemplating Christ's face, and among the mysteries of light I included the institution of the Eucharist. Mary can guide us towards this most holy sacrament, because she herself has a profound relationship with it.

At first glance, the Gospel is silent on this subject. The account of the institution of the Eucharist on the night of Holy Thursday makes no mention of Mary. Yet we know that she was present among the Apostles who prayed "with one accord" (cf. Acts 1:14) in the first community which gathered after the Ascension in expectation of Pentecost. Certainly Mary must have been present at the

Eucharistic celebrations of the first generation of Christians, who were devoted to "the breaking of bread" (Acts 2:42).

But in addition to her sharing in the Eucharistic banquet, an indirect picture of Mary's relationship with the Eucharist can be had, beginning with her interior disposition. Mary is a "woman of the Eucharist" in her whole life. The Church, which looks to Mary as a model, is also called to imitate her in her relationship with this most holy mystery.

54. *Mysterium fidei!* If the Eucharist is a mystery of faith which so greatly transcends our understanding as to call for sheer abandonment to the word of God, then there can be no one like Mary to act as our support and guide in acquiring this disposition.

In repeating what Christ did at the Last Supper in obedience to his command: "Do this in memory of me!", we also accept Mary's invitation to obey him without hesitation: "Do whatever he tells you" (Jn 2:5). With the same maternal concern which she showed at the wedding feast of Cana, Mary seems to say to us: "Do not waver; trust in the words of my Son.

If he was able to change water into wine, he can also turn bread and wine into his body and blood, and through this mystery bestow on believers the living memorial of his passover, thus becoming the 'bread of life'".

55. In a certain sense Mary lived her Eucharistic faith even before the institution of the Eucharist, by the very

fact that she offered her virginal womb for the Incarnation of God's Word. The Eucharist, while commemorating the passion and resurrection, is also in continuity with the incarnation.

At the Annunciation Mary conceived the Son of God in the physical reality of his body and blood, thus anticipating within herself what to some degree happens sacramentally in every believer who receives, under the signs of bread and wine, the Lord's body and blood.

As a result, there is a profound analogy between the Fiat which Mary said in reply to the angel, and the Amen which every believer says when receiving the body of the Lord. Mary was asked to believe that the One whom she conceived "through the Holy Spirit" was "the Son of God" (Lk 1:30-35). In continuity with the Virgin's faith, in the Eucharistic mystery we are asked to believe that the same Jesus Christ, Son of God and Son of Mary, becomes present in his full humanity and divinity under the signs of bread and wine.

"Blessed is she who believed" (Lk 1:45). Mary also anticipated, in the mystery of the incarnation, the Church's Eucharistic faith. When, at the Visitation, she bore in her womb the Word made flesh, she became in some way a "tabernacle" – the first "tabernacle" in history – in which the Son of God, still invisible to our human gaze, allowed himself to be adored by Elizabeth, radiating his light as it were through the eyes and the voice of Mary. And is not the enraptured gaze of Mary as she contemplated the face of the newborn Christ and cradled him in her arms that unparalleled model of love which should inspire us every time we receive Eucharistic communion?

True Devotion to Mary
by St. Louis de Montfort, Chapter XVII

Before Communion you must (a) humble yourself profoundly before God; (b) renounce your corrupted nature and your dispositions, however good your self-love makes them seem; (c) renew your consecration, saying: "I am all Thine, and all I have is Thine, Lord Jesus, through Mary, Thy holy Mother"; (d) ask Mary to lend you her heart that you may receive Jesus there, and with her dispositions.

Tell her the glory of her Son is at stake. He should not be placed in so corrupt and inconsistent a heart as yours. It might lessen His glory, or even destroy it. Tell her that, because of the dominion she has over the hearts of men, she can come into your heart—such as it is—and receive Jesus there. Then there will be no danger of His being unworthily received.

Tell her that all you have given her is nothing, but that now, through Holy Communion you wish to give her the same present God the Father gave her!

Tell her that Jesus, Who loves her with a divine love, a unique love, still desires to rest and delight in her, although He must come to your soul to do so...a soul filthier and poorer than the stable in which He was born, the mean little stable He loved because Mary was there.

And implore her to give you her heart, using these tender words: "I receive you as my all; give me your heart."

And he took bread, and when he had given thanks he broke it and gave it to them, saying, "This is my body which is given for you. Do this in remembrance of me." And likewise the cup after supper, saying, "This cup which is poured out for you is the new covenant in my blood." — Luke 22:19-20

Now review part of the *Gifts of the Holy Spirit and Infused Virtues* (#53L5) and reflect on part of Pope John Paul II's *Act of Entrustment to Mary* (#27b) in Appendix A. Pray 4 decades of the Rosary (#6a-9), preferably with your family, sometime during the day. If you already pray the daily family Rosary, you do not need to pray these 4 decades. Optional: reflect on paragraphs 52-54 of the *Dogmatic Constitution on the Church* (#65c).

Twenty-Fourth Day
Knowledge of Mary

Come Holy Spirit, please help us to know, understand and see Mary as you want us to. Please teach us to fully live our Total Consecration to Jesus through Mary in union with St. Joseph, and thus truly live as her children.

Rosarium Virginis Mariae (On the Holy Rosary) by Pope John Paul II

41. As a prayer for peace, the Rosary is also, and always has been, a prayer of and for the family. At one time this prayer was particularly dear to Christian families, and it certainly brought them closer together. It is important not to lose this precious inheritance. We need to return to the practice of family prayer and prayer for families, continuing to use the Rosary.

The family that prays together stays together. The Holy Rosary, by age-old tradition, has shown itself particularly effective as a prayer which brings the family together.

Individual family members, in turning their eyes towards Jesus, also regain the ability to look one another in the eye, to communicate, to show solidarity, to forgive one another and to see their covenant of love renewed in the Spirit of God.

Many of the problems facing contemporary families, especially in economically developed societies, result from their increasing difficulty in communicating. Families seldom manage to come together, and the rare occasions when they do are often taken up with watching television.

To return to the recitation of the family Rosary means filling daily life with very different images, images of the mystery of salvation: the image of the Redeemer, the image of his most Blessed Mother.

The family that recites the Rosary together reproduces something of the atmosphere of the household of Nazareth: its members place Jesus at the centre, they share his joys and sorrows, they place their needs and their plans in his hands, they draw from him the hope and the strength to go on.

42. It is also beautiful and fruitful to entrust to this prayer the growth and development of children. Does the Rosary not follow the life of Christ, from his conception to his death, and then to his Resurrection and his glory? Parents are finding it ever more difficult to follow the lives of their children as they grow to maturity.

In a society of advanced technology, of mass communications and globalization, everything has become hurried, and the cultural distance between generations is growing ever greater. The most diverse messages and the most unpredictable experiences rapidly make their way into the lives of children and adolescents, and parents can become quite anxious about the dangers their children face.

At times parents suffer acute disappointment at the failure of their children to resist the seductions of the drug culture, the lure of an unbridled hedonism, the temptation to violence, and the manifold expressions of meaninglessness and despair.

To pray the Rosary for children, and even more, with children, training them from their earliest years to experience this daily "pause for prayer" with the family, is admittedly not the solution to every problem, but it is a spiritual aid which should not be underestimated.

It could be objected that the Rosary seems hardly suited to the taste of children and young people of today. But perhaps the objection is directed to an impoverished method of praying it. Furthermore, without prejudice to the Rosary's basic structure, there is nothing to stop children and young people from praying it – either within the family or in groups – with appropriate symbolic and practical aids to understanding and appreciation. Why not try it? With God's help, a pastoral approach to youth which is positive, impassioned and creative – as shown by the World Youth Days! – is capable of achieving quite remarkable results.

If the Rosary is well presented, I am sure that young people will once more surprise adults by the way they make this prayer their own and recite it with the enthusiasm typical of their age group.

True Devotion to Mary
by St. Louis de Montfort, Chapter X

True devotion to Mary is an easy, short, perfect, and safe road to perfection, which means union with Christ. To a Christian, perfection is nothing else than such a union.

It is an easy road. It was opened by Jesus when He came to us. There are no obstacles there to prevent our using it to go to Him.

One may, it is true, arrive at union with God by other roads. But he will encounter many more crosses; he will find deadly perils; and he will have many difficulties to overcome. There will be dark nights, strange fights, bitter agonies. There will be steep mountains to climb, sharp patches of briars and brambles to traverse, and frightful deserts to cross.

The road of Mary is gentle, and more peaceful. One finds there, it is true, great difficulties and fierce battles. But our mother is ever near, to light the darkness, to clear away doubts, to give strength, to banish fear, to help in every way....

It is my belief that anyone who wishes to live truly in Christ, and carry his cross daily, can never carry a heavy cross—or bear one joyfully to the end—without a tender devotion to Our Lady.

The road is short. One does not get lost. He walks joyfully in it, and therefore speedily. One makes more progress, in a brief time of submission to Mary and dependence on her, than in years of self-will and self-reliance...

 True devotion is a safe road to Christ, and to that perfection which is union with Him. The practice I teach is not new. It is very old, but one cannot trace its beginnings with precision. It has been in existence though, for the last seven hundred years.

St. Odilo, abbot of Cluny, who lived in the eleventh century, was one of the first to practice it publicly in France. Cardinal Peter Damian tells us that in the year 1016 his brother, Blessed Marian, made himself the slave of Mary. He tied a rope around his neck, scourged himself, and placed a sum of money on the altar as a token of his consecration to Our Lady. This he did in the presence of his spiritual director. He remained so faithful to his consecration that Our Lady visited him on his deathbed and promised to reward him in heaven.

In the beginning was the Word, and the Word was with God, and the Word was God. He was in the beginning with God; all things were made through him, and without him was not anything made that was made. In him was life, and the life was the light of men. The light shines in the darkness, and the darkness has not overcome it. — John 1:1-5

Now review part of the *Gifts of the Holy Spirit and Infused Virtues* (#53L6) in Appendix A. Pray 4 decades of the Rosary (#6a-9), preferably with your family, sometime during the day. If you already pray the daily family Rosary, you do not need to pray these 4 decades. Optional: reflect on paragraphs 55-59 of the *Dogmatic Constitution on the Church* (#65c).

Twenty-Fifth Day
Knowledge of Mary

Come Holy Spirit, please help us to know, understand and see Mary as you want us to. Please teach us to fully live our Total Consecration to Jesus through Mary in union with St. Joseph, and thus truly live as her children.

Redemptoris Mater (Mother of the Redeemer)
by Pope John Paul II

18. This blessing reaches its full meaning when Mary stands beneath the Cross of her Son (cf. Jn. 19:25). The Council says that this happened "not without a divine plan": by "suffering deeply with her only-begotten Son and joining herself with her maternal spirit to his sacrifice, lovingly consenting to the immolation of the victim to whom she had given birth," in this way Mary "faithfully preserved her union with her Son even to the Cross."

It is a union through faith—the same faith with which she had received the angel's revelation at the Annunciation. At that moment she had also heard the words: "He will be great...and the Lord God will give to him the throne of his father David, and he will reign over the house of Jacob for ever; and of his kingdom there will be no end" (Lk. 1:32-33).

And now, standing at the foot of the Cross, Mary is the witness, humanly speaking, of the complete negation of these words. On that wood of the Cross her Son hangs in agony as one condemned. "He was despised and rejected by men; a man of sorrows...he was despised, and we esteemed him not": as one destroyed (cf. Is. 53:3- 5).

How great, how heroic then is the obedience of faith shown by Mary in the face of God's "unsearchable judgments"! How completely she "abandons herself to God" without reserve, offering the full assent of the intellect and the will" to him whose "ways are inscrutable" (cf. Rom. 11:33)! And how powerful too is the action of grace in her soul, how all-pervading is the influence of the Holy Spirit and of his light and power!

Through this faith Mary is perfectly united with Christ in his self-emptying. For "Christ Jesus, who, though he was in the form of God, did not count equality with God a thing to be grasped, but emptied himself, taking the form of a servant, being born in the likeness of men": precisely on Golgotha "humbled himself and became obedient unto death, even death on a cross" (cf. Phil. 2:5-8).

At the foot of the Cross, Mary shares through faith in the shocking mystery of this self-emptying. This is perhaps the deepest *"kenosis"* of faith in human history. Through faith the Mother shares in the death of her Son, in his redeeming death; but in contrast with the faith of the disciples who fled, hers was far more enlightened. On Golgotha, Jesus through the Cross definitively confirmed that he was the "sign of contradiction" foretold by Simeon. At the same time, there were also fulfilled on Golgotha the words which Simeon had addressed to Mary: "and a sword will pierce through your own soul also."

19. Yes, truly "blessed is she who believed"! These words, spoken by Elizabeth after the Annunciation, here at the foot of the Cross seem to re-echo with supreme eloquence, and the power contained within them becomes something penetrating.

From the Cross, that is to say from the very heart of the mystery of Redemption, there radiates and spreads out the prospect of that blessing of faith. It goes right back to "the beginning." and as a sharing in the sacrifice of Christ—the new Adam—it becomes in a certain sense the counterpoise to the disobedience and disbelief embodied in the sin of our first parents.

Thus teach the Fathers of the Church and especially St. Irenaeus, quoted by the Constitution *Lumen Gentium*: "The knot of Eve's disobedience was untied by Mary's obedience; what the virgin Eve bound through her unbelief, the Virgin Mary loosened by her faith." In the light of this comparison with Eve, the Fathers of the Church—as the Council also says—call Mary the "mother of the living" and often speak of "death through Eve, life through Mary."

In the expression "Blessed is she who believed," we can therefore rightly find a kind of "key" which unlocks for us the innermost reality of Mary, whom the angel hailed as "full of grace." If as "full of grace" she has been eternally present in the mystery of Christ, through faith she became a sharer in that mystery in every extension of her earthly journey. She "advanced in her pilgrimage of faith" and at the same time, in a discreet yet direct and effective way, she made present to humanity the mystery of Christ. And she still continues to do so.

Through the mystery of Christ, she too is present within mankind. Thus through the mystery of the Son the mystery of the Mother is also made clear.

True Devotion to Mary
by St. Louis de Montfort, Chapter XIV

Rest assured, my dear friends and neighbors, if you are faithful to the practices of true devotion, both interior and exterior—I will discuss them later—wonderful things will happen to you.

Through the light of the Holy Spirit—Mary, His spouse, will shine it on you—you will know yourself as you are. You will realize you are corrupted by original sin and incapable of performing any good action except through the grace of God ... But the humble Virgin will make you share in her humility. So, while you will despise yourself and love to be despised, you will not despise anyone else.

Our Lady will give you a share in her faith, which was greater than that of all the patriarchs, prophets, and saints. In heaven she does not need faith, for she sees all things in God through the light of glory. Yet God permitted that she should keep her faith, that she might give it to the Church Militant.

The more Mary loves you, the more surely you will act by faith. Yours will become a faith so pure you will scarcely bother about the extraordinary favors God sometimes gives His beloved, such as ecstasies, for instance. Yours will be a faith animated by charity. You will do everything through no other motive than pure love. It will be a faith firm as a rock, and as unshakable. And it will make you firm and constant in the most terrific storms.

It will be a positive faith, far-seeing. It will be a pass key into all the mysteries of Christ, into the very heart of God.

It will be a brave faith. You will hold it high, a burning torch. It will be your life, your secret treasure of divine wisdom, your all-powerful weapon. By it you will be able to enlighten those sitting in the darkness of the shadow of death, enkindle the lukewarm to renewed ardor, and restore life to those whose souls are dead through sin. By it you will be able, with soft and tender words, to transform hearts of marble and to overthrow the proud tall cedars of Lebanon.

But standing by the cross of Jesus were his mother, and his mother's sister, Mary the wife of Clopas, and Mary Magdalene. When Jesus saw his mother, and the disciple whom he loved standing near, he said to his mother, "Woman, behold, your son!" Then he said to the disciple, "Behold, your mother!" And from that hour the disciple took her to his own home. — John 19:25-27

Now review part of the *Gifts of the Holy Spirit and Infused Virtues* (#53L7) and pray the *Litany of Loretto* (#47a) in Appendix A. Pray 4 decades of the Rosary (#6a-9), preferably with your family, sometime during the day. If you already pray the daily family Rosary, you do not need to pray these 4 decades. Optional: reflect on paragraphs 60-65 of the *Dogmatic Constitution on the Church* (#65c).

Twenty-Sixth Day
Knowledge of Mary

Come Holy Spirit, please help us to know, understand and see Mary as you want us to. Please teach us to fully live our Total Consecration to Jesus through Mary in union with St. Joseph, and thus truly live as her children.

Rosarium Virginis Mariae (On the Holy Rosary)
by Pope John Paul II

14. Christ is the supreme Teacher, the revealer and the one revealed. It is not just a question of learning what he taught but of "learning him". In this regard could we have any better teacher than Mary? From the divine standpoint, the Spirit is the interior teacher who leads us to the full truth of Christ (cf. Jn 14:26; 15:26; 16:13). But among creatures no one knows Christ better than Mary; no one can introduce us to a profound knowledge of his mystery better than his Mother.

The first of the "signs" worked by Jesus – the changing of water into wine at the marriage in Cana – clearly presents Mary in the guise of a teacher, as she urges the servants to do what Jesus commands (cf. Jn 2:5). We can imagine that she would have done likewise for the disciples after Jesus' Ascension, when she joined them in awaiting the Holy Spirit and supported them in their first mission. Contemplating the scenes of the Rosary in union with Mary is a means of learning from her to "read" Christ, to discover his secrets and to understand his message.

This school of Mary is all the more effective if we consider that she teaches by obtaining for us in abundance the gifts of the Holy Spirit, even as she offers us the incomparable example of her own "pilgrimage of faith".

As we contemplate each mystery of her Son's life, she invites us to do as she did at the Annunciation: to ask humbly the questions which open us to the light, in order to end with the obedience of faith: "Behold I am the handmaid of the Lord; be it done to me according to your word" (Lk 1:38).

True Devotion to Mary
by St. Louis de Montfort, Chapters I and II

If you want to understand the Mother, try to understand the Son.

Let all tongues be silent here!

My heart dictated these words. I wrote them with a special joy to show that our most holy Mary still remains unknown. This is partly the reason why we do not know Jesus Christ as we should. He will be known, of course;

and His kingdom will come. This is certain. But this will happen only after the Blessed Virgin is known, and has begun to reign.

She gave Him birth the first time. She will bring Him forth when He comes to us again.

Mary, made by the hands of the Most High, is, we all acknowledge, merely a creature. Compared with God's infinite majesty she is less than an atom. We might say she is as nothing.

God alone is "He Who Is." He does not depend on anyone. He is sufficient unto Himself. He did not, and still does not, have any absolute need of Mary to accomplish His will and to manifest His glory. To do all things, He has only to will them. But He did will to begin and end His greatest works through her.

We may well believe He will not change. He is God and does not change either His sentiments or His conduct.

...God, Who gave her power over His only begotten Son by nature, also gave her power over all His children by adoption, not only of the body—which would be little—but of the soul as well. Mary is the queen of heaven and earth by grace, as Christ is king by nature and by conquest.

Now, as the kingdom of Jesus Christ consists principally in the heart, or interior, of man—according to the words, "the kingdom of God is within us"—so does the kingdom of Mary. The Blessed Virgin reigns principally in the interior of man, that is to say in his soul. And in souls she and her Son are more glorified than in all visible creatures; so that, with the saints, we may call her the Queen of All Hearts!

🕮 *Come to me, all who labor and are heavy laden, and I will give you rest. Take my yoke upon you, and learn from me; for I am gentle and lowly in heart, and you will find rest for your souls. For my yoke is easy, and my burden is light. — Matthew 11:28-30*

Now pray the *Prayer to Mary* (#27c) by Pope John Paul II in Appendix A. Pray 4 decades of the Rosary (#6a-9), preferably with your family, sometime during the day. If you already pray the daily family Rosary, you do not need to pray these 4 decades. Optional: reflect on sections 66–69 of the *Dogmatic Constitution on the Church* (#65c).

Eternal Father,
I offer you the Body and Blood,
Soul and Divinity of Your dearly beloved
Son, Our Lord Jesus Christ, in atonement for
our sins and those of the whole world.

Part 4: Knowledge of Jesus Christ
(Days 27-33)

Our Lord tells us, "I am the way, and the truth, and the life; no one comes to the Father, but by me. If you had known me, you would have known my Father also; henceforth you know him and have seen him (Jn 4:6-7)." This Scripture says it all.

Our Lord goes on to say in John 15:13, "Greater love has no man than this, that a man lay down his life for his friends."

Every time we look at the Cross, we see the greatest act of love there could ever be. Every time we look at the Eucharist, we see that God is with us, Body, Blood, Soul and Divinity, to give us the strength to fulfill our destinies—destinies far greater than any of us can imagine.

We all want to be loved. In love we find our security. But when we've been disappointed so often by human failures to love faithfully, we find it hard to love. But when we look at the Cross, we see our God showing us how much He loves us even though we have betrayed Him with our sins.

It was such a great gift to see in the movie, *The Passion of the Christ*, the role of Mary in offering her Son to the Father, and to see the total abandonment of the Son to the Father to atone for the sins of the world. It is precisely Jesus' Passion which opens up the gate of Heaven for those who believe in His love and strive to unite themselves directly or indirectly to the Holy Sacrifice of the Mass.

We need to realize that Jesus is both God and Man. As God, He could have stopped the Passion at any time with just an act of His Will, but He chose, both as God and as Man, to go through unbelievable torture. The Shroud of Turin shows that this torture was even worse than what was portrayed in the movie. Jesus could have stopped it but He didn't because He wanted us to know how much He loves us, loving us to the end (cf. John 13:1).

Every time we see the crucifix, we should thank God for His love. We should make an act of love to Him, and ask Him for the gift to increase our capacity for grace in our soul, in order to increase our capacity to love and serve Him.

These last days in our preparation for Total Consecration will offer us a special time for learning more about Jesus Christ.

Twenty-Seventh Day
Knowledge of Jesus Christ

*Come Holy Spirit, fill us and animate us. Please help us to know,
understand and see Jesus as you want us to. Help us to believe in
Him and in His love for us, to trust in Him and commit ourselves to
Him, and to return His love with all our love and persevering service
so that we will in fact live our total consecration to Him through
Mary in union with St. Joseph more and more faithfully everyday.*

Salvifici Dolores (On the Christian Meaning of
Human Suffering), by Pope John Paul II

16. In his messianic activity in the midst of Israel, Christ
drew increasingly closer to the world of human suffering.
"He went about doing good", and his actions concerned primarily those who were suffering and seeking help.

He healed the sick, consoled the afflicted, fed the
hungry, freed people from deafness, from blindness, from
leprosy, from the devil and from various physical disabil-
ities, three times he restored the dead to life. He was
sensitive to every human suffering, whether of the body
or of the soul.

And at the same time he taught, and at the heart of
his teaching there are the eight beatitudes, which are
addressed to people tried by various sufferings in their
temporal life. These are "the poor in spirit" and "the
afflicted" and "those who hunger and thirst for justice"
and those who are "persecuted for justice sake", when
they insult them, persecute them and speak falsely every
kind of evil against them for the sake of Christ.... (cf. Mt.
5:3-11). Thus according to Matthew; Luke mentions
explicitly those "who hunger now"(cf. Lk. 6:12).

At any rate, Christ drew close above all to the world of
human suffering through the fact of having taken this
suffering upon his very self.

During his public activity, he experienced not only
fatigue, homelessness, misunderstanding even on the part
of those closest to him, but, more than anything, he became
progressively more and more isolated and encircled by hostility and the preparations for putting him to death.

Christ is aware of this, and often speaks to his disciples of the sufferings and death that await him: "Behold, we are going up to Jerusalem; and the Son of man will be delivered to the chief priests and the scribes, and they will condemn him to death and deliver him to the Gentiles; and they will mock him, and spit upon him, and scourge him, and kill him; and after three days he will rise" (Mk. 10:33-34).

Christ goes towards his Passion and death with full awareness of the mission that he has to fulfill precisely in this way. Precisely by means of this suffering he must bring it about "that man should not perish, but have eternal life".

Precisely by means of his Cross he must strike at the roots of evil, planted in the history of man and in human souls. Precisely by means of his Cross he must accomplish the work of salvation. This work, in the plan of eternal Love, has a redemptive character.

And therefore Christ severely reproves Peter when the latter wants to make him abandon the thoughts of suffering and of death on the Cross. And when, during his arrest in Gethsemane, the same Peter tries to defend him with the sword, Christ says, "Put your sword back into its place... But how then should the scriptures be fulfilled, that it must be so?" (Mt. 26:52, 54).

And he also says, "Shall I not drink the cup which the Father has given me?" (Jn. 18:11). This response, like others that reappear in different points of the Gospel, shows how profoundly Christ was imbued by the thought that he had already expressed in the conversation with Nicodemus: "For God so loved the world that he gave his only Son, that whoever believes in him should not perish but have eternal life" (Jn 3:16).

Christ goes toward his own suffering, aware of its saving power; he goes forward in obedience to the Father, but primarily he is united to the Father in this love with which he has loved the world and man in the world. And for this reason Saint Paul will write of Christ: "He loved me and gave himself for me" (Gal. 2:20).

True Devotion to Mary
by St. Louis de Montfort, Chapter IV

Jesus Christ, our Savior, true God and true Man, must be the aim and end of all our devotions, otherwise they would be false. Christ to us is the beginning and end of all things; or, as scholars say, using the first and last letters of the Greek alphabet.

He is our Alpha and Omega. Our sole work, the Apostle reminds us, is to make every man perfect in Jesus Christ; because in Him is all the fullness of divinity, all graces, all virtues, all perfections.

Christ alone is our Master, our Lord, our Head, our Model, our Physician, our Shepherd. He is the Way we must follow, the Truth we must believe, the Life that gives us life. He is our All in all things. He alone is enough.

No other name under heaven has been given for our salvation than the name of Jesus. God has given us no other foundation for our redemption, our perfection, our glory. Any edifice not built on this strong Stone is built on quicksand and cannot endure. Any Christian who is not united to Him, as a branch to the vine, will wither and fall away—fit for nothing but burning.

If we are in Jesus Christ, and He in us, we need not fear damnation. No creature in heaven or earth or hell can harm us, and none can separate us from the love of God, which is in Jesus Christ. Through Christ, in Christ, and with Christ, we can do all things. We can render homage to the Father in unity with the Holy Spirit, we can make ourselves perfect, we can be a good influence on our neighbor leading him to eternal life.

If, then, we wish to establish a strong true devotion to Mary, it is only that we may the better establish a perfect devotion to her Son.

We wish only, through Mary, to find a sure and easy way of finding Jesus. If devotion to Mary could in any way lessen devotion to her Son we should have to reject it. But the contrary is true, as I have shown, and as I will show more clearly. Devotion to Mary is vital if we should discover, know, love, and faithfully serve Jesus Christ.

[We look to St. Joseph as a perfect model for this devotion to the Hearts of Jesus and Mary. We ask to be caught up in the current of love in the Holy Family where Joseph is the virgin father of Jesus who protects him and his true spouse. He is truly the protector of the "domestic Church," the family.]

Abide in me, and I in you. As the branch cannot bear fruit by itself, unless it abides in the vine, neither can you, unless you abide in me. I am the vine, you are the branches. He who abides in me, and I in him, he it is that bears much fruit, for apart from me you can do nothing. — John 15:4-5

Now review the introduction to "Part 4: Knowledge of Jesus" on pages 133–134 and pray the *Act of Reparation to the Sacred Heart of Jesus* (#22). Pray one 5-decade Rosary (#6a-9) sometime today, preferably with your family. Optional: reflect on sections 1–15 of *Secret of Mary* (#67).

Twenty-Eighth Day
Knowledge of Jesus Christ

Come Holy Spirit, fill us and animate us. Please help us to know, understand and see Jesus as you want us to. Help us to believe in Him and in His love for us, to trust in Him and commit ourselves to Him, and to return His love with all our love and persevering service so that we will in fact live our total consecration to Him through Mary in union with St. Joseph more and more faithfully everyday.

Dominum et Vivificantem (On the Holy Spirit)
by Pope John Paul II

19. Even though in his hometown of Nazareth Jesus is not accepted as the Messiah, nonetheless, at the beginning of his public activity, his messianic mission in the Holy Spirit is revealed to the people by John the Baptist. The latter, the son of Zechariah and Elizabeth, foretells at the Jordan the coming of the Messiah and administers the baptism of repentance.

He says: "I baptize you with water; he who is mightier than I is coming, the thong of whose sandals I am not worthy to untie; he will baptize you with the Holy Spirit and with fire" (Lk. 3:16; cf. Mt. 3:11; Mk. 1:7f; Jn. 1:33).

John the Baptist foretells the Messiah-Christ not only as the one who "is coming" in the Holy Spirit but also as the one who "brings" the Holy Spirit, as Jesus will reveal more clearly in the Upper Room. Here John faithfully echoes the words of Isaiah, words which in the ancient Prophet concerned the future, while in John's teaching on the banks of the Jordan they are the immediate introduction to the new messianic reality.

John is not only a prophet but also a messenger: he is the precursor of Christ. What he foretells is accomplished before the eyes of all. Jesus of Nazareth too comes to the Jordan to receive the baptism of repentance. At the sight of him arriving, John proclaims: "Behold, the Lamb of God, who takes away the sin of the world" (Jn 1:29).

He says this through the inspiration of the Holy Spirit, bearing witness to the fulfillment of the prophecy of Isaiah. At the same time he confesses his faith in the redeeming mission of Jesus of Nazareth. On the lips of John the Baptist, "Lamb of God" is an expression of truth about the Redeemer no less significant than the one used by Isaiah: "Servant of the Lord."

Thus, by the testimony of John at the Jordan, Jesus of Nazareth, rejected by his own fellow-citizens, is exalted before the eyes of Israel as the Messiah, that is to say the "One Anointed" with the Holy Spirit.

And this testimony is corroborated by another testimony of a higher order, mentioned by the three Synoptics. For when all the people were baptized and as Jesus, having received baptism, was praying, "the heaven was opened, and the Holy Spirit descended upon him in bodily form, as a dove" (Lk. 3:21f) and at the same time "a voice from heaven said 'This is my beloved Son, with whom I am well pleased'" (Mt. 3:17).

This is a Trinitarian theophany which bears witness to the exaltation of Christ on the occasion of his baptism in the Jordan. It not only confirms the testimony of John the Baptist but also reveals another more profound dimension of the truth about Jesus of Nazareth as Messiah. It is this: the Messiah is the beloved Son of the Father.

His solemn exaltation cannot be reduced to the messianic mission of the "Servant of the Lord." In the light of the theophany at the Jordan, this exaltation touches the mystery of the very person of the Messiah. He has been raised up because he is the beloved Son in whom God is well pleased. The voice from on high says: "my Son."

True Devotion to Mary
by St. Louis de Montfort, Chapter XVI

One must do everything with Mary. That is we must try to imitate, in our own human way, all the virtues—the perfection—the Holy Spirit fashioned in her.

We must, in each action, consider how Mary did this or that, or how she would do it in our circumstances.

Hence we must examine the virtues she practiced, and meditate on them. Particularly we must concern ourself with her lively faith, which made her believe the words of the angel, without the least hesitation; with her deep humility, which made her hide herself, be silent, submit to everything, and put herself in the last place; and with her truly divine purity which never had its equal and never will this side of heaven!

Here I must cry out again that Mary is the unique mold of God, most suitable to produce living images of God at little cost and in little time! A soul who has found this mold, and loses himself in it, is soon transformed into Jesus Christ, Whom this mold perfectly represents.

And he said to all, "If any man would come after me, let him deny himself and take up his cross daily and follow me. For whoever would save his life will lose it; and whoever loses his life for my sake, he will save it. — Luke 9:23-24

Now pray *The Apostolate's Act of Consecration* (#4) in Appendix A. Pray one 5-decade Rosary (#6a-9) sometime today, preferably with your family. Optional: reflect on sections 16–34 of *Secret of Mary* (#67).

Twenty-Ninth Day
Knowledge of Jesus Christ

Come Holy Spirit, fill us and animate us. Please help us to know, understand and see Jesus as you want us to. Help us to believe in Him and in His love for us, to trust in Him and commit ourselves to Him, and to return His love with all our love and persevering service so that we will in fact live our total consecration to Him through Mary in union with St. Joseph more and more faithfully everyday.

Redemptoris Missio (The Mission of the Redeemer)
by Pope John Paul II

13. Jesus of Nazareth brings God's plan to fulfillment. After receiving the Holy Spirit at his Baptism, Jesus makes clear his messianic calling: he goes about Galilee "preaching the Gospel of God and saying: 'The time is fulfilled, and the kingdom of God is at hand; repent and believe in the Gospel'" (Mk 1:14-15; cf. Mt 4:17; Lk 4:43).

The proclamation and establishment of God's kingdom are the purpose of his mission: "I was sent for this purpose" (Lk 4:43). But that is not all. Jesus himself is the "Good News," as he declares at the very beginning of his mission in the synagogue at Nazareth, when he applies to himself the words of Isaiah about the Anointed One sent by the Spirit of the Lord (cf. Lk 4;14-21).

Since the "Good News" is Christ, there is an identity between the message and the messenger, between saying, doing and being. His power, the secret of the effectiveness of his actions, lies in his total identification with the message he announces; he proclaims the "Good News" not just by what he says or does, but by what he is.

The ministry of Jesus is described in the context of his journeys within his homeland. Before Easter, the scope of his mission was focused on Israel. Nevertheless, Jesus offers a new element of extreme importance.

The eschatological reality is not relegated to a remote "end of the world," but is already close and at work in our midst. The kingdom of God is at hand (cf. Mk 1:15); its coming is to be prayed for (cf. Mt 6:10); faith can glimpse it already at work in signs such as miracles (cf. Mt 11:4-

5) and exorcisms (cf. Mt 12:25-28), in the choosing of the Twelve (cf. Mk 3:13-19), and in the proclamation of the Good News to the poor (cf. Lk 4:18).

Jesus' encounters with Gentiles make it clear that entry into the kingdom comes through faith and conversion (cf. Mk 1:15), and not merely by reason of ethnic background.

The kingdom which Jesus inaugurates is the kingdom of God. Jesus himself reveals who this God is, the One whom he addresses by the intimate term "Abba," Father (cf. Mk 14:36).

God, as revealed above all in the parables (cf. Lk 15:3-32; Mt 20:1-16), is sensitive to the needs and sufferings of every human being: he is a Father filled with love and compassion, who grants forgiveness and freely bestows the favors asked of him.

St. John tells us that "God is love" (1 Jn 4:8, 16). Every person therefore is invited to "repent" and to "believe" in God's merciful love. The kingdom will grow insofar as every person learns to turn to God in the intimacy of prayer as to a Father (cf. Lk 11:2; Mt 23:9) and strives to do his will (cf. Mt 7:21).

True Devotion to Mary
by St. Louis de Montfort, Chapter XVI

One must do everything *in* Mary.

To understand this, we must realize that Mary is the true paradise of the new Adam. The Eden from which the old Adam was expelled prefigured her.

Our paradise is filled with untold riches, with beauty, with delights, with all sorts of good things that the new Adam left there. He occupied this paradise for nine months, and was well pleased with it. He worked

His wonders there. He displayed there His riches, and with divine magnificence.

In this Eden, this weedless garden made fertile by the power of the Holy Spirit, its Tenant, one may find trees which were planted by God and sustained by His grace. There is the tree of life, which bore Jesus as its Fruit. And there is the tree of the knowledge of good and evil, whose fruit was Incarnate Wisdom, the Light of the world.

There are, in this most beautiful place, flowers of various kinds, flowers of virtue, whose fragrance thrills even the angels. There are fields of flowers there, meadows of hope, towers of strength, and mansions of simplicity and trust.

Only the Holy Spirit can make you understand the truth that lies behind these images.

The air is pure. It is the air of purity. Day reigns here. Day without night. A beautiful day, the day of the Sacred Humanity. The sun does not cast a shadow. It is the sun of the Divinity. It is a sun that melts base metals and changes them to gold. A clear spring, humility, here turns itself into four streams—the cardinal virtues—and waters the entire oasis.

The Holy Spirit, speaking through the ancient Fathers of the Church, refers to this garden as the eastern gate through which the High Priest, Jesus, entered the world.

There He came the first time. There He will come once more.

The Holy Spirit also speaks of Mary as the sanctuary of the Divinity, the resting place of the Trinity, the throne of God, the city of God, the altar of God, the temple of God, and the world of God.

What a privilege, what a glory, what a joy, what a rich blessing to be able to enter this new Garden of Eden—to dwell in Mary, where the Most High has placed His throne!

But how difficult it is for sinners like us to obtain the right to venture into a place so holy—and power and intelligence enough to use that right. This paradise is guarded not by a cherub, but by the Holy Spirit Himself. He wields absolute dominion over it. Mary is His closed garden.

"A garden enclosed is my sister, my spouse; a spring shut up; a fountain sealed."

Mary is enclosed. Mary is sealed. The miserable children of Adam and Eve, driven out of the old paradise, cannot enter this one except through permission of the Holy Spirit, a very special grace, which they must earn.

When one has succeeded, through his faithfulness, in obtaining this permission, this grace beyond compare, he must remain in the garden, in happiness, in peace, in trust, and in complete assurance. He must here abandon himself without reserve.

In the fair interior of Mary the soul will be fed on the milk of her grace and mercy. It will be freed from all its anxieties, fears, and scruples; it will be held safe from its enemies, the world, the devil, and the flesh. These enemies never had any entrance here. That is why Mary says that those who work in her will not sin. "He who lives by me will do no wrong." (Eccl. 24, 30.) Those who dwell in Our Lady in spirit will not commit any grievous sin.

In Mary the soul may be formed in Jesus, and Jesus in the soul. Her womb is, as the ancient Fathers say, the chamber of the sacraments of God, where Christ and all the elect were formed.

Do you not know that your body is a temple of the Holy Spirit within you, which you have from God? You are not your own; you were bought with a price. So glorify God in your body.
— *1 Corinthians 6:19-20*

Now pray the *Prayer to Jesus* (#50) in Appendix A. Pray one 5-decade Rosary (#6a-9) sometime today, preferably with your family. Optional: reflect on sections 35–49 of *Secret of Mary* (#67).

Thirtieth Day
Knowledge of Jesus Christ

Come Holy Spirit, fill us and animate us. Please help us to know, understand and see Jesus as you want us to. Help us to believe in Him and in His love for us, to trust in Him and commit ourselves to Him, and to return His love with all our love and persevering service so that we will in fact live our total consecration to Him through Mary in union with St. Joseph more and more faithfully everyday.

Dives in Misericordia (On the Mercy of God)
by Pope John Paul II

13. The Church must profess and proclaim God's mercy in all its truth, as it has been handed down to us by revelation. We have sought, in the foregoing pages of the present document, to give at least an outline of this truth, which finds such rich expression in the whole of Sacred Scripture and in Sacred Tradition.

In the daily life of the Church the truth about the mercy of God, expressed in the Bible, resounds as a perennial echo through the many readings of the Sacred Liturgy. The authentic sense of faith of the People of God perceives this truth, as is shown by various expressions of personal and community piety.

It would of course be difficult to give a list or summary of them all, since most of them are vividly inscribed in the depths of people's hearts and minds. Some theologians affirm that mercy is the greatest of the attributes and perfections of God, and the Bible, Tradition and the whole faith life of the People of God provide particular proofs of this.

It is not a question here of the perfection of the inscrutable essence of God in the mystery of the divinity itself, but of the perfection and attribute whereby man, in the intimate truth of his existence, encounters the living God particularly closely and particularly often.

In harmony with Christ's words to Philip (cf. Jn 14:9-10), the "vision of the Father"—a vision of God through faith finds precisely in the encounter with His mercy a unique moment of interior simplicity and truth, similar to that which we discover in the parable of the prodigal son.

"He who has seen me has seen the Father" (Jn 14:9). The Church professes the mercy of God, the Church lives by it in her wide experience of faith and also in her teaching, constantly contemplating Christ, concentrating on Him, on His life and on His Gospel, on His cross and resurrection, on His whole mystery.

Everything that forms the "vision" of Christ in the Church's living faith and teaching brings us nearer to the "vision of the Father" in the holiness of His mercy. The Church seems in a particular way to profess the mercy of God and to venerate it when she directs herself to the Heart of Christ. In fact, it is precisely this drawing close to Christ in the mystery of His Heart which enables us to dwell on this point—a point in a sense central and also most accessible on the human level—of the revelation of the merciful love of the Father, a revelation which constituted the central content of the messianic mission of the Son of Man.

The Church lives an authentic life when she professes and proclaims mercy—the most stupendous attribute of the Creator and of the Redeemer—and when she brings people close to the sources of the Savior's mercy, of which she is the trustee and dispenser.

Of great significance in this area is constant meditation on the Word of God, and above all conscious and mature participation in the Eucharist and in the Sacrament of Penance or Reconciliation. The Eucharist brings us ever nearer to that love which is more powerful than death: "For as often as we eat this bread and drink this cup," we proclaim not only the death of the Redeemer but also His resurrection, "until he comes" in glory (cf. 1 Cor. 11:26).

The same Eucharistic rite, celebrated in memory of Him who in His messianic mission revealed the Father to us by means of His words and His cross, attests to the inexhaustible love by virtue of which He desires always to be united with us and present in our midst, coming to meet every human heart.

It is the Sacrament of Penance or Reconciliation that prepares the way for each individual, even those weighed down with great faults. In this sacrament each person can experience mercy in a unique way, that is, the love which is more powerful than sin.

The contemporary Church is profoundly conscious that only on the basis of the mercy of God will she be able to carry out the tasks that derive from the teaching of the Second Vatican Council, and, in the first place, the ecumenical task which aims at uniting all those who confess Christ.

As she makes many efforts in this direction, the Church confesses with humility that only that love which is more powerful than the weakness of human divisions can definitively bring about that unity which Christ implored from the Father and which the Spirit never ceases to beseech for us "with sighs too deep for words."

True Devotion to Mary
by St. Louis de Montfort, Chapter XVI

And we must do everything *for* Mary. Inasmuch as one has given himself to her, it is right that he should do everything for her, as a servant and a slave. One does not, of course, regard her as the last end of his services—that end is Christ alone—but as a means to reach that end. As a good servant and slave one must not remain idle.

Depending on the protection of his august sovereign Lady—he must dare and do great things for her. He must defend her rights when they are disputed, and fight for her glory when it is assailed. He must attract the whole world to her service, if he can. He must lift his voice to denounce those who abuse her and outrage her Son. He must do everything in his power to spread true devotion.

And he must ask nothing of her, as a reward for what little he accomplishes, except the honor of belonging absolutely to her; and the joy of being united by her to Jesus, never to be separated from Him.

GLORY TO JESUS IN MARY!
GLORY TO MARY IN JESUS!
GLORY TO GOD ALONE!

So you also, when you have done all that is commanded you, say, "We are unworthy servants; we have only done what was our duty."— Luke 17:10

Now pray *The Holy Trinity Prayer in the Spirit of Fatima* (#21) in Appendix A. Pray one 5-decade Rosary (#6a-9) sometime today, preferably with your family. Optional: reflect on sections 50–64 of *Secret of Mary* (#67).

Thirty-First Day
Knowledge of Jesus Christ

*Come Holy Spirit, fill us and animate us. Please help us to know,
understand and see Jesus as you want us to. Help us to believe in
Him and in His love for us, to trust in Him and commit ourselves to
Him, and to return His love with all our love and persevering service
so that we will in fact live our total consecration to Him through
Mary in union with St. Joseph more and more faithfully everyday.*

Redemptor Hominis (Redeemer of Man)
by Pope John Paul II

13. When we penetrate by means of the continually
and rapidly increasing experience of the human family
into the mystery of Jesus Christ, we understand with
greater clarity that there is at the basis of all these ways
that the Church of our time must follow, in accordance
with the wisdom of Pope Paul VI, one single way: it is the
way that has stood the test of centuries and it is also the
way of the future.

Christ the Lord indicated this way especially, when, as
the Council teaches, "by his Incarnation, he, the Son of
God, in a certain way united himself with each man". The
Church therefore sees its fundamental task in enabling
that union to be brought about and renewed continually.

The Church wishes to serve this single end: that each
person may be able to find Christ, in order that Christ
may walk with each person the path of life, with the
power of the truth about man and the world that is contained in the mystery of the Incarnation and the
Redemption and with the power of the love that is radiated by that truth.

Against a background of the ever increasing historical
processes, which seem at the present time to have results
especially within the spheres of various systems, ideolog-
ical concepts of the world and regimes, Jesus Christ
becomes, in a way, newly present, in spite of all his
apparent absences, in spite of all the limitations of the
presence and of the institutional activity of the Church.
Jesus Christ becomes present with the power of the truth

and the love that are expressed in him with unique unrepeatable fullness in spite of the shortness of his life on earth and the even greater shortness of his public activity.

Jesus Christ is the chief way for the Church. He himself is our way "to the Father's house" and is the way to each man. On this way leading from Christ to man, on this way on which Christ unites himself with each man, nobody can halt the Church. This is an exigency of man's temporal welfare and of his eternal welfare.

Out of regard for Christ and in view of the mystery that constitutes the Church's own life, the Church cannot remain insensible to whatever serves man's true welfare, any more than she can remain indifferent to what threatens it. In various passages in its documents the Second Vatican Council has expressed the Church's fundamental solicitude that life in "the world should conform more to man's surpassing dignity" in all its aspects, so as to make that life "ever more human".

This is the solicitude of Christ himself, the good Shepherd of all men. In the name of this solicitude, as we read in the Council's Pastoral Constitution, "the Church must in no way be confused with the political community, nor bound to any political system. She is at once a sign and a safeguard of the transcendence of the human person" (*Gaudium et Spes*, 91).

Accordingly, what is in question here is man in all his truth, in his full magnitude. We are not dealing with the "abstract" man, but the real, "concrete", "historical" man. We are dealing with "each" man, for each one is included in the mystery of the Redemption and with each one Christ has united himself for ever through this mystery. Every man comes into the world through being conceived in his mother's womb and being born of his mother, and precisely on account of the mystery of the Redemption is entrusted to the solicitude of the Church. Her solicitude is about the whole man and is focussed on him in an altogether special manner.

The object of her care is man in his unique unrepeatable human reality, which keeps intact the image and likeness of God himself. The Council points out this very fact when, speaking of that likeness, it recalls that "man is the only creature on earth that God willed for itself."

Man as "willed" by God, as "chosen" by him from eternity and called, destined for grace and glory—this is "each" man, "the most concrete" man, "the most real"; this is man in all the fullness of the mystery in which he has become a sharer in Jesus Christ, the mystery in which each one of the four thousand million human beings living on our planet has become a sharer from the moment he is conceived beneath the heart of his mother.

True Devotion to Mary
by St. Louis de Montfort, Chapter XV

Slaves of Jesus in Mary will have a special devotion to the great mystery of the Incarnation of the Word, March 25th. This is the mystery proper to true devotion because it has been inspired by the Holy Spirit.

It was inspired that we might see—and honor and imitate—the utter dependence of God on the Virgin Mary for His Father's glory and for our salvation.

We must certainly use this occasion to thank God for the incomparable graces He has granted Mary in choosing her for His Mother—the choice celebrated in this feast day.

These are the two principal ends of the slavery of Jesus Christ in Mary.

(1) Since we live in a proud century among a great number of puffed-up scholars, and proud and critical minds, men who find fault with the best established customs of piety, it is better to say "slavery of Jesus in Mary" and to call oneself a slave of Jesus rather than a slave of Mary—naming the devotion after its Last End, Jesus, and not after the way to arrive at that End, Mary....

(2) As the principal mystery celebrated in this devotion is that of the Incarnation—Jesus made flesh in the womb of Mary—it is more fitting we should say "slavery of Jesus in Mary." By this we signify the mystery of Jesus abiding and reigning in Mary. And there is the prayer recited by so many great souls; "O Jesus living in Mary, come and live in us, in Thy spirit of sanctity...."

Slaves of Jesus in Mary will have a great love for the recitation of the Hail Mary, the Angelical Salutation. Few Christians, no matter how enlightened, know the excellence, the merit, and the value of this prayer. Nor are they aware of the necessity of saying it often.

No longer do I call you servants, for the servant does not know what his master is doing; but I have called you friends, for all that I have heard from my Father I have made known to you. You did not choose me, but I chose you and appointed you that you should go and bear fruit and that your fruit should abide; so that whatever you ask the Father in my name, he may give it to you. This I command you, to love one another. — John 15:15-17

Now reflect on *Spiritual Poverty is Worse than Physical Poverty* (#43b). Pray one 5-decade Rosary (#6a-9) sometime today, preferably with your family. Optional: reflect on sections 65–74 of *Secret of Mary* (#67).

Thirty-Second Day
Knowledge of Jesus Christ

*Come Holy Spirit, fill us and animate us. Please help us to know,
understand and see Jesus as you want us to. Help us to believe in
Him and in His love for us, to trust in Him and commit ourselves to
Him, and to return His love with all our love and persevering service
so that we will in fact live our total consecration to Him through
Mary in union with St. Joseph more and more faithfully everyday.*

Novo Millennio Ineunte (At the Beginning of the
New Millennium), by Pope John Paul II

24. This divine-human identity emerges forcefully
from the Gospels, which offer us a range of elements that
make it possible for us to enter that "frontier zone" of the
mystery, represented by Christ's self-awareness. The
Church has no doubt that the Evangelists in their
accounts, and inspired from on high, have correctly
understood in the words which Jesus spoke the truth
about his person and his awareness of it.

Is this not what Luke wishes to tell us when he
recounts Jesus' first recorded words, spoken in the
Temple in Jerusalem when he was barely twelve years
old? Already at that time he shows that he is aware of a
unique relationship with God, a relationship which properly belongs to a "son".

When his mother tells him how anxiously she and
Joseph had been searching for him, Jesus replies without
hesitation: "How is it that you sought me? Did you not
know that I must be about my Father's affairs?" (Lk 2:49).

It is no wonder therefore that later as a grown man his
language authoritatively expresses the depth of his own
mystery, as is abundantly clear both in the Synoptic
Gospels (cf. Mt 11:27; Lk 10:22) and above all in the
Gospel of John. In his self-awareness, Jesus has no
doubts: "The Father is in me and I am in the Father" (Jn
10:38).

However valid it may be to maintain that, because of
the human condition which made him grow "in wisdom
and in stature, and in favor with God and man' (Lk 2:52),
his human awareness of his own mystery would also

have progressed to its fullest expression in his glorified humanity, there is no doubt that already in his historical existence Jesus was aware of his identity as the Son of God.

John emphasizes this to the point of affirming that it was ultimately because of this awareness that Jesus was rejected and condemned: they sought to kill him "because he not only broke the sabbath but also called God his Father, making himself equal with God" (Jn 5:18).

In Gethsemane and on Golgotha Jesus' human awareness will be put to the supreme test. But not even the drama of his Passion and Death will be able to shake his serene certainty of being the Son of the heavenly Father.

Secret of Mary by St. Louis de Montfort, Part II

20. Happy, a thousand times happy, is the soul here below to which the Holy Spirit reveals the Secret of Mary in order that it may come to know her; to which He opens the "Garden Enclosed" that it may enter into it; to which He gives access to that "Fountain Sealed," that it may draw from it and drink deep draughts of the living waters of grace!

That soul will find God alone in His most loving creature. It will find God infinitely holy and exalted, yet at the same time adapting Himself to its own weakness.

Since God is present everywhere, He may be found everywhere, even in hell, but nowhere do we creatures find Him nearer to us and more adapted to our weakness than in Mary, since it was for that end that He came and dwelt in her. Everywhere else He is the Bread of the strong, the Bread of the angels, but in Mary He is the Bread of children.

Let us not imagine, then, as some do who are misled by erroneous teachings, that Mary, being a creature, is a

hindrance to our union with the Creator. It is no longer
Mary who lives, it is Jesus Christ, it is God alone Who
lives in her.

Her transformation into
God surpasses that of St.
Paul and of the other saints
more than the heavens surpass the earth by their
height. Mary is made for
God alone, and far from ever
detaining a soul in herself,
she casts the soul upon God
and unites it with Him so much the more perfectly as the
soul is more perfectly united to her.

Mary is the admirable echo of God. When we say,
"Mary," she answers, "God". When, with St. Elizabeth, we
call her, "Blessed," she glorifies God. If the falsely enlightened, whom the devil has so miserably illusioned, even in
prayer, had known how to find Mary, and through her, to
find Jesus, and through Jesus, God the Father, they
would not have had such terrible falls.

The saints tell us that when we have once found Mary,
and through Mary, Jesus, and through Jesus, God the
Father, we have found all good. He who says all, excepts
nothing: all grace and all friendship with God, all safety
from God's enemies, all truth to crush falsehoods, all
facility to overcome difficulties in the way of salvation, all
comfort and all joy amidst the bitterness of life.

*When the Spirit of truth comes, he will guide you into all
the truth; for he will not speak on his own authority, but whatever
he hears he will speak, and he will declare to you the things that
are to come. He will glorify me, for he will take what is mine and
declare it to you. All that the Father has is mine; therefore I said
that he will take what is mine and declare it to you.*
— *John 16:13-15*

Pray the *Litany of the Holy Spirit* (#46d) and read the *Twelve
Promises of the Sacred Heart* (#19). Also pray one 5-decade
Rosary (#6a-9) sometime today, preferably with your family.

Thirty-Third Day
Knowledge of Jesus Christ

*Come Holy Spirit, fill us and animate us. Please help us to know,
understand and see Jesus as you want us to. Help us to believe in
Him and in His love for us, to trust in Him and commit ourselves to
Him, and to return His love with all our love and persevering service
so that we will in fact live our total consecration to Him through
Mary in union with St. Joseph more and more faithfully everyday.*

Ecclesia de Eucharistia (On the Eucharist in Its
Relationship to the Church), by Pope John Paul II

15. The sacramental re-presentation of Christ's sacrifice, crowned by the resurrection, in the Mass involves a
most special presence which — in the words of Paul VI —
"is called 'real' not as a way of excluding all other types of
presence as if they were 'not real', but because it is a presence in the fullest sense: a substantial presence whereby
Christ, the God-Man, is wholly and entirely present"
(*Mysterium Fidei*).

This sets forth once more the perennially valid
teaching of the Council of Trent: "the consecration of the
bread and wine effects the change of the whole substance
of the bread into the substance of the body of Christ our
Lord, and of the whole substance of the wine into the substance of his blood. And the holy Catholic Church has
fittingly and properly called this change transubstantia-
tion".

Truly the Eucharist is a *mysterium fidei*, a mystery
which surpasses our understanding and can only be
received in faith, as is often brought out in the catechesis
of the Church Fathers regarding this divine sacrament:
"Do not see — Saint Cyril of Jerusalem exhorts — in the
bread and wine merely natural elements, because the
Lord has expressly said that they are his body and his
blood: faith assures you of this, though your senses suggest otherwise".

Adoro te devote, latens Deitas, we shall continue to sing
with the Angelic Doctor. Before this mystery of love,
human reason fully experiences its limitations. One under-

stands how, down the centuries, this truth has stimulated theology to strive to understand it ever more deeply.

These are praiseworthy efforts, which are all the more helpful and insightful to the extent that they are able to join critical thinking to the "living faith" of the Church, as grasped especially by the Magisterium's "sure charism of truth" and the "intimate sense of spiritual realities" which is attained above all by the saints.

There remains the boundary indicated by Paul VI: "Every theological explanation which seeks some understanding of this mystery, in order to be in accord with Catholic faith, must firmly maintain that in objective reality, independently of our mind, the bread and wine have ceased to exist after the consecration, so that the adorable body and blood of the Lord Jesus from that moment on are really before us under the sacramental species of bread and wine".

Redemptor Hominis (Redeemer of Man), by Pope John Paul II

20. It is an essential truth, not only of doctrine but also of life, that the Eucharist builds the Church, building it as the authentic community of the People of God, as the assembly of the faithful, bearing the same mark of unity that was shared by the Apostles and the first disciples of the Lord. The Eucharist builds ever anew this community and unity, ever building and regenerating it on the basis of the Sacrifice of Christ, since it commemorates his death on the Cross, the price by which he redeemed us. Accordingly, in the Eucharist we touch in a way the very mystery of the Body and Blood of the Lord, as is attested by the very words used at its institution, the words that, because of that institution, have become the words with which those called to this ministry in the Church unceasingly celebrate the Eucharist.

...Indeed, the Eucharist is the ineffable Sacrament! The essential commitment and, above all,

the visible grace and source of supernatural strength for the Church as the People of God is to persevere and advance constantly in Eucharistic life and Eucharistic piety and to develop spiritually in the climate of the Eucharist. With all the greater reason, then, it is not permissible for us, in thought, life or action, to take away from this truly most holy Sacrament its full magnitude and its essential meaning. *It is at one and the same time a Sacrifice-Sacrament, a Communion-Sacrament, and a Presence-Sacrament.* And, although it is true that the Eucharist always was and must continue to be the most profound revelation of the human brotherhood of Christ's disciples and confessors, it cannot be treated merely as an "occasion" for manifesting this brotherhood. When celebrating the Sacrament of the Body and Blood of the Lord, the full magnitude of the divine mystery must be respected, as must the full meaning of this sacramental sign in which Christ is really present and is received, the soul is filled with grace and the pledge of future glory is given

Secret of Mary by St. Louis de Montfort, Part I

Faithful soul, living image of God, redeemed by the Precious Blood of Jesus Christ, it is the will of God that you be holy like Him in this life and glorious like Him in the next. Your sure vocation is the acquisition of the holiness of God; and unless all your thoughts and words and actions, all the sufferings and events of your life tend to that end, you are resisting God by not doing that for which He has created you and is now preserving you.

Oh, what an admirable work! To change that which is dust into light, to make pure that which is unclean, holy that which is sinful, to make the creature like its Creator, man like God! Admirable work, I repeat, but difficult in itself, and impossible to mere nature; only God by His grace, by His abundant and extraordinary grace, can accomplish it. Even the creation of the whole world is not so great a masterpiece as this.

Predestinate soul, how are you to do it? What means will you choose to reach the height to which God calls you? The means of salvation and sanctification are known to all; they are laid down in the Gospel, explained by the masters of the spiritual life, practiced by the saints, and necessary to all who wish to be saved and to attain perfection. They are: humility of heart, continual prayer, mortification in all things, abandonment to Divine Providence, and conformity to the will of God.

To practice all these means of salvation and sanctification the grace of God is absolutely necessary. No one can doubt that God gives His grace to all, in a more or less abundant measure. I say in a more or less abundant measure, for God, although infinitely good, does not give equal grace to all, yet to each soul He gives sufficient grace.

The faithful soul will, with great grace, perform a great action, and with less grace a lesser action. It is the value and the excellence of the grace bestowed by God and corresponded to by the soul, that gives to our actions their value and their excellence. These principles are certain.

It all comes to this, then: that you should find an easy means for obtaining from God the grace necessary to make you holy; and this means I wish to make known to you. Now, I say that to find this grace of God, we must find Mary.

And from his fullness have we all received, grace upon grace. For the law was given through Moses; grace and truth came through Jesus Christ. No one has ever seen God; the only Son, who is in the bosom of the Father, he has made him known. — John 1:16-18

Pray the *Litany of the Holy Name of Jesus* (#23b) and the *Act of Faith and Intercession* (#29b). Also pray one 5-decade Rosary (#6a-9) sometime today, preferably with your family.

"How true it is that when we give all our merits to Mary,
she multiplies them by her own incalculable merits.
This puts into motion positive spiritual forces to repair the
damage due to sin and significantly change the course of history, if enough make this commitment. Mary's merits can
multiply the effects of one person's holiness and help countless souls. Only Heaven knows the depth of holiness a soul
must achieve to tip the scales for world peace...consecration
is not just a prayer or a devotion but a commitment to a way
of life which must be nourished through continuous
formation in the eternal truths of our faith."
— Mario Luigi Cardinal Ciappi, Papal Theologian Emeritus

Part 5: Consecration Day
Thirty-Fourth Day

Suggested meditations: John 17 (#50f).

Make the Act of Total Consecration by using prayer #49b.

How to Make Your Consecration

At the end of thirty-three days, you should go to Confession and Holy Communion with the intention of consecrating yourself to Jesus through Mary as His slave of love. After Communion, pray the Act of Consecration Prayer (#49b) — it is also good to write it out and sign it the same day you make the consecration.

It would be very becoming if on that day you offered some tribute to Jesus and His mother, either as a penance for past unfaithfulness to the promises made in Baptism or as a sign of your submission to Jesus and Mary. Such a tribute would be one in accordance with your ability and fervor, and may take the form of fasting if your state-in-life permits, an act of self-denial, a gift of an alms, or the offering of a votive candle. If you give only a pin as a token of your homage, provided it is given with a good heart, it would satisfy Jesus Who considers only the good intention.

Every year try to renew your consecration by following the same practices, beginning on February 20, the memorial day of Blesseds Francisco and Jacinta of Fatima (see schedule on pages 10–13).

After making your consecration, you may participate in further spiritual benefits for your family by enrolling as a Holy Family Cooperator of the Apostolate for Family Consecration and a member of the St. Louis de Montfort's Mary, Queen of All Hearts Association.* These unions will bring your family

---

* The Mary, Queen of All Hearts Association is a pious union of the faithful, without officers or meetings, organized to help the members live and publicize the Marian Way of Life as the easier and more secure means to sanctify themselves.

more grace and strength as you now strive to fully live your Total Consecration every day.

You may enroll on www.familyconsecration.org, under the tab "Deepening and Renewing Your Consecration." Click on the icon to register.** This enrollment entitles you to the spiritual benefits that are available to a Holy Family Cooperator and to membership in the Association of Mary, Queen of All Hearts.

Spiritual Benefits

On the occasion of the initial consecration or its renewal, a **plenary indulgence** (complete remission of all punishment due to sin) is granted under the usual conditions (Confession, Communion, prayer for the intentions of the Holy Father, and detachment from all sin).

A plenary indulgence is also granted under the usual conditions on the day of enrollment in the Association, on Holy Thursday and Christmas, and on the Feasts of the Annunciation, Immaculate Conception and St. Louis de Montfort, as well as on every first Saturday of the month.

As a Holy Family Cooperator, your family shares in all the prayers and good works of the Apostolate for Family Consecration and of all the associations and religious movements spiritually connected with the Family Apostolate, such as Blessed Teresa of Calcutta's Missionaries of Charity, the Dominican Sisters of the Perpetual Rosary in Fatima, and others. Also, your intentions are remembered at the Masses celebrated on the first Saturday of every month and on the Feast of the Holy Family.

Your name will also be included in the list of individuals and families who have made their Total Consecration to Jesus through Mary in union with St.

** You may also mail your enrollment to: **Apostolate for Family Consecration®** Catholic Familyland,® 3375 County Road 36, Bloomingdale, Ohio 43910-7903 U.S.A. or email at: consecration@familyland.org

Joseph. This list is presented every year to the Holy Father.

As a member of the Association of Mary Queen of All Hearts, your family will share in all the good works and prayers of the Montfort Fathers and Brothers, the Daughters of Wisdom, and the Brothers of St. Gabriel, which are the three congregations founded by St. Louis de Montfort. The Masses offered by the members of the Company of Mary on the first Monday of every month for the deceased of their Congregation are applied also to the deceased members of the Association.

Obligations

There are *no extraordinary obligations* of being a Holy Family Cooperator or a member of the Association of Mary, Queen of All Hearts. You are simply encouraged to strive to live more fully your Total Consecration and to enrich your life with a Marian spirit — doing all things with Mary, through Mary, in Mary, and for Mary. By this means, you will more perfectly live and act with, through, in, and for Christ. You are encouraged to renew your consecration faithfully and frequently, making a special practice of renewing it every morning at the beginning of each new day, when possible.

In the Apostolate for Family Consecration, members frequently renew their consecration by making a spiritual Communion by saying the two words "All for" as they make countless responses and choices throughout the day. In this way we are asking God for the grace to discern His Will and the grace to do it moment by moment...*All for the Sacred and Eucharistic Heart of Jesus, all through the Sorrowful and Immaculate Heart of Mary, all in union with St. Joseph.*

Enthroning the Holy Family in the Home

If you haven't already enthroned the Holy Family in your home using the Holy Family of Fatima portrait as a visible sign of your consecration, we encourage you to do so.

The materials and procedures for the enthronement are found at www.familyconsecration.org, under the "Enthronement" tab. The actual enthronement program and the beautiful portrait can be downloaded or purchased from the website. Please also see pages 507–508 for more information.

Enthroning the Holy Family in the home entitles your family to benefit from the Twelve Promises of the Sacred Heart (see section 19 in Appendix A), since the Holy Family of Fatima portrait is centered on the Sacred and Eucharistic Heart of the Boy Jesus.

Before the enthronement, the family should go to Confession. Examination of conscience formulas are provided on the website or in prayer section 53 of Appendix A.

You may enroll your enthronement of the Holy Family at www.familyconsecration.org, under the "Enthronement" tab. Upon enrollment, aside from the spiritual benefits mentioned above for Holy Family Cooperators, your family is remembered in all the Family Apostolate's Masses celebrated on the First Friday of every month. Your family is also included in the list which is presented to the Holy Father each year, consisting of the names of the families who have enthroned the Holy Family in their homes. You can also download the following images for veneration: Holy Trinity Vision at Fatima, Death of St. Joseph, and Divine Mercy.

To live out your family consecration, your family is encouraged to go to Confession regularly and to strive to pray the family Rosary daily. Rosary videos and other resources can be viewed online in the "Family Consecration" section of our website. Other resources that help facilitate praying the Rosary may be purchased from the same website. (See resource #115-378V for our Dramatized Rosary video.)

Be an apostle!

Ask other families to consecrate themselves to the Holy Family by making the Total Consecration to Jesus through Mary in union with St. Joseph. Get involved with several practical ways to effect a positive change in family life: Familyland TV Network, Consecration in Truth catechetical program, Lay Ecclesial Teams and Catholic Familyland events.

Information on these ministries is available at www.familyland.org. **We suggest that you send a personalized email to all those in your email address book to invite them to visit our website to learn more about Total Consecration.** Ask them to consider praying the short form consecration prayer and to register on-line. Great spiritual benefits can rapidly spread throughout the world and unleash a tremendous power of grace, if enough make this consecration. This grace can transform family life and bring about the era of peace promised by Our Lady at Fatima. You can make a difference! View our Mission Presentation on the homepage of www.familyland.org.

MONTFORT MISSIONARIES
101-18 104TH STREET
OZONE PARK, N.Y. 11416-2683

OFFICE OF THE PROVINCIAL

April 28, 1993

Most Rev. Gilbert J. Sheldon
Bishop of Steubenville
P.O. Box 969
Steubenville, OH 43952

Your Excellency,

Pursuant to your letter to me of November 26, 1992, re the establishing of a branch of the Association of Mary, Queen of All Hearts, at the Family Consecration Center in Bloomingdale, Ohio, it is my pleasant duty as the Provincial Superior of the American Province of the Montfort Missionaries to grant you all permissions needed for the establishment of a branch of The Association in your diocese.

As you may know, The Association is a spiritual organization having close ties with the Company of Mary (Montfort Missionaries). In the eyes of the Church, the members of this Association are attached to our Religious Congregation and enjoy the same spiritual privileges as any member of our Community. The Superior General of the Company of Mary is ultimately responsible for the Montfortian formation of all its members. It is up to him not only to erect the various centers but also to confirm the appointment of the directors. That is why all the branches of The Association are juridically attached to the Association in Rome.

The central branch of the Association of Mary, Queen of All Hearts, here in the United States is our Montfort Center, in Bay Shore, N.Y. 11706, with Father Roger M. Charest as the National Director.

It is my understanding that Mr. Jerry Coniker, the Founder of the Apostolate for Family Consecration will be the first Director of the Bloomingdale Branch of The Association and Father Kevin Barrett, its first Spiritual Director.

In the hope that this Center in your diocese will be a Center of Spiritual renewal and Marian Spirituality, in the spirit of Pope John Paul II's Marian Year encyclical, *Redemptoris Mater*, in which he wrote: "I would like to recall, among the many witnesses and teachers of this spirituality, the figure of Saint Louis Marie Grignion de Montfort, who proposes consecration to Christ through the hands of Mary, as an effective means for Christians to live faithfully their baptismal commitments."

Sincerely in Christ
Through Mary,

William J. Considine, S. M. M.
Provincial Superior

Now that you have made your consecration, you can receive the merits and indulgences of the St. Louis de Montfort's "Association of Mary, Queen of All Hearts" by enrolling at www.familyconsecration.org. Go under the "Deepening and Renewing Your Consecration" tab. Or you can email your enrollment to: consecration@familyland.org.

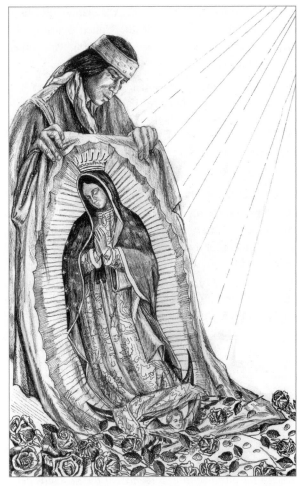

*"Am I not here who am your Mother? Are you not under
my shadow and protection? Am I not your fountain of life?
Are you not in the folds of my mantle? In the crossing
of my arms? Is there anything else you need?"*
– *Our Lady of Guadalupe to St. Juan Diego*

Part 6: Reparation and Consecration
(Days 35-37)

Thirty-Fifth Day
Reparation and Consecration

42a. Reparation and the Dual Dimension of Pope John Paul II's Consecration
by Jerome F. Coniker

1. Pope John Paul II has taught us how to enter into that era of peace promised by Our Lady of Fatima. While in New York in 1995, the Holy Father asked families to do two things: pray the Rosary and study the *Catechism of the Catholic Church*. He continues to tell us, "Take the Gospel to your neighbors!" By vigorously learning the Faith and teaching it to our children and our neighbors, we can truly renew family life and society.

If those of us who have been given the light of the Catholic faith do not make heroic sacrifices now to do what the Holy Father is telling us to do, our society will continue on its "free-fall" into the abyss of immorality, and we will see, before our very eyes, the fulfillment of the "conditional" prophecies of the approved apparitions of Our Lady in Fatima and Akita (Japan). I say "conditional" because that is what they are—conditional to the degree of how we sacrificially respond to Our Lady's requests.

First, let's reflect on what Pope John Paul II wrote in his book, *Crossing the Threshold of Hope,* with reference to Fatima:

"Perhaps this is also why the Pope was called from a faraway country, perhaps this is why it was necessary for the assassination attempt to be made in St. Peter's Square precisely on May 13, 1981, the anniversary of the first apparition at Fatima—so that all could become more transparent and comprehensible, so that the voice of God which speaks in human history through the 'signs of the times' could be more easily heard and understood." (p.131)

The Holy Father went on to write:

"On this universal level, if victory comes it will be brought by Mary. *Christ will conquer through her because he wants the Church's victories now and in the future to be linked to her....*

"I held this conviction even though I did not yet know very much about Fatima. I could see, however, that there was a certain continuity among La Salette, Lourdes, and Fatima—and, in the distant past, our Polish Jasna Gora." (p. 221)

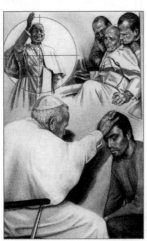

When the Pope was shot

2. "And thus we come to May 13, 1981, when I was wounded by gunshots fired in St. Peter's Square. At first, I did not pay attention to the fact that the assassination attempt had occurred on the exact anniversary of the day Mary appeared to the three children at Fatima in Portugal and spoke to them the words that now, at the end of this century, seem to be close to their fulfillment.

"With this event, didn't Christ perhaps say, once again, 'Be not afraid'? Did he repeat this Easter exhortation to the Pope, to the Church, and indirectly, to the entire human family?"

The Pope went on to say:

"At the end of the second millennium, we need, perhaps more than ever, the words of the Risen Christ: 'Be not afraid!' Man who, even after the fall of Communism, has not stopped being afraid and who truly has many reasons for feeling this way, needs to hear these words.

"Nations need to hear them, especially those nations that have been reborn after the fall of the Communist empire, as well as those that witnessed this event from the outside. Peoples and nations of the entire world need to hear these words.

"Their conscience needs to grow in the certainty that Someone exists who holds in His hands the destiny of this passing world; Someone who holds the keys to death and the netherworld (cf. Rev 1:18); Someone who is the Alpha and the Omega of human history (cf. Rev. 22:13)—be it the individual or collective history. And this Someone is Love (cf. 1 Jn 4:8,16)—Love that became man, Love crucified and risen, Love unceasingly present among men. It is Eucharistic Love. It is the infinite source of communion. He alone can give the ultimate assurance when He says 'Be not afraid!'" (pp. 221-222)

Fatima

3. When our family lived in Portugal from 1971–1973, we obtained a copy of a letter that Sister Lucia wrote to the Bishop of the Diocese of Leiria (where Fatima is located) about Our Lady's apparition of July 13, 1917. Sister Lucia was one of the seers of Fatima. She lived to be 97 years old, being called from this life on February 13, 2005, just two months before the passing of her friend and beloved Holy Father Pope John Paul II. The other two seers, Jacinta (age 7 at the time of the apparition) and Francisco (age 9), died shortly after they told Our Lady that they would be willing to offer their lives up for the conversion of sinners—for your family and my family.

The vision of hell

4. Lucia's words:

"Our Lady showed us a large sea of fire which seemed to be beneath the earth. Plunged in this fire were the demons and the souls, who were like embers, transparent and black or bronze-colored, with human forms which floated about in the conflagration, borne by the flames which issued from it with clouds of smoke, falling on all sides as sparks fall in great conflagrations, without weight or equilibrium, among shrieks and groans of sorrow and despair which horrified us and caused us to quake with fear.

"The demons were distinguished by horrible and loathsome forms of animals, frightful and unknown, but transparent and black. This vision vanished in a moment. Providentially, our good Heavenly Mother had promised us in the first apparition to take us to Heaven. Otherwise, I think we would have died of fright and horror." (Letter dated August 31, 1941 from Sr. Lucia to the Bishop of Leiria.)

The great Fatima prophecies

5. The following are Sister Lucia's words, published by the Bishop of Leiria. I have organized them in an outline with an *asterisk (*) to indicate the prophecies that have already been fulfilled*:

"Shortly afterwards, we raised our eyes to Our Lady, who said with goodness and sadness: 'You have seen hell, where the souls of poor sinners go.

- 'To save them, God wishes to establish in the world devotion to my Immaculate Heart.* [However, more should be done.]

- 'If they do what I will tell you, many souls will be saved, and there will be peace. The war is going to end.* [World War I]

- 'But if they don't stop offending God, another and worse one [World War II] will begin in the reign of Pius XI.*

- 'When you shall see a night illuminated by an unknown light [Jan 25-26, 1938]*, know that this is the great sign that God will give you, that He is going to punish the world by means of war, hunger and persecutions of the Church, and of the Holy Father.*

- 'To prevent this, I shall come to ask for the consecration of Russia to my Immaculate Heart; and for the Communion of Reparation on the First Saturdays.*

- 'If they listen to my request, Russia will be converted, and there will be peace.

- 'If not:

    'Russia will scatter her errors throughout the world,*

    'She will provoke wars and persecutions of the Church,*

    'The good will be martyred* [Note: there have been more martyrs in the 20th Century than in the entire 2000 year history of the Church],

    'The Holy Father will have much to suffer,*

    'And various nations will be annihilated. [This has not happened and does not have to happen if we consecrate ourselves in the dual dimension of Pope John Paul II's consecration.]

- 'In the end, my Immaculate Heart will triumph.

    'The Holy Father will consecrate Russia to me* [Pope John Paul II did this on May 13, 1982, in Fatima and on March 25, 1984, in Rome.],

    'And she will be converted,

    'And a certain period of peace will be granted to the world.'"

The miracle of the sun

6. Our Lady's final apparition at Fatima took place on October 13, 1917. This was the great "Miracle of the Sun." Cardinal Joseph Carberry once told me that never before in the history of the world has a public miracle, such as this, ever occurred, one that was prophesied in advance to occur on a specific day, at a specific place, and which was witnessed by over 70,000 people. *It was also documented as an historic fact by an atheistic press that was controlled by an atheistic government.*

When we lived near Fatima for two years, I had the privilege to study the Fatima message under the instruction of Father Gabriel Pausback, O'Carm., who was the assistant general of the Carmelite Order and author of *Saints of Carmel*. He introduced me to the Martos (Jacinta's and Francisco's family) and others who had witnessed the miracle of the sun.

The "Miracle of the Sun" was not like many other reported apparitions, where some could see the phenomenon and others could not. On October 13, 1917, everyone within a 20 mile radius saw the entire plateau of Fatima bathed in light-shafts of blue, red, yellow and green. Then they saw the sun spinning in the sky, and they ran for their lives when they saw it plummet towards the earth. The fire ball that appeared to be the sun stopped at the tree tops, hovered there for a few minutes and slowly went back into the heavens, leaving everyone present completely dry, when before the event they had been drenched from the rainfall.

Cardinal Carberry also told me that since there has never been a miracle such as this before, the message — which the miracle confirmed — must be of the greatest significance!

Approved Apparitions of Akita

7. Now let's consider the prophecies of the approved apparitions of Our Lady in Akita, Japan. Let me first give some background on these apparitions.

They started in 1973 and were approved, on April 22, 1984, by Bishop John Shojiro Ito, who at the time was Bishop of Niigata.

Bishop Francis Sato, the successor to Bishop Ito, also approved the apparitions. This approval was documented when our chaplain, Father Kevin Barrett, interviewed Bishop Sato on videotape in March of 1995 at his residence in Japan.

The seer, Sister Agnes Sasagawa, like Sr. Lucia of Fatima, submitted in total obedience to the bishop of the diocese where the apparitions occurred. It is important to note that this is the way of the Church, *that we are protected from deception by humbly submitting to Church authority.*

In the letter of approval issued by Bishop Ito, he quoted Our Blessed Mother as saying:

"As I told you, if men do not repent and better themselves, the Father will inflict a terrible punishment on all humanity. *It will be a punishment greater than the deluge, such as one will never have been seen before. Fire will fall from the sky and will wipe out a great part of humanity*, the good as well as the bad, sparing neither priests nor faithful. The survivors will find themselves so desolate that they will envy the dead. The only arms which will remain for you will be the Rosary and the Sign left by my Son. Each day recite the prayers of the Rosary. With the Rosary, pray for the Pope, the Bishops and the priests.

"...In order that the world might know His anger, the *Heavenly Father is preparing to inflict a great chastisement on all mankind*. With my Son, I have intervened so many times to appease the wrath of the Father. *I have prevented the coming of calamities by offering Him the sufferings of the Son on the Cross, His Precious Blood, and beloved souls who console Him and form a cohort of victim souls*. **Prayer, penance, and courageous sacrifices can soften the Father's anger**..." (taken from the letter of approval by Bishop John Shojiro Ito of April 22, 1984).

St. Kolbe on Obedience

8.   What is meant by the "penance" and "courageous sacrifices" which are necessary to prevent chastisement? **I believe that the penance and courageous sacrifices that God is asking of us is obedience to the Holy Father, the Pope.** The most difficult thing for man to do is to bend his will to lawful authority. This is the greatest reparation for sin we can offer.

The great Polish Marian saint and martyr of Auschwitz, St. Maximilian Kolbe, who started the Knights of the Immaculata movement shortly after he had a vision of Our Lady of Fatima standing over Moscow, said:

"Not in mortification, not in great prayer, not in labor, not in rest, but in *obedience is the essence and merit of holiness*" (*Aim Higher*, p. 84).

Obedience is the key. Doing penance and making sacrifices does not just mean praying and fasting. Although there are norms established by the Church for prayer and fasting, they are not the only thing we are supposed to do. ***Obedience to lawful authority represents the most pleasing penance and constitutes the most heroic sacrifices in order to repair for sin.***

As Catholics, we need to humble ourselves and bend our wills to the Holy Father if we want to be holy and receive an outpouring of God's mercy. *Obedience is the key to drawing down God's mercy upon the families of the world.*

Our Lord said in Matthew 7:21: "It is not those who say, 'Lord, Lord,' that will enter the kingdom of Heaven, *but those who do the will of My Father.*"

The Key to Hope and Mercy

9. Obedience to the Pope and reparation for sin gives us hope.

The messages of both Fatima and Akita have underscored the fact that reparation for sin is the formula for drawing down God's mercy upon our world. At the Apostolate's Catholic Familyland, we are seeking to teach families about reparation: what it means and how it should be effected in our daily lives. We have summarized what we call the Marian Multiplier "formula" for bringing down God's mercy.

Now I rejoice in my sufferings for your sake, and in my flesh I complete what is lacking in Christ's afflictions for the sake of his body, that is, the church — Colossians 1:24

Now pray the *Act of Spiritual Communion* (#11a) in Appendix A. Pray one 5-decade Rosary (#6a-9) sometime today, preferably with your family. Members and Discernment Cooperators: read sections 800–802 in Appendix C.

Thirty-Sixth Day
Reparation and Consecration

42a. Reparation and the Dual Dimension of Pope John Paul II's Consecration *(continued)*
by Jerome F. Coniker

10. First Point: <u>**Sin** is the cause of all unhappiness</u>. Every sin affects not only the sinner, but the entire world.

Second Point: <u>**Grace** is more powerful than sin</u>; the Redemption is greater than the Fall. Jesus has conquered satan. We have nothing to fear from the devil if we follow Christ (which also means following His Vicar on earth, the Pope, and the Teaching Magisterium of the Church), love God and neighbor and strive to grow in the grace Jesus won for us on Calvary.

Third Point: <u>**Personal holiness** is essential for salvation</u>. But our personal holiness alone is not enough to offset the effects of the sins of mankind and bring about a healing of families and world peace.

Fourth Point: <u>**Consecration** to Jesus through Mary</u>. When enough of us give the little holiness we have to Jesus through Mary, she will be able to purify and multiply it by her incalculable merits to most effectively repair for sins in our age and obtain grace from her Son to convert poor sinners and bring peace and healing into families and the world.

Every sin affects society

11. Reflecting on the First Point, let's look at what Pope John Paul II said in section 16 of his document *On Reconciliation and Penance*:

"In other words, there is no sin, not even the most intimate and secret one, the most strictly individual one that exclusively concerns the person committing it.

"With greater or lesser violence, with greater or lesser harm, *every sin has repercussions on the entire ecclesial body and on the whole human family.*"

In section 2 of the Apostolic Constitution on indulgences (*Indulgentiarum doctrina*), dated January 1, 1967, Pope Paul VI states:

"In fact, every sin upsets the universal order God, in His indescribable wisdom and limitless love, has established. Further, every sin does immense harm to the sinner himself and to the community of men."

This means that when someone sins, it not only hurts the sinner but the entire Mystical Body of Christ. It gives the devil more power to tempt us and to draw us away from God's will into venial sin, and eventually into mortal sin.

When we think about this, it can be very discouraging. We look around and see sin everywhere, and it seems that so few people are trying to do God's will. But there is hope.

Reparation—repairing for sin

12. If sin is the "bad news" then the Second Point (grace) is truly the heart of the "Good News" of the Gospel. Jesus, by His redemptive sacrifice, has won for us the grace to overcome and to repair for the sin in our lives and in our world.

I believe that the best definition of reparation for sin is from Pope Paul VI's Apostolic Constitution on indulgences. Providentially, former President Ronald Reagan quoted this definition in his welcoming address to Pope John Paul II when His Holiness visited the United States in 1987. In section 4, Pope Paul VI says:

"By the hidden and kindly mystery of God's will, a supernatural solidarity reigns among men. A consequence of this is that the sin of one person harms other people just as one person's holiness helps others."

In this same document, Pope Paul VI presents a more detailed explanation on reparation and what we must do to repair for sin. His Holiness states:

"The truth has been divinely revealed that sins are followed by punishments. God's holiness and justice inflict them. Sins must be expiated...

"The full taking away and, as it is called, reparation of sin requires two things:

"Firstly, friendship with God must be restored. Amends must be made for offending His wisdom and goodness. This is done by a sincere conversion of mind [repentance and formation].

"Secondly, all the personal and social values as well as those that are universal, which sin has lessened or destroyed, must be fully made good [evangelization and catechesis]" (Apostolic Constitution *Indulgentiarum doctrina*, sections 2–3).

Like the current of a river

13. You can compare the concept of reparation to a river in which people are swimming upstream, against the current, in order to get to Heaven. The more sin there is in the world, the stronger the current becomes (temptation), making it harder for everyone to reach Heaven.

However, when people grow in grace, they are repairing for their own sins and the sins of the whole world. They are helping to make the current run more slowly so that everyone in the family and in the world is able to swim more easily upstream (actual graces) and reach their heavenly goal if they truly will it.

Like a magnetic field

14. Another analogy can be made. Reparation may be compared with magnetic fields. God seeks to attract our free wills by His love and truth (actual grace). The devil seeks to seduce us by his lies and the empty pleasures of evil (temptation). By choosing to sin, man repels God and allows himself to be seduced by the devil. When many people sin, all society feels less attraction to God, and more and more people succumb to the corrupting seduction of the devil (temptation).

However, as more people renounce sin and allow themselves to be drawn to God, gaining grace and merit for their souls and the whole Mystical Body of Christ through their prayers and good works, they help to increase the attraction (actual grace) felt by all to God and His goodness.

In order for us to grow in grace (Second Point) and offset the effects of sin, we have to develop a prayer life, receive the sacraments and practice the virtues (Third Point). Naturally, the fervor and the love we have for God determines the amount of grace that we receive and therefore, determines the amount of reparation that is made for our own sins and for the sins of the world.

Consecration to Jesus through Mary

15. Now, if the devil is always actively trying to seduce souls away from God by his perverse influence, the Mother of Jesus, the woman of Genesis (cf. 3:15) and of Revelation (chapter 12), is ever more so attracting her children to God. She is the chosen vessel through whom God wishes to crush the head of Satan.

The late Cardinal Luigi Ciappi, who served the last five popes as personal theologian and was the primary theological advisor for The Apostolate, explained to us how, in the Fourth Point, our Blessed Mother's singular holiness helps us to more effectively repair for sin, especially through the power of consecration. In his letter of August 24, 1989, he said:

"How true it is when we give all of our merits to Mary, she multiplies them by her incalculable merits. This puts into motion positive spiritual forces to repair the damage due to sin and significantly change the course of history, if enough make this commitment.

"Mary's merits can multiply the effects of one person's holiness and help countless souls. Only heaven knows the depth of holiness a soul must achieve to tip the scales for world peace."

Mary never ceases to dispense the precious graces of Jesus, her Son, upon her children. And when we entrust to her our prayers, merits, and good works, through consecration, she purifies and multiplies their power to repair for sin and presents them to Jesus on our behalf.

Restoring Order through Reparation

16. When we live a life of reparation for sin, we are growing in union with God. Soon after founding the Apostolate for Family Consecration in 1975, I wrote the following explanation about the effects of "planting seeds" of prayer, charity, and sacrifice, accompa-

nied by the "water and sunshine" of our devout reception of the sacraments in our lives:

"Our meritorious actions help to bring back the spiritual balance in the universe by lessening the control of the forces of evil over our lives and those of our families, our neighborhoods, our schools, our parishes, our dioceses, and indeed, the entire world.

"Every supernaturally good act performed in the state of grace gives us a reward or merit, increasing our capacity for peace and our capacity to know, love and serve God for all eternity. In addition to, and through total consecration to Jesus through Mary, our merits are purified, multiplied and preserved for us throughout our entire pilgrimage on earth.

"Through consecration, we give to our Blessed Mother the privilege of directing our prayers. We more humbly acknowledge the reality that we are God's children, confident that Our Heavenly Mother knows better than we what we need in order to more perfectly accomplish God's will.

"Finally, because of the Church's intercessory power, many of our meritorious acts can be enriched by the Church through indulgences. Thus we have the power to help release a soul from Purgatory everyday through our plenary (full) indulgences, and relieve the suffering of the Holy Souls through our partial indulgences."

We need to better understand that indulgences are an added satisfactory effect given to our prayers and good works by the Church as part of the power of the "keys" entrusted to her by Christ in the person of the Apostle Peter (cf. Mt. 16:19 and Jn. 20:34). If we are in the state of grace and fulfill one of the norms laid down by the Church, we can continually earn plenary (no more than one a day) and partial indulgences for ourselves and for the souls in Purgatory.

Then he opened their minds to understand the scriptures, and said to them, "Thus it is written, that the Christ should suffer and on the third day rise from the dead and that repentance and forgiveness of sins should be preached in his name to all nations, beginning from Jerusalem. — Luke 24:45-47

Now pray one 5-decade Rosary (#6a-9) sometime today, preferably with your family. Members and Discernment Cooperators: read section 803 in Appendix C.

Thirty-Seventh Day
Reparation and Consecration

42a. Reparation and the Dual Dimension of Pope John Paul II's Consecration *(continued)*
by Jerome F. Coniker

17. The Third and Fourth Points are incorporated into the dual dimension of Pope John Paul II's consecration, which can bring the light of the truth into our dark world so that our families can live in the greatest era of peace and religion the world has ever known.

The dual dimension of Pope John Paul II's consecration is *Totus Tuus* and *Consecrate them in Truth.*

The first dimension

18. *Totus Tuus* (Latin for "Totally yours") refers to giving everything to Jesus through Mary, according to the formula of St. Louis de Montfort which the Holy Father wrote about in his book, *Crossing the Threshold of Hope* (p. 213).

If we follow this formula of consecration, which Pope John Paul proclaims and lives, we give the few merits that we have to our Blessed Mother who then takes them and multiplies them by her incalculable merits and presents them to Jesus on our behalf.

St. Louis de Montfort's formula

19. In his treatise, *True Devotion to the Blessed Virgin*, St. Louis wrote:

"For by it [this devotion] we show love for our neighbor in an outstanding way, since we give Him through Mary's hands all that we prize most highly— that is, the satisfactory and prayer value of all our good works, down to the least good thought and the least little suffering. We give our consent that all we have already acquired or will acquire until death should be used in accordance with our Lady's will for the conversion of sinners or the deliverance of souls from Purgatory" (section 171).

"It must be noted that our good works, passing through Mary's hands, are progressively purified. Consequently, their merit and their satisfactory and prayer value is also increased. That is why they become much more effective in relieving the souls in Purgatory and in converting sinners than if they did not pass through the virginal and liberal hands of Mary.

"Stripped of self-will and clothed with disinterested love, the little that we give to the Blessed Virgin is truly powerful enough to appease the anger of God and draw down His mercy. It may well be that at the hour of death a person who has been faithful to this devotion will find that he has freed many souls from Purgatory and converted many sinners, even though he performed only the ordinary actions of his state of life. Great will be his joy at the judgment. Great will be his glory throughout eternity" (section 172).

"Mary amassed such a multitude of merits and graces during her sojourn on earth that it would be easier to count the stars in heaven, the drops of water in the ocean or the sands of the seashore than count her merits and graces. She thus gave more glory to God than all the angels and saints have given or will ever give Him. Mary, wonder of God, when souls abandon themselves to you, you cannot but work wonders in them (section 222)!

"Our Blessed Lady, in her immense love for us, is eager to receive into her virginal hands the gift of our actions, imparting to them a marvelous beauty and splendor, presenting them herself to Jesus most willingly" (section 223).

St. Maximilian Kolbe's prophecy for modern times

20. "Modern times are dominated by Satan and will be more so in the future. The conflict with hell cannot be engaged by men, even the most clever. The Immaculata alone has from God the promise of victory over Satan. However, assumed into heaven, the Mother of God now requires our cooperation. She seeks souls who will consecrate themselves entirely to her, who will become in her hands effective instruments for the defeat of Satan and the spreading of God's kingdom upon earth."

The second dimension

21. Let's now consider the second dimension of Pope John Paul II's consecration, *Consecrate Them in Truth* or evangelization and catechesis, which represents his highest priority. Our Lord, in effect, defined consecration in John 17 when he said:

Verse 3: "Eternal life is this—to know you." [catechesis]

Verse 4: "I have glorified you on earth by finishing the work you gave me to do." [evangelization]

Verse 15: "Protect them from the evil one."

Verse 17: "Consecrate them in truth. Your word is truth."

Verse 19: "I consecrate myself so that they too may be consecrated in the truth.

Verse 21: "That they may be one as we are one."

When we steep ourselves in the truth, as put forth in Sacred Scripture, the Second Vatican Council documents, the *Catechism of the Catholic Church*, papal documents, etc., we are better disposed to pray, to receive the sacraments and practice virtue—in short, to be holy, gaining ever more grace and merit. Then we can give Our Blessed Mother many more of our graces and merits to multiply by her incalculable merits, putting into motion a tremendous spiritual power that can defeat Satan and bring about the era of peace which she promised at Fatima.

The Holy Father referred to this era in the last page of his book, *Crossing the Threshold of Hope*, when he wrote:

"André Malraux was certainly right when he said that the twenty-first century would be the century of religion or it would not be at all."

I believe that our Holy Father is telling us that if we do God's will and repair for sin, we will see a century of great religion and evangelization for our children and grandchildren to grow up in. But if we don't enter into a life of vigorous evangelization, catechesis and prayer, we will see, because of the evil use of modern technology, the darkest age of purification that the world has ever experienced.

Let's walk with His Holiness over the threshold of hope into the greatest period of light, evangelization, and peace that the world has ever known—that era of peace that Our Lady promised at Fatima.

A Summary —
Cardinal Mario Luigi Ciappi, O.P.

22.   The following article from the Pope's newspaper about the late papal theologian, Mario Luigi Cardinal Ciappi, gives you an idea of His Eminence's relationship with the papacy and his competency at reading the signs of the times.

Cardinal Ciappi was the master of the papal palace and papal theologian for the last five popes and was our primary theological advisor from 1979 until his death on April 22, 1996. Please read the following with great care.

*St. Dominic was the first papal theologian;
St. Thomas Aquinas was the fourth; and Cardinal
Luigi Ciappi was the eighty-fourth Dominican
Theologian of the Papal Household. His Eminence
was also the primary theological advisor of the
Apostolate for Family Consecration.*

Excerpts from Pope John Paul II's homily at Cardinal Ciappi's funeral, April 25, 1996

23. "Dear brothers and sisters, today in St. Peter's Basilica we are celebrating the funeral of beloved Cardinal Mario Luigi Ciappi, whom God called to himself last Monday evening after a long life spent in service to the Church and, in particular, to the Holy See. I have felt a personal bond with him since my studies, and I am pleased to honor his memory at this moment, so full of emotion, by my testimony of sincere esteem and deep gratitude.

"His brilliant and keen capacity for theological investigation grew and was quickly noticed.

"With a profound knowledge of the theological thought, he was himself a capable theologian who was able to serve the Church generously, first by teaching dogmatic theology and Thomistic aesthetics. The results he achieved in this task brought him to the attention of Pope Pius XII, who in 1955 wanted him at his side as Master of the Sacred Palace. He was confirmed in this office by Pope John XXIII and Pope Paul VI, who spelled out his duties in the Motu Proprio *Pontificalis Domus*, and appointed him Theologian of the Papal Household.

"His clear thinking, the soundness of his teaching and his undisputed fidelity to the Apostolic See, as well as his ability to interpret the signs of the times according to God, were qualities that made him a valued collaborator during the intense period of the Second Vatican Council to which he made a significant and balanced contribution.

"His careful scholarly work was always accompanied by an intense spiritual life and prayer, the first and fundamental nourishment of his whole life."

(Used by permission of L'Osservatore Romano)

Greatest miracle in the history of the world

24. Please read the letters on the next two pages from Cardinal Ciappi, which summarize this entire section. His Eminence talks about the greatest miracle in the history of the world and encourages consecration to Jesus through Mary.

For the days shall come upon you, when your enemies will cast up a bank about you and surround you, and hem you in on every side, and dash you to the ground, you and your children within you, and they will not leave one stone upon another in you; because you did not know the time of your visitation.
— Luke 19:43-44

Now pray the *Consecration to the Sacred Heart of Jesus* (#23) in Appendix A. Also pray one 5-decade Rosary (#6a-9) sometime today, preferably with your family. Members and Discernment Cooperators: read section 804 in Appendix C.

Vatican City
October 9, 1994

Dear Jerry and Gwen:

Once again, your Totus Tuus – "Consecrate Them in Truth" Conference will be serving the Church in a very timely way.

25. Your use of the social communications and the way in which you are using audio and video tape is **a 'fail-safe method' of teaching** and will allow families of today's media culture, which the Holy Father frequently mentions, to become powerful instruments of the Immaculata to bring about the era of peace she promised at Fatima.

26. *Yes, a miracle was promised at Fatima, the greatest miracle in the history of the world, second only to the Resurrection. And that miracle will be an era of peace which has never really been granted before to the world.*

27. *I believe that this peace will begin in the domestic church, the family, and go out to the parishes and into the diocese, the country, and the world. This lasting peace will be the fruit of a life of service and of evangelizing one's family and neighbors with the truth that will set them free!*

28. Our Blessed Mother promised us this era of peace if we say the daily Rosary, practice the First Saturday Communion of Reparation, and live lives consecrated in the truth. This consecration includes giving all of our possessions, both interior and exterior, to Jesus through the Immaculate Heart of Mary, and, as you know, in the Apostolate for Family Consecration, we like to add, "in union with St. Joseph."

29. As primary theological advisor to the Apostolate for Family Consecration since 1979, I have reminded its members frequently that **consecration is not just a prayer or a devotion but a commitment to a way of life which must be nourished through continuous formation in the eternal truths of our Faith**.

Yours in the Hearts of Jesus and Mary,

Mario Luigi Card. Ciappi, O.P.

Mario Luigi Cardinal Ciappi, O.P.
Papal Theologian Emeritus for Popes Pius XII, John XXIII, Paul VI, John Paul I, and John Paul II

Il Teologo Emerito
della Casa Pontificia

00120 Citta del Vaticano
Vatican City

August 24, 1989

Dear Jerry and Gwen Coniker and all the families of The Apostolate,

30. I wish to encourage your continued stress on total consecration to Jesus through Mary.

31. Paragraph 4 of Pope Paul VI's Apostolic Constitution on the Revision of Indulgences states:

> **"By the hidden and kindly mystery of God's will, a supernatural solidarity reigns among men. A consequence of this is that the sin of one person harms other people just as one person's holiness helps others."**

32. If this is true, how true it is that when we give all our merits to Mary, she multiplies them by Her own incalculable merits. This puts into motion positive spiritual forces to repair the damage due to sin and significantly change the course of history, if enough make this commitment.

33. Mary's merits can multiply the effects of one person's holiness and help countless souls. Only Heaven knows the depth of holiness a soul must achieve to tip the scales for world peace.

34. I agree that this apostolate of family consecration is the best way to defeat the scourge of abortion and renew family life.

The spiritual offensive must always be in the vanguard, presupposing all other activities.

35. The "Marian Era of Evangelization Campaign" can put into motion a chain of events to bring about that era of peace promised at Fatima.
Praying for the success of your most needed apostolate, I remain,

Yours in the Hearts of Jesus and Mary,

Mario Luigi Card. Ciappi, O.T.

Mario Luigi Cardinal Ciappi, O.P.
Pro-theologian of the Pontifical Household

To understand "Message of Hope" & Reparation, go to our web page at www.familyland.org and click on "Family Consecration", for a free presentation.

Part 7: Responsibility of the Present Moment

(Days 38-40)

A formula for renewing family life in the Third Millennium, through communion with the Holy Family

Thirty-Eighth Day

77. The Responsibility of the Present Moment
by Jerome F. Coniker

1.   In Pope John Paul II's *Letter to Families*, he wrote: "The family constitutes the fundamental 'cell' of society. But Christ—the 'vine' from which the 'branches' draw nourishment—is needed so that this cell will not be exposed to the threat of a *cultural uprooting* which can come both from within and from without. Indeed, although there is on the one hand the 'civilization of love,' there continues to exist on the other hand *the possibility of a destructive 'anti-civilization,'* as so many present trends and situations confirm. Who can deny that our age is one marked by a great crisis, which appears above all as *a profound crisis of truth*"? (sec. 13)

One of our most basic responsibilities as Catholics is to help build up the civilization of love initiated by Jesus Christ. This responsibility flows from our baptismal consecration, which makes us children of the God Who is love and Who calls us to live in a communion of love with Him and with each other in Him. This communion of love begins in our own families with the parents' communion of love, which is inspired by the Sacrament of Matrimony and which constantly grows to include others. It also moves us to live for God alone and to draw our family and others to Him.

As Catholic families, we are called to be instruments of the Holy Family to bring other families to God. If enough of us allow ourselves to be used by God, we will see the greatest period of peace and evangelization that the world has ever known. The Third Millennium can be a time when our children and grandchildren can grow up in a society of light and truth. At this point, you are probably thinking, "How can anyone talk this way when the evil we see today is so overwhelming and universal?"

I believe that many parents and grandparents are coming to the realization that unless we turn back to God in prayer and become virtuous, and then vigorously evangelize and catechize, we are going to slip into a totally dark age that will only be reversed after a long period of persecution and purification. This purification could last far beyond our lifetime.

In both the Old and New Testaments, we found 177 warnings from God to His people to stop sinning. Seventy times they responded with repentance and were blessed, rather than chastised. This should give us hope. But 107 times they didn't repent, and they were chastised. This should warn us.

A People of Hope

2.   The stakes are high, but we are a people of hope. We have been given a great gift for our troubled times—Pope John Paul II. If we follow his family-sensitive teachings and consciously cross the threshold of hope into this new millennium, our families can experience the greatest period of peace and religion that the world has ever known.

Let us respond to the late Holy Father's challenge, especially to the "sleeping giant" of the Catholic family, at this time in history.

Responsibility of the Present Moment

3.   Those who have visited Catholic Familyland in the United States and our St. Joseph Centers throughout the world hear about the *responsibility of the present moment*. In our particular charism, we believe that the essence of holiness consists in the love of God and the love of neighbor, which express themselves concretely in the fulfillment of one's responsibility of each present moment. Such practical love brings us into union with God's Will for us every moment of the day. When enough people live this way, we will see peace in our families and society.

How can we, as laymen, be deeply united with God? Haven't Catholics generally tended to think that only priests and religious sisters and brothers are called to be really united with God? Sometimes we assume that Catholic lay men or women who live in the world are actually part of the world and not really responsible for transforming it into God's kingdom on earth.

In his letter to the first Christians, St. Peter wrote, "You are a chosen race, a royal priesthood, a consecrated nation, a people set apart" (1 Peter 2:9). Consecration means to be set apart for the exclusive use of God. The whole world should be set apart for God.

Pope John Paul II referred to three vocations: the priesthood, religious, and the laity, all of which spring forth from and are nourished within the family.

The role of the ministerial priest is to be the bridge between heaven and earth. In the Holy Sacrifice of the Mass, only the ministerial priest brings down the Body, Blood, Soul and Divinity of Our Lord—the very center of our Faith. Only the ministerial priest can forgive sins in the name of Jesus Christ Our Lord.

The role of the religious and consecrated celibates (who are members of the common priesthood of the faithful) is to be outside of the world, but to serve the world.

The role of the laity (who are also members of the common priesthood of all the faithful) is to remain in the world, while *not being of the world, in order to transform the world into God's kingdom of love upon earth*—a kingdom where children are welcomed and family life is nourished within the parish Eucharistic community.

Our Vision — The Public Reign of Christ

4. Many lay people don't realize that as lay members of the Church, we are not called to be of the world, but rather to transform it. We are to help bring about the public reign of Christ so that the Faith will reign in our daily lives within our families and communities.

What does this mean—the public reign of Christ? First, that we will love God with all our hearts, all our soul and all our minds. I believe this means that nearly every parish will have Perpetual Adoration, where entire families come at specified times to adore and be with Our Eucharistic Lord. Churches will be left open for people to stop in and visit Our Lord 24 hours a day. Catholics will imitate some of their Protestant brethren in bringing their entire families to church for an evening of family worship during the week, and to participate in multimedia formation programs that feature some of the best teachers in the Church. This theologically fail-safe method will truly consecrate families in the Truth. It also means that our traditional devotions will be practiced by a large percentage of families.

Secondly, the Public Reign of Christ means that we will love our neighbor as ourselves. This means that employers will be fair with their employees, and that employees will do the very best at their jobs because they know they are doing it for the Lord, and not just for money. Neighbors will be there for each other. Clothing styles will be modest, and the media will be moral. And most of all, God's laws will prevail in all dimensions of our society. The Ten Commandments will be the standard by which decisions are made in our courts and legislatures.

What's so wrong with that?! Why can't we live and work for this goal? This is what we're called to do—to transform our world into God's kingdom on earth! Blessed Teresa of Calcutta said that God doesn't look for success, but for commitment. We plant the seeds or bring in the harvest when it's ready, but God brings about the miracle of growth.

We pray for the public reign of Christ every day in the Our Father: "Thy kingdom come, Thy will be done on earth as it is in heaven." This means we hope and pray for the reign of God's peace, the civilization of love of which Pope John Paul II often spoke about and asked us to work for. This can become a reality when we really do God's Will moment by moment, as it is done in heaven.

Is it Impossible?

5. Some may say that this goal is impossible! It isn't. It isn't if we really ask for the grace and work for it through heroic sacrifices. It is God's Will and His grace plus our wills that makes everything possible. We can't do it on our own strength. But anything is possible with God's grace (cf. Mark 10:27).

In many of our encounters with Blessed Teresa of Calcutta, she also told us that holiness is not the luxury of the few, but an obligation for all of us. It is God's Will plus our wills, combined with God's grace, that will transform us into His image.

But we have to make an act of the will, and actually choose to be holy with all of our hearts. We need to ask for it in prayer, and we have to prove that we have this desire by choosing to do God's Will. This is done by choosing to fulfill the responsibility of each present moment. When we are receptive to these graces and act upon them, God will make us holy. Holiness is union with God.

Today our society is anything but holy. This worldliness is due to the lack of adequate formation, along with many accepted misrepresentations of the Second Vatican Council and its directives. As a result of this and other factors, much confusion was wrought in the Church. However, we know that Vatican II was truly led by the Holy Spirit and made a special clarion call for the laity to become holy.

This is why it is so important for the Catholic laymen of today to prayerfully read Sacred Scripture, the *Catechism of the Catholic Church*, the documents of the Second Vatican Council, and papal documents. These teachings are so rich and put forth such clarity regarding the laity's call to sanctify their daily activities and to fulfill their obligation to evangelize.

The Truth Makes Us Free

6.   Our families have a responsibility to learn about the Truth. In many ways we become slaves to our own ignorance. We need to spend less time in leisure activities such as watching TV, and more time prayerfully reflecting on our Faith and Church teachings, and then systematically sharing these teachings. By reading the papal documents, we will learn what the Holy Father is telling the people of today.

Fatima—A Beginning, Not an End

7.   After living near Fatima in Portugal for two years, Gwen and I and the seven children we had at the time were privileged to have an audience with the Bishop of Fatima in the Leiria Diocese. He told us to go back

to America and use the Fatima message to get people's attention, so they could begin to live a spiritual life. The Bishop told us that the purpose of Our Lady's apparitions was to get our attention and bring us into the heart of the Church. He went on to say that the heart of the Church is where the Pope is.

Mary Draws Us to Jesus

8. The Hearts of Jesus and Mary are never to be separated. She is God's Mother and He has placed her in the dignified position as Mother of the Church.

Mary always draws us into the heart of the Church. We, as laymen, can reach the deepest degree of union with God by consecrating ourselves to Jesus through His mother, according to the formula of St. Louis de Montfort, which Pope John Paul II lived so faithfully (Totus Tuus). We develop a deep prayer life by prayerfully studying the truths of our Faith and fulfilling the responsibilities of our state in life for Jesus. Pope John Paul II gave us so many rich teachings about Mary and St. Joseph, who are perfect models for us to imitate, and about the Sacrament of Matrimony and family life.

St. Therese the Little Flower, Patroness of Missionaries

9. St. Therese has now been elevated to the authoritative position of Doctor of the Church. One of the books she read over and over during her short life was the classic by Fr. Pierre de Caussade, S.J., entitled, *Abandonment to Divine Providence*. In the Apostolate for Family Consecration we have coined the phrase "responsibility of the present moment" from the term used in this book, "grace of the present moment."

By fulfilling the responsibility of every moment— which means doing what we should be doing at the time that we should be doing it and in the way that we know we are supposed to do it in conscious union with the Holy Family—we can live a life of deep interior union with the Holy Family.

Attitude Makes the Difference

10. Our attitude makes all the difference in the world. When fulfilling our responsibilities, we can literally transform every act of our day into a meritorious act choosing to unite ourselves with Christ in love. This means that a mother at home who is cleaning the house or changing the diapers of her child, can, with love, transform these everyday tasks into great spiritual acts of mercy.

With love, we can transform the work that we do into a sacrificial offering to God, whether it be putting a wheel on a car in the factory or writing a procedure in the office. We can convert every act of our day into a meritorious act of love, if we do it for the Lord out of love and with a generous disposition— if we have that commitment!

God's Will

11. What does it mean to do God's Will? How does this impact on the Mystical Body of Christ? We know that we grow in sanctifying grace when we are in the state of grace and are doing God's Will out of love and other virtuous acts, when we are living a life of prayer and especially when we attend Mass and receive the sacraments. That is, we have the power to share in God's very own divine being and life so that God's presence grows within us. At the same time, we can also atone or repair for our sins and the sins of the world.

When anyone sins, that person gives the devil more power to tempt everyone else. This brings about more selfishness and evil in the world, along with more persecution of the innocent and the poor.

We also need to understand that we can gain no merit in the Mystical Body of Christ when we are not in the state of sanctifying grace; without God's grace in our souls, we cannot help to repair for the effects of sin in the world. That is why frequent reception of the Sacrament of Reconciliation is so essential. This sacrament helps keep our consciences from becoming so eroded that we can no longer discern good from evil in each present moment, or properly prepare to receive Our Eucharistic Lord.

Most people might ask, "How can a layman live the responsibility of the present moment in a practical way?" Our lives are so erratic, and we don't have the order of living like that which is found in a monastery, for instance, where the monks and nuns live in a strict

Our Supernatural House
to protect and nurture family life
in imitation of the Holy Family

6. OUR WORK

Formula
Faithfully fulfilling the responsibility of the present moment for the Sacred and Eucharistic Heart of Jesus, through the Sorrowful and Immaculate Heart of Mary, in union with St. Joseph.

7. EVANGELIZATION

2. PRAYER

3. FORMATION

4. FAMILY

5. COMMUNITY

Seven Dimensions of Our Lives

The Holy Family is the perfect reflection of the love of the Holy Trinity and is the perfect model of a family that lives the responsibility of the present moment. "All for."

1. SACRAMENTAL LIFE

If any one of the seven dimensions is missing, the house will collapse. Before we act or react throughout our day, we should get in the habit of making a spiritual communion by saying the two words "All for." By this we are acknowledging God's love for us while asking for the Eucharistic grace to discern and do God's will.

By "All for" we mean: "All for the Sacred and Eucharistic Heart of Jesus", Who loves us so that He died for us and Who is the center and source of our Faith, "all through the Sorrowful and Immaculate Heart of Mary", who purifies and multiplies our meager merits and distributes them to those most in need of God's mercy, "all in union with St. Joseph", who is the perfect model of living total consecration to Jesus through Mary.

Saying "All for" is also a great way to greet and say goodbye to family and friends.

routine. Laymen, on the contrary, should expect to experience a healthy tension in managing all the dimensions of their lives in order to do God's Will in each present moment, particularly in a family.

Seven Dimensions of the Spiritual House

12. There are seven dimensions to the concept of "responsibility of the present moment." This is depicted in the diagram of the "Supernatural House."

We need to maintain a balance of all seven responsibilities or dimensions. Otherwise, our "supernatural house" will collapse, and we and our families will have little protection from the onslaughts of the world, the flesh, and the devil.

These seven basic responsibilities that we must make time for in our lives are:

1. Sacramental life (foundation)
2. Prayer life (supporting wall)
3. Formation life (supporting wall)
4. Family life (supporting wall)
5. Community life (supporting wall)
6. Work in the home, factory, office, or field (first part of the roof)
7. Apostolic life — our grave responsibility to evangelize, to share our Faith with our families, neighbors, parish and the world (second part of the roof)

His divine power has granted us all things that pertain to life and godliness, through the knowledge of him who called us to his own glory and excellence, by which he has granted to us his precious and very great promises, that through these you may escape from the corruption that is in the world because of passion, and become partakers of the divine nature. For this very reason make every effort to supplement your faith with virtue, and virtue with knowledge, and knowledge with self-control, and self-control with steadfastness, and steadfastness with godliness, and godliness with brotherly affection, and brotherly affection with love. For if these things are yours and abound, they keep you from being ineffective or unfruitful in the knowledge of our Lord Jesus

Christ. For whoever lacks these things is blind and shortsighted and has forgotten that he was cleansed from his old sins. Therefore, brethren, be the more zealous to confirm your call and election, for if you do this you will never fall; so there will be richly provided for you an entrance into the eternal kingdom of our Lord and Savior Jesus Christ. — 2 Peter 1:3-11

Now and pray the *Memorare* (#30) in Appendix A. Also pray one 5-decade Rosary (#6a-9) sometime today, preferably with your family. Members and Discernment Cooperators: read sections 805–808 in Appendix C.

Thirty-Ninth Day

77. The Responsibility of the Present Moment
by Jerome F. Coniker *(continued)*

The First Dimension: Sacraments

13. The very foundation of our supernatural life is the sacraments, which confer on us the Holy Spirit and His gifts and charisms and the infused virtues, beginning with the theological virtues of faith, hope and charity and the cardinal virtues of prudence, justice, temperance and fortitude. In sections 798, under "The Church is the Temple of the Holy Spirit," the *Catechism of the Catholic Church* states:

"The Holy Spirit is "the principle of every vital and truly saving action in each part of the Body." He works in many ways to build up the whole Body in charity: by God's Word "which is able to build you up"; by Baptism, through which he forms Christ's Body; by the sacraments, which give growth and healing to Christ's members; by "the grace of the apostles, which holds first place among his gifts"; by the virtues, which make us act according to what is good; finally, by the many special graces (called "charisms"), by which he makes the faithful "fit and ready to undertake various tasks and offices for the renewal and building up of the Church."

In section 950, under "Communion of the Sacraments," the *Catechism of the Catholic Church* goes on to say:

"The fruit of all the sacraments belongs to all the faithful. All the sacraments are sacred links uniting the faithful with one another and binding them to Jesus Christ, and above all Baptism, the gate by which we enter into the Church. The communion of saints must be understood as the communion of the sacraments. The name 'communion' can be applied to all of them, for they unite us to God. But this name is better suited to the Eucharist than to any other, because it is primarily the Eucharist that brings this communion about."

God wants us to enter into communion with Him and to partake of His own divine nature, as stated in section 460 of the *Catechism of the Catholic Church*: "The Word became flesh to make us 'partakers of the divine nature': 'For this is why the Word became man, and the Son of God became the Son of man: so that man, by entering into communion with the Word and thus receiving divine sonship, might become a son of God.' **'For the Son of God became man so that we might become God.' 'The only-begotten Son of God, wanting to make us sharers in his divinity, assumed our nature, so that he, made man, might make men gods.'"**

But without frequent confession (at least monthly), we are building on sand. In section 1457, the *Catechism of the Catholic Church* goes on to teach:

"Anyone who is aware of having committed a mortal sin must not receive Holy Communion, even if he experiences deep contrition, without having first received sacramental absolution, unless he has a grave reason for receiving Communion and there is no possibility of going to confession. Children must go to the sacrament of Penance before receiving Holy Communion for the first time."

In section 1458, the *Catechism* continues to teach:

"Without being strictly necessary, confession of everyday faults (venial sins) is nevertheless strongly recommended by the Church. Indeed the regular confession of our venial sins helps us form our conscience, fight against evil tendencies, let ourselves be healed by Christ and progress in the life of the Spirit. By receiving more frequently through this sacrament the gift of the Father's mercy, we are spurred to be merciful as he is merciful."

Catechesis in churches and homes by using failsafe multimedia resources truly does form consciences and dispose families to go to Confession, which further disposes them to fervently adore and receive our Eucharistic Lord.

Second & Third Dimensions: Our Prayer & Formation Life

14. Two of the supporting walls of our "supernatural house" are our prayer life and formation life, meaning that we must pray every day and learn our Faith. The Church teaches us how to pray. She teaches about the great treasures of the Church found in Sacred Scripture, the *Catechism of the Catholic Church*, and the Vatican Council documents, as well as the writings of the saints, the Popes, and the Doctors of the Church—all presented in such a cohesive way in The Apostolate's Family Catechism and its Consecration in Truth catechetical program for homes and schools, and the Family Catechism Direct with Cardinal Arinze program for churches and homes. The family Rosary and the reflective reading of Scripture and other spiritual books will help the members of a family to enter into mental prayer as they work their way through the day while fulfilling their responsibilities of each present moment.

Pope John Paul II writes of St. Joseph's interior life in *Redemptoris Custos (Guardian of the Redeemer)*, sections 25–27:

"The same aura of silence that envelops everything else about Joseph also shrouds his work as a carpenter in the house of Nazareth. It is, however, a silence that reveals in a special way the inner portrait of the man. The Gospels speak exclusively of what Joseph 'did.' Still, they allow us to discover in his 'actions' — shrouded in silence as they are — an aura of deep contemplation. Joseph was in daily contact with the mystery 'hidden from ages past,' and which 'dwelt' under his roof. This explains, for example, why St. Teresa of Jesus, the great reformer of the Carmelites, promoted the renewal of veneration to St. Joseph in Western Christianity.

"The total sacrifice, whereby Joseph surrendered his whole existence to the demands of the Messiah's coming into his home, becomes understandable only in the light of his profound interior life. It was from this interior life that 'very singular commands and consolations came, bringing him also the logic and strength that belong to simple and clear souls, and giving him the power of making great decisions—such as the decision to put his liberty immediately at the disposition of the divine designs, to make over to them also his legitimate human calling, his conjugal happiness, to accept the conditions, the responsibility and the burden of a family, but, through an incomparable virginal love, to renounce that natural conjugal love that is the foundation and nourishment of the family.'"

"This submission to God, this readiness of will to dedicate oneself to all that serves him, is really nothing less than that exercise of devotion which constitutes one expression of the virtue of religion.

"The communion of life between Joseph and Jesus leads us to consider once again the mystery of the Incarnation, precisely in reference to the humanity of Jesus as the efficacious instrument of his divinity for the purpose of sanctifying man: 'By virtue of his divinity, Christ's human actions were salvific for us, causing grace within us, either by merit or by a certain efficacy.'

"Among those actions, the gospel writers highlight those which have to do with the Paschal Mystery, but they also underscore the importance of physical contact with Jesus for healing (cf. for example, Mk 1:41), and the influence Jesus exercised upon John the Baptist when they were both in their mothers' wombs (cf. Lk 1:41-44).

"As we have seen, the apostolic witness did not neglect the story of Jesus' birth, his circumcision, his presentation in the Temple, his flight into Egypt and his hidden life in Nazareth. It recognized the 'mystery' of grace present in each of these saving 'acts,' inasmuch as they all share the same source of love: the divinity of Christ. If through Christ's humanity this love shone on all mankind, the first beneficiaries were undoubtedly those whom the divine will had most intimately associated with itself: Mary, the Mother of Jesus, and Joseph, his presumed father.

"Why should the 'fatherly' love of Joseph not have had an influence upon the 'filial' love of Jesus? And vice versa why should the 'filial' love of Jesus not have had an influence upon the 'fatherly' love of Joseph, thus leading to a further deepening of their unique relationship? Those souls most sensitive to the impulses of divine love have rightly seen in Joseph a brilliant example of the interior life.

"Furthermore, in Joseph, the apparent tension between the active and the contemplative life finds an ideal harmony that is only possible for those who possess the perfection of charity. Following St. Augustine's well-known distinction between the love of the truth (caritas veritatis) and the practical demands of love (necessitas caritatis), we can say that Joseph experienced both love of the truth—that pure contemplative love of the divine Truth which radiated from the humanity of Christ—and the demands of love—that equally pure and selfless love required for his vocation to safeguard and develop the humanity of Jesus, which was inseparably linked to his divinity."

The Fourth & Fifth Dimensions: Our Family & Community

15. Family life and community life are the other two supporting walls of our "supernatural house." At the Second World Meeting of Families, the Holy Father said, "Today the basic struggle for human dignity is centered on the family and life." His theme for this world gathering was "The Family: Gift and Commitment, Hope for Humanity."

The destiny of the world depends on the family. If we do not have a good family life, we will be unstable in everything we do.

One of the reasons why there is so much confusion in our society today is that a stable family life is essentially non-existent. The family stabilizes society. When the family is not formed in the Truth, it loses its very moorings. If we neglect the family, everything will crumble. That is why the simultaneous renewal of the family and parish community is so necessary.

Pope John Paul II wrote of Joseph's fatherhood in *Redemptoris Custos (Guardian of the Redeemer)*, sections 7–8:

"Analyzing the nature of marriage, both St. Augustine and St. Thomas always identify it with an 'indivisible union of souls,' a 'union of hearts,' with 'consent.'(15) These elements are found in an exemplary manner in the marriage of Mary and Joseph. At the culmination of the history of salvation, when God reveals his love for humanity through the gift of the Word, it is precisely the marriage of Mary and Joseph that brings to realization in full 'freedom' the 'spousal gift of self' in receiving and expressing such a love. 'In this great undertaking which is the renewal of all things in Christ, marriage—it too purified and renewed—becomes a new reality, a sacrament of the New Covenant. We see that at the beginning of the New Testament, as at the beginning of the Old, there is a married couple. But whereas Adam and Eve were the source of evil which was unleashed on the world, Joseph and Mary arc the summit from which holiness spreads all over the earth. The Savior began the work of salvation by this virginal and holy union, wherein is manifested his all-powerful will to purify and sanctify the family—that sanctuary of love and cradle of life.'

"How much the family of today can learn from this! The essence and role of the family are in the final analysis specified by love. Hence the family has the mission to guard, reveal and communicate love, and this is a living reflection of and a real sharing in God's love for humanity and the love of Christ the Lord for the Church his bride.' This being the case, it is in the Holy Family, the original 'Church in miniature (*Ecclesia domestica*),' that every Christian family must be reflected. 'Through God's mysterious design, it was in that family that the Son of God spent long years of a hidden life. It is therefore the prototype and example for all Christian families.'

"St. Joseph was called by God to serve the person and mission of Jesus directly through the exercise of his fatherhood. It is precisely in this way that, as the Church's Liturgy teaches, he 'cooperated in the fullness of time in the great mystery of salvation' and is truly a 'minister of salvation.' His fatherhood is expressed concretely 'in his having made his life a service, a sacrifice to the mystery of the Incarnation and to the redemptive mission connected with it; in having used the legal authority which was his over the Holy Family in order to make a total gift of self, of his life and work; in having turned his human vocation to domestic love into a superhuman oblation of self, an oblation of his heart and all his abilities into love placed at the service of the Messiah growing up in his house.'

"In recalling that 'the beginnings of our redemption' were entrusted 'to the faithful care of Joseph,' the Liturgy specifies that 'God placed him at the head of his family, as a faithful and prudent servant, so that with fatherly care he might watch over his only begotten Son.' Leo XIII emphasized the sublime nature of this mission: 'He among all stands out in his august dignity, since by divine disposition he was guardian, and according to human opinion, father of God's Son. Whence it followed that the Word of God was subjected to Joseph, he obeyed him and rendered to him that honor and reverence that children owe to their father. Since it is inconceivable that such a sublime task would not be matched by the necessary qualities to adequately fulfill it, we must recognize that Joseph showed Jesus by a special gift from heaven, all the natural love, all the affectionate solicitude that a father's heart can know.'

"Besides fatherly authority over Jesus, God also gave Joseph a share in the corresponding love, the love that has its origin in the Father 'from whom every family in heaven and on earth is named.'

"The Gospels clearly describe the fatherly responsibility of Joseph toward Jesus. For salvation—which comes through the humanity of Jesus—is realized in actions which are an everyday part of family life, in keeping with that 'condescension' which is inherent in the economy of the Incarnation. The gospel writers carefully show how in the life of Jesus nothing was left to chance, but how everything took place according to God's predetermined plan. The oft-repeated formula, 'This happened, so that there might be fulfilled...,' in reference to a particular event in the Old Testament serves to emphasize the unity and continuity of the plan which is fulfilled in Christ.

"With the Incarnation, the 'promises' and 'figures' of the Old Testament become 'reality': places, persons, events and rites interrelate according to precise divine commands communicated by angels and received by creatures who are particularly sensitive to the voice of God. Mary is the Lord's humble servant, prepared from eternity for the task of being the Mother of God. Joseph is the one whom God chose to be the 'overseer of the Lord's birth,' the one who has the responsibility to look after the Son of God's 'ordained' entry into the world, in accordance with divine dispositions and human laws. All of the so-called 'private' or 'hidden' life of Jesus is entrusted to Joseph's guardianship."

Sixth Dimension: Our Work

16. Our work is half the roof of our "supernatural house." Very few of us consider work to be meritorious. Great leaders in the Church, like St. Josemaria Escrivá, have said that work is at the very heart of our holiness, because it is fulfilling one of our major responsibilities in life.

St. Escriva wrote: "We look at Our Lord's work at the same time as we examine our own. And we ask him, Lord, give us your grace. Open the door to the workshop at Nazareth so that we may learn to contemplate you, together with your holy Mother Mary, and the holy Patriarch St. Joseph…, the three of you dedicated to a life of work made holy. Then, Lord, our poor hearts will be enkindled, we shall seek you and find you in our daily work, which you want us to convert into a work of God, a labor of love" (*Friends of the Cross*, 72).

In fact, Pope John Paul II has written an encyclical on the dignity of work (*Laborem exercens*). Reading this encyclical helps us to better understand the tremendous gift that God has given us—that of bringing order into our world.

Therefore, a mom at home taking care of the family (the home manager), and a dad in the factory, office, or field can tremendously grow in merit just by offering their work to the Lord while doing the very best they can out of love for God. In this way, all of us can transform our work into a living sacrifice, a prayer, which enables us to grow in sanctifying grace (the power to become God's true children in whom He dwells and whom He causes to actually share in His very being and life as God), and to grow in our capacity to know, love and serve God throughout all eternity.

St. Paul said in Colossians 3:23: *"Whatever your work is, put your heart into it, as if it were for the Lord, and not for men, knowing that the Lord will repay you by making you his heirs."*

Pope John Paul II wrote of work as an expression of love in *Redemptoris Custos*, sections 22–24:

"Work was the daily expression of love in the life of the Family of Nazareth. The Gospel specifies the kind of work Joseph did in order to support his family: he was a carpenter. This simple word sums up Joseph's entire life. For Jesus, these were hidden years, the years to which Luke refers after recounting the episode that occurred in the Temple: 'And he went down with them and came to Nazareth, and was obedient to them' (Lk 2:51). This 'submission' or obedience of Jesus in the house of Nazareth should be understood as a sharing in the work of Joseph. Having learned the work of his presumed father, he was known as 'the carpenter's son.'

"If the Family of Nazareth is an example and model for human families, in the order of salvation and holiness, so too, by analogy, is Jesus' work at the side of Joseph the carpenter. In our own day, the Church has emphasized this by instituting the liturgical memorial of St. Joseph the Worker on May 1. Human work, and especially manual labor, receive special prominence in the Gospel. Along with the humanity of the

Son of God, work too has been taken up in the mystery of the Incarnation, and has also been redeemed in a special way. At the workbench where he plied his trade together with Jesus, Joseph brought human work closer to the mystery of the Redemption.

"In the human growth of Jesus 'in wisdom, age and grace,' the virtue of industriousness played a notable role, since 'work is a human good' which 'transforms nature' and makes man 'in a sense, more human.'

"The importance of work in human life demands that its meaning be known and assimilated in order to 'help all people to come closer to God, the Creator and Redeemer, to participate in his salvific plan for man and the world, and to deepen...friendship with Christ in their lives, by accepting, through faith, a living participation in his threefold mission as Priest, Prophet and King.'

"What is crucially important here is the sanctification of daily life, a sanctification which each person must acquire according to his or her own state, and one which can be promoted according to a model accessible to all people: 'St. Joseph is the model of those humble ones that Christianity raises up to great destinies;...he is the proof that in order to be a good and genuine follower of Christ, there is no need of great things—it is enough to have the common, simple and human virtues, but they need to be true and authentic.'

He was in the world, and the world was made through him, yet the world knew him not. He came to his own home, and his own people received him not. But to all who received him, who believed in his name, he gave power to become children of God. — John 1:10-12

Now pray *Mother Teresa's Nazareth Prayer for the Family* (#11b) in Appendix A. Pray one 5-decade Rosary (#6a-9) sometime today, preferably with your family. Members and Discernment Cooperators: read sections 838–840 in Appendix C.

Fortieth Day

77. The Responsibility of the Present Moment
by Jerome F. Coniker *(continued)*

Seventh Dimension: Evangelization

17. When looking at the diagram of the seven dimensions of our lives, we see that evangelization is the other half of the roof—meaning it is just as important as our work.

What does a roof do? It protects the structure from the rain and snow that can erode the foundation and the walls. Also, the roof holds the sides together. If you have ever seen the construction of a house, workers rapidly try to get the roof frame built in order to hold the walls together so that it doesn't collapse.

Evangelization is a basic responsibility. We must teach the Faith and share it with our families, neighbors, and all those within our spheres of influence. This is the area where most of us fail.

Our culture does not look at the apostolic life as an essential responsibility that must be carried out by the laity. In many instances, people feel that catechesis and evangelization are primarily the obligation of the priests and the religious and that while lay people are not needed, they can be invited to do it when they have time.

The Holy Father and the teachings of the Second Vatican Council make it very clear that it is not an option—we must evangelize and catechize! Pope John Paul II called it the "Catechesis of the New Evangelization."

It is true that at times we may have to modify the time we spend for evangelization because of involvement in extraordinary family or workplace circumstances, but we must never abandon it—we must see to it that this responsibility is carried out by someone.

We should look at our obligation to do apostolate—which is to evangelize and catechize—just as we look at our work and our careers. If we were in charge of a major task at work and a problem came up in our home life, we would still be responsible for calling our place of work and making sure that someone took care of that particular task.

We should place the same emphasis on evangelization that we place on our work and careers. If we don't, we will not be fulfilling our missionary mandate to evangelize and spread the "Good News" of the Gospel. We may try to find some excuse to walk away from the obligation to save souls. "Woe to me if I do not preach the Gospel," said St. Paul (1 Cor. 9:16). Likewise, Pope John Paul II said, "Woe to you if you do not preach it" (World Youth Day, Denver 1993).

A "Blueprint" for the Laity

18. Pope John Paul II has written so much for the laity. In his apostolic letter, *Christifideles Laici* (*Lay Members of Christ's Faithful People*), he gave us a complete blueprint on what we, as lay members, should do and how we should do it. This document is a synthesis of the Synod of Bishops' teachings about the laity, the Fathers of the Church, Scripture, and the rich teachings of the Second Vatican Council. It clearly shows us that we have a responsibility to evangelize. We recommend this as regular spiritual reading. It is available on the internet or through the Family Apostolate and other Catholic bookstores.

Our Lord teaches us in Matthew 7:21 and 10:28:

"It is not those who say Lord, Lord, who will enter the Kingdom of Heaven, but those who do the will of my Father."

"Do not fear those who can kill the body, but those who can kill both the body and the soul."

Our Lord also said in Luke 9:23,

"If anyone wishes to be a follower of mine, let him renounce himself, take up his cross every day and follow me."

Our Lord is saying that we must "take up our crosses" every day—accept our responsibilities and follow Him.

Evangelization is not easy, particularly for those busy parents who homeschool their children. However, it can be done! It is a matter of prioritizing and strategically setting time aside. Some of our members homeschool and still make time to evangelize others by helping conduct our *Be Not Afraid Family Hours* at their local parish church.

Our Bad Reputation

19. Laymen have a bad reputation in the Catholic Church for dropping the ball when it comes to this seventh dimension—evangelization. That is why when people go to talk to their parish priests and ask them if they can run an evangelization or catechetical

program in the parish church, in many cases the first thing the priest wonders is whether he will be the one left "holding the bag" as soon as some trouble at home occurs. Keep in mind that in some parishes where there were once five priests, there may now be only one or two. The laity must now do their part. Of course, one does not need anyone's permission to evangelize at work or to invite people into their homes to watch orthodox formation videos. Cardinal Arinze has told us that the Sacrament of Baptism commissions us to do this.

Become First-Class Evangelizers

20. Since its founding in 1975, the Apostolate for Family Consecration has developed multimedia evangelization and catechetical programs which the laity can confidently use, as first-class evangelizers and catechists, without having to obtain any type of degree in theology. These videos are theologically "failsafe" because they feature some of the Church's greatest teachers, such as Pope John Paul II, Mother Teresa, Cardinal Francis Arinze, Cardinal J. Francis Stafford, and Archbishop John Foley. And they are particularly effectively because the teachings are carried out through the vibrant means of video, oftentimes while Confessions are being heard.

As families are drawn into deeper union with Our Eucharistic Lord, they can grow in sanctifying grace. This can be a spiritual power that can change the course of history. It can play a major role in bringing about the Civilization of Love by unleashing the spiritual power of the Church that is in the Holy Eucharist and the sacrament of Penance.

A Complete Reversal

21. All of the harm that has been sown so deeply in family life over the past forty years can be reversed through the powerful means of the multimedia and the Vatican-approved *Apostolate's Family Catechism*.

The Family Catechism systematically draws the entire family into Scripture, Vatican II documents, the *Catechism of the Catholic Church*, *Veritatis Splendor*, and numerous papal documents.

The Holy Father and his Roman Curia have blessed our Family Catechism and this method of systematic catechesis. They have encouraged us year after year, both in writing and in person. We are praying that more and more people will truly live the responsibility of the present moment, and carry this great gift out to others.

The family has to be restored through a very aggressive evangelization and catechetical program that represents the teachings of the Pope and the Magisterium of the Church.

Moving with God

22. The seven dimensions of living the responsibility of the present moment bring us into a life of union with God.

Blessed Mother Teresa said that everything must begin with prayer (dimensions 1 & 2), and the fruit of prayer is a deepening of faith (dimension 3), and the fruit of faith is love (dimensions 3, 4 & 5), and the fruit of love is service (dimensions 4, 5, 6 & 7), and the fruit of service is peace (union with God).

We should be determined to do God's Will at every moment of the day, and to ask for the actual grace to do it as perfectly as we can. This is accomplished by making acts of faith in God's plans for us and in His absolute commitment to us and love for us, and by making acts of spiritual communion by saying "All for," which is a way of asking God for the grace to discern and to do His Will in every decision or reaction we make throughout the day. ("All for" is the short formula for: "all for the Sacred and Eucharistic Heart of Jesus, all through the Sorrowful and Immaculate Heart of Mary, all in union with St. Joseph.) Not only does this practice make us more aware of God's presence, it enables us to pray constantly (cf. 1 Thess 5:17) because we will be communing with God in a very natural way throughout our day. That's what prayer is—talking to God, and knowing that we are in His Presence, or as Cardinal Arinze says, "just loving Him!".

Sometimes we don't have to talk when we are with our loved ones in the family. We are just there in their presence. When we experience this with God, it can evolve into the highest form of prayer, which the Church calls contemplation.

A Formula for Family Life

23. The seven dimensions of living the responsibility of the present moment give a formula for true family life. They will frequently create a healthy tension that will help to keep family life in balance. We know that we're not in heaven yet! We're part of the Church militant on earth. We're going through spiritual military maneuvers all the time in order to do battle with the world, the flesh and the devil—by planting seeds of charity and by patiently accepting our own weaknesses and the weaknesses of others.

Spiritual Time Management

24. Keeping a balance among these seven dimensions basically amounts to spiritual time management (prudence). We need to ask Mary to obtain for us the

grace to plan our time wisely each day in order to give adequate attention to these seven dimensions.

Throughout the day we must challenge ourselves and qualify what we are doing. We must not go to extremes and focus too much on just one or two of the dimensions. We need to seek God's Will in union with Mary as St. Joseph did and with his help.

We will be more responsive to God's inspirations when we have an adequate prayer and formation life, and particularly when we make frequent "All for" spiritual communions to receive the grace to discern and do God's Will in every encounter, project, and decision we make throughout the day.

God will start to clearly show us what we should do. Married couples must take the time to dialogue with our spouses and children, to pray together, and to call on the graces of the Sacrament of Matrimony. As we all do this, God will give us and our families the grace to do His Will.

Universal Call to Holiness

25. The *Catechism of the Catholic Church* states in sections 2013–2015:

"'All Christians in any state or walk of life are called to the fullness of Christian life and to the perfection of charity.' All are called to holiness: 'Be perfect, as your heavenly Father is perfect.'

"'In order to reach this perfection the faithful should use the strength dealt out to them by Christ's gift, so that...doing the will of the Father in everything, they may wholeheartedly devote themselves to the glory of God and to the service of their neighbor. Thus the holiness of the People of God will grow in fruitful abundance, as is clearly shown in the history of the Church through the lives of so many saints.'

"Spiritual progress tends toward ever more intimate union with Christ. This union is called 'mystical' because it participates in the mystery of Christ through the sacraments — 'the holy mysteries' — and, in him, in the mystery of the Holy Trinity. God calls us all to this intimate union with him, even if the special graces or extraordinary signs of this mystical life are granted only to some for the sake of manifesting the gratuitous gift given to all.

"The way of perfection passes by way of the Cross. There is no holiness without renunciation and spiritual battle. Spiritual progress entails the ascesis and mortification that gradually lead to living in the peace and joy of the Beatitudes: 'He who climbs never stops going from beginning to beginning, through beginnings that have no end. He never stops desiring what he already knows.'"

Keep in mind what Our Lord said in the Gospel of St. John:

26. "My food is to do the will of the one who sent me and complete his work" (4:34).

That is our task—to do the Will of God by completing the work that He has given us to do. Pope John Paul II said that each of us is a unique gift of God with an unrepeatable mission. Each of us has a unique role to fulfill in the Church. This role cannot be carried out by anyone else. If we don't step up to the challenge and fulfill our particular responsibility, other souls will not be touched and will not reach their own full potential in God's plan. Some may even be lost because we did our own will instead of God's.

Our Lord said in John 17:15–17, *"Father, do not remove them from the world, but protect them from the evil one... Consecrate them in truth."*

The Family Apostolate's multimedia catechetical and evangelization programs, which are available to all families, parishes, and movements, will protect your family and neighbors from the evil one through the dual dimensions of Pope John Paul II's consecration: Totus Tuus and Consecrate them in Truth.

Take up the challenge and contact the Apostolate for Family Consecration (www.familyland.org) to find out more about consecrating your family and neighbors in the Truth.

Finally, be strong in the Lord and in the strength of his might. Put on the whole armor of God, that you may be able to stand against the wiles of the devil. For we are not contending against flesh and blood, but against the principalities, against the powers, against the world rulers of this present darkness, against the spiritual hosts of wickedness in the heavenly places. Therefore take the whole armor of God, that you may be able to withstand in the evil day, and having done all, to stand. Stand therefore, having girded your loins with truth, and having put on the breastplate of righteousness, and having shod your feet with the equipment of the gospel of peace; above all taking the shield of faith, with which you can quench all the flaming darts of the evil one. And take the helmet of salvation, and the sword of the Spirit, which is the word of God. Pray at all times in the Spirit, with all prayer and supplication. To that end keep alert with all perseverance, making supplication for all the saints, and also for me, that utterance may be given me in opening my mouth boldly to proclaim the mystery of the gospel, for which I am an ambassador in chains; that I may declare it boldly, as I ought to speak. — Eph. 6:10-20

Now renew your consecration by praying the *Act of Consecration to Jesus through Mary* (#50b) in Appendix A. Also pray one 5-decade Rosary (#6a-9) sometime today, preferably with your family. Members and Discernment Cooperators: read sections 850–860 in Appendix C.

Recommended Daily Themes and Theme Prayers

for Members and Discernment Cooperators of the Apostolate for Family Consecration

Also see section 805.9 on pages 571–575.

Sundays

Theme: Gratitude, the Resurrection, and the Church

Theme Prayer: Litany of Thanksgiving, #34

Mondays

Theme: The Holy Spirit & the Last Things

Theme Prayer: Veni Creator, #46, and pray for the Holy Souls in Purgatory

Tuesdays

Theme: The Church Triumphant

Theme Prayer: Litany of the Patrons of the Apostolate for Family Consecration, #40

Wednesdays

Theme: St. Joseph

Theme Prayer: Act of Consecration to St. Joseph, #14

Thursdays

Theme: The Holy Trinity & the Eucharist

Theme Prayer: Holy Trinity Prayer in the Spirit of Fatima, #21

Fridays

Theme: Reparation and the Sacred Heart

Theme Prayer: Act of Reparation to the Sacred Heart of Jesus, #22

Saturdays

Theme: Our Blessed Mother

Theme Prayer: The Magnificat, #2

Appendix A
Prayers and Meditations

Live your consecration by joyfully fulfilling
the responsibilities of each present moment
for Jesus, through His Immaculate Mother,
in union with St. Joseph.

Note: Daily prayers and practices include prayer series #2 through #11a, and #53a, plus the theme prayers listed on page 228. For a pray-along CD of most of these prayers, ask for resource #160-760CD.

2. The Magnificat (cf. Luke 1:46-55)
Saturday Meditation

My soul magnifies the Lord, and my spirit rejoices in God my Savior:

Because He has regarded the lowliness of His handmaid; for behold, henceforth all generations shall call me blessed;

Because He who is mighty has done great things for me, and holy is His Name;

And His mercy is from generation to generation on those who fear Him.

He has shown might with His arm, He has scattered the proud in the conceit of their hearts.

He has put down the mighty from their thrones, and has exalted the lowly.

He has filled the hungry with good things, and the rich He has sent away empty.

He has given help to Israel, His servant, mindful of His mercy, even as He spoke to our fathers, to Abraham and to his posterity for ever. Amen.

2a. The Morning Offering

Most Holy Trinity, Father, Son, and Holy Spirit, I adore You profoundly. Help me and all the members of my family, parish, and The Apostolate to take up our crosses this day and to be strengthened and guided by the Most Holy Family.

Give us the grace to fulfill our destinies and to have total trust in You. Help us not to be disturbed about the past *(provided that we are in the state of grace)* or worried about the future, but to realize that we are secure in Your Will when we fulfill the responsibilities of each present moment as perfectly and as mercifully as we can for the unique vision of the Apostolate for Family Consecration. Let The Apostolate fulfill its destiny while always abiding in Christ and remaining an obedient and fruitful branch of the Catholic Church.

Help us to gratefully offer our prayers, works, joys, and sufferings, along with our interior and exterior possessions, including the value of our good actions, past, present, and future, all for the Sacred and Eucharistic Heart of Jesus, all through the Sorrowful and Immaculate Heart of Mary, all in union with St. Joseph. Amen.

2b. Hail Holy Queen
Daily prayer for membership in the
Archconfraternity of Our Lady of Guadalupe

Hail Holy Queen, Mother of mercy; our life, our sweetness, and our hope. To thee do we cry, poor banished children of Eve. To thee do we send up our sighs, mourning, and weeping in this valley of tears.

Turn then, most gracious advocate, thine eyes of mercy toward us; and after this our exile, show unto us the blessed fruit of thy womb, Jesus. O clement, O loving, O sweet Virgin Mary.

Pray for us, O holy Mother of God, that we may be made worthy of the promises of Christ. Amen.

2c. The Angelus

(3 times daily, preferably at meals)

V.   The angel of the Lord declared unto Mary,
R.   And she conceived by the Holy Spirit.
Hail Mary…

V.   Behold the Handmaid of the Lord,
R.   Be it done unto me according to thy word.
Hail Mary…

V.   And the Word was made flesh,
R.   And dwelt among us.
Hail Mary…

V.   Pray for us, O holy Mother of God,
R.   That we may be made worthy of the promises of Christ.

Let us pray: Pour forth, we beseech Thee, O Lord, Thy grace into our hearts; that we, to whom the Incarnation of Christ Thy Son was made known by the message of an angel, may by His Passion and Cross be brought to the glory of His Resurrection. Through the same Christ our Lord. Amen.

2c.1 Regina Caeli

Prayed during the Easter Season in place of the Angelus

Queen of heaven, rejoice! Alleluia.
For he whom you merited to bear. Alleluia.
Has risen, as he said. Alleluia.
Pray for us to God. Alleluia.

V. Rejoice and be glad, O Virgin Mary. Alleluia.
R. Because the Lord is truly risen. Alleluia.

Let us pray: O God, who by the Resurrection of Your Son, our Lord Jesus Christ, granted joy to the whole world: grant, we beg You, that through the intercession of the Virgin Mary, His Mother, we may lay hold of the joys of eternal life, through the same Christ our Lord. Amen.

Regina caeli, laetare. Alleluia.
Quia quem meruisti portare. Alleluia.
Resurrexit, sicut dixit. Alleluia.
Ora pro nobis, Deum. Alleluia.

V. Gaude et laetare, Virgo Maria. Alleluia.
R. Quia surrexit Dominus vere. Alleluia.

Oremus: Deus, qui per resurrectionem Filii tui, Domini nostri Iesu Christi, mundum laetificare dignatus es: praesta, quaesumus; ut,pereius Genitricem Virginem Mariam, perpetuae capiamus gaudia vitae. Per eundem Christum Dominum nostrum. Amen.

2d. Prayer to the Holy Spirit

Most Holy Spirit, source of all holiness, we pray that humanity will soon recognize and embrace the Catholic Church's timeless teachings so that we will see, in our age, the public reign of Christ through Mary, in union with St. Joseph, for which we should be working and sacrificing.

Be our Union of Love with the Father, the Holy Family, and all of the people in our lives, especially with our families and community.

Mary our Mother please show us how to draw closer to your Spouse, the Holy Spirit. We ask all of this in your Son's Name, Jesus Christ. Amen.

(or see #46e Holy Spirit: Secret to Sanctity and Happiness)

2e. Immaculate Conception Prayer for the Apostolate

O Immaculate Conception, Mary, my Mother, live in me, my family, and all the members, benefactors, and candidates of the apostolate; act in us; speak in and through us. Think your thoughts in our minds, love through our hearts. Give us your own dispositions and feelings. Teach, lead, and guide us to Jesus. Correct, enlighten, and expand our thoughts and behavior. Possess our souls; take over our entire personalities and lives. Replace us with yourself. Incline us to constant adoration and thanksgiving; pray in and through us. Let us live in you and keep us in this union always. Amen.

2f. St. Joseph Prayer for the Apostolate

St. Joseph, unite my prayers with those of the other members and friends of the society of the Apostolate for Family Consecration throughout the world.

We know, St. Joseph, that Our Lord will refuse you nothing. Please ask God to bless The Apostolate and all of its members and friends. Ask Our Lord to help The Apostolate and its Lay Ecclesial Teams to make the best use of the modern means of communications to consecrate families, parishes, and movements in the Truth and to help families understand and imitate the Eucharistic, Marian, and family-centered spirituality of Pope John Paul II.

St. Joseph, we are confident that you will remove all obstacles in the path of this spiritual renewal program so that our society may be transformed through a chain reaction which will renew our families, neighborhoods, parishes, schools, country, and the entire world.

Form the society of the Apostolate for Family Consecration into a useful instrument of the Holy Family, and never let its members and leaders lose their holy zeal for souls or fall into the sin of spiritual pride like that of the Pharisees, which is so fatal to the work of God. Use The Apostolate as an instrument to bring about the social reign of the Most Holy Family in our age. Amen.

2g. St. Michael the Archangel

St. Michael the Archangel, defend us in battle; be our safeguard against the wickedness and snares of the devil. May God rebuke him, we humbly pray, and do you, O prince of the heavenly host, by the power of God, cast into hell, Satan and all the other evil spirits who prowl through the world seeking the ruin of souls. Amen.

2h. Guardian Angel

Angel of God, my guardian dear, to whom God's love commits me here, ever this day be at my side, to light, to guard, to rule, and to guide. Amen.

2i. First Corinthians 13

If I speak in the tongues of men and of angels, but have not love, I am a noisy gong or a clanging cymbal. [2]And if I have prophetic powers, and understand all mysteries and all knowledge, and if I have all faith, so as to remove mountains, but have not love, I am nothing. [3]If I give away all I have, and if I deliver my body to be burned, but have not love, I gain nothing.

[4]Love is patient and kind; love is not jealous or boastful; [5]it is not arrogant or rude. Love does not insist on its own way; it is not irritable or resentful; [6]it does not rejoice at wrong, but rejoices in the right. [7]Love bears all things, believes all things, hopes all things, endures all things.

[8]Love never ends; as for prophecies, they will pass away; as for tongues, they will cease; as for knowledge, it will pass away. [9]For our knowledge is imperfect and our prophecy is imperfect; [10]but when the perfect comes, the imperfect will pass away. [11]When I was a child, I spoke like a child, I thought like a child, I reasoned like a child; when I became a man, I gave up childish ways. [12]For now we see in a mirror dimly, but then face to face. Now I know in part; then I shall understand fully, even as I have been fully understood. [13]So faith, hope, love abide, these three; but the greatest of these is love.

2j. Prayer for Gwen and Family Unity

(#40c in some prayer books)
For Private Devotion

Heavenly Father, Gwen Coniker was a model for family fidelity. She taught parents and grandparents how to sacrifice everything to fulfill God's will and become persons and families for others. Thank you for her work in the spirit of Pope John Paul II for the renewal of the Church and society through family consecration.

Gwen was a person for others who joyfully lived Your Will by fulfilling the responsibilities of each present moment. She faithfully and lovingly carried out the duties and commitments of her state in life. She showed us how to be always grateful in the deepest of trials, and how to discern and do God's will moment by moment. Gwen also showed us how to gracefully die a prolonged and painful death without complaint or self-pity.

Heavenly Father, we ask you to glorify Gwen. May the Church raise her to the honor of the altars for the encouragement of "family and parish consecration in the truth" to the Holy Family, and for the protection of our families from the evil one (cf. John 17:15-17).

We make our prayer and petition for the work of the Apostolate for Family Consecration and our special requests (mention your intentions) through Christ our Lord. Amen.

Our Father. Hail Mary. Glory Be.

Nihil Obstat:	Rev. James M. Dunfee
	Censor Librorum
Imprimatur:	+ Most Rev. R. Daniel Conlon
	Bishop of Steubenville
	October 21, 2002

(See Appendix D for more information on Gwen Coniker.)

4. Apostolate's Act of Consecration
Try to say this prayer after Mass

Heavenly Father, grant that we, who are nourished by the Body and Blood of Your Divine Son, may die to our own selfishness and be one spirit with Christ, as we seek to fulfill Your distinctive plan for our lives. (pause)

Form me and all the members of my family, community, and the apostolate into instruments of atonement. Unite our entire lives with the Holy Sacrifice of Jesus in the Mass of Calvary, and accept our seed sacrifice offering of all of our spiritual and material possessions, for the Sacred and Eucharistic Heart of Jesus, through the Sorrowful and Immaculate Heart of Mary, in union with St. Joseph. *(pause)*

Our Father, let Sacred Scripture's Four "C's" of Confidence, Conscience, seed-Charity, and Constancy be our guide for living our consecration as peaceful children, and purified instruments of the Most Holy Family. *(pause)*

Let us live our consecration by remaining perpetually confident, calm, cheerful, and compassionate, especially with the members of our own family and community. *(pause)*

Please protect our loved ones and ourselves from the temptations of the world, the flesh, and the devil. Help us to become more sensitive to the inspirations of Your Holy Spirit, the Holy Family, our Patron Saints and Guardian Angels. *(pause)*

And now, Most Heavenly Father, inspire us to establish the right priorities for Your precious gift of time. And most of all, help us to be more sensitive to the needs and feelings of our loved ones. *(pause)*

Never let us forget the souls in Purgatory who are dependent upon us for help. Enable us to gain, for the Poor Souls of our loved ones and others, as many indulgences as possible. We ask You this, Our Father, in the Name of Our Lord and Savior Jesus Christ, Your Son and the Son of Mary. Amen.

5. Short Form Consecration Prayer

Most Holy Family, unite my daily life with the Holy Sacrifice of the Mass. Accept all of my spiritual and material possessions as my seed of sacrifice offered to the Sacred and Eucharistic Heart of Jesus, through the Sorrowful and Immaculate Heart of Mary, in union with St. Joseph. This shall be my commitment in life, in death, and in eternity. Amen.

6a–9 The Holy Rosary
Try to pray five decades daily

For the Church's teachings on the Rosary, see the Catechism of the Catholic Church, paragraphs 971, 2678, and 2708.

How to pray the Rosary:

Pray the Apostles' Creed (#6a) on the Crucifix. Then offer one Our Father (#6b) on the large bead, and three Hail Marys (#6c) on each of the three small beads for the Holy Father, the Pope. After the three Hail Marys, pray the Glory Be (#7a), the Fatima Rosary Prayer (#7b), and the Consecration Prayer (#7c).

Announce the Mystery for the decade (see #7d) and meditate on it while praying. Pray one Our Father on the large bead. Pray the Hail Mary on each of the ten small beads. On the next large bead, pray the Glory Be, the Rosary Prayer, and the Consecration Prayer. Then, on the same large bead, announce the next Mystery and begin again with the Our Father. Continue until you have prayed all five decades.

After the Rosary, pray #8, 8a, 9, 10 & 11a. (Note: Pope Leo XIII asked for a prayer to St. Joseph to be recited at the end of the Rosary.)

6a. Apostles' Creed

I believe in God, the Father Almighty, Creator of Heaven and earth; and in Jesus Christ, His only Son, our Lord; Who was conceived by the Holy Spirit, born of the Virgin Mary, suffered under Pontius Pilate, was crucified, died and was buried; He descended into hell, the third day He rose again from the dead, He ascended into Heaven, and is seated at the right hand of God, the Father Almighty. From thence He shall come to judge the living and the dead. I believe in the Holy Spirit, the Holy Catholic Church, the Communion of Saints, the forgiveness of sins, the resurrection of the body, and life everlasting. Amen.

For an explanation of the term "descended into hell," see paragraphs 631-637 of the Catechism of the Catholic Church. For a complete explanation of the Apostles' Creed, see paragraphs 198-1065.

6b. Our Father

Our Father Who art in Heaven, hallowed be Thy name. Thy Kingdom come. Thy will be done on earth, as it is in Heaven. Give us this day our daily bread, and forgive us our trespasses, as we forgive those who trespass against us, and lead us not into temptation, but deliver us from evil. Amen.

In the Philippines:

Our Father in Heaven, holy be Your Name. Your Kingdom come. Your Will be done on earth as it is in Heaven. Give us this day our daily bread; and forgive us our sins, as we forgive those who sin against us. Do not bring us to the test, but deliver us from evil. Amen.

For a detailed explanation of the Our Father, see paragraphs 2759–2865 of the Catechism of the Catholic Church.

6c. Hail Mary

Hail Mary, full of grace;
the Lord is with thee;
blessed art thou among
women and blessed is the
fruit of thy womb, Jesus.
Holy Mary, Mother of
God, pray for us sinners,
now and at the hour of
our death. Amen.

In the Philippines:

Hail Mary, full of grace;
the Lord is with you;
blessed are you among
women and blessed is the
fruit of your womb, Jesus.
Holy Mary, Mother of
God, pray for us sinners,
now and at the hour of
our death. Amen.

For teachings on Mary, see the Catechism of the Catholic Church, para. 411, 487–511, 721–726, 773, 829, 963–975, 2617–2619, 2622.

7a. Glory Be

Glory be to the Father, and to the Son, and to the Holy Spirit. As it was in the beginning, is now, and ever shall be, world without end. Amen.

For more on the Holy Trinity, see the Catechism of the Catholic Church's index, under "Trinity." Some key paragraphs are: 232-234, 238-246, 253-255, 683 and 687.

7b. Fatima Rosary Prayer
The prayer Our Lady of Fatima requested to be said after each decade of the Rosary.

O My Jesus, forgive us our sins; save us from the fires of hell; lead all souls to Heaven, especially those who are in most need of Your mercy.

7c. The Apostolate's Motto and Act of Spiritual Communion
Said after each decade of the Rosary following 7b.

We make a spiritual communion to discern and do God's Will in the present moment as we pray:

All for the Sacred and Eucharistic Heart of Jesus, all through the Sorrowful and Immaculate Heart of Mary, all in union with St. Joseph.

(or before each decision, simply pray "All for.")

7d. Mysteries of the Rosary

7d.1 The Joyful Mysteries

1. ***The Annunciation of the Archangel Gabriel to the Virgin Mary.*** We ask for the gifts of the Holy Spirit and an increase in the virtue of humility.

(Read St. Luke 1:28–38 and the Catechism of the Catholic Church, paragraphs 456–486.)

2. ***The Visitation of the Virgin Mary to Elizabeth, the Mother of St. John the Baptist.*** We ask for the gifts of the Holy Spirit and an increase in the virtue of generosity.

(Read St. Luke 1:39–56.)

3. ***The Birth of Our Lord at Bethlehem.*** We ask for the gifts of the Holy Spirit and an increase in the virtue of detachment from the things of this world.

(Read St. Luke 2:4–20 and the Catechism of the Catholic Church, paragraphs 437, 487–511, and 525.)

4. ***The Presentation of Our Lord in the Temple.*** We ask for the gifts of the Holy Spirit and an increase in the virtue of obedience.

(Read St. Luke 2:22–40 and the Catechism of the Catholic Church, paragraphs 144–152 and 527–530.)

5. ***The Finding of Our Lord in the Temple.*** We ask for the gifts of the Holy Spirit and an increase in the virtue of fear of the Lord, fear of ever losing God because of our sins.

(Read St. Luke 2:41–52 and the Catechism of the Catholic Church, paragraphs 531–534.)

7d.2 The Luminous Mysteries

1. ***The Baptism of Jesus in the Jordan.*** We ask for the gifts of the Holy Spirit and the grace to live our Baptismal Consecration.

(Read St. Matthew 4:3-17; St. Mark 1:9-13, St. Luke 3:21-22 and St. John 1:29-34 and the Catechism of the Catholic Church, paragraphs 1123-1225 and 535-537.)

2. **The Wedding at Cana.** We ask for the gifts of the Holy Spirit and the grace to keep our commitments.

(Read St. John 2:1-12 and the Catechism of the Catholic Church, paragraphs 1335, 1613 and 2618.)

3. **Our Lord's Proclamation of the Kingdom of God and His Call to Conversion.** We ask for the gifts of the Holy Spirit to proclaim the truths of our faith.

(Read St. Matthew 5, 6 and 7; St. Mark 1:21-22, St. Luke 4:14-30 and St. John 4:21-38 and the Catechism of the Catholic Church, paragraphs 541-546.)

4. ***The Transfiguration***. We ask for the gifts of the Holy Spirit and the grace to be transformed into the image of Christ, through Our Lady in union with St. Joseph.

(Read St. Matthew 17:1-13; St. Mark 9:2-13, St. Luke 9:28-36 and the Catechism of the Catholic Church, paragraphs 554-556, 568.)

5. ***Our Lord's Institution of the Holy Eucharist.*** We ask for the gifts of the Holy Spirit and the understanding that Eucharistic worship constitutes the soul of all Christian life.

(Read St. Matthew 26:26-29; St. Mark 14:22-25, St. Luke 22:19-20 and St. John 6:22-65 and chapters 13-17 and the Catechism of the Catholic Church, paragraphs 610-611, 1322-1327, 1337-1340.)

7d.3 The Sorrowful Mysteries

1. ***The Agony of Our Lord in the Garden of Gethsemane.*** We ask for the gifts of the Holy Spirit and the grace of abandonment to the will of the Father.

(Read St. Luke 22:39–46 and the Catechism of the Catholic Church, paragraph 612.)

2. ***The Scourging of Our Lord at the Pillar.*** We ask for the gifts of the Holy Spirit and an increase in the virtue of purity, of body and intention.

(Read St. Mark 14:55–15:20 and the Catechism of the Catholic Church, paragraphs 2517–2533.)

3. ***The Crowning of Our Lord with Thorns.*** We ask for the gifts of the Holy Spirit and an increase in the virtue of moral courage, by not striking back at those who hurt us.

(Read St. Mark 15:16–20, St. John 18:28-46 and 19:1-16; and the Catechism of the Catholic Church, paragraphs 2838–2845.)

4. ***The Carrying of the Cross by Our Lord to Calvary.*** We ask for the gifts of the Holy Spirit and an increase in the virtue of constancy.

(Read St. Luke 23:26–31 and St. Mark 15:21-22.)

5. ***The Crucifixion and Death of Our Lord.*** We ask for the gifts of the Holy Spirit and the grace to die to our own selfishness so that we can be one spirit with Christ.

(Read St. John 19:23–30, St. Matthew 27:32-56, and the Catechism of the Catholic Church, paragraphs 613–630.)

7d.4 The Glorious Mysteries

1. ***The Resurrection of Our Lord from the Dead.*** We ask for the gifts of the Holy Spirit and an increase in the virtue of faith.

(Read St. John 20:19–31, St. Luke 24:1-49, and the Catechism of the Catholic Church, paragraphs 631–658.)

2. ***The Ascension of Our Lord into Heaven.*** We ask for the gifts of the Holy Spirit and an increase in the virtue of hope.

> *(Read St. Mark 16:15–20, St. Matthew 28:16-20, and the Catechism of the Catholic Church, paragraphs 659–664.)*

3. ***The Descent of the Holy Spirit upon Mary and the Apostles.*** We ask for the gifts of the Holy Spirit and an increase in the virtue of charity.

> *(Read Acts 2:1–38 and the Catechism of the Catholic Church, paragraphs 731–747.)*

4. ***The Assumption of Our Blessed Mother into Heaven.*** We ask for the gifts of the Holy Spirit and the grace of a happy death for all the members of our family and The Apostolate.

(Read Wisdom 7:22–30 and 8:1–21; and the Catechism of the Catholic Church, paragraphs. 964–966.)

5. ***The Coronation of Our Blessed Lady as Queen of Heaven and Earth.*** We ask for the gifts of the Holy Spirit and an increase in true devotion to Mary to spread throughout the world.

(Read Revelation 12, Genesis 3:15, and the Catechism of the Catholic Church, paragraphs 966–975.)

8. St. Joseph Prayer after the Rosary

Glorious St. Joseph, spouse of the Immaculate Virgin, obtain for me and all the members of my family and loved ones, a confident, sinless, generous, and patient heart, and perfect resignation to the Divine Will.

Be our guide, father, and model throughout life, that we may merit a death like yours, in the arms of Jesus and Mary.

Help us, St. Joseph, in our earthly strife, to fulfill our responsibilities and ever to lead a pure and blameless life.

Heavenly Father, please ask the Holy Spirit, Who resides in the innermost recesses of my soul, to help me to call to mind all of my sins and faults. Help me to detach myself from these faults and sins so that I can be a useful instrument in the hands of the Most Holy Family, to achieve Your distinctive plan for my life.

Let me now pause for a few moments to think of my sins, faults, and omissions.

8a. Examination of Conscience Prayer

Mother Mary, please obtain for me, my family, and the members and families of the apostolate the gifts of the Holy Spirit and the grace to live the virtues which will help us overcome our primary faults. Let us be caught up in the Holy Spirit's love for the Father and the Holy Family.

9. Act of Contrition
Recited daily

O my God! I am heartily sorry for having offended Thee, and I detest all of my sins, because I dread the loss of Heaven and the pains of hell, but most of all because they have offended Thee, my God, Who art all-good and deserving of all my love. I firmly resolve with the help of Thy grace, to confess my sins, to do penance, and to amend my life. Amen.

Let us pray: Heavenly Father, in the Name of Our Lord Jesus Christ, we ask You to release a Poor Soul of one of our loved ones from Purgatory for each of us who have received Your Son in Holy Communion this day, *and we ask these souls being released to pray continually that our families and the members and families of The Apostolate do Your will.*

10. Seed-Charity Prayer in the Spirit of St. Francis
Try to reflect on one part each day

Lord, make me an instrument of Your peace;
Where there is hatred,
    let me sow seeds of love;
Where there is injury,
    let me sow seeds of pardon;
Where there is discord,
    let me sow seeds of union;
Where there is doubt,
    let me sow seeds of faith;
Where there is despair,
    let me sow seeds of hope;
Where there is darkness,
    let me sow seeds of light;
And where there is sadness,
    let me sow seeds of joy.

O Divine Master, grant that I may not so much seek to be consoled as to console You in others; to be loved, as to love You in others.

For it is in giving that we receive. It is in pardoning that we are pardoned, and it is in dying as a seed to our selfishness that we are born to eternal life. Amen.

11a. Act of Spiritual Communion
May be said throughout the day

My Jesus, I believe that You are in the Blessed Sacrament. I love You above all things, and I long for You in my soul.

Since I cannot now receive You sacramentally, come at least spiritually into my heart.

As though You have already come, I embrace You and unite myself entirely to You; never permit me to be separated from You. Amen.

11b. Mother Teresa's Nazareth Prayer for the Family
Recommended after the family Rosary.

Heavenly Father, You have given us a model of life in the Holy Family of Nazareth. Help us, O loving Father, to make our family another Nazareth where love, peace, and joy reign.

May it be deeply contemplative, intensely Eucharistic, and vibrant with joy. Help us to stay together in joy and sorrow through family prayer. Teach us to see Jesus in the members of our family, especially in their distressing disguise.

May the Eucharistic Heart of Jesus make our hearts meek and humble like His and help us to carry out our family duties in a holy way.

May we love one another as God loves each one of us more and more each day, and forgive each others' faults as You forgive our sins.

Help us, O loving Father, to take whatever You give and to give whatever You take with a big smile.

Immaculate Heart of Mary, cause of our joy, pray for us. St. Joseph, pray for us. Holy Guardian Angels, be always with us, guide and protect us. Amen.

14. Act of Consecration to St. Joseph
Recited on Wednesdays

St. Joseph, I consecrate myself, my entire family and all of my loved ones to you, that you may ever be our father, our patron, and our guide in the way of salvation. Obtain for us purity of heart and a fervent devotion to the spiritual life. Grant that, following your example, we may direct all our actions to the greater glory of God, in union with the Sacred Heart of Jesus, the Immaculate Heart of Mary, and in union with you.

Finally, St. Joseph, pray for my family, my loved ones, and the members of the apostolate, that we may be partakers in the peace and joy which were yours throughout your life and at the hour of your death. Amen.

(Note: On Wednesdays, we recommend praying the St. Joseph Chaplet [#14a] in place of the Rosary.)

14a. Seven Sorrows and Joys of St. Joseph Chaplet

Recommended devotion for
Wednesdays in place of the Rosary

1. Prayer

(All) Jesus and Mary, Saint Joseph loved you without bounds. He achieved a union with you that no other soul has been privileged to achieve. Use me as your earthly instrument to honor St. Joseph. I am reciting these prayers in union with You and the Holy Spirit.

2. Petition

(All) Glorious St. Joseph, accept this novena as our seed of faith in your powerful intercession with Almighty God and His Immaculate Mother. We are confident that God will multiply this seed of faith by helping us to fulfill the responsibilities we have taken upon ourselves. We pray that all the members of our families and loved ones will be spiritually and physically protected and guided to fulfill the vocations that God has predestined for them. We pray that all of our enterprises will be successful, and that our parish, diocese, and all apostolates flourish and be protected from error. And particularly we pray that God will grant us the favor we now ask of you, or if it is His will, one that is better for us.

(Pause and silently make your request.)

Pray the Apostles' Creed (#6a), one Our Father (#6b), three Hail Marys (#6c), and one Glory Be (#7a) for the Holy Father's intentions.

First Sorrow and Joy — *The Incarnation*

(Leader) St. Joseph, chaste spouse of the Immaculate Mother of God, by the deep SORROW which pierced your heart at the thought of quietly leaving Mary so that she would not be punished by the law when found to be with child; by the deep JOY that you felt when the angel revealed to you in a dream the mystery of the Incarnation of Jesus through the power of the Holy Spirit, and your vital role as the guardian of the Holy Family,

(All) St. Joseph, obtain for me, my family, and all the members and families of the apostolate, from the Hearts of Jesus and Mary, the grace for surmounting all anxiety and the grace of total and absolute trust in God. Win for us from the Sacred Heart of Jesus the indestructible peace of which He is the eternal source.

Pray one Our Father, Seven Hail Marys, and one Glory Be.

(All) O My Jesus, forgive us our sins; save us from the fires of hell; lead all souls to Heaven, especially those who are in most need of Your mercy.

[We make a spiritual communion to discern and do God's Will in each present moment as we say:]
(All) All for the Sacred and Eucharistic Heart of Jesus, all through the Sorrowful and Immaculate Heart of Mary, all in union with St. Joseph.

Second Sorrow and Joy — *The Birth of Jesus*

(Leader) St. Joseph, faithful guardian of Jesus, by the bitter SORROW which your heart experienced in seeing the Child Jesus lying in a manger, and by the deep JOY which you did feel at seeing the Wise Men recognize and adore Him as their God,

(All) Grant through your prayers that my conscience and the consciences of all the members of my family and all the members and families of the apostolate, purified by your protection, may become sinless cribs, where the Savior of the world may be received with love and respect.

Pray one Our Father, Seven Hail Marys, and one Glory Be.

(All) O My Jesus, forgive us our sins; save us from the fires of hell; lead all souls to Heaven, especially those who are in most need of Your mercy.

[We make a spiritual communion to discern and do God's Will in each present moment as we say:]

(All) All for the Sacred and Eucharistic Heart of Jesus, all through the Sorrowful and Immaculate Heart of Mary, all in union with St. Joseph.

Third Sorrow and Joy — *The Circumcision*

(Leader) St. Joseph, by the SORROW with which your heart was pierced at the sight of the blood which flowed from the infant Jesus in the circumcision, and by the JOY that filled your soul at the privilege of bestowing the sacred and mysterious Name of Jesus,

(All) Intercede for us, that the merits of this Precious Blood, poured out as a Seed-Sacrifice offering for our salvation, may be applied to my family and all the members and families of the apostolate, so that the Divine Name of Jesus may be engraved forever in our hearts.

Pray one Our Father, Seven Hail Marys, and one Glory Be.

(All) O My Jesus, forgive us our sins; save us from the fires of hell; lead all souls to Heaven, especially those who are in most need of Your mercy.

[We make a spiritual communion to discern and do God's Will in each present moment as we say:]
(All) All for the Sacred and Eucharistic Heart of Jesus, all through the Sorrowful and Immaculate Heart of Mary, all in union with St. Joseph.

Fourth Sorrow and Joy — *The Presentation*

(Leader) St. Joseph, by your deep SORROW when Simeon declared that the heart of Mary would be pierced with the sword of sorrow at the time that her Divine Son generously sacrificed Himself for our sins, and by your JOY when Simeon added that the Seed-Sacrifice offering of Jesus was to bear an abundant harvest of redeemed souls,

(All) Obtain for me, my family, and all the members and families of the apostolate, the grace to unite ourselves with the sorrows of Mary and to share in the salvation which Jesus brought to the earth.

Pray one Our Father, Seven Hail Marys, and one Glory Be.

(All) O My Jesus, forgive us our sins; save us from the fires of hell; lead all souls to Heaven, especially those who are in most need of Your mercy.

[We make a spiritual communion to discern and do God's Will in each present moment as we say:]

(All) All for the Sacred and Eucharistic Heart of Jesus, all through the Sorrowful and Immaculate Heart of Mary, all in union with St. Joseph.

Fifth Sorrow and Joy — *The Flight into Egypt*

(Leader) St. Joseph, by your SORROW when told to flee into the foreign and hostile land of Egypt, and by your JOY in seeing their satanic idols fall to the ground as the Living God passed by,

(All) Grant that I, the members of my family, and all the members and families of the apostolate will not fear to do God's will, which is distinct for each one of us, and will always trust in Him as the total source of both our spiritual and material security.

Pray one Our Father, Seven Hail Marys, and one Glory Be.

(All) O My Jesus, forgive us our sins; save us from the fires of hell; lead all souls to Heaven, especially those who are in most need of Your mercy.

[We make a spiritual communion to discern and do God's Will in each present moment as we say:]

(All) All for the Sacred and Eucharistic Heart of Jesus, all through the Sorrowful and Immaculate Heart of Mary, all in union with St. Joseph.

Sixth Sorrow and Joy – *The Return from Egypt*

(Leader) St. Joseph, by the SORROW of your heart caused by the fear of the son of Herod after your obedient return from Egypt, and by your JOY in sharing the company of Jesus and Mary at Nazareth,

(All) Grant for us that, freed from all fear, we may enjoy the peace of a good conscience, live securely in union with Jesus and Mary, and experience your assistance at the hour of our death.

Pray one Our Father, Seven Hail Marys, and one Glory Be.

(All) O My Jesus, forgive us our sins; save us from the fires of hell; lead all souls to Heaven, especially those who are in most need of Your mercy.

[We make a spiritual communion to discern and do God's Will in each present moment as we say:]

(All) All for the Sacred and Eucharistic Heart of Jesus, all through the Sorrowful and Immaculate Heart of Mary, all in union with St. Joseph.

Seventh Sorrow and Joy – *The Finding in the Temple*

(Leader) St. Joseph, by the bitter SORROW with which the loss of the Child Jesus crushed your heart, and by the holy JOY which filled your soul in recovering your treasure when you re-entered the Temple,

(All) I beg you not to permit me, any member of my family, or any member or family of the apostolate to lose our Savior Jesus through sin. Yet, should this misfortune befall any of us, grant that we may share your eagerness in seeking him, and obtain for us the grace of finding Him, and never losing Him again.

Pray one Our Father, Seven Hail Marys, and one Glory Be.

(All) O My Jesus, forgive us our sins; save us from the fires of hell; lead all souls to Heaven, especially those who are in most need of Your mercy.

(All) All for the Sacred and Eucharistic Heart of Jesus, all through the Sorrowful and Immaculate Heart of Mary, all in union with St. Joseph.

(Leader) Behold the faithful and prudent servant,

(All) Whom the Lord set over His house.

Conclude by praying the Prayer to St. Joseph after the Rosary (#8), making an examination of conscience (#8a), and praying an Act of Contrition (#9).

16a. Go to St. Joseph Novena

For a special intention, pray this novena for nine days or nine times in one day or on nine consecutive Wednesdays.

16a.1 Glorious St. Joseph, most pure spouse of the Virgin Mary, pray every day for me, my family, and all of my loved ones to Jesus, the Son of God, whom God Himself placed under your loving care and protection, that we, being defended by the power of His grace and sincerely trying to live a good life, may be crowned by Him at the hour of our death. Please, St. Joseph pray that we receive the grace to successfully fulfill the responsibilities we have taken upon ourselves, and grant us the favor we now ask of you, or if it is God's will, one that is better for us.

(Pause and silently make your request.)

16a.2 In the terrible anxieties of this life, to whom shall we have recourse, if not to you, to whom your beloved spouse, Mary, entrusted all her rich treasures, that you might keep them to our advantage.

"Go to my spouse, Joseph," Mary seems to say to us, "and he will comfort you. He will deliver you from the misfortunes which now oppress you and will make you happy and content."

Have pity on us, St. Joseph; have pity on us through that love which you did cherish toward a spouse so worthy and pure.

All for the Sacred and Eucharistic Heart of Jesus, all through the Sorrowful and Immaculate Heart of Mary, all in union with St. Joseph.

16a.3 We are fully conscious that we have deeply hurt God with our sins and therefore have given the devils more power over ourselves, our loved ones and the entire temporal world.

Now, what shall be our place of refuge? In what haven shall we find ourselves in safety?

"Go to Joseph," Jesus seems to say to us. "Go to Joseph, in whom I was well pleased, and whom I had for My chaste father. To him as to a real father, I have communicated all power, that he may use it for your good according to his own desire and My plan for you."

Pity us, therefore, blessed Joseph; pity us, for the great love you did bear toward a Son so admirable and dear.

All for the Sacred and Eucharistic Heart of Jesus, all through the Sorrowful and Immaculate Heart of Mary, all in union with St. Joseph.

16a.4   Unhappily, the sins of the world, added to our own weaknesses, introduce a painful disorder into our lives and make it more difficult to gain salvation. In what shelter can we take refuge in order to be saved? Where shall we find the security that shall give us strength, order, and hope in the midst of our afflictions?

"Go to Joseph," the eternal Father seems to say to us. "Go to him who took My place on earth with regard to My Son made man. I entrusted to his keeping My Son, Who is the unfailing source of grace; every help necessary for your well-being is in his hands."

Pity us then, St. Joseph; pity us by your great love for Almighty God the Father, Who has been so generous to you.

All for the Sacred and Eucharistic Heart of Jesus, all through the Sorrowful and Immaculate Heart of Mary, all in union with St. Joseph.

16a.5   St. Joseph, help me and all the members of my family and loved ones to use the gifts we have received from Almighty God; to work with confidence, order, peace, moderation and patience, without ever shrinking from responsibilities and difficulties; to work, above all, with a pure intention and with detachment from self, having always before our eyes the hour of death and the accounting which we must then make of time ill-spent, of talents unemployed, of good undone and of our empty pride or complacency in success, which is so fatal to the work of God.

All for the Sacred and Eucharistic Heart of Jesus, all through the Sorrowful and Immaculate Heart of Mary, all in union with St. Joseph. This shall be our motto in life, in death, and in eternity. Amen.

17a. Prayer for the Divine Communion of Love

Heavenly Father grant that—

Our feet may walk together with the feet of the Holy Family.

Our hands may gather together with the hands of the Holy Family.

Our hearts may beat together with the Hearts of the Holy Family.

Our inner most beings may feel together with the beings of the Holy Family.

The thoughts of our mind may be one with the thoughts of the Holy Family.

Our ears may listen together to the silence with the Holy Family.

Our eyes may look at each other in unity with the eyes of the Holy Family.

Our lips may pray together with the lips of the Holy Family to You, Eternal Father, for mercy. Amen.

19. The Twelve Promises of the Sacred Heart to Saint Margaret Mary

1. I will give them the graces necessary in their state of life.

2. I will establish peace in their houses.

3. I will comfort them in all of their afflictions.

4. I will be their secure refuge during life, and above all in death.

5. I will bestow a large blessing upon all their undertakings.

6. Sinners shall find in My Heart the source and the infinite ocean of mercy.

7. Tepid souls shall grow fervent.

8. Fervent souls shall quickly mount to high perfection.

9. I will bless every place where a picture of My Heart shall be set up and honored.

10. I will give to the priests the gift of touching the most hardened hearts.

11. Those who shall promote this devotion shall have their names written in My Heart, never to be blotted out.

12. I promise you in the excessive mercy of My Heart that My all-powerful love will grant to all those who communicate on the First Friday in nine consecutive months the grace of final penitence; they shall not die in my disgrace nor without receiving the Sacraments; My Divine Heart shall be their safe refuge in this last moment.

20f. The Chaplet of Divine Mercy

Our Lord taught Blessed Faustina a prayer for mercy that she was to pray "unceasingly": The Chaplet of Divine Mercy (cf. Diary, 476). He told her that, if she prayed in this way, her prayers would have great power for the conversion of sinners, for peace for the dying, and even for controlling nature. We, too, can pray this chaplet, using ordinary rosary beads of five decades.

Begin with the Our Father, the Hail Mary and the Apostles' Creed (see prayer #6b, 6c and 6a).

Then, on the large beads pray:

Eternal Father, I offer you the Body and Blood, Soul and Divinity of Your Dearly Beloved Son, Our Lord, Jesus Christ, in atonement for our sins and those of the whole world.

On the small beads pray:

For the sake of His sorrowful Passion, have mercy on us and on the whole world.

At the end, pray three times:

Holy God, Holy Mighty One, Holy Immortal One, have mercy on us and on the whole world.

21. Holy Trinity Prayer
in the Spirit of Fatima
Also an adoration prayer.
Recommended for Thursdays.

Most Holy Trinity, Father, Son, and Holy Spirit, I adore You profoundly. I offer you the most precious Body, Blood, Soul, and Divinity of Jesus Christ, present in all the tabernacles of the world, in reparation for the outrages, sacrileges, and indifferences by which he is offended. By the infinite merits of His Most Sacred Heart and through the Immaculate Heart of Mary, in union with St. Joseph, I beg the conversion of poor sinners. Amen.

22. Act of Reparation to the Sacred Heart of Jesus

In the Spirit of Blessed Mother Teresa
Recommended for Fridays.

Sacred Heart of Jesus, humbly prostrate before You, we come to renew our consecration, with the resolution of repairing, by an increase of love and fidelity to You, all the outrages unceasingly offered You. We firmly resolve that:

The more your mysteries are blasphemed, the more firmly we shall believe in them, O Sacred Heart of Jesus!

The more impiety endeavors to extinguish our hopes of immortality, the more we shall trust in Your Heart, sole Hope of mortals!

The more hearts resist Your divine attractions, the more we shall love You, O infinitely amiable Heart of Jesus!

The more Your divinity is attacked, the more we shall adore it, O Divine Heart of Jesus!

The more Your holy Laws are forgotten and transgressed, the more we shall observe them, O most Holy Heart of Jesus.

The more Your sacraments are despised and abandoned, the more we shall receive them with love and respect, O Most Liberal Heart of Jesus.

The more Your adorable virtues are forgotten, the more we shall endeavor to practice them, O Heart, Model of every virtue!

The more Your holy vows of Marriage are neglected and broken, the more we shall observe them with love and fidelity, O Heart most faithful.

The more the demon labors to destroy the life of prayer and purity in consecrated souls, the more we will try to keep Purity – pure, Chastity – chaste, Virginity – virginal, O most pure Heart of Jesus.

The more mothers destroy the presence and image of God through abortion, the more we shall save them by caring for them or by giving them in adoption, O tender Heart of Jesus.

O Sacred Heart, give us so strong and powerful a grace that we may be Your apostles in the midst of the world, and Your crown in a happy eternity. Amen.

23. Consecration to the Sacred Heart of Jesus

Most Sweet Jesus, humbly at your feet, we renew the consecration of our family to Your Divine Heart. Be our King forever! In you we have full and entire confidence. May Your spirit penetrate our thoughts, our desires, our words, and our works. Bless our undertakings, share in our joys, in our trials, and in our labors. Grant us to know You better, to love You more, to serve You without faltering.

By the Immaculate Heart of Mary, Queen of Peace, set up Your Kingdom in our country. Enter closely into the midst of our families and make them Your own through the solemn enthronement of Your Sacred Heart, so that soon one cry may resound from home to home: *May the triumphant Heart of Jesus be everywhere loved, blessed, and glorified forever!* Honor and glory be to the Sacred Heart of Jesus and Mary in union with St. Joseph! Sacred Heart of Jesus, protect our families.

(Read the "Catechism of the Catholic Church," paragraphs 478 and 2669.)

23b. Litany of the Holy Name of Jesus

Leader: Lord, have mercy on us.
All: *Christ, have mercy on us*

Leader: Lord, have mercy on us; Jesus hear us.
All: *Jesus, graciously hear us*

Leader   **Response**

God the Father of heaven,
God the Son, Redeemer of the world,
God the Holy Spirit,
Holy Trinity, one God,
Jesus, Son of the living God,
Jesus, splendor of the Father,
Jesus, brightness of eternal light,
Jesus, King of glory,
Jesus, sun of justice,
Jesus, Son of the Virgin Mary,
Jesus, most amiable
Jesus, most admirable,
Jesus, mighty God,
Jesus,Father of the world to come,
Jesus, angel of the great counsel,
Jesus, most powerful,
Jesus, most patient,
Jesus, most obedient,
Jesus, meek and humble of heart,
Jesus, lover of chastity,
Jesus, lover of us
Jesus, God of peace,
Jesus, author of life,
Jesus, model of virtues,
Jesus, lover of souls,
Jesus, our God,
Jesus, our refuge,
Jesus, Father of the poor,
Jesus, treasure of the faithful,
Jesus, Good Shepherd,

Have mercy on us

Jesus, true light,
Jesus, eternal wisdom,
Jesus, infinite goodness,
Jesus, our way and our life,
Jesus, joy of angels
Jesus, King of patriarchs
Jesus, master of Apostles,
Jesus, teacher of Evangelists,
Jesus, strength of martyrs,
Jesus, light of confessors,
Jesus, purity of virgins,
Jesus, crown of all saints,

Have mercy on us

Be merciful,   *Spare us, O Jesus*
Be merciful,   *Graciously hear us, O Jesus*

From all evil,
From all sin,
From Your wrath,
From the snares of the devil,
From the spirit of fornication,
From everlasting death,
From the neglect of Your inspirations
Through the mystery of Your holy Incarnation,
Through Your nativity
Through Your infancy,
Through Your most divine life
Through Your labors,
Through Your agony and Passion,
Through Your cross and dereliction
Through Your sufferings,
Through Your death and burial,
Through Your Resurrection
Through Your Ascension,
Through Your institution of the most Holy
    Eucharist
Through Your joys,
Through Your glory,

Jesus, deliver us

Leader: Lamb of God, Who takes away the sins of the
world,
All: *Spare us, O Jesus*

Leader: Lamb of God, Who takes away the sins of the
world,
All: *Graciously hear us, O Jesus*

Leader: Lamb of God, Who takes away the sins of the
world,
All: *Have mercy on us, O Jesus*

Leader: Jesus, hear us
All: *Jesus, graciously hear us*

Leader: Let us pray:

O Lord Jesus
Christ, Who has said:
Ask and you shall
receive; seek and you
shall find; knock and it
shall be opened unto
you; grant, we beseech
You, to us who ask the
gift of Your divine love,
that we may ever love
You with all our hearts,
and in all our words
and actions, and never
cease praising You.

Give us, O Lord, a
perpetual fear and love
of Your holy Name; for
You never fail to govern those whom You do solidly establish in Your love. Who lives and reigns world without
end. Amen.

24. Scripture Passages for the Enthronement of the Sacred Heart and the Holy Family in the Home
(can also be used for reflection on Fridays)

John 17:15-19	Luke 19:1-10
1 Corinthians 13:4-7	Ephesians 6:10-17
Galatians 4:1-2 & 6	Luke 1:26-33

Exodus 24:7 *All that the Lord has spoken we will do.*

Psalm 29:10 *The Lord sits enthroned as king for ever.*

Matthew 6:33-34 *But seek first his kingdom and his righteousness, and all these things shall be yours as well. Therefore do not be anxious about tomorrow, for tomorrow will be anxious for itself.*

John 18:37 *Pilate said to him, "So you are a king?" Jesus answered, "You say that I am a king."*

Luke 19:5 *I must stay at your house today.*

Revelation 3:20 *I stand at the door and knock.*

Revelation 22:20 *Surely I am coming soon.*

For a free Holy Family of Fatima portrait and download of the enthronement devotion on video with Blessed Teresa of Calcutta, go to www.familyconsecration.org.

24a. Family Covenant with the Holy Family

Lord Jesus, Your hidden years with Your Blessed Mother and St. Joseph at Nazareth showed us the beauty of the community of life and love that the family is meant to be. You taught us the value of selfless love, humble obedience, and silent sacrifice. You showed us how to sanctify the daily give-and-take of family life.

Today, we, the members of the _____ family, publicly acknowledge You as the true Head of our family and the King of our home. We pledge ourselves to model our family after the Holy Family of Jesus, Mary, and Joseph of Nazareth.

We consecrate to You, Most Sacred Heart of Jesus, through the Immaculate Heart of Your Mother, in union with St. Joseph, our work, our play, our sorrows, and our joys, along with our interior and exterior possessions, including the value of our good actions — past, present, and future. This is the covenant we make with You, Lord.

In return, Lord Jesus, we ask You to bless and protect us, keeping us ever faithful to this Covenant, and helping us to sanctify our lives by faithfully fulfilling the responsibility of each present moment only for Your glory.

Jesus, King of Families, come and reign over our family! Mary, Queen of Families, take possession of our hearts!   St. Joseph, Protector of Families, help us to be absorbed in and reflect the love of the Holy Family!

26. Ceremony of Conferral of the Holy Medal of the Blessed and Immaculate Virgin Mary

Commonly known as the "Miraculous Medal"
(See note on page 10)

When the people have gathered, the celebrant enters during the singing of a hymn suited to the particular celebration. After the singing, the celebrant says:

Celebrant: In the Name of the Father, and of the Son, and of the Holy Spirit.

All *(Make the sign of the Cross and reply)*: Amen.

The celebrant greets those present in the following or other suitable words, taken mainly from Sacred Scripture.

Celebrant: Through the Son, born of Mary, every blessing comes to us from God our Father. May His grace and peace be with you all.

All: And also with you.

Celebrant: God uses ordinary things as signs to express his extraordinary mercy toward us. Through simple things as well we express our gratitude, declare our willingness to serve God, and profess the resolve to live up to our baptismal consecration.

This medal is a sign of entrance into the Association of the Blessed and Immaculate Virgin Mary, approved by the Church. The medal thus expresses our intention of sharing in the spirit of this Association. That intention renews our baptismal resolve to put on Christ with the help of Mary, whose own greatest desire is that we become more like Christ, in praise of the Trinity, until, dressed for the wedding feast, we reach our home in Heaven.

Reading of the Word of God

A reader, one of those present or the celebrant, reads a text of Sacred Scripture, taken preferably from the reading in the Lectionary for Mass for the mysteries of Mary. The text chosen may also be one of those particularly related to the spirit of the Association.

1. Revelation 11:19a; 12:1, 5, 14-17. "A great sign appeared in the heavens." God's temple in heaven opened...

2. John 2:1-11. "The first of the signs given by Jesus was at Cana in Galilee." There was a wedding at Cana in Galilee...

After the reading, the celebrant gives a homily in which he explains to those present the meaning of this celebration.

Intercessions

The intercessions are then said. From the following intercessions the celebrant may choose those which seem best suited to the occasion, or may add others which address the particular needs of the faithful.

Celebrant: Because the Medal of the Immaculate Conception is rightly considered to be a pre-eminent sign of our devotion to the Virgin Mary, let us call upon the Name of the Lord through the intercession of this Blessed Virgin:

All: Through Mary, O Lord, join us more closely to Christ.

Celebrant: Most compassionate Father, through the redemptive merits of your only begotten Son you preserved your mother Mary beforehand from all stain of sin; keep us free from sin.

All: Through Mary, O Lord, join us more closely to Christ.

Celebrant: When Mary consented to your word, you chose her as the companion of the Redeemer; grant through the intercession of this Blessed Virgin that your Church may abound in the fruits of Christ's redemption.

All: Through Mary, O Lord, join us more closely to Christ.

Celebrant: You joined the Virgin Mary to your Son in a close and unbreakable bond and showered her with the fullness of your grace; grant that we may always find her to be our advocate, pleading for the graces we need.

All: Through Mary, O Lord, join us more closely to Christ.

Celebrant: In the Virgin Mary you have provided us with the perfect example of following Christ; help us to strive to reflect in our lives the mysteries of our salvation.

All: Through Mary, O Lord, join us more closely to Christ.

Celebrant: You taught the Virgin Mary to keep all your words in her heart; grant that, by following her example, we may hold fast to the words of your Son in faith and carry them out in our lives.

All: Through Mary, O Lord, join us more closely to Christ.

Celebrant: You gave the Holy Spirit to your Apostles as they were at prayer with Mary, the Mother of Jesus; grant that, persevering in prayer, we may walk in the spirit even as we live in the spirit.

All: Through Mary, O Lord, join us more closely to Christ.

Prayer of Blessing

With hands outstretched, the celebrant continues:

Celebrant: O God, the author and perfecter of all holiness, you call all who are reborn of water and the Holy Spirit to the fullness of the Christian life and the perfection of charity. Look with kindness on those who devoutly receive this medal in honor of the Blessed and Immaculate Virgin Mary. As long as they live, let them become sharers in the image of Christ your Son, and, after they have fulfilled their mission on earth with the help of Mary, the Virgin Mother, receive them into the joy of your heavenly home. We ask this through Christ our Lord.

All: Amen.

Or (the following is adapted from Collection Rituum)

Celebrant: Almighty and merciful God, in virtue of the many apparitions on earth of the Immaculate Virgin Mary, it has pleased You to work miracles again and again for our salvation. Kindly pour out Your blessing † upon this medal (these medals). May all who piously reverence it (them) and devoutly wear it (them) experience the patronage of Mary

Immaculate and obtain mercy from you through
Christ our Lord.

All: Amen.

Conferral of the Medal

The celebrant puts the medal on each of the candidates, saying:

Celebrant: Receive this medal as the sign of your
acceptance into the Association of the Blessed and
Immaculate Virgin Mary. Live in such a way that,
with the help of the Mother of God, you may more and
more put on Christ and manifest Christ living in you,
for the glory of the Trinity, and for the service of the
Church and your neighbor.

All: Amen.

Or (adapted from Collection Rituum):

Celebrant: Receive this holy medal; wear it in faith,
and handle it with suitable devotion. May the most
holy and Immaculate Queen of Heaven protect and
defend you. She is ever ready to renew her wondrous
acts of kindness. May her intercession obtain for you
whatever you humbly ask of God. Both in life and
death may you rest securely in her motherly arms.

All: Amen.

*As circumstances suggest, the celebrant may, in a clear voice,
pronounce the formulas of conferral once for all the recipi-
ents. They all join in replying Amen, then go one by one to
receive the medal from the celebrant. The celebrant, in silence,
sprinkles all present with holy water.*

Concluding Rite

The celebrant continues the rite, saying:

Celebrant: God through the Immaculate Virgin
Mary, so inexpressibly united with your Son, you cause
us to rejoice in your great goodness. As we are supported by her motherly protection, may we never be
without your providential love, and be always dedicat-

ed to the mystery of your redemption with unbounded faith. We ask this through Christ our Lord.

All: Amen.

It is preferable to end the celebration with a suitable song.

(Except as indicated, Rite translated from Latin text approved by the Office of the Congregation for Divine Worship and the Discipline of the Sacraments, September 14, 1990. Permission to reprint granted by Rev. Charles F. Shelby, C.M., director of the Association of the Miraculous Medal, Perryville, Missouri.)

27b. Act of Entrustment to Mary

On October 8, 2000, during the Jubilee of Bishops, Pope John Paul II knelt before a statue of Our Lady of Fatima in St. Peter's Square and led the following prayer in union with over 1500 of the bishops of the world and 80 cardinals, to entrust the entire world and the Church to Mary.

"Woman, behold your Son!" (Jn 19:26).

As we near the end of this Jubilee Year,
when you, O Mother, have offered us Jesus anew,
the blessed fruit of your womb most pure,
the Word made flesh, the world's Redeemer,
we hear more clearly the sweet echo of his words
entrusting us to you, making you our Mother:

"Woman, behold your Son!"

When he entrusted to you the Apostle John,
and with him the children of the Church and all people,
Christ did not diminish but affirmed anew
the role which is his alone as the Savior of the world.

You are the splendor which in no way dims
the light of Christ,
for you exist in him and through him.
Everything in you is fiat: you are the Immaculate One,
through you there shines the fullness of grace.
Here, then, are your children, gathered before you
at the dawn of the new millennium.

The Church today, through the voice of the
Successor of Peter,
in union with so many Pastors assembled here
from every corner of the world,
seeks refuge in your motherly protection
and trustingly begs your intercession
as she faces the challenges which lie hidden
in the future.

In this year of grace, countless people have known
the overflowing joy of the mercy
which the Father has given us in Christ.
In the particular Churches throughout the world,
and still more in this center of Christianity,
the widest array of people have accepted this gift.
Here the enthusiasm of the young rang out,
here the sick have lifted up their prayer.
Here have gathered priests and religious,
artists and journalists,
workers and people of learning,
children and adults,
and all have acknowledged in your beloved Son
the Word of God made flesh in your womb.

O Mother, intercede for us,
that the fruits of this Year will not be lost
and that the seeds of grace will grow

to the full measure of the holiness
to which we are all called.

Today we wish to entrust to you
the future that awaits us,
and we ask you to be with us on our way.

We are the men and women of an extraordinary time,
exhilarating yet full of contradictions.
Humanity now has instruments of
unprecedented power:
we can turn this world into a garden,
or reduce it to a pile of rubble.
We have devised the astounding capacity
to intervene in the very well-springs of life:
man can use this power for good, within the
bounds of the moral law,
or he can succumb to the short-sighted pride
of a science which accepts no limits,
but tramples on the respect due to every human
    being.

Today as never before in the past,
humanity stands at a crossroads.
And once again, O Virgin Most Holy,
salvation lies fully and uniquely in Jesus, your Son.
Therefore, O Mother, like the Apostle John,
we wish to take you into our home (cf. Jn 19:27),
that we may learn from you to become like your Son.

"Woman, behold your son!"

Here we stand before you
to entrust to your maternal care
ourselves, the Church, the entire world.
Plead for us with your beloved Son
that he may give us in abundance the Holy Spirit,
the Spirit of truth which is the fountain of life.
Receive the Spirit for us and with us,
as happened in the first community gathered round you
in Jerusalem on the day of Pentecost (cf. Acts 1:14).
May the Spirit open our hearts to justice and love,

and guide people and nations to mutual understanding
and a firm desire for peace.

We entrust to you all
people, beginning
with the weakest:
the babies yet
unborn,
and those born into
poverty and
suffering,
the young in search
of meaning,
the unemployed,
and those suffering
hunger and disease.
We entrust to you all
troubled families,
the elderly with no
one to help them,
and all who are alone and without hope.

O Mother, you know the sufferings
and hopes of the Church and the world:
come to the aid of your children in the daily trials
which life brings to each one,
and grant that, thanks to the efforts of all,
the darkness will not prevail over the light.

To you, Dawn of Salvation, we commit
our journey through the new Millennium,
so that with you as guide
all people may know Christ,
the light of the world and its only Savior,
who reigns with the Father and the Holy Spirit
for ever and ever. Amen.

27c. Prayer to Mary from Christifidelis Laici
by Pope John Paul II

(same as prayer #65e in some prayer books)

O Most Blessed Virgin Mary, Mother of Christ and Mother of the Church, With joy and wonder we seek to make our own your Magnificat, joining you in your hymn of thankfulness and love.

With you we give thanks to God, "whose mercy is from generation to generation", for the exalted vocation and the many forms of mission entrusted to the lay faithful.

God has called each of them by name to live his own communion of love and holiness and to be one in the great family of God's children.

He has sent them forth to shine with the light of Christ and to communicate the fire of the Spirit in every part of society through their life inspired by the gospel.

O Virgin of the Magnificat, fill their hearts with a gratitude and enthusiasm for this vocation and mission.

With humility and magnanimity you were the "handmaid of the Lord"; give us your unreserved willingness for service to God and the salvation of the world.

Open our hearts to the great anticipation of the Kingdom of God and of the proclamation of the Gospel to the whole of creation. Your mother's heart is ever mindful of the many dangers and evils which threaten to overpower men and women in our time.

At the same time your heart also takes notice of the many initiatives undertaken for good, the great yearning for values, and the progress achieved in bringing forth the abundant fruits of salvation.

O Virgin full of courage, may your spiritual strength and trust in God inspire us, so that we might know how to overcome all the obstacles that we encounter in accomplishing our mission. Teach us to treat the affairs of the world with a real sense of Christian responsibility and a joyful hope of the coming of God's Kingdom, and of a "new heaven and a new earth".

You who were gathered in prayer with the Apostles in the Cenacle, awaiting the coming of the Spirit at Pentecost, implore his renewed outpouring on all the faithful, men and women alike, so that they might more fully respond to their vocation and mission, as branches engrafted to the true vine, called to bear much fruit for the life of the world.

O Virgin Mother, guide and sustain us so that we might always live as true sons and daughters of the Church of your Son. Enable us to do our part in helping to establish on earth the civilization of truth and love, as God wills it, for his glory. Amen.

29b. Act of Faith and Intercession
*A Fatima prayer often prayed during Mass
at the Consecration*

My Jesus, I believe, I adore, I trust, and I love You. I ask pardon for those who do not believe, do not adore, do not trust, and do not love You. Amen.

30. The Memorare

Remember, O most gracious Virgin Mary, that never was it known that anyone who fled to your protection, implored your help or sought your intercession was left unaided. Inspired by this confidence, we fly unto you, O Virgin of virgins, our Mother. To you do we come, before you we stand sinful and sorrowful. O Mother of the Word Incarnate, despise not our petitions but in your mercy hear and answer us. Amen.

32. Miraculous Medal Prayer
Expanded by St. Maximilian Kolbe

O Mary, conceived without sin, pray for us who have recourse to you, and for those who do not have recourse to you, especially the enemies of the Church and those who are recommended to you.

32a. Meditation Prayer with the Miraculous Medal
by Fr. Bernard Geiger, OFM Conv.

Mary, this medal is a sign and a guarantee of your presence. You are present because your power is present, your voice is present and your love is present.

Therefore, O wonderful, sinless Woman and our mystical Mother, we call on you now to fulfill your guarantee.

Bring us the great graces you promised to those who carry this medal, especially to those who wear it around the neck. Make us perceive your presence now and always. Make us consciously experience your power, your love and your guidance, that in their strength, we may begin to share in your perfect response to God, and to each of His creatures and join in your war with the ancient Serpent.

Help us utterly abandon our self-centered feelings and preoccupations. Help us hear and understand you. Teach us to listen and learn. Help us respond to you today and always, that made one with you, we might more fully respond with the rest of the Church to the Father, Son and Holy Spirit, participating in their life and unity. Amen.

33. First Saturdays Reparation Promise

In December, 1940, Sister Lucia (one of the seers of Fatima) wrote to Pope Pius XII: "Most Holy Father...in a revelation [our Lady] asked that a Communion for the purpose of reparation on the First Saturday of five consecutive months be propagated throughout the world and also for the same purpose, Confession (if necessary), meditation for a quarter of an hour on one or more of the mysteries of the Rosary, and the meditative recitation of five decades of the Rosary, all for the purpose of making reparation for the insults, sacrileges and indifferences committed against her Immaculate Heart."

According to Sister Lucia, our Lady promised to assist at the hour of death with all the graces necessary for salvation all those who would fulfill the aforementioned acts of reparation on the First Saturday of five consecutive months.

34. Litany of Joyful Thanksgiving
Try to recite part or all on Sundays

Before retiring, thank God for something specific and possibly reflect on one of the following points. The key is to have a thankful and joyful disposition in good times and in bad.

Jesus, help us now to pause for a few moments and to think of all the spiritual and material gifts that You have showered upon us, our families, and the entire human race.

- Lord, You have given us an immortal life.

- Lord, You took upon Yourself our nature, and have

made us members of your royal family and heirs of the thrones in Heaven.

- Lord, You loved us so, that You died for us on Calvary, so that we could be with you for all eternity.

- You created Your Mother immaculate and You loved her above all creation, yet You shared Mary with us by making her our Mother as well.

- You created St. Joseph and allowed him to be the guardian of Your children on earth.

- You created the billions of angels and saints and allowed them to help us in our earthly pilgrimage.

- You allow us to be present at Your sacrificial offering to the Father at Mass every day.

- You humble yourself in the Holy Eucharist to become our daily bread. Your Eucharistic Presence in all the tabernacles of the world continually intercedes for us with our Father.

- You instituted the other sacraments to give us strength, while Your Church guides us on the narrow path to eternal paradise.

- You have given us many sacramentals, such as the Brown Scapular of Our Lady of Mount Carmel, to remind us of the spiritual realities that affect our lives, and to properly dispose us for the reception of special graces You want to confer on us.

- And most of all, Jesus, You sent Your Most Holy Spirit to dwell within us. Through Baptism, You have made an interior heaven within us. You have truly made us a temple of the Holy Spirit of the Father and Yourself. You daily give us opportunities to become one spirit with You by interiorly uniting ourselves with Your Spirit who dwells within us closer than our very breath (cf. 1 Corinthians 3:16-17).

- Indeed Lord, what else can You do for us that You have not already done?

Pause and thank God for His specific blessings. You may want to reflect on just one of these gifts each day.

34c. Canticle of the Lord's Day in Honor of the Holy Family

Recommended as the prayer before dinner on Saturday evening

All stand for the Angelus. (On Easter until Pentecost, the Angelus is replaced by the Regina Caeli.)

(1) The Angelus

L: The Angel of the Lord declared unto Mary,
All: And she conceived by the Holy Spirit.
Hail Mary...

L: Behold the handmaid of the Lord,
All: Be it done unto me according to Your word.
Hail Mary...

L: And the Word was made flesh, (all genuflect)
All: And dwelt among us.
Hail Mary...

L: Pray for us, O Holy Mother of God,
All: That we may be made worthy of the promises of Christ.

L: Let us pray,
All: Pour forth, we beseech Thee, O Lord, Thy grace into our hearts, that we to whom the Incarnation of Christ Thy Son was made known by the message of an angel, may by His Passion and Cross be brought to the glory of His Resurrection, through the same Christ Our Lord. Amen.

(1a) Regina Caeli (from Easter until Pentecost)

All: Queen of heaven, rejoice! Alleluia.
For he whom you merited to bear. Alleluia.
Has risen, as he said. Alleluia.
Pray for us to God. Alleluia.

L: Rejoice and be glad, O Virgin Mary. Alleluia.
All: Because the Lord is truly risen. Alleluia.

L: Let us pray,
All: O God, Who by the Resurrection of Your Son, our Lord Jesus Christ, granted joy to the whole world: grant we beg You, that through the intercession of the Virgin Mary His Mother, we may lay hold of the joys of eternal life, through the same Christ our Lord. Amen.

(2) **Announcement of the Lord's Day**

L: Brothers and sisters, this is the Lord's Day.

All: Let us welcome it in joy and peace.

L: Today we set aside our concerns of the week that we may honor the Lord and celebrate His Resurrection. Today we cease from our work in order to worship God and to remember the eternal life to which He has called us.

All: The Lord Himself is with us to refresh and strengthen us.

(3) **A Sung Grace** (to the tune of *Edelweiss*)

Bless our friends, bless our food.
Come, O Lord and sit with us.
May our talk glow with peace,
Bring Your love to surround us.
Friendship and peace, may it bloom and grow,
Bloom and grow forever.
Bless our friends, bless our food,
Bless our dear home forever.

(4) **Lighting of the Candle**

All are seated. As the candle is lit, the following is prayed:

L: Blessed are You, Lord our God, who created light on the first day and raised Your Son, the Light of the World, to begin the new creation.

All: We are the light of the world, and the salt of the earth.

(5) **Meditation on the Holy Family**

L: At this time we call to mind the unity of the Holy Family of Nazareth. We recall that the Boy Jesus, after He was found in the temple by His earthly parents, Joseph and Mary, "went down with them, and came to Nazareth and was subject to them" (Luke 2:51). Sacred Scripture also tells us that under the care of Joseph and Mary, Jesus "advanced in wisdom and age and favor before God and man" (Luke 2:52).

All: "O Gentle Jesus, let every worthy feeling of ours show You love, take delight in You, and admire You. O God of our hearts and our inheritance, Christ Jesus, may our hearts mellow before the influence of Your Spirit, and may You live in us. May the flame of Your love burn in our souls." (Prayer of St. Augustine)

L: We honor Mary, the Immaculate Mother of Jesus Christ. St. Luke tells us in his Gospel, that the words and actions of the Child Jesus made deep impressions on the interior life of Mary, since it states twice that she "kept all these things, reflecting on them in her heart" (Luke 2:19, 52).

All: "Most Holy Spirit, give us a great trust in Mary's maternal heart, and a continuous access to her compassion, so that with her, You may truly form Jesus, great and powerful, in us, until we attain the fullness of His perfect age. Amen." (Prayer of St. Louis de Montfort)

L: We also honor St. Joseph because, due to his "trustworthiness and meekness, God selected him from all mankind" to be the foster-father of Jesus, the Incarnate Wisdom. (Sirach 45:4)

L: "Behold the faithful and prudent servant,

All: Whom the Lord set over His House." (Preface for the Solemnity of St. Joseph)

(6) Reflection on the Unity of the Holy Family and Thanksgiving

The bread is passed. Each person tears off a piece of the bread. All eat while reflecting on the unity of the Holy Family and the ways in which this unity may be imitated in his/her family. The leader then reads the following.

L: Let us reflect in the four following points which culminate in the "Marian Multiplier":

1. Sin is the cause of all unhappiness.
2. Grace is more powerful than sin.
3. Our holiness is essential, but it is not enough to convert the world.

4. Therefore we need Mary, because "our good works passing through Mary's hands are progressively purified. Consequently, their merit and satisfactory and prayer value is also increased." (St. Louis de Montfort, *True Devotion to the Blessed Virgin,* 172)

The wine or juice is passed. Each person pours a little into his/her glass, but does not drink it yet. Then each person takes a turn saying something for which he/she is thankful, ending with "Amen." All respond, "Amen." He/she then takes a drink. When all are done, the leader says the following.

L: God Our Father, may the bread we have shared be a sign of the unity we are called to live, and may we live in a manner worthy of our calling. Pope John Paul II reminds us that "the future of the world and the Church, passes through the family." Pour out upon us Your Mercy, and keep all families one in the fellowship of love. May the members and friends of the Apostolate for Family Consecration be used as your instruments to make your Church a living presence in the midst of our world.

All: Amen. All for the Sacred and Eucharistic Heart of Jesus, all through the Sorrowful and Immaculate Heart of Mary, all in union with St. Joseph. Amen.

(7) **End of the Meal Song** (to the tune of *Edelweiss*)
When everyone has finished eating their dinner, stand and sing the following song of thanksgiving.

Hear our thanks, Father God,
Thanks, O Son for You're with us.
Thanks for words giving peace,
Making our love sincere.
Friendship and peace, let it bloom and grow,
Bloom and grow forever.
Thanks for friends, thanks for food,
Thanks for our home, dear Father.

40. Litany of the Patrons of the Apostolate for Family Consecration
Try to recite on Tuesdays

Petition-Leader

Response

God the Father, Our Creator,

God the Son, our Redeemer,

God the Holy Spirit, our Consoler,

Holy Trinity, One God,

Most Sacred and Eucharistic Heart of Jesus,

Have mercy on my family and The Apostolate.

Most Sorrowful and Immaculate Heart of Mary,

St. Joseph, our Guardian,

Most Holy Family, our Example,

St. Anne and St. Joachim,

St. John the Baptist,

Form my family and The Apostolate.

St. Michael, Prince of Angels,

St. Raphael, Guardian of married couples,

St. Gabriel, Guardian of those consecrated to Mary,

Holy Choir of the Seraphim, Standard for a God-centered life,

Holy Choir of the Cherubim, Pillar of Faith and Purity,

Holy Choir of the Thrones, Mainstay for higher units of authority,

Holy Choir of the Dominions, Pillar of spiritual authority,

Holy Choir of the Virtues, Advocate of the spiritual life,

Holy Choir of the Powers, Mainstay against the demons,

Holy Choir of the Principalities, Protector of parishes, lay ecclesial teams, and spiritual associations,

Protect my family and The Apostolate.

Holy Choir of the Archangels, Advocate of religious and lay apostles,

Holy Choir of the Angels, Guardians of the People of God,

Our own guardian angels,

Protect my family and The Apostolate.

St. Peter, our first Holy Father,

St. Paul the Evangelist,

St. John the Evangelist,

St. James the Apostle,

St. Andrew the Apostle,

St. Philip the Apostle,

St. Bartholomew the Apostle,

St. Thomas the Apostle,

St. Matthew the Apostle,

St. James the Less,

St. Simon the Apostle,

St. Jude the Apostle, and Patron of desperate cases,

St. Matthias the Apostle,

Intercede for my family and The Apostolate.

St. Tarsicius, standard for Eucharistic devotion,

St. Maria Goretti, patroness of purity,

St. Francis of Assisi, standard for Christian renewal,

St. Dominic, patron of the Holy Rosary,

St. Thomas Aquinas, patron of Catholic education,

St. John Neumann, patron of catechists,

St. Ignatius Loyola, defender of the Faith,

St. Jerome, patron of Scripture studies,

St. Patrick, patron of God-centered countries,

St. Teresa of Avila, model for the interior life and devotion to St. Joseph,

St. Therese, the Little Flower, patroness of the active apostolate, and the Little Way,

Pray for my family and The Apostolate.

St. Margaret Mary, patroness of devotion to the Sacred Heart,

St. Catherine of Siena, model for lay celibates,

St. Louis de Montfort, patron of total consecration,

St. Martin de Porres, patron of the suffering,

St. John Bosco, patron of youth,

St. Nicholas, patron of those in financial need,

St. Dominic Savio, patron of youthful deaths,

St. Maximilian Kolbe, model for Marian devotion,

St. Vincent Pallotti, patron of the lay apostolate,

St. John Vianney, patron of parish priests,

St. Elizabeth Ann Seton, patroness of Catholic schools,

St. Thomas More, patron of fidelity to the Holy Father,

St. Juan Diego, patron of the Catholic Corps Men's Community and model for lay evangelists,

St. Faustina, model for devotion to Divine Mercy,

St. Pio of Pietrelcina, model for obedience,

St. Josemaria Escriva, model for sanctification of one's daily work,

St. Catherine Laboure, patroness of the Miraculous Medal,

St. Simon Stock, patron of the Brown Scapular of Mount Carmel

Blessed Teresa of Calcutta, model for acceptance

Blessed Kateri Tekakwitha, model for humility and patroness of the Catholic Corp Women's Community,

Blessed Jacinta and Francisco, patrons of the Fatima message,

Our own Patron Saints,

Amen.

Pray for my family and The Apostolate.

41. The Scapular Confraternity

41a. Indulgences Granted to the Order of Carmel on the 17th of September, 1968

All Scapular Confraternity members and Lay Carmelites are included in two Plenary Indulgences: the "Portiuncula Indulgence" on August second, and "The Solemn Commemoration of Our Lady of Mt. Carmel" on July sixteenth.

Notes

The official and most complete teaching of the meaning of indulgences is contained in the Apostolic Constitution of Pope Paul VI *On Indulgences* (1967).

Indulgences are best understood in the context of our Christian faith and the doctrine of the Communion of Saints. Death does not end our relationships with those we love and with those who have died in the spirit of faith. We have spiritual responsibilities to our deceased Carmelites, relatives, and friends, as well as all the Faithful Departed. We can assist them through our prayers and good works. Indulgences when seen in this way and not as an accumulation of spiritual "treasures" are a dispensing and application of the merits of Christ and the saints.

Scapular Confraternity

The Confraternity of the Brown Scapular is an association of people with a common dedication to the following of Jesus Christ under the loving protection of Our Lady of Mount Carmel. Membership in the Confraternity occurs when a person is enrolled in the Brown Scapular. Due to large numbers, the listing of members is open; no records are maintained of membership.

Wearing the brown scapular promises the wearer a share in the prayers and good works of the entire Carmelite family. Not only a privileged sign of affiliation to the Carmelite Order, the scapular is also a highly indulgenced sacramental. It inspires those who wear it, committing them to live their lives in the spirit of Our Lady.

Tradition tells us that Our Lady appeared to St. Simon Stock at Aylesford, England, in 1251, holding out to him the Scapular and making the "great promise," *"This shall be a sign for you and for Carmelites. Whoever dies in this shall not suffer eternal fire."*

A second Scapular promise concerns prompt deliverance from Purgatory. Known as the Sabbatine Privilege, it links the Scapular to Saturday, Our Lady's day. It spells out the requirements of a genuine Christian life: prayer, penance, purity, and fidelity to the sacraments.

The Brown Scapular, as well as the Rosary, is also linked to the appearances of Our Lady to three young children in Fatima, Portugal. Her final appearance on October 13, 1917, was as Our Lady of Mount Carmel with the Scapular.

Part of the message of Fatima is the Scapular as a means of "entrusting" ourselves to the Immaculate Heart of Mary, consecrating ourselves as she did to the following of her Son, Jesus Christ.

41b. Some Scapular Facts

1. The cloth Scapular may be made of any cloth material, brown in color.

2. The strings connecting the two pieces of cloth may be of any color or material, e.g., silver chain.

3. The scapular is worn over the shoulders, one piece in front and one in back. It is not necessary to wear it next to the skin; it may be worn over one's clothes or enclosed in a covering or locket, front and back.

4. Enrollment in the Brown Scapular need only be done once. If one who is enrolled in the Scapular should put it aside for a time, even for years, a new enrollment is not necessary. The person simply puts it on and begins again to share in Our Lady's promise and the indulgences granted by the Church.

5. Though the Sabbatine Privilege has been questioned historically, it is approved by the Church and it has been believed by the faithful for over six centuries.

6. The scapular medal may be substituted for the cloth scapular, according to a permission granted by St. Pius X.

Editor's Note: Sabbatine Privileges for Members of the Apostolate for Family Consecration

On July 15, 1976, Reverend Howard Rafferty, O.Carm., the National Director of the Brown Scapular Confraternity and member of the Apostolate's Advisory Council, extended the Sabbatine Privilege to all of the members and benefactors of the Apostolate for Family Consecration who fulfill the following conditions:

- Wear the Brown Scapular or Scapular Medal of Our Lady of Mount Carmel faithfully;

- Observe chastity according to one's state in life;

- Daily perform one of the following spiritual exercises:
  – at least a half hour adoration of the Blessed Sacrament,

   – or recite five decades of the Rosary,
   – or walk the Stations of the Cross,
   – or read or listen to Sacred Scripture for half an
       hour.

Note: These are the same conditions as those for gaining a plenary indulgence. See section 45a.

Privileges

The Brown Scapular is a sign of an interior life, a sign of consecration to Jesus through Mary, who is the Immaculate Conception and perfect model for all of us to imitate.

When we wear the Scapular faithfully and devoutly, we will have Our Lady's protection in life and her special help at the hour of death. The Sabbatine or Saturday Privilege is based on a bull said to have been issued on March 3, 1322, by Pope John XXII. The privilege is commonly understood to mean that those who wear the Scapular and fulfill the other conditions will be freed from Purgatory on the first Saturday after death.

However, the Church officially states in explanation of this privilege, in its decree on the Congregation of Index, January 20, 1613, and later called by Pope Benedict XIV a "very wise decree," is that those who fulfill the conditions will be released from Purgatory through the intercession of Our Lady soon after death, and especially on Saturdays.

One of the advantages to members of the Family Apostolate who are properly enrolled and wear the Brown Scapular of Our Lady is that they share not only in the combined good works of all the members of the Family Apostolate, but also in the good works of the entire Carmelite Order throughout the world and of the more than 200 million members of the Scapular Confraternity.

41c. Blessing and Conferral of the
Brown Scapular
(See note on page 10)

Introduction

The blessing and conferral of the Brown Scapular should, if at all possible, be carried out in a communal celebration. The blessing and clothing with the Scapular of the Blessed Virgin Mary of Mt. Carmel enrolls the individual in the Scapular Confraternity. All priests have the faculty to enroll.

On the occasion of the blessing and conferral, the cloth scapular itself must be used; afterwards a blessed medal may replace the scapular.

Ceremony of Clothing

Blessing and clothing with the Scapular of the Blessed Virgin Mary of Mt. Carmel enrolls the individual in the Scapular Confraternity, a prayer organization almost as large as the Church itself. This Ceremony is usually performed after the reception of First Holy Communion. Today many converts ask to be enrolled in the Brown Scapular of Our Lady.

The following Ceremony, in English, is used by the priest. If Scapulars, only, are to be blessed, the priest begins the blessing with "Show us, O Lord, Your mercy" and ends the blessing with the prayer "O Lord Jesus Christ...."

The Short Formula of Enrollment and Blessing

Priest: Show us, O Lord, Your mercy.

All: And grant us Your salvation.

Priest: O Lord, hear my prayer.

All: And let my cry come to You.

Priest: The Lord be with you.

All: And also with you.

Priest: Let us pray:

O Lord Jesus Christ, Savior of mankind, * by Your right hand sanctify these Scapulars [this Scapular] * which Your servants will devoutly wear for the love of You * and of Your Mother, the Blessed Virgin Mary of Mt. Carmel; * so that, by her intercession, * they may be protected from the wickedness of the enemy and persevere in Your grace until death; * Who live and reign for ever and ever.

All: Amen.

The priest now sprinkles the Scapular with Holy Water, after which he places the Scapular on each one saying:

Priest: Receive this blessed Scapular and ask the Most Holy Virgin that, by her merits, it may be worn with no stain of sin and may protect you from all harm and bring you into everlasting life.

All: Amen.

Priest: By the power granted to me, I admit you to a share in all the spiritual works performed, with the merciful help of Jesus Christ, by the Religious of Mount Carmel; in the name of the Father, and of the Son † and of the Holy Spirit.

All: Amen.

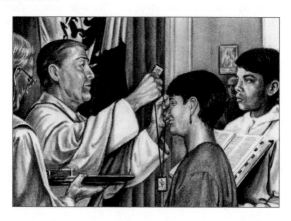

Priest: May Almighty God, Creator of heaven and earth, bless † you * whom He has been pleased to receive into the Confraternity of the Blessed Virgin Mary of Mount Carmel. * We beg her to crush the head of the ancient serpent in the hour of your death, * and, in the end, to obtain for you a palm and the crown of your everlasting inheritance. * Through Christ Our Lord.

All: Amen.

The priest now sprinkles those enrolled with Holy Water.

Note: From Carmel's Call, 9th Edition, Edited by Rev. Howard Rafferty, O. Carm.Used with permission.

41d. Pope John Paul II Speaks on the Scapular

On Sunday, July 24, 1988, at Castel Gandolfo, the Holy Father, Pope John Paul II, introduced the midday Angelus and spoke about Our Lady, Flos Carmeli, [the Flower of Carmel], as possessing all the virtues. His words are as follows.

"In this month of July we have commemorated Our Lady of Mount Carmel, so dear to the piety of the Christian people throughout the world, and linked in a special way to the great Carmelite religious family.

"Our thoughts go to the holy mountain which in the biblical world is always considered as a symbol of grace, blessing and beauty. On this mountain the Carmelites dedicated their first church to the Virgin Mother of God, *"Flos Carmeli,"* who possesses the beauty of all the virtues. They thus expressed their desire to entrust themselves completely to her, and to link indissolubly their service of Mary with that "in submission to Christ" (cf. Carmelite Rule, Prologue).

"The great Carmelite mystics have understood the experience of God in their lives as a "way of perfection" (St. Teresa of Jesus), as an "ascent of Mount Carmel" (St. John of the Cross). On this itinerary Mary is present. Invoked by the Carmelites as Mother, Patroness, and Sister, as the Most Pure Virgin she becomes a model of contemplation, sensitive to hearing and contemplating God's word, and obedient to the Father's will through Christ in the Holy

Spirit. For this reason, in Carmel and in every deeply Carmelite soul, there flourishes a life of intense communion and familiarity with the Blessed Virgin, as a "new way" of living for God and of continuing here on earth the love of Jesus the Son for his Mother Mary.

"A particular favor of Our Lady for the Carmelites, associated with St. Simon Stock according to a venerable tradition, has spread among the Christian people with many spiritual fruits. It is the scapular of Carmel, a means of affiliation to the Carmelite Order through sharing in its spiritual benefits and an instrument of tender filial Marian devotion (cf. Pius XII, Apostolic Letter *Nemini Profecto Latet*).

"Through the scapular, those devoted to Our Lady of Mount Carmel express their desire to mould their existence on the example of Mary as Mother, Patroness, Sister, and Most Pure Virgin; to accept God's word with a purified heart and to devote themselves to the zealous service of others.

"I now invite all those devoted to the Blessed Virgin to offer a fervent prayer so that through her intercession she may obtain that everyone travel safely along life's journey and 'successfully reach the Holy Mountain, Jesus Christ Our Lord' (cf. Prayer of the Mass of Our Lady of Mount Carmel, July 16)."

L'Osservatore Romano, English Edition, August 1, 1988, p. 12. Used with permission. Printed with Ecclesial Approbation

See Cardinal Ciappi's letter in Day 37 on page 194.

42a. Reparation and the Dual Dimension of Pope John Paul II's Consecration

See Days 35–37 on pages 171–194.

43b. Spiritual Poverty is Worse than Physical Poverty: Reflections by Blessed Mother Teresa of Calcutta and Fr. John A. Hardon, S.J.

Excerpts from videotaped interviews by Jerry and Gwen Coniker

Jerry Coniker: Sin is the cause of all unhappiness in the world. And Bishop Sheen said it once—that the starving people in the Third World were suffering for the sins of Western civilization. Fr. Hardon, I know you said this many times. And Mother, I think that it's so hard for us in this part of the world, but here you deal with the poor—and the real hunger is the spiritual hunger, isn't it?

Mother Teresa: I find that this hunger and this poverty much much harder than the hunger of our poor people. I have been to Ethiopia for a fortnight with our sisters there, and we have many houses. The people are dying of hunger, but they are dying with such dignity. No cursing.

Fr. Hardon: Mother, as you know, whenever there is spiritual hunger, there must be somebody who can provide spiritual food.

Mother Teresa: Exactly.

Fr. Hardon: Now material food we can get. But, Mother, where do you find who is willing and able to supply the spiritual food? That's why I have been encouraging the Apostolate for Family Consecration. In other words you cannot give what you do not have.

Mother Teresa: Exactly.

Fr. Hardon: Unless people have a deep faith, a deep love of God, they can not give it to others. So these people are hungry, but there must be somebody who can provide a spiritual nourishment.

Mother Teresa: Yes, but that's why Jesus made Himself the Bread of Life, to satisfy that hunger. That's why we must bring them to Jesus. He's the answer. He will satisfy that hunger. He will satisfy with peace and with joy, and He will give unity.

Jerry Coniker: So you are saying that the hunger here in America is worse because of the spiritual poverty?

Mother Teresa: **Oh yes. Because there's a terrible hunger for love.** They are just left alone, unwanted, unloved. Left alone. And so I find that much more difficult to forgive because it's in the heart, and they find it difficult to forgive. That's a terrible hunger.

But there must be somebody to bring Christ, to bring the soul that is destroyed by many sins—to help him to go to Confession, no? We go to Confession a sinner full of sin. And we come from Confession a sinner without sin.

In a later videotaped interview with Jerry Coniker, Dr. Burns Seeley, and Fr. John A. Hardon, SJ:

Fr. Hardon: In fact John Chrysostom, one of the Church's great doctors, declares the principal meaning of the 25th Chapter of Matthew's Gospel—that the last day **is not, says Chrysostom**, feeding the hungry and giving drink to the thirsty and clothing the naked in body. It is mainly feeding the hungry and giving drink to the thirsty and clothing the naked in spirit!

What people mainly need is love, generosity, faith, sharing our spirit with others, especially the supernatural gifts of the spirit that God has given to us.

In fact, this is my definition of the Apostolate for Family Consecration: sharing supernatural gifts, period. Sharing supernatural gifts!

Jerry Coniker: Remember when we met with Mother Teresa in the Bronx, and we videotaped her there, and she said she had many communities in Ethiopia, but the spiritual poverty in America was worse than the starvation in Ethiopia?

Fr. Hardon: Undoubtedly.

Jerry Coniker: Mother Teresa said that.

Fr. Hardon: Undoubtedly. **And the both marvelous and frightening thing is that we who have the Faith, who have been so graced by God, how can we ever have gotten to the point that we are not eager, anxious, restless, burning with zeal to give to others what God has given to us.**

45a. Summary of Norms for Gaining Indulgences for the Holy Souls in Purgatory or Oneself
Issued by Pope Paul VI on January 1, 1967
Try to partially review on Mondays

A **plenary indulgence** is a complete release from the temporal punishment due for sins already forgiven (as far as their guilt is concerned). Only one plenary indulgence may be obtained a day for oneself or a Holy Soul in Purgatory (see #51b, questions 11 and 19).

Conditions for a plenary indulgence:

A. One must be baptized and in the state of grace.

B. One must receive Holy Communion each time a plenary indulgence is sought.

C. One must go to Confession several days preceding or following the indulgenced action. A single sacramental Confession suffices for gaining several plenary indulgences.

D. One must have a disposition of mind and heart which totally excludes all attachment to sin, even venial sin, otherwise one can only gain a partial indulgence.

E. One must pray for the intentions of the Holy Father, the Pope, preferably one "Our Father" and one "Hail Mary," however, any other pious prayer may be substituted.

F. One must have at least a general intention to gain a plenary indulgence.

G. One must perform the indulgenced work (see below and section 45b).

A plenary indulgence may be obtained every day by completing *one* of the following works, provided the conditions mentioned above have been fulfilled:

- At least a half hour of adoration of the Blessed Sacrament;

- *or* the private recitation of the Rosary before the Blessed Sacrament or with others in your family, religious community, or pious association;

- *or* at least a half hour of pious reading of or listening to Sacred Scripture (via tape, CD, radio, etc.);*

- *or* walking the Stations of the Cross in a church or with a properly erected display of the Stations.

A partial indulgence removes part of the temporal punishment due for sins already forgiven. Several partial indulgences may be obtained each day.

Conditions for a partial indulgence:

A. One must be baptized and in the state of grace.

B. One must be inwardly contrite [have at least a striving intention to cut oneself off from all attachment to sin].

C. One must have a general intention to gain an indulgence.

D. One must fulfill the action prescribed in *one* of the following three general grants of indulgences:

- Raise one's mind in humble prayer to God while fulfilling one's responsibilities and enduring the trials of life.

- Give of one's time or goods as a charitable act to assist people who are in need of spiritual comfort or instruction or who are in need of material assistance (donation of time and resources to the work of the Church are, therefore, indulgenced).

- Voluntarily deprive oneself of what is lawful and pleasing, such as giving up dessert or a favorite TV program.

For more information on indulgences, see the "Catechism of the Catholic Church," sections 1030-1032, 1471-1479, and 1498. See *pages 316–320 for additional grants for indulgences.*

---

* See Francis Cardinal Stafford's letter on page 314.

TRIBUNALE
DELLA
PENITENZIERIA APOSTOLICA
Prot. N. 337/04/I   October 26, 2004

Dear Mr. Coniker,

...This Apostolic Penitentiary will do its best to answer
your questions about indulgences. It would take a commentary on the Apostolic Constitution *Indulgentiarum doctrina,*
on Indulgences, 1 January 1967: AAS (1967) 5-24 of Pope
Paul VI, to do justice to questions on indulgences.

1. The norm for gaining a partial indulgence
In the above-mentioned Apostolic Constitution, Pope Paul
VI re-presented the Church's doctrine and discipline regarding indulgences. We read under Norm 5: *Any of the faithful
who, being at least inwardly contrite, perform a work carrying with it a partial indulgence, receive through the Church
the remission of temporal punishment equivalent to what
their own act already receives.* This is what Fr. William
Most meant when he said that indulgences are an added satisfactory power over and above the merits of good acts and
the reception of the sacraments. The more intense the fervor
of charity with which the faithful fulfill their obligations etc.,
proportionately greater is the partial indulgence granted
through the Church.

This is clearly seen in the three general types of indulgenced
grants which *have for their purpose to encourage the
Christian faithful to structure into the texture of their everyday activities a Christian spirit and to gear their lives
toward the perfection of charity* (Handbook of Indulgences
Catholic Book Publishing Co. 1991, n.1, p.25).

Grant I: *A partial indulgence is granted to the Christian
faithful who, while performing their duties and enduring the
difficulties of life, raise their minds in humble trust to God and
make, at least mentally, some pious invocation.*

Grant II: *A partial indulgence is granted to the
Christian faithful who, prompted by a spirit of faith, devote*

themselves or their goods in compassionate service to their brothers and sisters in need.

Grant III: *A partial indulgence is granted to the Christian faithful who, in a spirit of penitence, voluntarily abstain from something which is licit for and pleasing to them.*

2. As regards the reading of Sacred Scripture Cardinal William Wakefield Baum had mentioned to you that this "is under study and will no doubt be incorporated into the new edition of the manual of Indulgences". Since the latest edition of the manual of indulgences has not as yet been published in English, we give you a running translation of the new norm, added as paragraph two, to the grant regarding the reading of Sacred Scripture (n.30): *if for a reasonable cause one is unable to read, the plenary or partial indulgence as above, is granted if the text of Sacred Scripture is followed while another person reads it, or write it is transmitted by television or radio.*

3. Shut–ins reciting the rosary together with one actually being broadcast Regarding the possibility of gaining a plenary indulgence for the recitation of the rosary by one who is physically alone but united to those who are actually reciting the rosary on the radio or television, this, at the present moment, is only foreseen when the rosary is recited in union with the Holy Father: 1. *The plenary indulgence is granted to the Christian faithful who... 2°Piously unites himself to the above mentioned prayer while it is being said by the Holy Father and transmitted by television or radio* (n. 17, §1, 2°).

With prayerful best wishes to you, we are

Sincerely yours in the Lord Jesus,

James Francis Card. Stafford

James Francis Cardinal Stafford
Major Penitentiary

P. Gianfranco Girotti, O.F.M.Conv.

P. Gianfranco Girotti, O.F.M.Conv.
Regent

45b. Additional Grants for Indulgences

The following grants are taken from The Handbook of Indulgences, *the authorized English edition published by Catholic Book Publishing Co. (Resource #506-555-22, see page 515). The indulgences are granted in accord with the norms summarized in section 45a.*

(13) Visiting a Cemetery

An indulgence is granted the Christian faithful who devoutly visit a cemetery and pray, if only mentally, for the dead. This indulgence is applicable only to the souls in purgatory. This indulgence is a *plenary* one from November 1 through November 8 and can be gained on each one of these days. On the other days of the year this indulgence is a *partial* one.

(15) Act of Spiritual Communion

An act of spiritual communion, expressed in any devout formula whatsoever, is endowed with a *partial indulgence*.

(17) Adoration of the Cross

A *plenary indulgence* is granted the Christian faithful who devoutly take part in the adoration of the cross during the solemn liturgy of Good Friday.

(20) Teaching or Studying Christian Doctrine

A *partial indulgence* is granted the Christian faithful who either teach or study Christian doctrine.

N.B.—A person who teaches Christian doctrine prompted by a spirit of faith and charity can acquire a partial indulgence in accord with the second general type of indulgenced grant mentioned on page 312.

This present grant, number 20, restates the *partial indulgence* as regards the teacher but extends it also to include the person who studies Christian doctrine.

(25) Retreats

A *plenary indulgence* is granted the Christian faithful who spend at least three full days of spiritual exercises during a retreat.

(34) Novena Prayers

A *partial indulgence* is granted the Christian faithful who devoutly take part in a publicly celebrated novena before the solemnity of Christmas, Pentecost, or the Immaculate Conception of the Blessed Virgin Mary.

(35) Use of Devotional Objects

The Christian faithful obtain a *partial indulgence* when they make devout use of a devotional object (such as a crucifix or cross, a rosary, a scapular, or a medal) which has been rightly blessed by any priest or deacon.

If the devotional object has been blessed by the Pope or by any bishop, the Christian faithful can obtain a *plenary indulgence* while making devout use of it on the solemnity of the holy apostles, Peter and Paul, provided they add it its use a profession of faith made in any legitimate formula.

This grant is taken from the apostolic constitution *Indulgentiarum doctrina*, norm 16.

(38) Mental Prayer

A *partial indulgence* is granted the Christian faithful who devoutly spent time in mental prayer.

(41) Listening to Preaching

A *partial indulgence* is granted the Christian faithful who attentively and devoutly assist at the preaching of the Word of God.

A *plenary indulgence* is granted the Christian faithful who on the occasion of a mission have heard some of the sermons and are present for its solemn conclusion.

(45) Monthly Period of Recollection

A *partial indulgence* is granted the Christian faithful who participate in a monthly period of recollection. [In the Apostolate for Family Consecration, we recommend this take place on the first Saturday of every month, as part of the First Saturday Fatima devotion.]

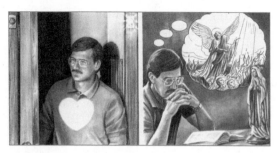

(65) Visiting a Parish Church

A *plenary indulgence* is granted the Christian faithful who devoutly make a visit to a parish church:

1) on its titular feast day

2) on August 2, the day on which the *Portiuncula* indulgence occurs.

These same indulgences can be obtained either on the days mentioned above or on other days determined by the Ordinary [diocesan bishop] so that the faithful can take better advantage of them.

The same indulgences are also attached to the cathedral church and, if there be one, to the co-cathedral church, even if neither of these is a parish church. They are also attached to a quasi-parish church.

These *indulgences are already contained in the apostolic constitution,* Indulgentiarum doctrina, *norm 15. They are included here in light of the Sacred Penitentiary's deliberations since the constitution was issued.*

*According to norm 16 of the apostolic constitution, this visit is to include the "recitation of the Lord's Prayer and the Creed (*Pater *and* Credo*).*

(67) Visiting a Church or an Oratory on All Souls Day, November 2

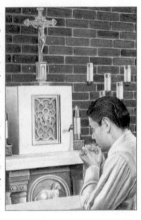

A *plenary indulgence* which is applicable only to the souls in purgatory is granted the Christian faithful who devoutly visit a church or an oratory on All Souls Day.

This indulgence can be obtained either on the day mentioned above or, with the consent of the ordinary, on the preceding or following Sunday or on the solemnity of All Saints.

This indulgence is already contained in the apostolic constitution, Indulgentiarum doctrina, *norm 15. It is included here in light of the Sacred Penitentiary's deliberations since the constitution was issued.*

According to norm 16 of the apostolic constitution, this visit is to include the "recitation of the Lord's Prayer and the Creed (Pater and Credo).

Note: For the complete authorized English Edition of the Handbook of Indulgences: Norms and Grants, *published by Catholic Book Publishing Company, call 1-800-77-FAMILY and ask for Resource #506-555-22, or order online at www.familyland.org.*

46. Veni Creator
Try to recite on Mondays.

Come, O Creator Spirit blest,
And in our souls take up Thy rest;
Come with Thy grace and heavenly aid
To fill the hearts which Thou hast made.

Great Paraclete, to Thee we cry,
O highest gift of God most high!
O font of life! O fire of love!
And sweet anointing from above.

Thou in Thy sevenfold gifts art known,
The finger of God's hand we own;
The promise of the Father, Thou!
Who dost the tongue with power endow.

Kindle our senses from above,
And make our hearts o'erflow with love;
With patience firm and virtue high
The weakness of our flesh supply.

Far from us drive the foe we dread,
And grant us Thy true peace instead;
So shall we not, with Thee for guide,
Turn from the path of life aside.

O may Thy grace on us bestow
The Father and the Son to know,
And Thee through endless times confessed
Of both the eternal Spirit blest.

All glory while the ages run
Be to the Father and the Son,
Who rose from death; the same to Thee,
O Holy Ghost, eternally. Amen.

46d. Litany of the Holy Spirit

Leader: Lord, have mercy on us.
All: Christ, have mercy on us

Leader: Lord, have mercy on us; Christ hear us.
All: Christ, graciously hear us

Leader: Father, all powerful,
All: Have mercy on us

Leader: Jesus, Eternal Son of the Father, Redeemer of
the world,
All: Save us

Leader: Spirit of the Father and the Son, boundless life
of both,
All: Sanctify us

Leader: Holy Trinity,
All: Hear us

Leader: Holy Spirit, Who proceeds from the Father and
the Son,
All: Enter our hearts

Leader: Holy Spirit, Who are equal to the Father and
the Son,
All: Enter our hearts

Leader   **Response**

Promise of God the Father,	*Have mercy on us*
Ray of heavenly light,	
Author of all good,	
Source of heavenly water,	
Consuming Fire,	
Ardent Charity,	
Spiritual unction,	
Spirit of love and truth,	
Spirit of wisdom and understanding,	
Spirit of counsel and fortitude,	
Spirit of knowledge and piety,	
Spirit of the fear of the Lord,	
Spirit of grace and prayer,	
Spirit of peace and meekness,	
Spirit of modesty and innocence,	
Holy Spirit, the Comforter,	
Holy Spirit, the Sanctifier,	
Holy Spirit, Who governs the Church,	
Gift of God, the Most High,	
Spirit Who fills the universe,	
Spirit of the adoption of the children of God,	

Holy Spirit,	*Inspire us with horror of sin*
Holy Spirit,	*Come and renew the face of the earth*
Holy Spirit,	*Shed Your light in our souls*
Holy Spirit,	*Engrave Your law in our hearts*
Holy Spirit,	*Inflame us with the flame of Your love*
Holy Spirit,	*Open to us the treasures of Your graces*
Holy Spirit,	*Teach us to pray well.*
Holy Spirit,	*Enlighten us with Your heavenly inspirations*
Holy Spirit,	*Lead us in the way of salvation*
Holy Spirit,	*Grant us the only necessary knowledge*
Holy Spirit,	*Inspire in us the practice of good*
Holy Spirit,	*Grant us the merits of all virtues*
Holy Spirit,	*Help us persevere in justice*
Holy Spirit,	*Be our everlasting reward*

Leader: Lamb of God, Who takes away the sins of the world,

All: *Send us Your Holy Spirit*

Leader: Lamb of God, Who takes away the sins of the world,

All: *Pour down into our souls the gifts of the Holy Spirit*

Leader: Lamb of God, Who takes away the sins of the world,

All: *Grant us the Spirit of wisdom and piety*

Leader: Let us pray:

V/. Come, Holy Spirit! Fill the hearts of Your faithful.
R/. *And enkindle in them the fire of Your love.*

Leader: Let us pray:

Grant, O merciful Father, that Your Divine Spirit enlighten, inflame and purify us, that He may penetrate us with His heavenly dew and make us fruitful in good works; through our Lord Jesus Christ, Your Son, Who with You, in the unity of the same Spirit, lives and reigns forever and ever. Amen.

46e. The Holy Spirit: Secret to Sanctity and Happiness
by Cardinal Mercier

Five minutes every day keep your imagination quiet. Shut your eyes to all things of sense and close your ears to all the sounds of earth, so as to be able to withdraw into the sanctuary of your baptized soul, the temple of the Holy Spirit. Speak there to the Holy Spirit, saying:

O Holy Spirit, Soul of my soul, I adore You. Enlighten, guide, strengthen and console me. Tell me what I ought to do [today] and command me to do it. I promise to be submissive to everything that You permit to happen to me. Show me only what is Your will.

If you do this, your life will be happy and at peace. Consolation will abound, even in the midst of troubles. Grace will be given in proportion to the trial as well as strength to bear it, bringing you to the Gates of Paradise.

47. Ave Maris Stella

Hail, bright star of ocean,
God's own Mother blest,
Ever sinless Virgin,
Gate of heavenly rest.

Taking that sweet Ave
Which from Gabriel came,
Peace confirm within us,
Changing Eva's name.

Break the captives' fetters,
Light on blindness pour;
All our ills expelling,
Every bliss implore.

Show thyself a mother;
May the Word Divine,
Born for us thy Infant,
Hear our prayers through thine.

Virgin all excelling,
Mildest of the mild,
Freed from guilt, preserve us,
Pure and undefiled.

Keep our life all spotless,
Make our way secure,
Till we find in Jesus
Joy forevermore.

Through the highest Heaven
To the Almighty Three,
Father, Son, and Spirit,
One same glory be. Amen.

47a. The Litany of Our Lady of Loreto

Leader: Lord, have mercy on us.
All: *Christ, have mercy on us*

Leader: Lord, have mercy on us; Christ hear us.
All: *Christ, graciously hear us*

Leader   Response

God, the Father of Heaven,
God, the Son, Redeemer of the world,
God, the Holy Spirit,
Holy Trinity, One God,

Have mercy on us

Holy Mary,
Holy Mother of God,
Holy Virgin of virgins,
Mother of Christ,
Mother of the Church,
Mother of divine grace,
Mother most pure,
Mother most chaste,
Mother inviolate,
Mother undefiled,
Mother immaculate,
Mother most amiable,
Mother most admirable,
Mother of good counsel,
Mother of our Creator,
Mother of our Savior,
Mother of the Church,
Virgin most prudent,
Virgin most venerable,
Virgin most renowned,
Virgin most powerful,
Virgin most merciful,
Virgin most faithful,
Mirror of justice,
Seat of wisdom,
Cause of our joy,

Pray for us

Spiritual vessel,
Vessel of honor,
Singular vessel of devotion,
Mystical rose,
Tower of David,
Tower of ivory,
House of gold,
Ark of the covenant,
Gate of Heaven,
Morning star,
Health of the sick,
Refuge of sinners,
Comforter of the afflicted,
Help of Christians,
Queen of angels,
Queen of Patriarchs,
Queen of Prophets,
Queen of Apostles,
Queen of Martyrs,
Queen of Confessors,
Queen of Virgins,
Queen of all saints,
Queen conceived without original sin,
Queen assumed into Heaven,
Queen of the Most Holy Rosary,
Queen of the family,
Queen of peace,

Pray for us

Leader: Lamb of God, Who takes away the sins of the world,
All: *Spare us, O Lord*

Leader: Lamb of God, Who takes away the sins of the world,
All: *Graciously hear us, O Lord*

Leader: Lamb of God, Who takes away the sins of the world,
All: *Have mercy on us*

Leader: Pray for us, O Holy Mother of God,
All: *That we may be made worthy of the promises of Christ.*

Leader: Let us pray:

Grant, we beg you, O Lord God, to your servants, that we may rejoice in continual health of mind and body; and, by the glorious intercession of blessed Mary ever Virgin, may we be delivered from present sadness, and enter into the joy of Your eternal gladness. Through Christ our Lord. Amen.

48. **Prayer to Mary**
by St. Louis de Montfort

Hail Mary, beloved Daughter of the Eternal Father! Hail Mary, admirable Mother of the Son! Hail Mary, faithful Spouse of the Holy Spirit! Hail Mary, my dear Mother, my loving mistress, my powerful sovereign! Hail my joy, my glory, my heart, and my soul. You are all mine by mercy, and I am all yours by justice.

But I am not yet fully yours. I now give myself wholly to you without keeping anything back for myself or others. If you still see in me anything which does not belong to you, I beg you to take it and to make yourself the absolute mistress of all that is mine.

Destroy in me all that may be displeasing to God, root it up and bring it to nothing, place and cultivate in me everything that is pleasing to you. May the light of your faith dispel the darkness of my mind; may your profound humility take the place of my pride; may your sublime contemplation check the distractions of my wandering imagination; may your continuous sight of God fill my memory with His presence; may the burning love of your heart inflame the lukewarmness of mine; may your virtues take the place of my sins; may your merits be my only adornment in the sight of God and make up all that is lacking in me.

Finally, dearly beloved Mother, grant, if it be possible, that I may have no other spirit but yours to know Jesus and His divine will; that I may have no other soul but yours to praise and glorify the Lord; that I may have no other heart but yours to love God with a love as pure and ardent as yours.

I do not ask you for visions, revelations, sensible devotion, or spiritual pleasures.

It is your privilege to see God clearly; it is your privilege to enjoy heavenly bliss; it is your privilege to triumph gloriously in Heaven at the right hand of your Son and to hold absolute sway over angels, men, and demons; it is your privilege to dispose of all the gifts of God just as you desire.

Such is, O heavenly Mary, the "best part" which the Lord has given you and which shall never be taken away from you — and this thought fills my heart with joy.

As for my part here below, I wish for no other than that which was yours: to believe sincerely without spiritual pleasures; to suffer joyfully without human consolation; to die continually to myself without respite; and to work zealously and unselfishly for you until death as the humblest of your servants.

The only grace I beg you to obtain for me is that every day and every moment of my life I may say: Amen — Amen — so be it, to all that you are now doing in Heaven; Amen — so be it, to all that you are doing in my soul, so that you alone may fully glorify Jesus in me for time and eternity. Amen.

48a. Chaplet of the Immaculate Heart of Mary
Using the Rosary

Make the sign of the cross 5 times in honor of the 5 wounds of Jesus while praying the following:

1. Jesus, I praise and venerate the wound of Your sacred right hand in the name of the Father and the Son and the Holy Spirit.
2. I praise and venerate the wound of Your sacred left hand in the name of the Father and the Son and the Holy Spirit.
3. I praise and venerate the wound of Your sacred right foot in the name of the Father and the Son and the Holy Spirit.
4. I praise and venerate the wound of Your sacred left foot in the name of the Father and the Son and the Holy Spirit.
5. I praise and venerate the wound in Your sacred side and heart in the name of the Father and the Son and the Holy Spirit.

On the large beads of the Rosary pray: Sorrowful and Immaculate Heart of Mary pray for us who seek refuge in you.

On the small beads pray: Holy Mother save us through your Immaculate Heart's Flame of Love.

At the end say 3 times: Glory be to the Father and to the Son and to the Holy Spirit, as it was in the beginning, is now, and ever shall be, world without end. Amen.

48b. Prayer to Blind Satan

O Mary, flood the whole human race* with grace from your Immaculate Heart's Flame of Love, now and at the hour of our death. Amen.

[You may substitute "the whole human race" with your name or the name of someone for whom you are praying.]*

49b. Consecration to Jesus Christ, the Incarnate Wisdom, through the Blessed Virgin Mary, in Union with St. Joseph

in the spirit of St. Louis de Montfort
(Try to meditatively recite on First Saturdays)

Eternal and Incarnate Wisdom! O sweet and most adorable Jesus! True God and true man, only Son of the eternal Father, and of Mary and St. Joseph, always virgins!

I adore You profoundly in the bosom and splendor of Your Father throughout eternity; and I adore You also in the virginal bosom of Mary, Your most worthy Mother, in the time of Your Incarnation.

I adore you in the holy house of Nazareth where You honored St. Joseph, Your virgin father. And I adore you in all the tabernacles throughout the world.

Jesus, I give You thanks for emptying Yourself, taking the form of a slave in order to rescue me from the cruel slavery of the devil. I praise and glorify You for being pleased to submit Yourself to Mary, Your holy Mother, in all things, in order to make me Your consecrated instrument through her.

But alas! Ungrateful and faithless as I have been, I have not kept the promises which I made so solemnly to You in my Baptism and Confirmation; I have not fulfilled my obligations; I do not deserve to be called Your child, nor yet Your slave of love; and as there is nothing in me which does not merit Your anger and Your repulsion, I dare not come by myself before Your most holy and august majesty.

It is on this account that I have recourse to the intercession of Your most holy Mother, whom You have given me for a mediatrix with You. It is through her that I hope to obtain from You contrition, the pardon of my sins, and the acquisition and preservation of wisdom.

Hail, then, Immaculate Mother Mary, living tabernacle of the Divinity, where the Eternal Wisdom willed to be hidden and to be adored by angels and by men! Hail, O Queen of Heaven and earth, to whose empire everything is subject which is under God.

Hail, O sure refuge of sinners, whose mercy fails no one. Hear the desires which I have of the Divine Wisdom; and for that end receive the vows and offerings which in my lowliness I present to you.

I, N., a faithless sinner, renew and ratify today in your hands the vows of my Baptism and Confirmation; I renounce forever satan, his pomps and works, and I give myself entirely to Jesus Christ, the Incarnate Wisdom, to carry my cross after Him all the days of my life, and to be more faithful to Him than I have ever been before.

In the presence of all the heavenly court, I choose you this day for my Mother and Queen. I deliver and consecrate to you, as your child and slave of love, my body and soul, my goods, both interior and exterior and even the value of all my good actions, past, present, and future; leaving to you the entire and full right of disposing of me, and all that belongs to me, without exception, according to your good pleasure, for the greater glory of God in time and in eternity. I also choose you, St. Joseph as my spiritual father, protector and guide in the way of salvation. Please show me how to be faithful and constant in living my consecration to Jesus through your Immaculate Spouse.

Receive, most kind Virgin, this little offering of my slavery of love and spiritual childhood, in honor of, and in union with, that subjection which the Eternal Wisdom willed to your maternal guidance, in homage to the power which both of You have over this poor sinner, and in thanksgiving for the privileges with which the Holy

Trinity has favored you. Mary and Joseph, I declare that I wish henceforth, as your true slave of love and spiritual child, to seek your honor and to obey you in all things.

Mother, I declare that I wish henceforth to enter into a "consecration in truth" way of life through ongoing formation in the eternal truths of our Catholic faith. Please help me to enter more deeply into these truths so that I may come to a greater love of your divine Son, Who is "the way, the truth and the life".

St. Joseph, protector and virgin father of the Word Incarnate and protector and virgin father of the Church, please intercede for me and guide me on my path of formation and evangelization so that I can be a more perfect instrument in Mary's hands for the glory of her Son and the salvation of souls. St. Joseph, obtain for me the grace to always fulfill the responsibilities of every present moment all for the Sacred and Eucharistic Heart of Jesus, all through the Sorrowful and Immaculate Heart of Mary, all in union with you, O Faithful Head of the Holy Family.

St. Joseph, Guardian of the Redeemer, I choose you this day as my guardian and model for living this total consecration of everything I have or will have, including all of my merits and indulgences, to the Ever-virgin Mary. Help me and my family to be caught up in the current of love between Jesus and Mary as you were and to serve them with fidelity and constancy as you did, for the rest of my life. Help me to really show this love by planting seeds of charity in my daily encounters with my family, community and all the souls that God providentially puts into my life.

I entrust to you, O St. Joseph, my passing from this life into eternity. Please bring Jesus and Mary to the hour of my death and the deaths of all the members of my family and those families that work to spread this consecration.

Admirable Mother, present me to your dear Son as His eternal slave of love and instrument, so that as He has redeemed me through you, by you He may receive me! O Mother of mercy, grant me the grace to obtain the true Wisdom of God; and for that end receive me among those whom you love, lead, nourish, and protect as your children and your slaves of love.

O faithful Virgin, make me in all things so perfect a disciple, imitator, and spiritual child and slave of love of the Incarnate Wisdom, Jesus Christ your Son, that I may attain, through your intercession and by your example, to the fullness of His age on earth and of His glory in Heaven. Amen.

A plenary indulgence, under the usual conditions, on the feast of the Immaculate Conception and April 28. (Preces et Pia Opera, 75.)

50. Prayer to Jesus
by St. Louis de Montfort

O most loving Jesus, allow me to pour forth my gratitude before You for the grace You have bestowed upon me in giving me to Your holy mother through the devotion of Holy Bondage, that she may be my advocate in the presence of Your majesty and my support in my extreme misery.

Alas, O Lord! I am so wretched that without this dear Mother I should be certainly lost. Yes, Mary is necessary for me at Your side and everywhere; that she may save me from the eternal punishment which I deserve; that she may contemplate You, speak to You, pray to You, approach You, and please You; that she may help me to save my soul and the souls of others; in short, Mary is necessary for me that I may always do Your holy will and see Your greater glory in all things.

O that I might proclaim throughout the whole world the mercy that You have shown to me! O that everyone might know I would already be damned, were it not for

Mary! O that I might offer worthy thanksgiving for so great a blessing! Mary is in me, O, what a treasure! O, what a consolation! And shall I not be entirely hers?

O, what ingratitude! My dear Savior, send me death rather than such a calamity, for I would rather die than live without belonging entirely to Mary.

With St. John the Evangelist at the foot of the Cross, I have taken her a thousand times for my own and as many times have given myself to her; but if I have not yet done it as You, dear Jesus, wish, I now renew this offering as You desire me to renew it.

And if you see in my soul or my body anything that does not belong to this august princess, I ask You to take it and cast it far from me, for whatever in me does not belong to Mary is unworthy of You. O Holy Spirit, grant me all these graces. Plant in my soul the Tree of True Life, which is Mary; cultivate it and tend it so that it may grow and blossom and bring forth the fruit of life in abundance.

O Holy Spirit, give me great devotion to Mary, Your faithful spouse; give me great confidence in her maternal heart and an abiding refuge in her mercy so that, by her, You might truly form Jesus Christ in me, great and mighty, unto the fullness of His perfect age. Amen.

50a. O Jesus Living in Mary
by St. Louis de Montfort

O Jesus Living in Mary
Come and live in Your servants,
In the spirit of Your holiness,
In the fullness of Your might,
In the truth of Your virtues,
In the perfection of Your ways,
In the communion of Your mysteries,
Subdue every hostile power in Your spirit,
for the glory of the Father. Amen

O Imr
of sinners a
entrust the

I, N., a
humbly imp
have, wholl
Please make
whole life, de

If it plea
reserve, who
will crush yo
heresies in th

we are and have, wholly to yours
and property. Please make of us
and body, of our whole lives, d
most pleases you.
If it pleases you
without reserve, wh
you: "She will cr
destroyed all
Let th
your im
incre
st

Let me b .... in your immaculate and
merciful hands for introducing and increasing your glory
to the maximum in all the many strayed and indifferent
souls, and thus help extend as far as possible the blessed
kingdom of the most Sacred Heart of Jesus.

For wherever you enter you obtain the grace of conversion and growth in holiness, since it is through your
hands that all graces come to us from the most Sacred
Heart of Jesus. Amen.

V/. Allow me to praise you, O Sacred Virgin.
R/. Give me strength against your enemies.

50b.1 Consecration of Children
to Jesus through Mary at Baptism
in the spirit St. Maximilian Kolbe, OFM Conv.
adapted by Fr. Bernard Geiger, OFM Conv.

O Immaculata, Queen of Heaven and earth, refuge
of sinners and our most loving Mother, God has willed to
entrust the entire order of mercy to you.

We, the __(name)__ family, repentant sinners, cast ourselves at your feet humbly imploring you to take us, and
especially our new (son/daughter) __(name)__, with all that

elf as your possession
, of all our powers of soul
eaths, and eternity, whatever

, use all that we are and have
olly to accomplish what was said of
ush your head," and, "You alone have
eresies in the whole world."

s child and our family be a fit instrument in
maculate and merciful hands for introducing and
easing your glory to the maximum in all the many
rayed and indifferent souls, and thus help extend as far
as possible the blessed kingdom of the most Sacred Heart
of Jesus.

For wherever you enter you obtain the grace of conversion and growth in holiness, since it is through your hands that all graces come to us from the most Sacred Heart of Jesus. Amen.

V/. Allow us to praise you, O Sacred Virgin.
R/. Give us strength against your enemies.

Note: Consecrating children to Jesus through Mary explicitly entrusts them to Mary, to whom they already belong by their Baptism in Jesus. This entrustment explicitly calls on Mary to fulfill her role as their mystical mother, and nurture their growth in Jesus and in his Bride-Church and Mystical Body.

When parents have consecrated their children to God by Baptism, it is their responsibility to help them grow as children of God the Father by using the graces, Gifts of the Holy Spirit and Infused Virtues that Baptism gives us to imitate Christ and to develop all these acts little by little into strong habits. Later, as the children receive the other Sacraments and learn to participate in the Sacred Liturgy, the parents' responsibility is to help them use the graces and charisms of the Holy Spirit that these impart to perform other acts of virtue and of service, learn to accept and fulfill responsibilities, grow in healthy, holy relationships, and develop all these into strong habits as well.

Admittedly this is a daunting task. However, the parents' consecration of themselves and their children to Jesus through Mary will bring them her strong practical assistance, providential help and grace to persevere. This greatly simplifies their task, for then their responsibility will be to act as best they can as her instruments and cooperators to help her fulfill her responsibility as the Mother of her Son's Bride-Church and Mystical Body to raise and form its members.

50b.2 Renewal of Baptismal Vows

Do you reject sin so as to live in the freedom of God's children?   **I do.**

Do you reject the glamour of evil and refuse to be mastered by sin?   **I do.**

Do you reject Satan, father of sin and prince of darkness?   **I do.**

Do you reject Satan and all his works?   **I do.**

And all his empty promises?   **I do.**

Do you believe in God, the Father almighty, creator of heaven and earth?   **I do.**

Do you believe in Jesus Christ, his only Son, our Lord, who was born of the Virgin Mary, was crucified, died, and was buried, rose from the dead, and is now seated at the right hand of the Father?   **I do.**

Do you believe in the Holy Spirit, the holy catholic Church, the communion of saints, the forgiveness of sins, the resurrection of the body, and life everlasting?   **I do.**

50c. Implementing the Sacraments of Baptism and Confirmation with Mary
by Fr. Bernard Geiger, OFM Conv.

Through the Seven Sacraments of the Catholic Church—those momentous reciprocal oaths that form the core of God's New Covenant with all believers—God makes each of us sharers in the New Covenant—the Covenant that saves all believers, forms them into his Church, and confers on them a destiny of eternal life.

The word *sacrament* comes from the Latin word *sacramentum* which means, "that by which a person binds oneself or another to do something"—as, for instance, when a person joins the military by swearing an oath of allegiance. In each Sacrament that we receive, therefore, God swears something to us and we swear something to God, which results in our becoming more and more deeply involved in God's New Covenant with his Church.

The first and most fundamental of all the Sacraments is Baptism. As a person is baptized, God swears He is incorporating that person into Jesus Christ, his Incarnate Son, and is thus making that person His own adopted son or daughter in Christ who actually shares His own divine being and nature as God.

The second most fundamental Sacrament is the one that completes Baptism, namely, Confirmation. In this Sacrament, God swears He is giving the person being confirmed the exact same full outpouring of the Holy Spirit He once gave to the Apostles and disciples on the day of Pentecost. He swears that with this outpouring He makes that person a witness of Jesus Christ and gives that person a mission to spread and defend the Catholic Faith by word and action.

Each person receiving these two Sacraments swears something to God, too. By receiving them we swear that we accept the identities, relationships and responsibilities they confer on us, and that we will do our best to live out these identities and relationships, and fulfill the responsibilities they entail.

Once we have received these Sacraments and sworn these oaths, we are gravely obliged to fulfill them. God for his part does not fail to give us the graces we need to do this in proportion as we desire them, ask for them and open our hearts to receive them.

Ordinarily we need the help of the Church and our fellow Christians to implement and live God's Plan for our salvation, membership in his Church, and destiny of eternal life. Unfortunately, it often happens that we do not receive the help, instruction, spiritual formation and training we need to live the identities and relationships, and fulfill the responsibilities that the Sacraments confer.

To help supply this aid and meet this need, the Holy Spirit and his Immaculate Spouse, the Blessed Virgin Mary, have given the Church two very powerful means. These are the teachings and the devotions of total consecration to Mary formulated by Saints Louis Marie Grignon de Montfort and Maximilian Maria Kolbe.

St. Louis de Montfort's teaching and formula for consecrating oneself to Jesus through Mary under her title as Mother of God are specifically designed to help us live out the promises we made to God by our Baptisms. We will in fact keep these promises and implement the Sacrament of Baptism by utilizing the graces Baptism makes available, and by growing in the communion of faith, hope and love with the Mother of God that our total consecration of ourselves to her makes possible.

Our consecration of ourselves to the Mother of God enables her to instruct, form and train us to live as God's and her precious sons and daughters, as the precious sisters and brothers of their Divine Son, Jesus, and as signs and temples of the Holy Spirit.

St. Maximilian Maria Kolbe's teachings and formula for consecrating oneself to Mary under her titles as the Immaculate Conception and Spouse of the Holy Spirit are specifically effective for helping us to live out and fulfill the identity, relationships and responsibilities conferred on us in the Sacrament of Confirmation.

Although St. Maximilian did not expressly present his teachings and formula of self-consecration to the Immaculata as a means for implementing the Sacrament of Confirmation, this is in fact what they most effectively do. For Mary is, herself, her Son's first and most effective witness and evangelist—a fact illustrated by her Visitation to St. Elizabeth and her witness at the Marriage Feast of Cana.

In his formula of self-consecration to the Immaculata, Kolbe has us entrust ourselves to Mary as her property and possession, and beg her to make us fit instruments in her immaculate and merciful hands for continuing her work of evangelizing all peoples, especially the straying and the indifferent, and of bringing about the kingdom of the Most Sacred Heart of her Son, Jesus.

She does this by directly helping us implement the Sacrament of Confirmation we have received, that is, she transforms us into witnesses for Christ with her. As his witnesses, we are to help spread and defend the faith in every possible way with every legitimate means available. Mary brings about this transformation in proportion as we live lives of total consecration to her in complete self-surrender, obedience and the fulfillment of whatever contemplative or active apostolate she calls us to engage in.

The de Montfort and Kolbean self-consecration formulas, then, complement each other by providing us with effective ways to implement the Sacraments of Baptism and Confirmation. (The Holy Eucharist is the third most *fundamental* Sacrament and, of course, the most important of all the Sacraments; with Baptism and Confirmation it forms the Sacraments of Christian Initiation, "whose unity must be safeguarded." —*Catechism of the Catholic Church,* 1285)

50f. Jesus Defines Consecration
The Gospel of St. John Chapter 17

Jesus raised His eyes to Heaven and said:
"Father, the hour has come:
glorify Your Son
so that Your Son may glorify You;
[2] and, through the power over all mankind
that You have given Him,
let Him give eternal life to all
those you have entrusted to Him.

[3] And eternal life is this:
to know You, the only true God,
and Jesus Christ whom You have sent.
[4] I have glorified You on earth
by finishing the work
that You gave Me to do.
[5] Now, Father, it is time for you to glorify Me
with that glory I had with You

before ever the world was.
[6]I have made Your name known
to the men You took from the world to give Me.
They were Yours and You gave them to Me,
and they have kept Your word.
[7]Now at last they know
that all You have given Me
comes indeed from You;
[8]for I have given them
the teaching You gave to Me,
and they have truly accepted this,
that I came from You,
and have believed that it was You who sent Me.

[9]I pray for them;
I am not praying for the world
but for those You have given Me,
because they belong to You:
[10]all I have is Yours
and all You have is mine,
and in them I am glorified.
[11]I am not in the world any longer,
but they are in the world,
and I am coming to You.

Holy Father,
keep those You have given
Me true to Your name,
so that they may be one like us.
[12]While I was with them,
I kept those You had given Me true to Your name.
I have watched over them and not one is lost
except the one who chose to be lost,
and this was to fulfill the scriptures.

[13]But now I am coming to You
and while still in the world I say these things
to share my joy with them to the full.
[14]I passed Your word on to them,
and the world hated them,

because they belong to the world
no more than I belong to the world.
[15]I am not asking You to remove them from the world,
but to protect them from the evil one.
[16]They do not belong to the world
any more than I belong to the world.

[17]Consecrate them in the truth;
Your word is truth.
[18]As You sent Me into the world,
I have sent them into the world,
[19]and for their sake I consecrate myself
so that they too may be consecrated in truth.
[20]I pray not only for these,
but for those also
who through their words will believe in Me.

[21]May they all be one.
Father, may they
be one in us,
as You are in Me and
I am in You,
so that the world may believe it was You
who sent Me.
[22]I have given them the glory You gave to Me,
that they may be one as we are one.
[23]With Me in them and You in Me,
may they be so completely one
that the world will realize that it was You who sent Me
and that I have loved them as much as You loved Me.

[24]Father,
I want those You have given Me
to be with Me where I am,
so that they may always see the glory
You have given Me
because You loved Me
before the foundation of the world.

[25]Father, Righteous One,
the world has not known You,

but I have known You,
and these have known
that You have sent Me.
[26] I have made Your name known to them
and will continue to make it known,
so that the love with which You loved Me
may be in them,
and so that I may be in them."

Excerpts from the Jerusalem Bible ©1966 by Darton Longman & Todd, Ltd. and Doubleday and Co., Inc., used by permission of the publisher.

51b. Catechism on True Devotion to Mary
by Rev. Ralph W. Beiting

Imprimi potest: *Roger M. Charest, S.M.M.*
                      Superior Provincialis
Nihil obstat: *Francis J. Reine, S.T.D.*
                      Censor librorum
Imprimatur: *Paul C. Schulte, D.D.*
                      Archbishop of Indianapolis
                      Feast of the Immaculate Conception, 1952
Printed with permission.

Introduction

To fully appreciate the meaning and greatness of a man's work one must know and experience something of the life that formed and fashioned the man. So it is in the case of Louis Marie Grignion De Montfort. His beautiful works on our Blessed Mother have aroused the sleeping hearts of thousands the world over, yet almost nothing is ever mentioned of his life.

Louis Marie was born in 1673 to a simple peasant family of Montfort-la-Canne in Brittany, France. As the second oldest of 18 children he learned early to love the virtues of poverty, mortification and blind attachment to the will of God that were so characteristic of his later life. His devotion to the Mother of God was a thing that went back to the days of earliest childhood. It formed and molded the thinking and plans of his life. The realization of his vocation to the priesthood came as he knelt in prayer before the statue of our Lady in the Carmelite church of the village, and from that day on he promised Mary that he would be an untiring preacher of her wondrous dignity.

After years of hardship and poverty he was ordained priest in 1700, after attending the seminary of St. Sulpice, Paris. He immediately went to the poor and the forgotten. To them he brought the message of divine love. The response to his life and teaching was enthusiastic, and hundreds returned to the practice of their faith. But to the forces of Jansenism, that infected so much of France at this time, he was a man to be feared and hated. De Montfort accepted their challenge by going to Rome and placing his case at the feet of the Holy Father, Clement XI. His Holiness gave him the title of Missionary Apostolic and the commission to combat Jansenism throughout France. Up and down the countryside he went preaching, giving missions, consoling, teaching catechism. Every-where he enkindled the desire for sanctity and at the same time implanted in the minds of his listeners that the best way of reaching God is to have His Mother lead you. For sixteen years he was a familiar figure on the countryside of France, untiring in his devotion to Jesus and Mary, but at last the fire of his own zeal and the attacks of his enemies brought his short priestly life to an end. On the evening of April 28, 1716, death overtook him. Calmly he waited for it, having in his hands the crucifix of Our Lord and a small statue of the Virgin while from his lips came those beautiful words, "Jesus and Mary are with me, I have finished my course, I shall never sin again."

When men of later times came and read the wonders of his sixteen years of priestly life, they wondered how a man could do so much. There were the two religious congregations he founded, the Montfort Fathers and the Montfort Sisters; there were the hundreds and hundreds of missions he gave and the two wonderful books he wrote to show unto others the secret of his success. These books are *True Devotion to the Blessed Virgin*, and *The Secret of Mary*.

In the years that followed his death many souls continued to experience the intercession of this humble priest. Miracles gave divine approval to his teachings and, before long, the recognition of the Church gave final assurance of his continued greatness. In September, 1838, Pope Gregory XVI bestowed on him the title of Venerable and on September 29, 1869, Pope Pius IX proclaimed his virtues heroic. He was beatified by Leo XIII on January 22, 1888, and was canonized by Pius XII on July 20, 1947.

If one phrase can be said to sum up his life surely it is the phrase "to Jesus through Mary," while his two works, *The Secret of Mary*, and *True Devotion to the Blessed Virgin* form a gospel of Marian spirituality. It was in an effort to help everyone clearly understand the meaning of St. Louis De Montfort's teachings that this simple catechism was written. It is also hoped that it will answer some of the difficulties that may arise in the mind of an interested reader who loves Mary and wishes to honor her as perfectly as he can.

Ralph Beiting

1. In what does True Devotion to the Blessed Virgin consist?

Saint Louis De Montfort says: "It consists in giving oneself entirely and as a slave to Mary, and to Jesus through Mary" *(The Secret of Mary, 28)*. "And to do all our actions by Mary, with Mary, in Mary, and for Mary; so that we may do them all the more perfectly by Jesus, with Jesus, in Jesus, and for Jesus" *(True Devotion, 257)*.

2. What is meant when De Montfort says that we are to give ourselves entirely and as a slave to Jesus through Mary?

By a total gift he means that we give to Jesus by means of Mary:

(1) our body, with its senses and its members,

(2) our exterior goods of fortune, whether present or to come,

(3) our soul, with all its powers, and

(4) our interior and spiritual goods, which are our merits and our virtues and our good works, past, present, and future.

3. How do we give to Mary our body with its senses and its members?

Of course, even after the act of consecration, we retain the use of our bodies, but from the moment of consecration, we show our body special respect, for now we have given it to Mary in a special way. We will keep it clean and neatly attired, for it belongs to Mary. We will mortify it and check the evil tendencies it has, for it is now an instrument of Mary. We will accept all sickness and evil that befall it, and especially the death that will destroy it, for it is now Mary's property, and she may use it as she sees fit.

4. How can we give Mary our exterior goods of fortune?

This does not mean that we take the vow of poverty, but it does mean that, by our surrender, we make our Lady the real owner of all we have. We are now her representatives, using our external possessions as she would use them. We give alms with our money, for Mary is the most charitable of God's creatures. We are not spend-thrifts or misers with our goods. We take proper care of our rooms, our clothes, our car, our typewriter, etc., because they are Mary's and we are using them as she would if she were living her earthly life now.

5. What is meant by giving Mary our soul?

The soul is that principle in us by which we live, and move, and are. Therefore, when we give our soul to Mary, we really give her our very life. Our life is hers to direct as she sees fit. If she makes it a hard existence or an easy one, if she fills it with interest and shows it forth before all men, or hides it in some quiet corner, it is all the same to us. Mary is the one who owns and directs our life; we are happy in the fact that we live it under her loving care.

6. What are the faculties of the soul and how can we use them for Mary?

The faculties of the soul are the intellect and the will. It is by means of the intellect that man understands the meaning of things, that he forms ideas and makes plans. So, when we give Mary our intellect, we give her the ideas and plans that we shall form, and we promise her that we will use our minds only to know the truth, and to seek God's will in all things. We renounce at the same time any study or inquiry that might lead us from God.

By means of the will, we love persons and things. When we hand our will over to our Lady, we tell her in effect that we will do nothing that may hinder the good of souls or imperil our own sanctification and salvation. We may still seek to know and do things that are not essentially religious. For example, a teacher may still study literature or science; a mechanic may investigate the problems and the make-up of engines, and desire to have a business of his own. He will, however, do so for Mary and work under the direction of Mary. In a word, he will give his mind and his will to Mary, asking her to give him the ideas she knows will be best, and whatever success may come to him by reason of his actions, he gives to Mary.

7. What are merits?

When a person is in the state of grace, Christ is so pleased with him that He says to him, "Every time you do good, I will reward you; I will pay you for this good you have done Me." Jesus goes even further and gives us the right to buy things with our wages, something we could not do before. Part of our pay must be put aside for ourselves. It is to constitute our bank account for the day on which we can work no longer, the day when we will go home to Our Father's house in heaven. This part of our pay, we call "merit" in the strict sense of the word. Another part of our wages can be used for paying our debts.

We incur debts every time we commit sin, and we have to pay for all the debts we run up by our sins before we can enter heaven. For this we have what is known as satisfactory-value money. We can use it pretty much as we see fit. Finally we may use it to ask God for a favor for ourselves; we can ask Him to help our friends and relatives with it, or that the Church may spread; that peace will come to the world, etc. Theologians call this the impetratory power of our good deeds. Such, in brief, are the meaning and three different kinds of merit.

8. How can we give our merits, virtues, and good works to Mary?

Our virtues are good habits by means of which we perform good works, and the reward of these good works we call merit. We give our virtues to Mary to guard and protect for us. She cannot give our virtue of charity or faith to someone else, but she does watch over it, and sees that nothing destroys it. We give virtue to her for safe-keeping. Our merits are of three kinds, as previously noted. The first kind, the kind that forms our bank account for heaven, we give to Mary to keep, augment and embellish for us, just as we did with our virtues. The second kind of merit, by which we pay the debts for our sins, we give to Mary to use as she wishes. If she sees fit, she can pay the debt of someone else. Perhaps she will use it to free a soul from purgatory or to aid someone here on earth. It is entirely hers to use in the way from which God will get the greatest honor and glory. We also give her the third kind of merit, which we called "spending money." We give up the right of determining the application of our good works, the right of saying for what the value of our works shall go. All we suffer, all we think, all the good we say or do, we now give to Jesus through Mary, in order that she may dispose of it according to the will of her Son and His greatest glory.

9. Why do we say our good actions, past, present, and future?

By this we show the completeness of our gift. All the merits we stored up before we made the Act of Consecration, we give to Mary either to protect or to dispose of, as well as the merits we shall get in the future. Even the satisfaction we make by our sufferings in purgatory, we give to Mary to use as she sees fit.

10. How can Mary sanctify, augment, and embellish the merits and virtues we give her to guard for us?

Once we have performed a good action, we receive a reward from God. This reward we call merit. This merit is given because of the work done here and now; so once the good work is completed, the merit of that action cannot be increased, not even by Mary. However, once we have made the Act of Consecration to Mary as her slave, the same act performed will now be more meritorious than it would have been before we bound ourself to Mary. *In this sense, Mary increases and purifies our merits. The reason for this is that we now belong to Mary; we are doing things for her intentions, which are the purest imaginable.* Mary is partner with us in all our activities, and, therefore, our acts carry the stamp of Mary's love. Jesus, seeing our actions permeated with Mary's love and grace, gives them a far higher reward than He would if we had only our intention expressed in them. It is the same way with our virtues. Virtues are augmented and embellished by God alone. However, God gives this increase because of the good acts we perform. So when Mary purifies our acts by inspiring us to unite our intentions with hers, and to put the same love into them that she did, she thereby augments and embellishes our virtues.

11. If I give to Mary the merits by which I pay the debt I owe for my sins, will I not spend an extra long time in Purgatory?

It is true that by this Act of Consecration we give all to Mary, even the indulgences we may gain, having nothing for ourselves. So, in itself, it could be possible that we should still have all our debt to pay. But remember, when we gave all to Mary, she also gave herself to us, and it is morally impossible for Mary to abandon one who is her child in a very special way. Mary loves us much more than we love ourselves. So we shall not have to worry about being too generous with her. She simply cannot be outdone in generosity.

12. If we give our indulgences to Mary, can we still make spiritual bouquets?

Spiritual bouquets can still be made as in the past, but with this difference. Before, you stated without reserve that you wanted the prayers and indulgences to go for a particular person, but now you make this request conditionally, which means if Mary sees that this will be for the greatest glory and honor of God. We now leave it to her to decide. We ask only; we do not demand.

13. Does not the total gift of my merits put me in a state of incapacity to assist the souls of parents, relatives, friends, pupils, benefactors?

It is true that we have given up the right of specifying for whom our prayers and good works will go, but this does not mean that our friends and relatives will suffer. We have given ourselves as slaves to Mary; all that we can call our own, in any way at all, now belongs to her. Our parents, friends, and relatives belong to us; so by our Act of Consecration, they, too, are brought into closer relationship with our Mother. She is bound to take a more loving care of them now that they are closer to her than she would have taken before we gave them to her as her special charges. Priests who give themselves to Mary as slaves thereby bring greater blessings on their flock. Sisters and Religious draw their pupils closer to Mary by their Act of Consecration. The same is true of parents in regard to their families.

14. Does Saint Louis De Montfort consider the question of praying for others?

Yes, he does. Here are his exact words: "This practice does not hinder us from praying for others, whether living or dead, although the application of our good works depends on the will of our Blessed Lady. On the contrary, it is this very thing which will lead us to pray with more confidence" *(True Devotion, 132).*

15. If we can no longer specify definitely for whom we wish our prayers and good works to go, how can we say this practice leads us to pray with more confidence?

Our confidence can come from two sources. Either it is from our own actions or it comes from something outside ourselves. By the Act of Consecration we have given up our own interests and intentions and have united ourselves with Jesus and Mary. From now on, Mary will be the cause of our hope with God. When Our Lord looks at us, He will not see us so much as Mary, our Mistress. We no longer count on our own merits, but rely on the graces of Mary, and our confidence will be greatly increased.

16. How can this act give me more hope of obtaining what I ask?

God can give His merits and favors in two ways. In the first case, He gives them because we have worked for them, and therefore have a right to them. In the second, it is His pure and free love that prompts Him to give us the things we need. When we give up our right to our merits, our hope of obtaining what we ask is not directly increased by this gift, but indirectly it does give us greater certitude. The reason is a simple one. No longer are we entering into a business deal with God, demanding petty wages. Instead, we tell Mary to take our wages and use them for the things she knows are best. God is now so pleased with us that He showers down on us and the persons for whom we pray blessings over and above those we could ever have hoped to obtain by our own individual works.

17. When we have given all to Mary, does it not seem contrary to the spirit of True Devotion to ask for individual favors?

If we asked for individual favors without making the reservation that it is up to Mary to grant them or not, then our petitions would be contrary to the spirit of True Devotion. But when we made our Act of Consecration, we became united with Mary in all things; we became sharers of the mission her Son gave her, which is the sanctification of mankind. So, we can see that we also become sharers in her apostolic prayer, and her prayer is a constant, ever-living, all-embracing prayer. Our prayers must be molded on hers, or, rather, should be a part of hers. So, instead of True Devotion decreasing the number of our prayers, it will rather increase them, make them greater and more intensive.

18. If we give all our merits to Mary, will this not interfere with the duties of our state in life?

Saint De Montfort clearly states: "We make the offering of this devotion only according to the order of God, and the duties of our state" *(True Devotion, 124).* So, a priest could make the Act of Consecration and still apply the satisfactory and impetratory value of the Holy Sacrifice of the Mass to some private person. The same thing is true of Consecrated who by the rules of their Community are bound to offer certain prayers for benefactors, and other specified intentions. the explanation lies in the fact that by reason of our state in life, these actions are no longer ours to give, and we can give only what we ourselves have a strict right to.

19. Could one practice True Devotion and at the same time make the heroic act of charity?

According to the definition of the Sacred Congregation of Indulgences, Dec. 1885, the Heroic Act of Charity consists in this, that a member of the Church Militant offers to God for the souls in purgatory all the satisfactory works which he will perform during his lifetime, and also all the suffrages which may accrue to him after his death. It can be seen at once that this Heroic Act does not go as far as De Montfort's slavery of love. After making the Heroic Act we still keep our merits, strictly so called, as well as the right to pray for anyone we wish. By the Holy Slavery, however, we give Mary our merits in the strict sense also, as well as our right to determine for whom our prayers are to be offered. Even in the Heroic Act, we still specify that the satisfactory value of our works shall go to the souls in purgatory. But, by the Act of Consecration, we leave it all up to Mary to aid whom she wills. So, one would not be living the life of slavery if he merely made the Heroic Act. De Montfort asks for the complete gift of oneself, nothing less.

20. Why does Saint Louis De Montfort tell us to be slaves of Jesus and Mary when we should be their loving children?

It must be remembered that Saint Louis De Montfort calls his devotion the Holy Slavery of Love. By it, we are loving children of Jesus and Mary, and more besides. To bring out that we are children of Mary he uses the word, "love" and to show that we are to exceed the duty imposed on even loving children, he uses the word "slave." It is the only term that we have to express this idea of complete surrender. It is the same slavery which Saint Paul prized so highly. Indeed, he found his honor in being a "slave of Jesus Christ." When he wrote to his converts to congratulate them on their entrance into the Church, he gave them the same glorious title of slaves: "But now being made free from sin and become slaves of God, you have your fruit unto sanctity and the end, life everlasting." This is a slavery that only the most perfect can conceive.

21. What is the difference between this devotion and religious duties that every Christian has by reason of his Baptism?

It is true that at the time of our Baptism, our sponsors in our name dedicated our lives to God and promised we would forsake the slavery of sin and evil for the holy slavery of Jesus. So, it is not surprising to hear De Montfort say, "This devotion may rightly be called a perfect renewal of the vows or promises of holy Baptism" *(True Devotion, 126)*. Attention must, however, be called to the word "perfect" renewal, for herein lies the difference between the two.

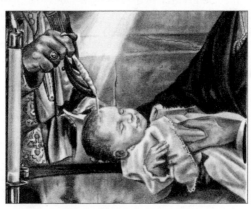

22. How is the practice of True Devotion a more perfect renewal of our Baptismal promises?

Saint De Montfort gives the following reasons why his way of renewing our Baptismal promises is more perfect. "In Baptism, we ordinarily speak by the mouth of another, our godfather or godmother, and so we give ourselves to Jesus Christ not by ourselves, but through another. But in this devotion, we do it by ourselves, voluntarily, knowing what we are doing. Moreover, in holy Baptism, we do not give ourselves to Jesus by the hands of Mary, at least not in an explicit manner; and we do not give Him the value of our good actions. We remain entirely free after Baptism, either to apply them to whom we please, or to keep them for ourselves. But, by this devotion, we give ourselves to our Lord explicitly by the hands of Mary, and we consecrate to Him the value of our good actions" *(True Devotion, 126)*.

23. Are we not, by reason of our Baptism, bound always to work for the glory of God?

Most assuredly we are. But De Montfort would have us go even further than this. He wants us to work for the greater honor and glory of God. Christ has told us that if we pray in the proper way for the proper thing, He will infallibly answer our petition. However, the fact that we have asked for a good thing does not mean that we asked for the best thing, and De Montfort wants us to ask for the best thing. Now, we do not always ask what is best for us, and as a result, we spend our merits on inferior products instead of putting them to their best use. These inferior products are good, however; if they were not, God would not have answered our prayer. But we could have done more with the same merit, if we had known how to spend it. Apart from God Himself, Mary alone knows what things contribute most to the glory of

God. For example, it may give God more glory at this time to have a sinner converted than to free a soul from purgatory. We are finite; we do not know what, in this particular case, is the better thing to ask for. Instead of asking for one or the other favor as we ordinarily do, we now leave it to Mary to use our prayers or fastings as she knows best.

24. Why is it best to offer our merits to Jesus through Mary?

Four reasons can be given for this practice. The first and most important reason is that such is the Will of God. The second is, that in so doing, we imitate most perfectly the example of Jesus Himself. It is also more perfect because it is more humble, and lastly, because of the blessings such an offering brings down upon us.

25. How do we know it is God's Will that we should come to Him through Mary?

We know God's Will in something from what He has done. Now, in regard to our Blessed Lady, He has made her our spiritual Mother. Mary is our spiritual Mother because she cooperated with Jesus in giving us our spiritual life of grace. She did this by her cooperation with Jesus in the work of redemption. But

God has done even greater things for our Lady.
Besides using her as His helper in giving us grace, He
has deemed that she should intercede for, and dispense to us, every grace that we receive. In other
words, God sent His only begotten Son to us by means
of Mary. He began the work of our salvation by means
of Mary. He continues and completes the work of our
sanctification even now by means of Mary. He has
placed her as the Mediatrix between Himself and us;
for us to refuse to go back to Him by means of Mary,
would be to ignore His Will in the matter.

26. In what way did Jesus give us an example of dependence on Mary?

Jesus showed His desire to depend on Mary in the
following manner. He became man for our salvation,
but it was only in Mary and by Mary. As God He could
have chosen a thousand other ways of redeeming us.
He willed to be presented to His Father in the Temple
by means of the virginal hands of His Mother. For
over thirty years He was "subject" to her in all things,
and gave only three years to the preaching of the
kingdom. As De Montfort expressed it, "Jesus Christ
gave more glory to God the Father by submission to
His Mother during those thirty years, than He would
have given Him in converting the whole world by the
working of the most stupendous miracles," a thing He
would have done if it would have given more honor to
God. Then, too, Jesus performed His first miracles of
grace and of nature only at the word of Mary. Saint
John the Baptist was sanctified, and the water at
Cana was made wine because of Mary's word. And at
the end of His life, He tells us simply, "I have given
you an example that as I have done...so you also
should do" *(John 13:15)*. Thus, it was all this that made
St. De Montfort cry out, "O, how highly we glorify God
when, to please Him, we submit ourselves to Mary
after the example of Jesus Christ, our sole Exemplar"
(True Devotion, 18).

27. How do we practice greater humility by going to Jesus through Mary?

The Curé of Ars often used to remark that we sprinkle pride like salt on everything we do; and yet, we seldom reflect on the condition of our soul. By going to Jesus through Mary, we recognize our nothingness and wickedness, and ask her to be our suppliant with Our Lord.

28. Will not the great emphasis laid on the position of the Blessed Virgin cause us at least in some measure to forget Jesus?

Such a thought was totally foreign to the mind of Saint De Montfort, as can be gathered from his own words, "If we establish solid devotion to our Blessed Lady, it is only to establish more perfectly devotion to Jesus Christ, and to provide an easy and secure means for finding Jesus Christ." *(True Devotion, 62)*. Mary is loved only because she is so intimately connected with Jesus. As De Montfort puts it, "You, Lord, are always with Mary, and Mary is always with You, and she cannot be without You, else she would cease to be what she is...She is so intimately united with You that it were easier to separate the light from the sun, the heat from the fire, than to separate Mary from You" *(True Devotion, 63)*.

29. Even though Mary is closely united to Jesus, does there not still seem danger of neglecting Jesus?

Saint Thomas says that when we will the means to an end, we, by that very act, will also the end. Now, Mary is sought as a means of union with Jesus. Her position in regard to Jesus may be likened to that of direction signs on a highway. Do we ignore these signs, and say, "I want to concentrate on the road itself, and I do not want the signs to interfere with my attention?" This would be silly. For the entire purpose of road signs is to call attention to the road. They tell us of the hills and curves, how fast to go, and a thousand other things that make us know the road more thoroughly. The same construction company that built the road, put up the signs, and they placed the signs there to help us. God the Father, generated the Son, our Way. And this same God gave us Mary as a sign along the way so that the more we investigate the sign, the better will be our knowledge of the road.

30. Does it not seem fitting that we should honor Jesus first, and then speak of loving Mary?

This would certainly be true if we were praising Mary without considering Christ, but we must remember that in reality, we honor and love Jesus when we salute Mary. We go to her only as the way by which we are to find the end we are seeking, which is Jesus. As De Montfort remarks, "The Church, with the Holy Spirit, blesses our Lady first, and our Lord second, 'Blessed art thou among women, and blessed is the Fruit of thy womb, Jesus.' It is not that Mary is more than Jesus, or even equal to Him—that would be intolerable heresy. But it is that, in order to bless Jesus more perfectly, we must begin by blessing Mary. If we praise or glorify her, she immediately praises and glorifies Jesus as of old, when Saint Elizabeth praised her, 'My soul doth magnify the Lord'" *(True Devotion, 95, 148)*.

31. How can we perform all our actions by Mary?

To act BY MARY means to be completely dependent on her. Before I decide on a course of action, I will ask for her guidance and direction. As I begin my meditation, I ask her to draw my thoughts along the lines she knows will do me the most good. When I act by Mary, I make my intentions hers. I perform the duties of my life in the same spirit that she performed her daily tasks. When I pray, it will be for Mary's intention. My Mass, my Communion, my duties in life, my acts of charity, and my sufferings are all for her intention. I can form particular intentions, and I should, but they will be formed in the same spirit that our Lady formed hers.

32. How can we do all our actions with Mary?

Saint De Montfort answers this when he writes, "We must do all our actions With Mary, that is to say, we must in all our actions, regard Mary as an accomplished model of every virtue and perfection. We must, therefore, in every action, consider how Mary has done it, or how she would have done it, had she been in our place" *(True Devotion, 260)*.

33. How can we perform all our actions in Mary?

We do this by trying to enter into Mary's interior and stay there, adopting her views and feelings. Mary must become, as it were, the place and atmosphere in which we live; her influence must penetrate us. In our plans and hopes, we naturally consider her, and assign her a place in all our affairs. In a word, companionship with her becomes the constant state of our soul. As De Montfort says, "Mary will be the only means used by our souls in dealing with God" *(Secret of Mary, 47)*.

34. How can we perform all our actions for Mary?

When we do all our actions For Mary, we recall the fact that we are now slaves of the Queen of Heaven. Seeing that our Queen is so very good, we will continue to offer her love and praise. With the words of De Montfort, we will address ourselves to Mary, "O my dear Mother, it is for thee that I go here or there; for thee that I do this or that; for thee that I suffer this pain or that wrong" *(Secret of Mary, 49)*. Our love will lead us to seek out opportunities that she may use them to spread the kingdom of her Son. Hand in hand with our own personal love and service for her, will come the desire to have others know her. We will spend ourselves in bringing others to the love of Jesus in Mary. All the world must be given the opportunity and privilege of serving our Lady.

35. When De Montfort says "Mary will be the only means used by our soul in dealing with God," does he mean to say that we are no longer to pray directly to Jesus?

No, he does not mean that at all. The entire purpose of his devotion is to cultivate a more intimate union with Jesus, and the constant conversation of our soul with God is one of the best ways of being united to Him. It is Mary's part to bring us together and to purify us that we be more fit for this union with Jesus. Before we pray, we tell Jesus that we are offering Him these prayers through Mary and that we wish to speak with Him just as she did.

36. If we perform all our actions through Mary, can we still pray to other Saints?

We may, and should pray to the Saints after we have made this consecration. Remember that Mary is Queen of all Saints, and that they all serve her as their loving Mistress. When we ask the Saints for a favor, we are, in reality, asking them to intercede for us with our Lady. "In vain," says Saint Bernard, "would a person ask other Saints for a favor, if Mary did not interpose to obtain it." The Saints received all their virtues and graces by the intercession of Mary; so, when we ask them to obtain a special favor for us, we are using them as our advocates with Mary, our Queen.

37. If we make the Act of Consecration, do we always have to be thinking of Mary?

Since we are all humans, it is impossible for us actually and distinctly to think of Mary in each of our actions. It is sufficient to make our Act of Consecration to Mary with the intention of doing all things for, with, and in, and by her, and then not to retract that intention. A mother is not always actually thinking of her family as she goes about washing, cleaning, etc., but if we should stop her, and ask her why she is doing all this, she would answer, "Out of love for my family." It is the same in our relationship with Mary. Dependence on her is the habitual state of our soul. However, we should remember that the more often we think of her, the more perfect will be our devotion. De Montfort says: "We must, from time to time, both during and after the action, renew our act of offering and union. The more often we do so, the sooner we shall be sanctified, and attain to union with Jesus Christ, which always follows necessarily on our union with Mary" *(True Devotion, 259)*.

38. If I now say the Rosary and pray to our Lady, why should I add True Devotion?

First of all, True Devotion is not a matter of commandment. It is merely a question of love. One would not, by any means, be damned, if he did not practice True Devotion. De Montfort himself tells us that all forms of true devotion to Mary are "good, holy, and praise-worthy." But he adds that they are "not so perfect, nor so efficient in severing our soul from creatures, or in detaching us from ourselves, in order to be united with Jesus Christ," *(Secret of Mary, 26)*, as is the practice of Holy Slavery. It is a question of generosity. De Montfort asks for the complete gift of self to Jesus Christ through the best means, Mary.

39. Will not the addition of another devotion only tend to confuse?

True Devotion is not "another devotion"; it is a consecration, a way of life that embraces all other devotions. Thus, it is not something different from devotion to the Sacred Heart, the Precious Blood, or the Eucharist. It is a part of every holy practice in the Church; it permeates every devotion and makes us see the hidden and holy things they contain. It makes us live the Mass as Mary lived it. In short, it means that Mary is with us, teaching us what all of these other devotions mean, and making us love them as she did.

40. Does not a person have to be very holy before he can practice this devotion to Jesus and Mary?

It must be remembered that Saint Louis De Montfort taught this devotion not to a chosen few, but to all the people who attended the various missions that he conducted. The entire idea of his slavery of love was to obtain union with Jesus. Therefore, it is a way of perfection, and not a reward for virtue. He gives it to all that they might find an "easy, short, and secure" path to Jesus. Surely, one does not show another how to get to a place if he is already there. When De Montfort says that we are to give this devotion only "to those who deserve it by their prayers, their alms-deeds, and mortification," he is laying stress on one point only, and that is, that the person must have a desire for bettering himself spiritually. This is only common sense, for you do not teach someone a more perfect way of sanctifying himself if he is not interested in sanctifying himself at all. If you really want to be more like Jesus, practice True Devotion. If you are not interested particularly in attaining holiness, please do not begin to practice this holy slavery of love.

Conclusion

The foregoing, in brief outline, is the teaching of
Saint Louis Grignion De Montfort on our Blessed
Mother. Since his time, people by the thousands from
every walk and vocation of life have used him as their
guide to heavenly living. They have found in this
teaching the joy and peace that Christ promised to all
"men of good will." A selection of some of their trib-
utes of praise has been made so that we may see the
high value that these individuals have set on the
faithful practice of Saint Louis De Montfort's *True
Devotion to the Blessed Virgin Mary*.

Tributes to Saint Louis De Montfort's
True Devotion to the Blessed Virgin

Popes

Pope Pius IX declared that
Saint Louis De Montfort's devotion to Mary is best and is the
most acceptable to our Lady.

Leo XIII granted a Plenary
Indulgence to those who make
Saint Louis De Montfort's Act
of Consecration to the Blessed
Virgin Mary. On his deathbed he
renewed the Act himself and
invoked the heavenly aid of
Saint Louis De Montfort whom he himself had beatified in 1888.

Pius X: "I heartily recommend *True Devotion to the
Blessed Virgin Mary*, so admirably written by Blessed
De Montfort, and to all who read it, I grant the
Apostolic Benediction."

In his famous encyclical "Ad diem illum" where
Pius X clearly sets forth the doctrine of the universal
mediation of Mary, he not only uses the thoughts and
words of Saint De Montfort, but in places even quotes

him directly. Pius X himself confessed this to Father Lhoumeau, Superior General of the Company of Mary.

Benedict XV: "The book on *True Devotion to the Blessed Virgin* is small in size, but of high authority and unction. We rejoice that it has already been so widely spread...May it spread still more, and ever revive the Christian spirit in an ever-increasing number of souls."

Pius XI: "Not only am I acquainted with it *(True Devotion)* but I have practiced it since my youth." On another occasion this same Pontiff acknowledged to Cardinal Charost, late Archbishop of Rheims, that he knew its contents almost by heart.

Pius XII: "The force and unction of the words of Mary's servant (De Montfort), have not only touched, but have captivated and converted many souls."

John Paul II: see pages 1-3, 99-101, and 379.

Cardinals

Cardinal Vaughn: "I have recommended 'True Devotion to the Blessed Virgin' to the clergy of this diocese as I recommended it some years ago to the clergy of the diocese of Salford: and I distributed copies of it to the priests who attended the first Synod which was held in Westminster. I should be glad to see it in the hands of every priest, as experience has taught me the power of this most persuasive treatise in propagating a solid devotion to the Blessed Mother of God...In our humble judgement no one can do better then spread the knowledge of this golden treatise on devotion to our Blessed Mother."

Cardinal Mercier: "Not only do I greatly esteem the *True Devotion* according to Blessed De Montfort, but for many years I have tried my best to put it into practice." This same Cardinal addressed a pastoral letter to the clergy and laity of his archdiocese on the subject of Montfort's *True Devotion to the Blessed Virgin* urging them to embrace it.

Cardinal O'Connell: "It is my happy privilege to recommend to everyone, following therein the example of our late Holy Father of blessed memory, Pius X, *True Devotion to the Blessed Virgin.* I have known this form of devotion for many years and I never hesitated to recommend it to those in whom the grace of God seemed at work, drawing them to a deeper and more intense spiritual life. As Rector of the American College in Rome, I proposed and taught it to the seminarians as an excellent means of acquiring the holiness of the priestly ideal. It was with my encouragement that there was formed among them a Blessed De Montfort Society."

Cardinal Lauri: "This book is a masterpiece."

Cardinal De Berulle: Founder of the Oratory in France and whose memory is held in veneration throughout all France, was most zealous in spreading this devotion in that country.

Theologians

Garrigou-Lagrange, O.P.: "Any one who willingly allows himself to be conducted in his prayers and in all phases of his life by Mary Mediatrix will attain to true humility which will draw upon him the grace of contemplation and of divine union." He then adds, quoting from De Montfort, "Without a great love for her, a soul will attain union with God only with extreme difficulty."

"One of the best means of spreading throughout the Christian people a devotion to Mary the universal Mediatrix, and of making understood the full import and the full compass of this title...is to broadcast the admirable doctrine of Blessed De Montfort....Those who propagate this devotion and those who love it have in their lives a sign of predestination."

Tanquerey: "It is an act of holy abandonment, of self-surrender excellent in itself and containing, moreover, acts of the highest virtues, religion, humility, and confiding love....By this act we glorify God and Mary in an unparalleled manner....We therefore also insure our individual sanctification and a third fruit of his Act of Consecration to Mary is the sanctification of our neighbor....It may be said that this Act of Consecration, if rightly made and correctly renewed, is of even greater worth than the Heroic Act."

Lemkuhl: "What can be truer than these principles of Blessed De Montfort? And if they be true, what can be more desirable, in these our times, in which indifference for Christ and His Church has spread throughout the world, than to possess in this devotion to Mary so excellent a means to lead souls back again to Christ?"

The Examinee of the Holy Office whose duty it was to investigate De Montfort's work to be sure that it contained nothing contrary to Faith, had this to say: "I must begin by confessing the impression made in me by reading the precious writing of this venerable servant of God. I have experienced an interior unction, a peace, and a consolation which the writings of highly favored servants of God, of servants of God endowed with light and sanctity of an extraordinary kind are known frequently to produce....This impression was profound and sweet to the highest degree."

Spiritual Writers

Father Faber: "I cannot think of a higher work or a broader vocation for any one than the simple spreading of this devotion of Grignion De Montfort.

Let a man but try it for himself and his surprise at the graces it brings with it, and the transformation it causes in his soul, will soon convince him of its otherwise almost incredible efficacy as a means for the salvation of men, and for the coming of the kingdom of Christ. Oh, if Mary were but known, there would be no coldness to Jesus then!...I would venture to warn the reader that one perusal will be very far from making him a master of it. If I may dare to say so, there is a growing feeling of something inspired and supernatural about it as we go on studying it; and with that we cannot help experiencing, after repeated readings of it, that its novelty never seems to wear off, nor its fullness to be diminished nor the fresh fragrance and sensible fire of its unction to abate."

Father Price (co-founder of Maryknoll): "I celebrate this day (25th anniversary of his ordination to the priesthood), Mother, by consecrating myself to you as Blessed De Montfort recommends."

Dom Chautard (author of *The Soul of the Apostolate*): "Obliged to limit myself and still wishing to offer my confreres in the Apostolate a sort of summing up of the advice of Saint Bernard to become true children of Mary, I think I cannot do better than to invite them to read carefully the solid and precious volume – The Spiritual Life according to the teaching of Blessed Grignion De Montfort."

Outstanding Catholic Laymen

Frank Duff (founder of the Legion of Mary): "De Montfort's book has a place of its own in the Church. There is nothing else quite like it. In its doctrine it is eminently theological and profound....It is certain that everyone who studies *True Devotion* will fall beneath its spell, for the book has everything. It has style, it has fervor, it has intense conviction, solidity, soaring eloquence, the air of authority and inspiration....Nowadays, there is no competent writer on the subject of Mary who does not pay tribute to the *True Devotion* and its influence on Mariology."

Handbook of the Legion of Mary: "It can be safely asserted that no saint has played a greater part in the development of the Legion than he (Saint De Montfort). The handbook is full of his spirit. The prayers re-echo his very words. He is really the Tutor of the Legion. The practice of True Devotion deepens the interior life, sealing it with the special character of unselfishness and purity of intention. There is a sense of guidance and protection: a joyful certainty that now one's life is being employed to the best advantage. There is a supernatural outlook, a definite courage, a firmer faith, which makes one a mainstay of any enterprise."

Saints Who Have Practiced True Devotion

As True Devotion was known before the time of Saint De Montfort, we should not be surprised to find many of the great Saints of the Church finding Jesus through Mary by the slavery of love. A few can be mentioned: Saints Ephrem, Bonaventure, Anselm, Bernardine, Leonard of Port Maurice. After De Montfort the greatest slave of Jesus in Mary is Saint Alphonsus. But it is in the last century especially that we find true followers of De Montfort's Devotion. Blessed Peter Eymard, the Apostle of the Eucharist, knew no better way of adoring Jesus in the Eucharist than by becoming a slave of Mary. The Saintly Curé of Ars was a fervent advocate of True Devotion to our Lady. Saint Gabriel was a model for all seminarians in his love for Mary. By means of this slavery to Mary he reached the highest sanctity after five years in the Passionist seminary. Perhaps the most inspiring story of all the Saints of our Lady is the story of the Little Flower and Blessed Theophane Venard. Therese in her monastery and Theophane in his Mission were both slaves of our Lady and bound themselves together as brother and sister in the service of Mary. The results of both of their lives stand as a divine approval to this secret of grace that they found in *True Devotion to our Lady*.

The Maternity of Mary

"God could create more perfect angels, a more perfect heaven, a greater universe than ours, but He could not create a greater Mother than the Mother of God," so wrote Saint Bonaventure, many centuries ago. Today, we have the privilege of celebrating this Feast of Mary's Maternity, and of studying the "great things" that God has done to her.

It is from her motherhood of God that all her other dignities stem. The Immaculate Conception prepared her for it, while the Nativity was the outward manifestation of it. Because she is the Mother of God, it follows that she is the universal *Mediatrix of All Grace*. In a word, everything good and holy that can be said of our Lady belongs to her because she brought forth the God-Man.

Consider what a work of perfection she is. God the Father claims her as His daughter; God the Son calls her His Mother; and of God the Holy Spirit, she is the Spouse. She was a creature whose whole being was tied up intimately with Divinity. God made her the perfect workshop, the place where nothing evil could claim entrance, for in her was to be formed the greatest perfection of which the Holy Spirit was capable – the formation of the God-Man.

We stand back and look in loving rapture. "O Mary, thou art all beautiful," we cry out, "If only we could belong to you." Christ knew our desires and in

His great act of love on Mount Calvary, He answered our prayer even before we formed it. He turned to Saint John who took your place and mine, and said, "Behold thy Mother." Jesus, if we did not have Your word for it, could we ever hope to have the Mother of God as our Mother as well! We do have Your word for it, and, like Saint John, we know what to do. We will take her to ourselves, and spend our lives in loving service to her. O thank You, Jesus, for giving me Your very own Mother. Holy Mary, Mother of God, pray for me a sinner, now and at the hour of my death. Amen.

Pope John Paul II

"Marian *spirituality*, like its corresponding *devotion*, finds a very rich source in the historical experience of individuals and of the various Christian communities present among the different peoples and nations of the world. In this regard, I would like to recall, among the many witnesses and teachers of this spirituality, the figure of Saint Louis Marie Grignion de Montfort, who proposes consecration to Christ through the hands of Mary, as an effective means for Christians to live faithfully their baptismal commitments" *(Mother of the Redeemer, 48).*

THE END

"I am all Thine and all I have is Thine, O most loving Jesus, through Mary, Thy holy Mother."

The above illustration and others in this meditation book are taken from *The Apostolate's Family Catechism* and the "Consecration in Truth" catechetical program, which includes over 1000 illustrations. These unique pictures unite the mind with the heart and help parents and teachers to discuss the faith with their children and students.

53a. Examination of Conscience: Scripture's Four C's

53a.1 Confidence:

— How well have I trusted God?

— Have I given into anxiety and fear because I have not chosen to trust in God's love and Providence?

— Do I really believe that God loves me?

— *There is no fear in love, but perfect love casts out fear. For fear has to do with punishment, and he who fears is not perfected in love.* (1 John 4:18)

— *Humble yourselves therefore under the mighty hand of God, that in due time he may exalt you. Cast all your anxieties on him, for he cares about you.* (1 Pet. 5:6-7)

53a.2 Conscience:

— How well have I prayed, practiced silence and the Presence of God, and listened to God?

— Do I pause and mentally say "All for" before every decision, activity, or reaction?

— Do I mean when I say "All for" that I am making a spiritual communion and asking for the graces to discern and do God's will for the present moment?

— Do I truly strive to fulfill the responsibility of the present moment?

— Have I used my spiritual and material resources as God has called me to do?

— Have I thanked God for all that He has given me, including the graces to carry my crosses?

— Have I obeyed my superiors, which is a true test of my willingness to surrender my will to God, or do I try to manipulate them?

— Have I fallen from grace by using artificial contraceptives? (All contraceptives are forbidden.)

— Have I sought spiritual counsel from someone who fully subscribes to the teachings of *Humane Vitae* before using natural family planning? (This document clearly outlines the Church's teaching on marriage and life.)

— *He himself bore our sins in his body on the tree, that we might die to sin and live to righteousness.* (1 Pet. 2:24)

53a.3 Charity:

— How well have I treated others, particularly those in my family?

— Have I taught by good example and loving authority, or have I abused my authority by showing my anger and by not being charitable or just?

— Do I try too hard to change others rather than change myself?

— Have I been a hypocrite by talking about others or looking down on others? The only people with whom Christ really grew angry were the Pharisees when they judged others, St. Peter when he tried to talk Jesus out of carrying the Cross, and those who made irreverent use of God's house!

— How well have I lived my total consecration (i.e., total giving of oneself to Jesus through Mary in union with St. Joseph)?

— Do I guard lawful confidences? *(One would not keep confident that which a parent or superior should know).*

— *Clothe yourselves, all of you, with humility toward one another, for "God opposes the proud, but gives grace to the humble."* (1 Pet. 5:5)

— *If I speak in the tongues of men and of angels, but have not love, I am a noisy gong or a clanging cymbal. And if I have prophetic powers, and understand all mysteries and all knowledge, and if I have all faith, so as to remove mountains, but have not love, I am nothing. If I give away all I have, and if I deliver my body to be burned, but have not love, I gain nothing. Love is patient and kind; love is not jealous or boastful; it is not arrogant or rude. Love does not insist on its own way; it is not irritable or resentful; it does not rejoice at wrong, but rejoices in the right. Love bears all things, believes all things, hopes all things, endures all things.* (1 Cor. 13:1-7)

53a.4 Constancy:

— How well have I applied myself to my tasks and responsibilities? Have I carried my cross and gone the extra mile for God?

— Have I remembered that I am in God's presence by turning my mind to Him frequently during the day? "All for"

— Have I maintained a positive and patient attitude, looking for the harvest of graces which will enable me to fulfill God's providential plan in His due season?

— Do I realize that God has a providential plan for each day in my life. This is what we mean by "Divine Providence". We need to persevere and stay alert for "All for" opportunities to plant seeds of Faith and charity in our daily lives.

— Have I used the grace offered to me in each present moment to say "All for" to God, or do I allow the world, the flesh, or the devil to distract me and therefore offend God by regretting the past or feeling sorry for myself? In other words, do I get caught up in the teeter-totter of fearing the future and regretting the past and miss the grace of the now? (Graces, both sanctifying and actual, are only given to us in the present moment.)

— Do I offend God by worrying about the future? I must remember that the only moment over which I have control is the present moment; which should be offered with fervent love to God!

— *Therefore do not be anxious about tomorrow, for tomorrow will be anxious for itself. Let the day's own trouble be sufficient for the day.* (Mt. 6:34)

53b. Examination of Conscience: The Seven Capital Virtues and Seven Capital Sins

In our prayer we ask for the grace to overcome our faults by practicing the virtue that is the opposite of each of our faults.

1.   Let the virtue of *humility* (acknowledgment of my total dependence on God for what is good) overcome my tendency toward pride and egoism and my desire for fullness and recognition.

2.   Let the virtue of *liberality* overcome my tendency toward spiritual and material avarice and my desire for security and prosperity.

3.   Let the virtue of *temperance* overcome my tendency toward gluttony and uncontrolled self-indulgence in food, television, and other forms of normally licit pleasures.

4.   Let the virtues of *chastity* and self-control overcome my tendency toward mental and physical lust.

5.   Let the virtue of *meekness* overcome my tendency toward anger, which manifests itself when my human plans (no matter how good they may be) are upset. Often I may fail to use trials as stepping stones toward that total detachment which, as Pope John Paul II has said, purifies our feelings and lifts our spirits so that we can hear the voice of God and train our consciences.

6.   Let the virtue of *brotherly love* overcome my tendency toward envy. Let me understand that the vision of The Apostolate promotes the truth with great intensity so that authentic brotherly love will be manifested

through the systematic transformation of neighborhoods into strong God-centered communities, in the joyful spirit of Pope John Paul II.

7.　　Let the virtue of *diligence* overcome my tendency toward sloth (laziness). Let me not fall into the trap of feeling sorry for myself when others appear to be doing less work than myself; rather, let me go the extra mile and fulfill my responsibilities better than I have to, because I do it for God, not for man.

53c. Examination of Conscience: The Spiritual Works of Mercy
(see #43b for Blessed Teresa of Calcutta and Fr. John Hardon's interview)

The spiritual works of mercy are a form of Christian charity in favor of the soul or spirit of one's neighbor. Let's check to see how we have been following these norms:

1. Converting the sinner (clothing the spiritually naked with grace)
2. Instructing the ignorant (feeding the spiritually hungry and thirsty)
3. Counseling the doubtful
4. Comforting the sorrowful
5. Bearing wrongs patiently
6. Forgiving injury
7. Praying for the living and the dead

53d. Examination of Conscience: The Corporal Works of Mercy

Christ taught us that the corporal works of mercy, which overlap into the spiritual works of mercy, will be the criteria for salvation at the Last Judgment. (cf. Mt. 25:34-46 and the *Catechism of the Catholic Church*, section 2447; also see #43b)

1. Feeding the hungry
2. Giving drink to the thirsty
3. Clothing the naked
4. Giving shelter to the homeless
5. Visiting the sick
6. Visiting those in prison
7. Burying the dead

53e. Examination of Conscience: The Precepts of the Church

What is expected of Catholic Christians, as found in the Catechism of the Catholic Church

2041   The precepts of the Church are set in the context of a moral life bound to and nourished by liturgical life. The obligatory character of these positive laws decreed by the pastoral authorities is meant to guarantee to the faithful the indispensable minimum in the spirit of prayer and moral effort, in the growth in love of God and neighbor:

2042   The first precept ("You shall attend Mass on Sundays and holy days of obligation.") requires the faithful to participate in the Eucharistic celebration when the Christian community gathers together on the day commemorating the Resurrection of the Lord.

The second precept ("You shall confess your sins at least once a year.") ensures preparation for the Eucharist by the reception of the sacrament of reconciliation, which continues Baptism's work of conversion and forgiveness.

The third precept ("You shall humbly receive your Creator in Holy Communion at least during the Easter season.") guarantees as a minimum the reception of the Lord's Body and Blood in connection with the Paschal feasts, the origin and center of the Christian liturgy.

2043   The fourth precept ("You shall keep holy the holy days of obligation.") completes the Sunday observance by participation in the principal liturgical feasts which honor the mysteries of the Lord, the Virgin Mary, and the saints.

The fifth precept ("You shall observe the prescribed days of fasting and abstinence.") ensures the times of ascesis* and penance which prepare us for the liturgical feasts; they help us acquire mastery over our instincts and freedom of heart.

The faithful also have the duty of providing for the material needs of the Church, each according to his abilities.

53f . Examination of Conscience: The Seven Gifts of the Holy Spirit

Father John Hardon, S.J., writes that the seven gifts of the Holy Spirit are "the seven forms of supernatural initiatives conferred with the reception of sanctifying grace. They are in the nature of supernatural reflexes or reactive instincts that spontaneously answer to divine impulses of grace, almost without reflection but always with full consent."

---

*Ascesis is a spiritual effort or exercise to help one grow in virtue.

Wisdom

Most Holy Spirit, help me, my family, and all the members of The Apostolate to respond well to Your will by judging all things according to Your spiritual standards. Help us to contemplate Your truths and to apply them, in a practical manner, to our daily lives.

Understanding

Most Holy Spirit, help me, my family, and all the members of The Apostolate to go beyond faith and to penetrate the very core of revealed truths by giving us insights into their meaning. Confirm us in our faith by giving us great confidence in the revealed word of God.

Knowledge

Most Holy Spirit, give me, my family, and all the members of The Apostolate the ability to judge everything from a supernatural point of view. Help us to see the providential purpose of whatever enters our lives and to discern clearly between impulses of temptation and inspirations of grace.

Fortitude

Most Holy Spirit, help me, my family, and all the members of The Apostolate to persevere in carrying out Your distinctive plan for our lives. Make us ready to sacrifice whatever is truly necessary in order to do Your will.

Counsel

Most Holy Spirit, help me, my family, and all the members of The Apostolate to judge properly and rightly, by a sort of supernatural intuition, what should be done, especially in difficult situations. Please speak to our hearts and enlighten us as to what we should do in each present moment. Help us to think of Mat. 10:19-20: *When they deliver you up, do not be anxious how you are to speak or what you are to say; for what you are to say will be given to you in that hour; for it is not you who speak, but the Spirit of your Father speaking through you.*

Help us to understand that counsel refers to conducting ourselves, primarily, prudently and, secondarily, to the advice we might give to others about their conduct. Enlightened by the Holy Spirit, a person will know what to do in a specific case, what advice to give someone when he is consulted, or what command to make when he is in authority.

Piety

Most Holy Spirit, infuse into my soul, and into the souls of all of my family members and the members of The Apostolate, a profound respect for God, a generous love for Him, and an affectionate obedience to legitimate authority; thus I may show others the most perfect way to please God.

Fear of the Lord

Most Holy Spirit, confirm in me, my family, and all of the members of The Apostolate a profound respect for the majesty of God, a loving sorrow for the least fault committed, and a vigilant love in order that we may avoid all occasions of sin.

53g. Examination of Conscience: The Eight Beatitudes
Catechism of the Catholic Church, section 1716
(cf. Mt. 5:3-12 and Lk. 6:20-23)

Lord, help me, my family, and all of the members of The Apostolate to practice the Beatitudes and to realize that they are expressions of the New Covenant, where the peace that only God can give is assured already in this life, provided that a person totally gives himself to the imitation of Christ.

The Beatitudes are:

1. Blessed are the poor in spirit, for theirs is the kingdom of heaven.

2. Blessed are those who mourn, for they shall be comforted.

3. Blessed are the meek, for they shall inherit the earth.

4. Blessed are those who hunger and thirst for righteousness, for they shall be satisfied.

5. Blessed are the merciful, for they shall obtain mercy.

6. Blessed are the pure in heart, for they shall see God.

7. Blessed are the peacemakers, for they shall be called sons of God.

8. Blessed are those who are persecuted for righteousness' sake, for theirs is the kingdom of heaven. Blessed are you when men revile you and persecute you and utter all kinds of evil against you falsely on my account. Rejoice and be glad, for your reward is great in heaven, for so men persecuted the prophets who were before you.

53h. Examination of Conscience: In Light of the Ten Commandments
Refer to Exodus 20:1-17, Deuteronomy 5:6-21

The First Commandment

53h.1 I am the Lord your God: you shall not have strange gods before me.

- Have I received Holy Communion in the state of mortal sin?

- Have I neglected to confess a mortal sin in a previous confession to a priest, when I was aware of having committed one?

- Have I practiced superstition?

- Have I been engaged in occult practices such as consulting horoscopes, tarot cards, or ouija boards?

- Have I participated in seances, or in satanic or demonic services and/or prayers?

- Have I refused to accept any teaching of the Church?

- Have I put my soul in danger by reading, viewing, or listening to material that attacks the teachings of the Catholic Church in matters of faith or morals?

- Do I belong to any anti-Catholic organizations such as the Freemasons (Shriners)?

- Have I attended the meetings or gatherings of any anti-Catholic organizations?

- Have I profaned (desecrated) or spoken sinfully against a sacred person, place, or thing?

- Have I sought an unhealthy relationship with a person who is a consecrated celibate?

- Have I been slow or reluctant to perform my duties toward God?

- Have I neglected to pray?

- Have I neglected to prepare myself properly for Holy Communion?

- Have I made a false god of money, career, or possessions?

- Have I made a false god of pleasure, sports, internet, video games, or television, etc.?

The Second Commandment

53h.2 You shall not take the Name of the Lord your God in vain.

- Have I taken the Holy Name of God in vain?

- Have I spoken His Name in anger?

- Have I jokingly or irreverently spoken about God?

- Have I been a baptismal or confirmation sponsor in a non-Catholic ceremony?

- Have I broken any promises (oaths) in which I invoked God's Name?

The Third Commandment

53h.3 Remember to keep holy the Lord's Day.

- Have I failed to attend Mass on Sundays or holy days of obligation without just cause (for example, serious illness or impassible roads or pathways)?

- Have I arrived at Mass on Sundays or holy days of obligation after the Liturgy of the Word without just cause?

- Have I worn improper attire to Mass, or have I otherwise distracted others from paying attention at Mass?

- Do I fast (one full meal and two lighter meals) and abstain from eating meat on the days or at times which are appointed by the Church (for example, fast and abstain from eating meat on Ash Wednesday and Good Friday, and abstain from eating meat on all Fridays during Lent).

- Have I maintained the one-hour fast (including gum) before receiving Holy Communion (except for health reasons). Water is permissible.

- Have I fulfilled the Church's precept to confess my sins at least once a year? *(Catechism of the Catholic Church, 2042)*

- Have I fulfilled my yearly Easter duty of receiving Holy Communion and Confession?

- Have I performed (or required others to perform) servile or manual labor on Sundays (not including work to save souls or work required by your employer, enjoyable gardening, or acts of mercy such as helping a neighbor in need or milking cows and feeding livestock)?

- Have I deliberately failed to pay attention at Mass?

- Am I generous in helping the Church and contributing to the financial support of her ministries that are laboring to save souls? Do I try to follow the biblical exhortation to tithe, that is, to give back to God, through His Church and her ministries, one tenth of the income He blesses me with (cf. Malachi 3:6-12)?

The Fourth Commandment

53h.4 Honor your father and your mother.

For Parents:
- Have I set a bad example for my children?

- When I do correct my children's faults, is it done with charity?

- Have I made sure that my children make their First Confession and First Communion at about the age of seven?

- Have I failed to take my children to Mass on Sundays and holy days of obligation; or neglected to provide them with an orthodox Catholic education; or neglected to teach them how to pray; or failed to lead them to the sacraments?

- Have I failed to supervise my children with respect to the friends they choose and the entertainment they pursue?

- Do I monitor my children in their choice of reading material, in the shows they watch on television, or in the movies or concerts they attend?

- Have I separated from or divorced my spouse civilly without consultation of a priest who follows the mind of the Church?

- Do I seek God's help every day to fulfill my duties as a parent?

For Children:
- Have I disobeyed my parents, or been disrespectful to them in other ways?

- Do I nurse angry feelings or show resentment when I am corrected by my parents?

- Have I been moody, sour, or bad-tempered towards other people?

- Do I desire to leave my parents' household when I am too young or for other improper reasons?

- Am I a financial burden to my parents when I can take care of my own financial needs and am old enough to help support the household?

- Do I fight and/or quarrel with my brothers and sisters?

- Have I failed to express my love for my parents?

- Have I failed to help my parents when they were unable to meet their basic needs?

- Do I faithfully perform—without complaining—the household and outdoor chores my parents give me to do?

The Fifth Commandment

53h.5 You shall not kill.

- Have I lost my temper or become unjustly angry at others?

- Have I neglected to loved my neighbor as Our Lord has loved me?

- Have I murdered or otherwise unjustly injured (no matter how slight) anyone?

- Have I been a reckless driver?

- Have I tempted others to sin by my bad example or sinful conversation?

- Have I encouraged others to read or watch sinful materials or programs or to otherwise do sinful things?

- Have I failed to make up for, or repair for, the bad example I may have given others?

- Have I been jealous of others? Have I been envious of the possessions of others?

- How many people have I led into sin? What type of sins were they?

- Have I tried to, or nurtured the thoughts to, commit suicide?

- Have I failed to take proper care of my health?

- Have I mutilated myself or someone else?

- Have I been drunk or intoxicated on alcohol or other substances?

- Have I intentionally overindulged in food or drink (gluttony)?

- Have I participated in gang fights or other illegal gang activities?

- Have I been a bully or picked fights with others?

- Have I consented to a sterilization or encouraged others to do so, or actively taken part in someone else's sterilization?

- Have I practiced contraception or encouraged others to do so?

- When using Natural Family Planning, have I prayed with my spouse and truly sought God's will?

- Have I recommended, consented to, advised, or actively taken part in an abortion?

- Am I aware of the Church's teaching that abortion is a mortal sin, and that those who actively take part (for example, doctor, nurse, and mother) in an abortion are automatically excommunicated? (However, most priests have the authority to lift that excommunication.)

- Have I harmed anyone's reputation by my speech or actions?

- Have I desired to take revenge of anyone who offended me?

- Have I hated or nursed bad feelings toward any person?

- Have I maliciously teased or insulted others?

- Have I refused to forgive anyone who may have offended me?

- Have I sought pardon of those whom I have offended?

The Sixth and Ninth Commandments

53h.6 You shall not commit adultery.

53h.9 You shall not covet your neighbor's wife.

- Have I entertained impure thoughts? Have I deliberately recalled impure thoughts or images? Do I watch soap operas or other impure programs?

- Have I had sexual relations with a member of the opposite sex when we weren't married to each other (fornication)?

- Have I had sexual relations with a married person who is not my spouse (adultery)?

- Although I may never have fully carried them out, have I consented to impure desires?

- Were any circumstances present to make the sin of impurity even more serious, for example, having impure relations with someone who is consecrated to God by vows (sacrilege), or who is married to someone other than myself (adultery), or who is a member of my family (other than my spouse if I am married) (incest)?

- Have I engaged in impure conversations? Did I begin them?

- Have I sought to have a good time by engaging in entertainment which placed me in proximate [close] occasions of sin, such as sensual dances; sexually suggestive movies, plays, and reading material; evil company; houses of prostitution; and massage parlors?

- Am I aware of the fact that I might already be sinning by simply placing myself in a proximate occasion of sin? Such circumstances can include carelessly accessing or surfing the web, sharing of a room with a member of the opposite sex, being alone with a member of the opposite sex with whom I have continually sinned with, or deliberately taking such a person to a secluded place.

- Have I neglected to dress modestly or to otherwise safeguard purity? Have I guarded my eyes?

- Have I willfully looked at immodest pictures, impure movies, or pornographic sites on the web?

- Have I immodestly looked or glanced at others?

- Did I do any of the above things, knowing that they involved gravely sinful matter?

- Have I led others to commit the sins of immodesty or impurity? Specifically speaking, what were they?

- Have I committed impure acts by myself (masturbation)? Did I do so deliberately and freely, knowing that serious matter was involved? Did I know that masturbation freely and willfully performed is a mortal sin?

- Have I committed impure acts with someone else either of the opposite or the same sex (homosexual acts)? How many times did I do so? Were there any circumstances (such as impure acts with members of my family other than my spouse, or with persons consecrated to God by vows or promises) which could have made the sin especially serious?

- Do I have evil or immoral friendships? Have I taken steps to break these friendships?

- Do I respect and guard my exclusive relationship with my spouse by not getting too familiar with someone of the opposite sex, whether it be in a work or social setting?

- Have I been engaged in immodest conduct or conversation with someone I am seriously thinking of marrying?

- Have I used my fiance, spouse, or another person as an object for my pleasure, rather than a person created in

God's image and likeness whom God has placed in my life to respect and reverence and help get to heaven?

- Have I engaged in acts of intimate affection reserved for spouses (such as passionate kissing, embraces, petting, etc.) with someone other than my spouse, arousing lustful thoughts and desires as well?

- Have I failed to protect my spouse, fiance, or friend from sinning?

- Have I failed to investigate beforehand the sinful potentials of watching a particular show or reading a particular book or magazine?

For Married People:
- Have I denied my spouse of her or his marital right?

- Have I engaged in adulterous acts or desires?

- Have I used or consented to the use of artificial contraceptives?

- Have I suggested that others do so? (On sterilization, abortion, etc., refer to the Fifth Commandment.)

- Do I practice natural means of conception control without justifiable reasons before God for doing so? (See the *Catechism of the Catholic Church*, 2368-2371, and *Humane Vitae*, 16.)

The Seventh and Tenth Commandments

53h.7 You shall not steal.

53h.10 You shall not covet your neighbor's goods.

- Have I stolen anything? What was it worth?

- Have I returned the stolen item, or do I intend to return it?

- Have I damaged or been responsible for the damage of another person's property? What would be the cost of repairing or replacing it?

- Have I caused harm to anyone in business dealings by means of fraud, deception, or coercion?

- Have I spent beyond my means?

- Have I deprived others of their needs by spending too little?

- Have I supported the Church and charitable organizations according to my means?

- Have I honored my debts?

- Have I taken stolen property or refused to seek the owner of property that I have found?

- Have I seriously entertained temptations to steal?

- Have I been lazy with respect to my employment, household chores, work, or studies?

- Have I been greedy?

- Have I placed too high a value on material goods?

- Have I failed to help those whom I know are truly needy?

- Have I been irresponsible with money or other means of wealth which God has entrusted to me?

- Have I excessively gambled?

- Have I been envious of the wealth or material goods of another person?

- Have I realized that sins of omission are just as serious, if not more, than sins of comission, as taught by Our Lord in Matthew 25? (also see section 43b)

The Eighth Commandment

53h.8 You shall not bear false witness against your neighbor.

- Have I lied?

- Have I sought to make up for the damage caused by my lies?

- Have I accused others of wrongdoing without sufficient evidence?

- Have I been guilty of detraction (to speak about the faults of others without having a good reason for doing so)?

- Have I been guilty of calumny (to falsely accuse someone of sinful conduct)?

- Have I gossiped about another person?

- Have I too hastily judged someone of improper conduct?

- Have I, without sufficient cause, suspected someone to be guilty of misconduct?

- Have I been excessively critical, negative, or uncharitable in my speech?

- Have I failed to honor the confidences or secrets entrusted to me by another? Have I revealed them to someone else without permission or without due or serious cause?

- Have I used the technique of binding others to secrecy about something that should be revealed to lawful authority?

- Have I failed to defend the good name or honor of others?

53i. Examination of Conscience Reflections
by Jerome F. Coniker

Most Holy Family, help me to call to mind the instances in the past few hours or days when I sowed bad seeds and lost my peaceful union with God, and when I did not make full use of Scriptures Four C's for Peaceful Seed Living (Confidence, Conscience, Seed-Charity, and Constancy) as part of my daily life.

Please uproot these negative seeds and help me to purify my conscience, which is the seedbed for the growth of grace in my soul.

Purify me so that my virtuous acts and sacrifices will be used to atone for sin. Allow me to peacefully rise above my problems and grow into a worthy instrument by becoming one spirit with the Lord and the Holy Family.

Help me, Most Holy Family, to forgive others. Inspire me to be respectful to those over whom I have authority and to praise their good points more than I point out their faults (cf. 2 Cor. 10:8).

Enable me to see the causes of my daily sins and faults, and to give them to Jesus so that He can wash them in His Precious Blood and transform them into virtues.

Never let me forget that it is God's power of grace combined with my good works that will overpower my sinful nature. Help me to see that without God as my Source, salvation would be impossible (cf. Lk. 18:26-27).

(Pause to reflect)

Inspire me, Most Holy Family, to make and to keep practical resolutions for the amendment of my life. Never let me forget that I primarily teach others by the example of my daily life, and that I will be held accountable for every thought, word, and action during my test on earth (cf. Mat. 12:36-37).

Help me to be as good to all the members of my family as I am to those whom I meet outside my home. Now, Most Holy Family, please let me picture myself as the person I want to become, a person who mirrors your virtues.

Help me to visualize how you would act if you were in my place at this time; and how you would treat the members of my family or community, especially those who need my time and undivided attention and those who have hurt me. (pause)

Help me to show affection rather than anger to all whom you bring into my life, especially those in my own family or community. (pause)

> *...put on the new nature, which is being renewed in knowledge after the image of its creator. (Col. 3:10)*

Pause and imagine Jesus, Mary, or Joseph living your life. Visualize yourself as a virtuous person who is perpetually confident, calm, cheerful, and compassionate, especially under pressure and with the members of your own family and community.

Visualize how you should have handled yourself the last time you lost your peaceful union with God by your faults, willful sins, and selfishness.

> *Let everyone who names the name of the Lord depart from iniquity. (2 Tim. 2:19)*
>
> *...do not let the sun go down on your anger, and give no opportunity to the devil. (Eph. 4:26-27)*

Most Holy Spirit of the Father and the Son, dwelling deep within the innermost recesses of my soul (cf. 1 Cor. 2:10-16), help me to realize that sin is the cause of all unhappiness because it gives the forces of evil more power over my life and over the entire world.

Inspire me to encourage others to help those who suffer. We can do this, not only by our much needed almsgiving which represents a true sacrifice of the fruits of our work and security, but also by our supernaturally good acts of prayer and charity and by the fervent reception of the sacraments.

Help me to unite the trials I encounter in the faithful fulfillment of the responsibilities of my state in life with the Holy Sacrifice of the Mass, which is continually being offered throughout the world.

Never let me forget, Most Holy Spirit, that You dwell within me. If I unite every act of my daily life with You and the Holy Family, I become a useful instrument to counteract the unhappy effects of sin. This can help to bring true peace and happiness not only into my life, but into the lives of the people in my family, my community, my school, my parish, and the entire Mystical Body of Christ on earth.

Because there is one bread, we who are many are one body, for we all partake of the one bread. (1 Cor. 10:17)

Most Holy Spirit, You are the Source of truth and enlightenment. Teach me the truths of my faith, and then give me the grace to believe and live them.

These things I have spoken to you, while I am still with you. But the Counselor, the Holy Spirit, whom the Father will send in my name, He will teach you all things, and bring to your remembrance all that I have said to you. (Jn. 14:25-26)

For just as the body is one and has many members, and all the members of the body, though many, are one body, so it is with Christ. For by one Spirit we were all baptized into one body — Jews or Greeks, slaves or free — and all were made to drink of one Spirit. (1 Cor. 12:12-13)

He is the head of the body, the church. (Col. 1:18)

Remember those who are in prison, as though in prison with them; and those who are ill-treated, since you also are in the body. (Heb. 13:3)

He has put all things under his feet and has made him the head over all things for the church, which is his body, the fullness of him who fills all in all. (Eph. 1:22-23)

...that is, how the Gentiles are fellow heirs, members of the same body, and partakers of the promise in Christ Jesus through the gospel. (Eph. 3:6)

Therefore, putting away falsehood, let every one speak the truth with his neighbor, for we are members one of another. (Eph. 4:25)

For no man ever hates his own flesh, but nourishes and cherishes it, as Christ does the church, because we are members of his body. (Eph. 5:29-30)

53j. Examination of Conscience: Excerpt from Veritatis Splendor
by Pope John Paul II

When examining your conscience, please read one of the Scripture references indicated in this excerpt.

26. In the *moral catechesis* of the Apostles, besides exhortations and directions connected to specific historical and cultural situations, we find an ethical teaching with precise rules of behavior. This is seen in their Letters, which contain the interpretation, made under the guidance of the Holy Spirit, of the Lord's precepts as they are to be lived in different cultural circumstances (cf. Rom. 12-15; 1 Cor. 11-14; Gal. 5-6; Eph. 4-6; Col. 3-4; 1 Pt. and Jas.).

53L. Examination of Conscience: Gifts of the Holy Spirit and Infused Virtues

© *MCMXCVI Rev. Bernard M. Geiger, O.F.M., Conv.*
(Used with permission)

The Gifts of the Holy Spirit supply, as it were, the forms and paths which our spiritual development and our service of God will take, while the *Infused Virtues* drive and bring about that development and service. If we choose to give in to the Capital Sins, they will block or kill the life of the Gifts and Virtues. If we choose to develop the habits of the Gifts and Virtues, they will put to death the seven capital tendencies to sin in us.

Gifts of the Holy Spirit—permanent capacities to receive and use particular lights from Jesus' fullness of Truth.
Infused Virtues—permanent capacities to receive and use particular powers from Jesus' fullness of Grace.
Capital Sins and their Effects—tendencies in us which lead to sin and bondage to Satan if not curbed.

Part I: Theological Virtues
Unite us directly to God

53L1. Gift of Knowledge
Permanent capacity to receive the light of Jesus' knowledge, so that we can use it to make acts of, and develop habits of, supernatural knowledge. We need these acts and habits to become informed and conscious of God's call, His plan for our salvation and divine adoption, and the New Covenant which activates the plan.

Virtue of Faith

Permanent capacity to receive the power of Jesus' absolute adherence and obedience to the Truth, so that we can use it to make acts of, and develop habits of, supernatural faith. We need these acts and habits to believe firmly that God's revelation of Himself and of His Kingdom of Love are true, that God is infinite goodness;

faith enables us to grow in our consciousness and celebration of the truth about God.

Capital Sins: Covetousness & Avarice

Darkens the mind, produces indifference to God, which leads to ignorance of God, God's call, His plan for our salvation, our divine adoption, and the New Covenant. Covetousness addicts us to worldly treasures as cheap substitutes for the treasure of God's Kingdom of Love.

Read the Catechism of the Catholic Church, paragraphs 31–38, 153–165, 2087–2089, 2535–2536, 2541, and 2552.

53L2. Gift of Understanding

Permanent capacity to receive the light of Jesus' understanding, so that we can use it to make acts of, and develop habits of, supernatural understanding. We need these acts and habits to understand our relationships with the Divine Persons, Mary, the Angels, the Saints, and each other in His Kingdom of Love, and what it means for each of us personally.

Virtue of Hope

Permanent capacity to receive the power of Jesus' commitment to His Father's Will and plan, so that we can use it to make acts of, and develop habits of, supernatural hope. We need these acts and habits to resolutely and perseveringly commit ourselves to God and His Kingdom of Love. This commitment incorporates us into the Kingdom.

Capital Sin: Gluttony

Numbs the mind and prevents understanding of God's plan and Covenant, and so forestalls commitment to them. Gluttony addicts us to pleasures of food, drink, and even television as cheap substitutes for the true meaning of life and for commitment to God.

Read the Catechism of the Catholic Church, paragraphs 84–95, 1817–1821, 2090– 2092, 2548–2549, and 2705.

53L3. Gift of Piety

Permanent capacity to receive the light of Jesus' piety—His habit of mentally identifying with the Father and with each of us—so that we can use it to make acts of, and develop habits of, supernatural piety. These acts and habits enable us to identify with God and each of our neighbors in God's Kingdom of Love—to see God as my Father and myself as His son or daughter; Jesus as my Brother and Redeemer; and Mary as my Mother, etc.

Virtue of Charity/Love

Permanent capacity to receive the power of Jesus' love and self-giving, so that we can use it to make acts of, and develop habits of, supernatural charity. By these acts and habits we can always say "yes" to Him and to all He wants to give us and ask of us. This "yes" allows Jesus to begin living in us and allows us to live in Him.

Capital Sin: Lust

Lust is a kind of false love. It causes alienation and isolation from others, and prevents real love of God, self, and neighbor. Lust addicts us to illicit sexual gratification as a cheap substitute for authentic Christian friendship and unselfish affectionate love.

Read the Catechism of the Catholic Church, paragraphs 1822–1829, 1889, 2093–2094, and 2514–2533.

Part II: Cardinal Virtues
Enable us to express, prove, and grow in our love of God by implementing His plan and Covenant in a practical way

53L.4 Gift of Wisdom

Permanent capacity to receive the light of Jesus' wisdom, so that we can use it to make acts of, and develop habits of, supernatural wisdom. They enable us to see where we have come from, where we are going in God's plan, and how to get there; and how to discern the poten-

tial, the means, and the opportunities which God gives us
to achieve our destiny.

Virtue of Prudence

Permanent capacity to receive Jesus' power of prudence, so that we can use it to make acts of, and develop
habits of, supernatural prudence. These acts and habits
enable us to set and prioritize goals for implementing
God's plan for us, and to plan or choose projects and programs which help us achieve these goals.

Capital Sin: Pride (Self-Worship)

Produces false self-image and delusions, refusal to
serve God. Addicts us to lying, empty boasting, possessing
power over others and dominating them, and doing whatever we please as perverse substitutes for true wisdom
and prudence.

Read the Catechism of the Catholic Church, paragraphs
1786–1789, 1806, 1950, 2094, and 2779.

53L5.   Gift of Counsel

Permanent capacity to receive the light of Jesus'
counsel, so that we can use it to make acts of, and develop
habits of, supernatural counsel. These acts and habits
enable us to discern what God wants us to think, say, or
do at each moment; and to plan a daily agenda, along
with the ways and means to carry it out.

Virtue of Justice

Permanent capacity to receive Jesus' power of justice, so that we can use it to make acts of, and develop
habits of, supernatural justice. These acts and habits
enable us to always do the right thing, consistently giving
ourselves firm, effective self-commands to always do
God's Will, and keep our New Covenant with Him.

Capital Sin: Envy

Tendency to sadness at others' good fortune, success,
talents, etc.— inspired by pride. Envy produces cunning

in efforts to cut others down, spoil their success, manipulate them, and exalt self. It addicts us to cunning and hypocrisy as perverse substitutes for true counsel and justice.

Read the Catechism of the Catholic Church, paragraphs 1807, 2479, 2484–2487, 2538–2540, and 2846–2849.

53L.6 Gift of Fear of the Lord

Permanent capacity to receive the light of Jesus' sensitivity to what pleases or displeases God and of his reverence for God and his compassion for others; so that we can use it to make acts of, and develop habits of, this gift. These acts and habits enable us to control our imaginations with images of Jesus, Mary, and the Saints, which turn on or turn off the emotions of delight, desire, joy, dismay, aversion, and sorrow.

Virtue of Temperance

Permanent capacity to receive Jesus' power of temperance, so that we can use it to make acts of, and develop habits of, supernatural temperance. These acts and habits enable us to toughen our wills and commitments by focusing the power of Jesus' or Mary's own delight, desire, and joy on them; and their dismay or disgust, aversion, and sorrow on any temptation to neglect or abandon these commitments.

Capital Sin: Sloth

Unwillingness to make the effort to develop fear of the Lord and temperance. Sloth produces insensitivity to what pleases and displeases God; insensitivity to our neighbor's feelings, needs, and condition. It addicts us to avoiding difficulties, suffering, and sacrifice, and leads to cynicism as a perverse substitute for sensitivity, compassion, and healthy toughness of will regarding what is good.

Read the Catechism of the Catholic Church, paragraphs 1453, 1809, 2094, 2341, and 2427.

53L.7   Gift of Fortitude

Permanent capacity to receive the light of Jesus' mental fortitude (fortitude of mind), so that we can use it to make acts of, and develop habits of, this gift. They enable us to use our imagination and memories to produce or recall images of Jesus which turn on or turn off emotions of courage, confident commitment, enthusiasm, fear, despair, and anger.

Virtue of Fortitude

Permanent capacity to receive Jesus' power of "intestinal" fortitude (fortitude of heart), so that we can use it to make acts of, and develop habits of, supernatural fortitude. These acts and habits enable us to focus Jesus' and Mary's emotions of courage, confident commitment, and enthusiasm on doing God's Will; and their emotions of fear, despair, and anger on sin, false hopes, Satan, etc.

Capital Sin: Anger (cruel/vicious/uncontrolled)

Produces a false conscience and moral weakness. Addicts us to murderous, insane, vindictive, and vengeful thoughts, speech, and actions as perverse substitutes for fortitude of mind and heart.

Read the "Catechism of the Catholic Church," sections 1808, 2262, 2302, 2473, and 2848–2849.

53m. Five Steps to Confession

1. Examine your conscience. (You may want to use #53a–53L in this prayer book.)

2. Be sorry for your sins; try to have perfect sorrow. Try to make an act of contrition (see #9) before going to Confession.

3. Make a firm resolution not to sin again and to avoid the occasions of sin.

4. Tell your sins to a priest and receive absolution (all mortal sins must be confessed).

5. Perform your penance promptly.

You can begin your confession by saying "Bless me Father for I have sinned, my last confession was _____ (weeks/months/years) ago." Then tell your sins. Say an "Act of Contrition" (see #9) when asked by the priest, before the absolution.

We need to rid ourselves of our desires for possessions, power, and pleasure.

59. The Way of the Cross with Reflections on Divine Mercy

(Kneel) Begin by offering one Our Father, one Hail Mary, and the Apostles' Creed for the intentions of our Holy Father in order to partially fulfill the Church's requirements for obtaining a plenary indulgence.

Our Father

Our Father Who art in Heaven, hallowed be Thy name. Thy Kingdom come. Thy will be done on earth, as it is in Heaven. Give us this day our daily bread, and forgive us our trespasses, as we forgive those who trespass against us, and lead us not into temptation, but deliver us from evil. Amen.

Hail Mary

Hail Mary, full of grace; the Lord is with thee; blessed art thou among women and blessed is the fruit of thy womb, Jesus. Holy Mary, Mother of God, pray for us sinners, now and at the hour of our death. Amen.

Apostles' Creed

I believe in God, the Father Almighty, Creator of Heaven and earth; and in Jesus Christ, His only Son, our Lord; Who was conceived by the Holy Spirit, born of the Virgin Mary, suffered under Pontius Pilate, was crucified, died and was buried; He descended into hell, the third day He rose again from the dead, He ascended into Heaven, and is seated at the right hand of God, the Father Almighty. From thence He shall come to judge the living and the dead. I believe in the Holy Spirit, the Holy Catholic Church, the Communion of Saints, the forgiveness of sins, the resurrection of the body, and life everlasting. Amen.

All: Eternal Father, I offer You the Body and Blood, Soul, and Divinity of Your dearly beloved Son, Our Lord Jesus Christ, in atonement for our sins and those of the whole world.

Leader: For the sake of His sorrowful Passion,

All: Have mercy on us and on the whole world. *(One time)*

All: *(Stand and sing)*

At the Cross her sta-tion keep-ing, stood the mourn-ful
Mo-ther weep-ing, close to Je-sus to the last.

FIRST STATION
Jesus is Condemned to Death

Leader: We adore You, O Christ, and we praise You,

(All genuflect)

All: Because by Your holy Cross You have redeemed the world.

Leader: *(All stand)* Consider how Jesus, after having been scourged and crowned with thorns, was unjustly condemned by Pilate to die on the Cross.

All: My adorable Jesus, it was not Pilate, no, it was my sins that condemned You to die. * I beg You, by the merits of this sorrowful journey, * to assist my soul and the souls of all the members of my family and of the apostolate in our journey towards eternity. * We love You, our beloved Jesus; * we ask for the grace to love You more than ourselves; * we repent with our whole heart for ever having offended You. * Never permit us to separate ourselves from You again. * Grant that we may love You always, and then do with us what You will. *

All: *(Kneel)* Eternal Father, I offer You the Body and Blood, Soul, and Divinity of Your dearly beloved Son, our Lord Jesus Christ, in atonement for our sins and those of the whole world.

Leader: For the sake of His sorrowful Passion, *(Repeat four times with response below)*

All: Have mercy on us and on the whole world. *(Four times)*

All: Jesus, I trust in You.

All: *(Stand and sing)*

Through her heart His sor-row shar-ing, all His bit-ter
an-guish bear-ing; now at length the sword had passed.

SECOND STATION
Jesus Accepts His Cross

Leader: We adore You, O Christ, and we praise You,

(All genuflect)

All: Because by Your holy Cross You have redeemed the world.

Leader: *(All stand)* Consider how Jesus, in making this journey with the Cross on His shoulders, thought of us, and for us offered to His Father the death He was about to undergo.

All: My most beloved Jesus, * I embrace all the tribulations You have destined for me until death. * I beseech You, by the merits of the pain You did suffer in carrying Your Cross, * to give me and all the members of my family and of the apostolate the necessary help to carry our crosses with perfect patience and resignation. * We love You, our beloved Jesus; * we ask for the grace to love You more than ourselves; * we repent with our whole heart for ever having offended You. * Never permit us to separate ourselves from You again. * Grant that we may love You always, * and then do with us what You will.

All: *(Kneel)* Eternal Father, I offer You the Body and Blood, Soul, and Divinity of Your dearly beloved Son, our Lord Jesus Christ, in atonement for our sins and those of the whole world.

Leader: For the sake of His sorrowful Passion, *(Repeat four times with response below)*

All: Have mercy on us and on the whole world. *(Four times)*

All: Jesus, I trust in You.

All: *(Stand and sing)*

Oh, how sad and sore di- stressed was that Mo-ther high- ly bl - est of the sole be- got- ten One.

THIRD STATION
Jesus Falls the First Time

Leader: We adore You, O Christ, and we praise You,

(All genuflect)

All: Because by Your holy Cross You have redeemed the world.

Leader: *(All stand)* Consider this first fall of Jesus under His Cross. His flesh was torn by scourges, His head was crowned with thorns, and He had lost a great quantity of blood. He was so weakened that He could scarcely walk, and yet He had to carry this great load upon His shoulders. The soldiers struck Him rudely, and thus He fell several times in His journey.

All: My beloved Jesus, it is not the weight of the Cross but my sins which have made You suffer so much pain. *

By the merits of this first fall, deliver me, my family, and all of the members of the apostolate from the misfortune of falling into mortal sin. * We love You, our beloved Jesus; * we ask for the grace to love You more than ourselves; * we repent with our whole heart for ever having offended You. * Never permit us to separate ourselves from You again. * Grant that we may love You always, and then do with us what You will.

All: *(Kneel)* Eternal Father, I offer You the Body and Blood, Soul, and Divinity of Your dearly beloved Son, our Lord Jesus Christ, in atonement for our sins and those of the whole world.

Leader: For the sake of His sorrowful Passion, *(Repeat four times with response below)*

All: Have mercy on us and on the whole world. *(Four times)*

All: Jesus, I trust in You.

All: *(Stand and sing)*

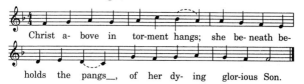

Christ a- bove in tor-ment hangs; she be- neath be- holds the pangs__, of her dy- ing glor-ious Son.

FOURTH STATION
Jesus Meets His Mother

Leader: We adore You, O Christ, and we praise You,

(All genuflect)

All: Because by Your holy Cross You have redeemed the world.

Leader: *(All stand)* Consider the meeting of the Son and the Mother which took place on this journey, Jesus and Mary looked at each other, and their looks became as so many arrows to wound those hearts which loved each other so tenderly.

All: My most loving Jesus, * by the sorrow You experienced in this meeting, * grant me and all the members of my family and of the apostolate the grace of a truly devoted love for your Most Holy Mother. * And you our

Queen, * who was overwhelmed with sorrow, obtain for us, by your intercession, a continual and tender remembrance of the Passion of your Son. * We love You, our beloved Jesus; * we ask for the grace to love You more than ourselves; * we repent with our whole heart for ever having offended You. * Never permit us to separate ourselves from You again. * Grant that we may love You always, and then do with us what You will.

All: *(Kneel)* Eternal Father, I offer You the Body and Blood, Soul, and Divinity of Your dearly beloved Son, our Lord Jesus Christ, in atonement for our sins and those of the whole world.

Leader: For the sake of His sorrowful Passion, *(Repeat four times with response below)*

All: Have mercy on us and on the whole world. *(Four times)*

All: Jesus, I trust in You.

All: *(Stand and sing)*

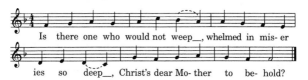

Is there one who would not weep__, whelmed in mis- er ies so deep__, Christ's dear Mo- ther to be- hold?

FIFTH STATION
Jesus is Helped by Simon

Leader: We adore You, O Christ, and we praise You,

(All genuflect)

All: Because by Your holy Cross You have redeemed the world.

Leader: *(All stand)* Consider how the executioners, seeing that at each step Jesus from weakness was on the point of expiring, and fearing that He would die on the way, when they wished Him to die the ignominious death of the Cross, constrained Simon the Cyrenian to carry the Cross behind Our Lord.

All: My most sweet Jesus, * I pray for the grace not to draw back from the cross as the Cyrenian did, * and for the grace to accept it and embrace it. * I pray to accept in particular the death You have destined for me, with all the pains that may accompany it; * I unite it to Your death, I offer it to You. * You have died for love of me; I will die for love of You, and to please You. * Help me and all the members of my family and of the apostolate by Your grace. * We love You, our beloved Jesus; we ask for the grace to love You more than ourselves; * we repent with our whole heart for ever having offended You. * Never permit us to separate ourselves from You again. * Grant that we may love You always, and then do with us what You will.

All: *(Kneel)* Eternal Father, I offer You the Body and Blood, Soul, and Divinity of Your dearly beloved Son, our Lord Jesus Christ, in atonement for our sins and those of the whole world.

Leader: For the sake of His sorrowful Passion, *(Repeat four times with response below)*

All: Have mercy on us and on the whole world. *(Four times)*

All: Jesus, I trust in You.

All: *(Stand and sing)*

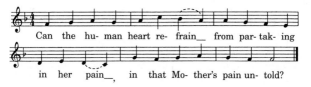

Can the hu-man heart re-frain__ from par-tak-ing in her pain__, in that Mo-ther's pain un-told?

SIXTH STATION
Jesus is Consoled by Veronica

Leader: We adore You, O Christ, and we praise You,

(All genuflect)

All: Because by Your holy Cross You have redeemed the world.

Leader: *(All stand)* Consider how the holy woman named Veronica, seeing Jesus so afflicted and His face bathed in sweat and blood, presented Him with a towel, with which He wiped His adorable face, leaving on it the impression of His holy countenance.

All: My most beloved Jesus, * Your face was beautiful before, but in this journey it has lost all its beauty, * and wounds and blood have disfigured it. * Alas, our souls were once beautiful when we received Your grace in

Baptism, * but we have disfigured them since by our sins. * You alone, our Redeemer, can restore our souls to their former beauty by Your Passion. * We love You, our beloved Jesus; * we ask for the grace to love You more than ourselves; * we repent with our whole heart for ever having offended You. * Never permit us to separate ourselves from You again. * Grant that we may love You always, and then do with us what You will.

All: *(Kneel)* Eternal Father, I offer You the Body and Blood, Soul, and Divinity of Your dearly beloved Son, our Lord Jesus Christ, in atonement for our sins and those of the whole world.

Leader: For the sake of His sorrowful Passion, *(Repeat four times with response below)*

All: Have mercy on us and on the whole world. *(Four times)*

All: Jesus, I trust in You.

All: *(Stand and sing)*

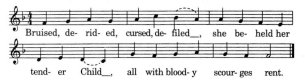

Bruised, de- rid- ed, cursed, de- filed__, she be- held her tend- er Child__, all with blood- y scour- ges rent.

SEVENTH STATION
Jesus Falls the Second Time

Leader: We adore You, O Christ, and we praise You,

(All genuflect)

All: Because by Your holy Cross You have redeemed the world.

Leader: *(All stand)* Consider the second fall of Jesus under the Cross, a fall which renews the pain of all the wounds of the head and members of our afflicted Lord.

All: My most gentle Jesus, * how many times You have pardoned me, and how many times have I fallen again and begun again to offend You! * By the merits of this new fall, * give me and all the members of my family and of the apostolate the necessary help to persevere in Your grace until death. * Grant that, in all temptations which assail us, we may always commend ourselves to You. * We love You, our beloved Jesus; * we ask for the grace to love You more than ourselves; * we repent with our whole heart for ever having offended You. * Never permit us to separate ourselves from You again. * Grant that we may love You always, and then do with us what You will.

All: *(Kneel)* Eternal Father, I offer You the Body and Blood, Soul, and Divinity of Your dearly beloved Son, our Lord Jesus Christ, in atonement for our sins and those of the whole world.

Leader: For the sake of His sorrowful Passion, *(Repeat four times with response below)*

All: Have mercy on us and on the whole world. *(Four times)*

All: Jesus, I trust in You.

All: *(Stand and sing)*

O thou Mo-ther, fount of love__, touch my spir-it from a-bove__; make my heart with thine ac-cord.

EIGHTH STATION
Jesus Meets the Women of Jerusalem

Leader: We adore You, O Christ, and we praise You,

(All genuflect)

All: Because by Your holy Cross You have redeemed the world.

Leader: *(All stand)* Consider how those women wept with compassion at seeing Jesus in such a pitiable state, streaming with blood as He walked along; but Jesus said to them: *Weep not for Me, but for your children.* (Lk. 23:28)

All: My Jesus, laden with sorrows, * I weep for the offenses I have committed against You, * because of the pains they have deserved, * and still more because of the displeasure they have caused You, Who have loved me so much. * It is Your love, more than the fear of hell, * which causes me to weep for my sins and the sins of all the members of my family and of the apostolate. * We love You, our beloved Jesus; * we ask for the grace to love You more than ourselves; * we repent with our whole heart for ever having offended You. * Never permit us to separate ourselves from You again. Grant that we may love You always, and then do with us what You will.

All: *(Kneel)* Eternal Father, I offer You the Body and Blood, Soul, and Divinity of Your dearly beloved Son, our Lord Jesus Christ, in atonement for our sins and those of the whole world.

Leader: For the sake of His sorrowful Passion, *(Repeat four times with response below)*

All: Have mercy on us and on the whole world. *(Four times)*

All: Jesus, I trust in You.

All: *(Stand and sing)*

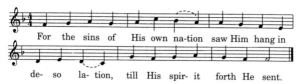

For the sins of His own na-tion saw Him hang in de- so la- tion, till His spir- it forth He sent.

NINTH STATION
Jesus Falls the Third Time

Leader: We adore You, O Christ, and we praise You,

(All genuflect)

All: Because by Your holy Cross You have redeemed the world.

Leader: *(All stand)* Consider the third fall of Jesus Christ. His weakness was extreme, and the cruelty of His executioners excessive, who tried to hasten His steps when He had scarcely strength to move.

All: My outraged Jesus, * by the merits of the weakness You suffered in going to Calvary, * give me and all the members of my family and of the apostolate strength sufficient to conquer all human respect * and all our wicked passions, which have led us to despise Your friendship. *

We love You, our beloved Jesus; * we ask for the grace to love You more than ourselves; * we repent with our whole heart for ever having offended You. * Never permit us to separate ourselves from You again. * Grant that we may love You always, and then do with us what You will.

All: *(Kneel)* Eternal Father, I offer You the Body and Blood, Soul, and Divinity of Your dearly beloved Son, our Lord Jesus Christ, in atonement for our sins and those of the whole world.

Leader: For the sake of His sorrowful Passion, *(Repeat four times with response below)*

All: Have mercy on us and on the whole world. *(Four times)*

All: Jesus, I trust in You.

All: *(Stand and sing)*

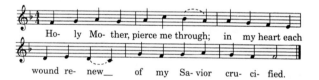

Ho- ly Mo- ther, pierce me through; in my heart each wound re- new__ of my Sa- vior cru- ci- fied.

TENTH STATION
Jesus is Stripped of His Garments

Leader: We adore You, O Christ, and we praise You,

(All genuflect)

All: Because by Your holy Cross You have redeemed the world.

Leader: *(All stand)* Consider the violence with which the executioners stripped Jesus. His inner garments adhered to His torn flesh, and they dragged them off so roughly that the skin came with them. Compassionate your Savior thus cruelly treated, and say to Him,

All: My innocent Jesus, * by the merits of the torment You have felt, * help me and all the members of my family and of the apostolate to strip ourselves of all affection to things of earth, * in order that we may place all our love in You, Who are so worthy of our love. * We love You, our beloved Jesus; * we ask for the grace to love You more than ourselves; * we repent with our whole heart for ever having offended You. * Never permit us to separate ourselves from You again. * Grant that we may love You always, and then do with us what You will.

All: *(Kneel)* Eternal Father, I offer You the Body and Blood, Soul, and Divinity of Your dearly beloved Son, our Lord Jesus Christ, in atonement for our sins and those of the whole world.

Leader: For the sake of His sorrowful Passion, *(Repeat four times with response below)*

All: Have mercy on us and on the whole world. *(Four times)*

All: Jesus, I trust in You.

All: *(Stand and sing)*

Make me feel as thou hast felt__, make my soul to glow and melt__ with the love of Christ my Lord.

ELEVENTH STATION
Jesus is Nailed to the Cross

Leader: We adore You, O Christ, and we praise You,

(All genuflect)

All: Because by Your holy Cross You have redeemed the world.

Leader: *(All stand)* Consider how Jesus, after being thrown on the Cross, extended His hands and offered to His Eternal Father the sacrifice of His death for our salvation. These barbarians fastened Him with nails, and then, raising the Cross, allowed Him to die with anguish on this infamous tree.

All: My Jesus, filled with rejection, * nail my heart and the hearts of all the members of my family and of the apostolate to Your feet, * that they may ever remain there to love You and never leave You again. * We love You, our beloved Jesus; * we ask for the grace to love You more than ourselves; * we repent with our whole heart for ever having offended You. * Never permit us to separate ourselves from You again. * Grant that we may love You always, * and then do with us what You will.

All: *(Kneel)* Eternal Father, I offer You the Body and Blood, Soul, and Divinity of Your dearly beloved Son, our Lord Jesus Christ, in atonement for our sins and those of the whole world.

Leader: For the sake of His sorrowful Passion, *(Repeat four times with response below)*

All: Have mercy on us and on the whole world. *(Four times)*

All: Jesus, I trust in You.

All: *(Stand and sing)*

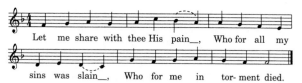

Let me share with thee His pain__, Who for all my
sins was slain__, Who for me in tor-ment died.

TWELFTH STATION
Jesus Dies on the Cross

Leader: We adore You, O Christ, and we praise You,

(All genuflect)

All: Because by Your holy Cross You have redeemed the world.

Leader: *(All stand)* Consider how Jesus, after three hours' agony on the Cross, consumed at length with anguish, abandons Himself to the weight of His body, bows His head, and dies.

All: O my dying Jesus, * I kiss devoutly the Cross on which You died for love of me, and for all the members of my family and of the apostolate. * We have merited by our sins to die a miserable death; * but Your death is our hope. * Ah, by the merits of Your death, * give us grace to

die embracing Your feet and burning with love for You. *
We yield our souls into Your hands. * We love You, our
beloved Jesus; * we ask for the grace to love You more
than ourselves; * we repent with our whole heart for ever
having offended You. * Never permit us to separate ourselves from You again. * Grant that we may love You
always, * and then do with us what You will.

All: *(Kneel)* Eternal Father, I offer You the Body and
Blood, Soul, and Divinity of Your dearly beloved Son, our
Lord Jesus Christ, in atonement for our sins and those of
the whole world.

Leader: For the sake of His sorrowful Passion, *(Repeat
four times with response below)*

All: Have mercy on us and on the whole world. *(Four
times)*

All: Jesus, I trust in You.

All: *(Stand and sing)*

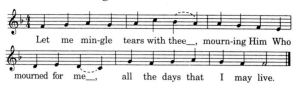

Let me min-gle tears with thee__, mourn-ing Him Who
mourned for me__, all the days that I may live.

THIRTEENTH STATION
Jesus' Body is Laid in the Arms of His Mother

Leader: We adore You, O Christ, and we praise You,

(All genuflect)

All: Because by Your holy Cross You have redeemed the world.

Leader: *(All stand)* Consider how, after the death of Our Lord, two of His disciples, Joseph and Nicodemus, took Him down from the Cross and placed Him in the arms of His afflicted Mother, who received Him with unutterable tenderness and pressed Him to her bosom.

All: O Mother of Sorrows, * for the love of this Son, accept me and all the members of my family and of the apostolate as your obedient children, * and pray to Him for us. * And You, our Redeemer, * since You have died for us, permit us to love You; * for we wish but You, and nothing more. * We love You, our beloved Jesus; * we ask for the grace to love You more than ourselves; * we repent with our whole heart for ever having offended You. * Never permit us to separate ourselves from You again. * Grant that we may love You always, * and then do with us what You will.

All: *(Kneel)* Eternal Father, I offer You the Body and Blood, Soul, and Divinity of Your dearly beloved Son, our Lord Jesus Christ, in atonement for our sins and those of the whole world.

Leader: For the sake of His sorrowful Passion, *(Repeat four times with response below)*

All: Have mercy on us and on the whole world. *(Four times)*

All: Jesus, I trust in You.

All: *(Stand and sing)*

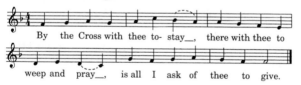

By the Cross with thee to-stay__, there with thee to weep and pray__, is all I ask of thee to give.

FOURTEENTH STATION
Jesus' Body is Laid in the Tomb

Leader: We adore You, O Christ, and we praise You,
(All genuflect)

All: Because by Your holy Cross You have redeemed the world.

Leader: *(All stand)* Consider how the disciples carried the body of Jesus to bury it, accompanied by His holy Mother, who arranged it in the sepulcher with her own hands. They then closed the tomb and all withdrew.

All: Oh, my buried Jesus, * I kiss the stone that enclosed You; * but You rose again on the third day. * I beseech You by Your Resurrection, * make me and the members of my family and of the apostolate rise gloriously with You on the last day, * to be always united with You in

Heaven, * to praise You, and love You forever. * We love You, our beloved Jesus; * we ask for the grace to love You more than ourselves; * we repent with our whole heart for ever having offended You. * Never permit us to separate ourselves from You again. * Grant that we may love You always, * and then do with us what You will.

All: *(Kneel)* Eternal Father, I offer You the Body and Blood, Soul, and Divinity of Your dearly beloved Son, our Lord Jesus Christ, in atonement for our sins and those of the whole world.

Leader: For the sake of His sorrowful Passion, *(Repeat four times with response below)*

All: Have mercy on us and on the whole world. *(Four times)*

All: Jesus, I trust in You.

All: *(Kneel and sing)*

Vir- gin of all vir- gins blest__, li- sten to my fond re- quest__: let me share thy grief di-vine.

All: *(Remain kneeling)* Holy God, Holy Mighty One, Holy Immortal One, have mercy on us and on the whole world. *(Three times)*

Jesus, I trust in You.

65b. Mother of the Redeemer
Sections 42-48

Mary in the life of the Church and of every Christian

42. Linking itself with Tradition, the Second Vatican Council brought new light to bear on the role of the Mother of Christ in the life of the Church. "Through the gift...of divine motherhood, Mary is united with her Son, the Redeemer, and with his singular graces and offices. By these, the Blessed Virgin is also intimately united with the Church: the Mother of God is a figure of the Church in the matter of faith, charity and perfect union with Christ." We have already noted how, from the beginning, Mary remains with the Apostles in expectation of Pentecost and how, as "the blessed one who believed," she is present in the midst of the pilgrim Church from generation to generation through faith and as the model of the hope which does not disappoint (cf. Rom. 5:5).

Mary believed in the fulfillment of what had been said to her by the Lord. As Virgin, she believed that she would conceive and bear a son: the "Holy One," who bears the name of "Son of God," the name "Jesus" (= God who saves). As handmaid of the Lord, she remained in perfect fidelity to the person and mission of this Son. As Mother, "believing and obeying...she brought forth on earth the Father's Son. This she did, knowing not man but overshadowed by the Holy Spirit."

For these reasons Mary is honored in the Church "with special reverence. Indeed, from most ancient times the Blessed Virgin Mary has been venerated under the title of 'God-bearer.' In all perils and needs, the faithful have fled prayerfully to her protection." This cult is altogether special: it bears in itself and expresses the profound link which exists between the Mother of Christ and the Church. As Virgin and Mother, Mary remains for the Church a "permanent model." It can therefore be said that especially under this aspect, namely as a model, or rather as a "figure," Mary, present in the mystery of Christ, remains constantly present also in the mystery of the Church. For the Church too is "called mother and virgin," and these names have a profound biblical and theological justification.

43. The Church "becomes herself a mother by accepting God's word with fidelity." Like Mary, who first believed by accepting the word of God revealed to her at the Annunciation and by remaining faithful to that word in all her trials even unto the Cross, so too the Church becomes a mother when, accepting with fidelity the word of God, "by her preaching and by baptism she brings forth to a new and immortal life children who are conceived of the Holy Spirit and born of God." This "maternal" characteristic of the Church was expressed in a particularly vivid way by the Apostle to the Gentiles when he wrote: "My little children, with whom I am again in travail until Christ be formed in you!" (Gal. 4:19) These words of Saint Paul contain an interesting sign of the early Church's awareness of her own motherhood, linked to her apostolic service to mankind. This awareness enabled and still enables the Church to see the mystery of her life and mission modeled upon the example of the Mother of the Son, who is "the first-born among many brethren" (Rom. 8:29).

It can be said that from Mary the Church also learns her own motherhood: she recognizes the maternal dimension of her vocation, which is essentially bound to her sacramental nature, in "contemplating Mary's mysterious sanctity, imitating her charity and faithfully fulfilling the Father's will." If the Church is the sign and instrument of intimate union with God, she is so by reason of her motherhood, because, receiving life from the Spirit, she "generates" sons and daughters of the human race to a new life in Christ. For, just as Mary is at the service of the mystery of the Incarnation, so the Church is always at the service of the mystery of adoption to sonship through grace.

Likewise, following the example of Mary, the Church remains the virgin faithful to her spouse: The Church herself is a virgin who keeps whole and pure the fidelity she has pledged to her Spouse." For the Church is the spouse of Christ, as is clear from the Pauline Letters (cf. Eph. 5:21-33; 2 Cor. 11:2), and from the title found in John: "bride of the Lamb" (Rev. 21:9). If the Church as spouse "keeps the fidelity she has pledged to Christ," this fidelity, even though in the Apostle's teaching it has become an image of marriage (cf. Eph. 5:23-33), also has value as a model of total self-giving to God in celibacy "for the kingdom of heaven," in virginity consecrated to God (cf. Mt. 19:11-12; 2 Cor. 11:2). Precisely such virginity, after the example of the Virgin of Nazareth, is the source of a special spiritual fruitfulness: it is the source of motherhood in the Holy Spirit.

But the Church also preserves the faith received from Christ. Following the example of Mary, who kept and pondered in her heart everything relating to her divine Son (cf. Lk. 2:19, 51), the Church is committed to preserving the word of God and investigating its riches with discernment and prudence, in order to bear faithful witness to it before all mankind in every age.

44. Given Mary's relationship to the Church as an exemplar, the Church is close to her and seeks to become like her: "Imitating the Mother of her Lord, and by the power of the Holy Spirit, she preserves with virginal purity an integral faith, a firm hope, and a sincere charity." Mary is thus present in the mystery of the Church as a model. But the Church's mystery also consists in generating people to a new and immortal life: this is her motherhood in the Holy Spirit. And here Mary is not only the model and figure of the Church; she is much more. For, "with maternal love she cooperates in the birth and development" of the sons and daughters of Mother Church. The Church's motherhood is accomplished not only according to the model and figure of the Mother of God but also with her "cooperation." The Church draws

abundantly from this cooperation, that is to say from the maternal mediation which is characteristic of Mary, insofar as already on earth she cooperated in the rebirth and development of the Church's sons and daughters, as the Mother of that Son whom the Father "placed as the first-born among many brethren."

She cooperated, as the Second Vatican Council teaches, with a maternal love. Here we perceive the real value of the words spoken by Jesus to his Mother at the hour of the Cross: "Woman, behold your son" and to the disciple: "Behold your mother" (Jn. 19:26-27). They are words which determine Mary's place in the life of Christ's disciples and they express—as I have already said—the new motherhood of the Mother of the Redeemer: a spiritual motherhood, born from the heart of the Paschal Mystery of the Redeemer of the world. It is a motherhood in the order of grace, for it implores the gift of the Spirit, who raises up the new children of God, redeems through the sacrifice of Christ that Spirit whom Mary too, together with the Church, received on the day of Pentecost.

Her motherhood is particularly noted and experienced by the Christian people at the Sacred Banquet—the liturgical celebration of the mystery of the Redemption—at which Christ, his true body born of the Virgin Mary, becomes present.

The piety of the Christian people has always very rightly sensed a profound link between devotion to the Blessed Virgin and worship of the Eucharist: this is a fact that can be seen in the liturgy of both the West and the East, in the traditions of the Religious Families, in the modern movements of spirituality, including those for youth, and in the pastoral practice of the Marian Shrines. Mary guides the faithful to the Eucharist.

45. Of the essence of motherhood is the fact that it concerns the person. Motherhood always establishes a unique and unrepeatable relationship between two people: between mother and child and between child and mother. Even when the same woman is the mother of

many children, her personal relationship with each one
of them is of the very essence of motherhood. For each
child is generated in a unique and unrepeatable way, and
this is true both for the mother and for the child. Each
child is surrounded in the same way by that maternal
love on which are based the child's development and
coming to maturity as a human being.

It can be said that motherhood "in the order of grace"
preserves the analogy with what "in the order of nature"
characterizes the union between mother and child. In the
light of this fact it becomes easier to understand why in
Christ's testament on Golgotha his Mother's new motherhood is expressed in the singular, in reference to one
man: "Behold your son."

It can also be said that these same words fully show
the reason for the Marian dimension of the life of Christ's
disciples. This is true not only of John, who at that hour
stood at the foot of the Cross together with his Master's
Mother, but it is also true of every disciple of Christ, of
every Christian. The Redeemer entrusts his mother to
the disciple, and at the same time he gives her to him as
his mother. Mary's motherhood, which becomes man's
inheritance, is a gift: a gift which Christ himself makes
personally to every individual. The Redeemer entrusts

Mary to John because he entrusts John to Mary. At the
foot of the Cross there begins that special entrusting of
humanity to the Mother of Christ, which in the history of
the Church has been practiced and expressed in different
ways. The same Apostle and Evangelist, after reporting
the words addressed by Jesus on the Cross to his Mother
and to himself, adds: "And from that hour the disciple
took her to his own home" (Jn. 19:27). This statement certainly means that the role of son was attributed to the
disciple and that he assumed responsibility for the
Mother of his beloved Master. And since Mary was given
as a mother to him personally, the statement indicates,
even though indirectly, everything expressed by the intimate relationship of a child with its mother. And all of
this can be included in the word "entrusting." Such
entrusting is the response to a person's love, and in particular to the love of a mother.

The Marian dimension of the life of a disciple of Christ
is expressed in a special way precisely through this filial
entrusting to the Mother of Christ, which began with the
testament of the Redeemer on Golgotha. Entrusting himself to Mary in a filial manner, the Christian, like the
Apostle John, "welcomes" the Mother of Christ "into his
own home" and brings her into everything that makes up
his inner life, that is to say into his human and Christian
"I": he "took her to his own home." Thus the Christian

seeks to be taken into that "maternal charity" with which the Redeemer's Mother "cares for the brethren of her Son," "in whose birth and development she cooperates" in the measure of the gift proper to each one through the power of Christ's Spirit. Thus also is exercised that motherhood in the Spirit which became Mary's role at the foot of the Cross and in the Upper Room.

46. This filial relationship, this self-entrusting of a child to its mother, not only has its beginning in Christ but can also be said to be definitively directed towards him. Mary can be said to continue to say to each individual the words which she spoke at Cana in Galilee: "Do whatever he tells you." For he, Christ, is the one Mediator between God and mankind; he is "the way, and the truth, and the life" (Jn. 14:6); it is he whom the Father has given to the world, so that man "should not perish but have eternal life" (Jn. 3:16). The Virgin of Nazareth became the first "witness" of this saving love of the Father, and she also wishes to remain its humble handmaid always and everywhere. For every Christian, for every human being, Mary is the one who first "believed," and precisely with her faith as Spouse and Mother she wishes to act upon all those who entrust themselves to her as her children. And it is well known that the more her children persevere and progress in this attitude, the nearer Mary leads them to the "unsearchable riches of Christ" (Eph. 3:8). And to the same degree they recognize more and more clearly the dignity of man in all its fullness and the definitive meaning of his vocation, for "Christ...fully reveals man to man himself."

This Marian dimension of Christian life takes on special importance in relation to women and their status. In fact, femininity has a unique relationship with the Mother of the Redeemer, a subject which can be studied in greater depth elsewhere. Here I simply wish to note that the figure of Mary of Nazareth sheds light on womanhood as such by the very fact that God, in the sublime event of the Incarnation of his Son, entrusted himself to the ministry, the free and active ministry of a woman. It can thus be said that women, by looking to Mary, find in her the secret of living their femininity with dignity and of achieving their own true advancement. In the light of Mary, the Church sees in the face of women the reflection of a beauty which mirrors the loftiest sentiments of which the human heart is capable: the self-offering totality of love; the strength that is capable of bearing the greatest sorrows; limitless fidelity and tireless devotion to work; the ability to combine penetrating intuition with words of support and encouragement.

47. At the Council Paul VI solemnly proclaimed that Mary is the Mother of the Church, "that is, Mother of the entire Christian people, both faithful and pastors." Later, in 1968, in the Profession of faith known as the "Credo of the People of God," he restated this truth in an even more forceful way in these words: "We believe that the Most Holy Mother of God, the new Eve, the Mother of the Church, carries on in heaven her maternal role with regard to the members of Christ, cooperating in the birth and development of divine life in the souls of the redeemed."

The Council's teaching emphasized that the truth concerning the Blessed Virgin, Mother of Christ, is an effective aid in exploring more deeply the truth concerning the Church. When speaking of the Constitution Lumen Gentium, which had just been approved by the Council, Paul VI said: "Knowledge of the true Catholic doctrine regarding the Blessed Virgin Mary will always be a key to the exact understanding of the mystery of Christ and of the Church." Mary is present in the Church as the Mother of Christ, and at the same time as that Mother whom Christ, in the mystery of the Redemption, gave to humanity in the person of the Apostle John. Thus, in her new motherhood in the Spirit, Mary embraces each and every one in the Church, and embraces each and every one through the Church. In this sense Mary, Mother of the Church, is also the Church's model. Indeed, as Paul VI hopes and asks, the Church must draw "from the Virgin Mother of God the most authentic form of perfect imitation of Christ."

Thanks to this special bond linking the Mother of Christ with the Church, there is further clarified the mystery of that "woman" who, from the first chapters of the Book of Genesis until the Book of Revelation, accompanies the revelation of God's salvific plan for humanity. For Mary, present in the Church as the Mother of the Redeemer, takes part, as a mother, in that monumental struggle; against the powers of darkness" which continues throughout human history. And by her ecclesial identification as the "woman clothed with the sun" (Rev. 12:1), it can be said that "in the Most Holy Virgin the Church has already reached that perfection whereby she exists without spot or wrinkle." Hence, as Christians raise their eyes with faith to Mary in the course of their earthly pilgrimage, they "strive to increase in holiness." Mary, the exalted Daughter of Sion, helps all her children, wherever they may be and whatever their condition, to find in Christ the path to the Father's house.

Thus, throughout her life, the Church maintains with the Mother of God a link which embraces, in the saving mystery, the past, the present and the future, and venerates her as the spiritual mother of humanity and the advocate of grace.

48. It is precisely the special bond between humanity and this Mother which has led me to proclaim a Marian Year in the Church, in this period before the end of the Second Millennium since Christ's birth. A similar initiative was taken in the past, when Pius XII proclaimed 1954 as a Marian Year, in order to highlight the exceptional holiness of the Mother of Christ as expressed in the mysteries of her Immaculate Conception (defined exactly a century before) and of her Assumption into heaven.

Now, following the line of the Second Vatican Council, I wish to emphasize the special presence of the Mother of God in the mystery of Christ and his Church. For this is a fundamental dimension emerging from the Mariology of the Council, the end of which is now more than twenty years behind us. The Extraordinary Synod of Bishops held in 1985 exhorted everyone to follow faithfully the teaching and guidelines of the Council. We can say that these two events—the Council and the synod—embody what the Holy Spirit himself wishes "to say to the Church" in the present phase of history.

In this context, the Marian Year is meant to promote a new and more careful reading of what the Council said about the Blessed Virgin Mary, Mother of God, in the mystery of Christ and of the Church, the topic to which the contents of this Encyclical are devoted. Here we speak not only of the doctrine of faith but also of the life of faith, and thus of authentic "Marian spirituality," seen in the light of Tradition, and especially the spirituality to which the Council exhorts us. Furthermore, Marian spirituality, like its corresponding devotion, finds a very rich source in the historical experience of individuals and of the various Christian communities present among the different peoples and nations of the world. In this regard, I would like to recall, among the many witnesses and teachers of this spirituality, the figure of Saint Louis Marie Grignion de Montfort, who proposes consecration to Christ through the hands of Mary, as an effective means for Christians to live faithfully their baptismal commitments. I am pleased to note that in our own time too new manifestations of this spirituality and devotion are not lacking.

65c. Lumen Gentium
(Dogmatic Constitution on the Church)
Chapter VIII

*The Second Vatican Council held Mary in great esteem. In
fact, the entire eighth chapter of the Dogmatic Constitution
on the Church (Lumen Gentium), included below, is devoted
to her. It is the longest treatment of Our Lady contained in
any of the Ecumenical Councils.*

I. Introduction

52. Wishing in his supreme goodness and wisdom to
effect the redemption of the world, "when the fullness of
time came, God sent his Son, born of a woman...that we
might receive the adoption of sons" (Gal. 4:4). "He for us
men, and for our salvation, came down from heaven, and
was incarnated by the Holy Spirit from the Virgin Mary."
This divine mystery of salvation is revealed to us and
continued in the Church, which the Lord established as
his body. Joined to Christ the head and in communion
with all his saints, the faithful must in the first place reverence the memory "of the glorious ever Virgin Mary,
Mother of God and of our Lord Jesus Christ."

53. The Virgin Mary, who at the message of the angel
received the Word of God in her heart and in her body and
gave Life to the world, is acknowledged and honored as
being truly the Mother of God and of the redeemer.
Redeemed, in a more exalted fashion, by reason of the

merits of her Son and united to him by a close and indissoluble tie, she is endowed with the high office and dignity of the Mother of the Son of God, and therefore she is also the beloved daughter of the Father and the temple of the Holy Spirit. Because of this gift of sublime grace she far surpasses all creatures, both in heaven and on earth. But, being of the race of Adam, she is at the same time also united to all those who are to be saved; indeed, "she is clearly the mother of the members of Christ... since she has by her charity, joined in bringing about the birth of believers in the Church, who are members of its head." Wherefore she is hailed as pre-eminent and as a wholly unique member of the Church, and as its type and outstanding model in faith and charity. The Catholic Church taught by the Holy Spirit, honors charity. The Catholic Church taught by the Holy Spirit, honors her with filial affection and devotion as a most beloved mother.

54. Wherefore this sacred synod, while expounding the doctrine on the Church, in which the divine Redeemer brings about our salvation, intends to set forth painstakingly both the role of the Blessed Virgin in the mystery of the Incarnate Word and the Mystical Body, and the duties of the redeemed towards the Mother of God, who is mother of Christ and mother of men, and most of all those who believe. It does not, however, intend to give a complete doctrine on Mary, nor does it wish to decide those questions which the work of theologians has not yet fully clarified. Those opinions therefore may be lawfully retained which are propounded in Catholic schools con-

cerning her, who occupies a place in the Church which is the highest after Christ and also closest to us.

II. The Function of the Blessed Virgin in the Plan of Salvation

55. The sacred writings of the Old and New Testaments, as well as venerable tradition, show the role of the Mother of the Saviour in the plan of salvation in an ever clearer light and call our attention to it. The books of the Old Testament describe the history of salvation, by which the coming of Christ into the world was slowly prepared. The earliest documents, as they are read in the Church and are understood in the light of a further and full revelation, bring the figure of a woman, Mother of the Redeemer, into a gradually clearer light. Considered in this light, she is already prophetically foreshadowed in the promise of victory over the serpent which was given to our first parents after their fall into sin (cf. Gen. 3:15). Likewise she is the virgin who shall conceive and bear a son, whose name shall be called Emmanuel (cf. Is. 7:14; Mic. 5:2-3; Mt. 1:22-23). She stands out among the poor and humble of the Lord, who confidently hope for and receive salvation from him. After a long period of waiting the times are fulfilled in her, the exalted Daughter of Sion and the new plan of salvation is established, when the Son of God has taken human nature from her, that he might in the mysteries of his flesh free man from sin.

56. The Father of mercies willed that the Incarnation should be preceded by assent on the part of the predestined mother, so that just as a woman had a share in bringing about death, so also a woman should contribute to life. This is pre-eminently true of the Mother of Jesus, who gave to the world the Life that renews all things, and who was enriched by God with gifts appropriate to such a role. *It is no wonder then that it was customary for the Fathers to refer to the Mother of God as all holy and free from every stain of sin, as though fashioned by the Holy Spirit and formed as a new creature. Enriched from the*

*first instant of her conception with the splendor of an
entirely unique holiness, the virgin of Nazareth is hailed
by the heralding angel, by divine command, as "full of
grace" (cf. Lk. 1:28), and to the heavenly messenger she
replies: "Behold the handmaid of the Lord, be it done unto
me according to thy word" (Lk. 1:38).*

Thus the daughter of Adam, Mary, consenting to the
word of God, became the Mother of Jesus. Committing
herself wholeheartedly and impeded by no sin to God's
saving will, she devoted herself totally, as a handmaid of
the Lord, to the person and work of her Son, under and
with him, serving the mystery of redemption, by the
grace of Almighty God. Rightly, therefore, the Fathers see
Mary not merely as passively engaged by God, but as
freely cooperating in the work of man's salvation through
faith and obedience.

For, as St. Irenaeus says, she "being obedient, became
the cause of salvation for herself and for the whole
human race." Hence not a few of the early Fathers gladly
assert with him in their preaching: "the knot of Eve's disobedience was untied by Mary's obedience: what the
virgin Eve bound through her disbelief, Mary loosened by
her faith." Comparing Mary with Eve, they call her
"Mother of the living," and frequently claim: "death
through Eve, life through Mary."

57. This union of the mother with the Son in the work
of salvation is made manifest from the time of Christ's
virginal conception up to his death; first when Mary,
arising in haste to go to visit Elizabeth, is greeted by her
as blessed because of her belief in the promise of salvation and the precursor leaped with joy in the womb of his
mother (cf. Lk. 1:41-45); then also at the birth of Our
Lord, who did not diminish his mother's virginal integrity
but sanctified it, the Mother of God joyfully showed her
firstborn son to the shepherds and the Magi: when she
presented him to the Lord in the temple, making the
offering of the poor, she heard Simeon foretelling at the
same time that her Son would be a sign of contradiction

and that a sword would pierce the mother's soul, that out of many hearts thoughts might be revealed (cf. Lk. 2:34-35); when the child Jesus was lost and they had sought him sorrowing, his parents found him in the temple, engaged in the things that were his Father's, and they did not understand the words of their Son. His mother, however, kept all these things to be pondered in her heart (cf. Lk. 2:41-51).

58. In the public life of Jesus, Mary appears prominently; at the very beginning when at the marriage feast of Cana, moved with pity, she brought about by her intercession the beginning of miracles of Jesus the Messiah (cf. Jn. 2:1-11). In the course of her Son's preaching she received the words whereby, in extolling a kingdom beyond the concerns and ties of flesh and blood, he declared blessed those who heard and kept the word of God (cf. Mk. 3:35; par. Lk. 11:27-28) as she was faithfully doing (cf. Lk. 2:19; 51).

Thus the Blessed Virgin advanced in her pilgrimage of faith, and faithfully persevered in her union with her Son unto the cross, where she stood, in keeping with the divine plan, enduring with her only begotten Son the intensity of his suffering, associated herself with his sacrifice in her mother's heart, and lovingly consenting to the immolation of this victim which was born of her. Finally, she was given by the same Christ Jesus dying on the cross as a mother to his disciple, with these words: "Woman, behold thy son" (Jn. 19:26-27).

59. But since it had pleased God not to manifest solemnly the mystery of the salvation of the human race before he would pour forth the Spirit promised by Christ, we see the apostles before the day of Pentecost "persevering with one mind in prayer with the women and Mary the Mother of Jesus, and with his brethren" (Acts 1:14), and we also see Mary by her prayers imploring the gift of the Spirit, who had already overshadowed her in the Annunciation. Finally the Immaculate Virgin preserved free from all stain of original sin, was taken up body and soul into heavenly glory, when her earthly life was over, and exalted by the Lord as Queen over all things, that she might be the more fully conformed to her Son, the Lord of lords, (cf. Apoc. 19:16) and conqueror of sin and death.

III. The Blessed Virgin and the Church

60. In the words of the apostle there is but one mediator: "for there is but one God and one mediator of God and men, the man Christ Jesus, who gave himself a redemption for all" (1 Tim. 2:5-6). But Mary's function as mother of men in no way obscures or diminishes this unique mediation of Christ, but rather shows its power. But the Blessed Virgin's salutary influence on men originates not in any inner necessity but in the disposition of

God. It flows forth from the superabundance of the merits of Christ, rests on his mediation, depends entirely on it and draws all its power from it. It does not hinder in any way the immediate union of the faithful with Christ but on the contrary fosters it.

61. The predestination of the Blessed Virgin as Mother of God was associated with the incarnation of the divine word: in the designs of divine Providence, she was the gracious mother of the divine Redeemer here on earth, and above all others and in a singular way the generous associate and humble handmaid of the Lord. She conceived, brought forth, and nourished Christ, she presented him to the Father in the temple, shared her Son's sufferings as he died on the cross. Thus, in a wholly singular way, she cooperated by her obedience, faith, hope, and burning charity in the work of the Savior in restoring supernatural life to souls. For this reason she is a mother to us in the order of grace.

62. This motherhood of Mary in the order of grace continues uninterruptedly from the consent which she loyally gave at the Annunciation and which she sustained without wavering beneath the cross, until the eternal fulfillment of all the elect. Taken up to heaven, she did not lay aside this saving office but by her manifold intercession continues to bring us the gifts of eternal salvation. By her maternal charity, she cares for the brethren of her Son, who still journey on earth surrounded by dangers and difficulties, until they are led into their blessed home. Therefore the Blessed Virgin is invoked in the Church under the titles of Advocate, Helper, Benefactress, and Mediatrix. This, however, is so understood that it neither takes away anything from nor adds anything to the dignity and efficacy of Christ the one Mediator.

No creature could ever be counted along with the Incarnate Word and Redeemer; but just as the priesthood of Christ is shared in various ways both by his ministers and the faithful, and as the one goodness of God is radiated in different ways among his creatures, so also the unique mediation of the Redeemer does not exclude but rather gives rise to a manifold cooperation which is but a sharing in this one source.

The Church does not hesitate to profess this subordinate role of Mary, which it constantly experiences and recommends to the heartfelt attention of the faithful, so that encouraged by this maternal help they may the more closely adhere to the Mediator and Redeemer.

63. By reason of the gift and role of her divine motherhood, by which she is united with her Son, the Redeemer, and with her unique graces and functions, the Blessed Virgin is also intimately united to the Church. As St. Ambrose taught, the Mother of God is a type of the Church in the order of faith, charity, and perfect union with Christ. For in the mystery of the Church, which is itself rightly called mother and virgin, the Blessed Virgin stands out in eminent and singular fashion as exemplar both of virgin and mother. Through her faith and obedience she gave birth on earth to the very Son of the Father, not through the knowledge of man but by the overshadowing of the Holy Spirit, in the manner of a new Eve who placed her faith, not in the serpent of old but in God's messenger without wavering in doubt. The Son whom she brought forth is he whom God placed as the first-born among many brethren (Rom. 8:29), that is, the faithful, in whose generation and formation she cooperates with a mother's love.

64. The Church indeed contemplating her hidden sanctity, imitating her charity and faithfully fulfilling the Father's will, by receiving the word of God in faith becomes herself a mother. By preaching and baptism she brings forth sons, who are conceived of the Holy Spirit and born of God, to a new and immortal life. She herself is a virgin, who keeps in its entirety and purity the faith she pledged to her spouse. Imitating the mother of her Lord, and by the power of the Holy Spirit, she keeps intact faith, firm hope and sincere charity.

65. But while in the most Blessed Virgin the Church
has already reached that perfection whereby she exists
without spot or wrinkle (cf. Eph. 5:27), the faithful still
strive to conquer sin and increase in holiness. And so they
turn their eyes to Mary who shines forth to the whole
community of the elect as the model of virtues. Devoutly
meditating on her and contemplating her in the light of
the Word made man, the Church reverently penetrates
more deeply into the great mystery of the Incarnation
and becomes more and more like her spouse. Having
entered deeply into the history of salvation, Mary, in a
way, unites in her person and re-echoes the most important doctrines of the faith: and when she is the subject of
preaching and worship she prompts the faithful to come
to her Son, to his sacrifice, and to the love of the Father.
Seeking after the glory of Christ, the Church becomes
more like her lofty type, and continually progresses in
faith, hope, and charity, seeking and doing the will of God
in all things. The Church, therefore, in her apostolic work
too, rightly looks to her who gave birth to Christ, who was
thus conceived of the Holy Spirit and born of a virgin, in
order that through the Church he could be born and
increase in the hearts of the faithful. In her life the Virgin
has been a model of that motherly love with which all
who join in the Church's apostolic mission for the regen-
eration of mankind should be animated.

IV. The Devotion of the Blessed Virgin in the Church

66. Mary has by grace been exalted above all angels and men to a place second only to her Son, as the most holy Mother of God who was involved in the mysteries of Christ: she is rightly honored by a special devotion in the Church. From the earliest times the Blessed Virgin is honored under the title of Mother of God, whose protection the faithful take refuge together in prayer in all their perils and needs. Accordingly, following the Council of Ephesus, there was a remarkable growth in the devotion of the People of God towards Mary, in veneration and love, in invocation and imitation, according to her own prophetic words: "all generations shall call me blessed, because he that is mighty hath done great things to me" (Luke 1:48). This devotion, as it has always existed in the Church, for all its uniqueness, differs essentially from the devotion of adoration, which is offered equally to the Incarnate Word and to the Father and the Holy Spirit, and it is most favorable to it. The various forms of piety towards the Mother of God, which the Church has approved within the limits of sound and orthodox doctrine, according to the dispositions and understanding of the faithful, ensure that while the mother is honored, the Son through whom all things have their being (cf. Col. 1:15-16) and in whom it has pleased the Father that all fullness should dwell (cf. Col. 1:19) is rightly known, loved and glorified and his commandments are observed.

67. The sacred synod teaches this Catholic doctrine advisedly and at the same time admonishes all the sons of the Church that the devotion, especially the liturgical devotion, of the Blessed Virgin, be generously fostered, and that the practices and exercises of devotion towards her, recommended by the teaching authority of the Church in the course of centuries be highly esteemed, and that those decrees, which were given in the early days regarding the devotional images of Christ, the Blessed Virgin and the saints, be religiously observed. But it strongly urges theologians and preachers of the word of God to be careful to refrain as much from all false exaggeration as from too summary an attitude in considering the special dignity of the Mother of God. Following the study of Sacred Scripture, the Fathers, the doctors and liturgy of the Church, and under the guidance of the Church's magisterium, let them rightly illustrate the duties and privileges of the Blessed Virgin which always refer to Christ, the source of all truth, sanctity, and devotion. Let them carefully refrain from whatever might by word or deed lead the separated brethren or any others whatsoever into error about the true doctrine of the Church. Let the faithful remember moreover that true devotion consists neither in sterile nor transitory affection, nor in a certain vain credulity, but proceeds from true faith, by which we are led to recognize the excellence of the Mother of God, and we are moved to a filial love towards our mother and to the imitation of her virtues.

V. Mary, Sign of True Hope and Comfort for the Pilgrim People of God

68. In the meantime the Mother of Jesus in the glory which she possesses in body and soul in heaven is the image and beginning of the Church as it is to be perfected in the world to come. Likewise she shines forth on earth, until the day of the Lord shall come (cf. 2 Pet. 3:10), a sign of certain hope and comfort to the pilgrim People of God.

69. It gives great joy and comfort to this sacred synod that among the separated brethren too there are those who give due honor to the Mother of Our Lord and Saviour, especially among the Easterns, who with devout mind and fervent impulse give honor to the Mother of God, ever virgin. The entire body of the faithful pours forth urgent supplications to the Mother of God and of men that she, who aided the beginnings of the Church by her prayers, may now, exalted as she is above all the angels and saints, intercede before her Son in the fellowship of all the saints, until all families of people, whether they are honored with the title of Christian or whether they still do not know the Saviour, may be happily gathered together in peace and harmony into one People of God, for the glory of the Most Holy and Undivided Trinity.

For #65e. Prayer to Mary from Christifidelis Laici, by Pope John Paul II, see #27c.

67. The Secret of Mary
by St. Louis Marie de Montfort

Imprimi potest: A. Josselin, S.M.M.
                  Superior Generalis
Nihil obstat: Thomas W. Smiddy, S.T.L.
Imprimatur: † Thomas Edmundus Molloy, S.T.D.
                  Episcopus Brooklyniensis
                  Brooklyni, die IV Junii, 1947

Printed with permission.

Introduction: A Secret of Sanctity

Conditions

1. Predestinate soul, here is a secret the Most High has taught me, which I have not been able to find in any book old or new.[1] I confide it to you, by the inspiration of the Holy Spirit, on condition:

(1) That you communicate it only to those who deserve it by their prayers, their alms-deeds, and mortifications, by the persecutions they suffer, by their detachment from the world, and their zeal for the salvation of souls.[2]

(2) That you make use of it for your personal sanctification and salvation; for this secret works its effects in a soul only in proportion to the use made of it. Beware, then, of remaining inactive while possessing my secret; it would turn into a poison and be your condemnation.*

(3) That you thank God all the days of your life for the grace He has given you to know a secret you do not deserve to know.

---

* "This solemn warning of the Saint is an application of the Parable of the Talents reported in Mt. 25:26. The unfaithful servant buried the talent he received and was condemned by the Master for his culpable negligence and for his disdain for the gifts of God. It is also a condemnation of the passivity or inertia taught by the false spirituality of Quietism or Semiquietism which existed in St. Louis de Montfort's time and which was condemned by Rome. The saint does not mean that one is obliged to follow his plan of Spiritual Life in order to be saved, for in his Treatise on the True Devotion to Mary, which is a development of the Secret of Mary, he explicitly says that we can attain divine union by other roads, but that his method is an Easy, Short, Perfect, and Secure Way that leads us to union with Our Lord."

As you go on making use of this secret in the ordinary actions of your life, you will comprehend its value and its excellence which at first you will not fully understand because of your many and grievous sins and because of your secret attachment to self.[3]

2. Before you read any further, lest you should be carried away by a too eager and natural desire to know this truth, kneel down and say devoutly the Ave Maris Stella[4] and the Veni Creator[5] in order to understand and appreciate this divine mystery.[6] As I have not much time for writing, nor you for reading, I shall say everything as briefly as possible.

I. Our Sanctification: Necessity of Sanctifying Ourselves

The Will of God

3. Faithful soul, living image of God, redeemed by the Precious Blood of Jesus Christ, it is the will of God that you be holy like Him in this life and glorious like Him in the next. Your sure vocation is the acquisition of the holiness of God; and unless all your thoughts and words and actions, all the sufferings and events of your life tend to that end, you are resisting God by not doing that for which He has created you and is now preserving you.[7] Oh, what an admirable work! To change that which is dust into light, to make pure that which is unclean, holy that which is sinful, to make the creature like its Creator, man like God! Admirable work, I repeat, but difficult in itself, and impossible to mere nature; only God by His grace, by His abundant and extraordinary grace, can accomplish it. Even the creation of the whole world is not so great a masterpiece as this.

Means of Sanctification

4. Predestinate soul, how are you to do it? What means will you choose to reach the height to which

God calls you? The means of salvation and sanctification are known to all; they are laid down in the Gospel, explained by the masters of the spiritual life, practiced by the saints, and necessary to all who wish to be saved and to attain perfection. They are: humility of heart, continual prayer, mortification in all things, abandonment to Divine Providence, and conformity to the will of God.

5. To practice all these means of salvation and sanctification the grace of God is absolutely necessary. No one can doubt that God gives His grace to all, in a more or less abundant measure. I say in a more or less abundant measure, for God, although infinitely good, does not give equal grace to all, yet to each soul He gives sufficient grace. The faithful soul will, with great grace,

perform a great action, and with less grace a lesser action. It is the value and the excellence of the grace bestowed by God and corresponded to by the soul, that gives to our actions their value and their excellence. These principles are certain.

An Easy Means

6. It all comes to this, then: that you should find an easy means for obtaining from God the grace necessary to make you holy; and this means I wish to make known to you. Now, I say that to find this grace of God, we must find Mary.[8]

II. Our Sanctification Through Mary[9]: A Necessary Means

Mary Alone Has Found Grace with God

7. (1) Mary alone has found grace with God, both for herself and for every man in particular. The patriarchs and prophets and all the saints of the Old Law were not able to find that grace.

Mother of Grace

8. (2) Mary gave being and life to the Author of all grace and that is why she is called the Mother of Grace.

Mary Has Received the Plenitude of Grace

9. (3) God the Father, from Whom every perfect gift and all grace comes, as from its essential source, has given all graces to Mary by giving her His Son: so that, as St. Bernard says, "With His Son and in Him, God has given His will to Mary."

Universal Treasurer of God's Graces

10. (4) God has entrusted Mary with the keeping, the administration, and distribution of all His graces, so that all His graces and gifts pass through her hands; and (according to the power she has received over them), as St. Bernardine teaches, Mary gives to whom she wills, the way she wills, when she wills, and as much as she wills the graces of the Eternal Father, the virtues of Jesus Christ, and the gifts of the Holy Spirit.

Mother of God's Children

11. (5) As in the order of nature, a child must have a father and a mother, so likewise in the order of grace, a true child of the Church must have God for his Father and Mary for his Mother; and if any one should glory in having God for his Father and yet has not the love of a true child for Mary, he is a deceiver and the only father he has is the devil.

Mary Forms the Members of Jesus

12. (6) Since Mary has formed Jesus Christ, the Head of the elect, it is also her office to form the members of that Head, that is to say, all true Christians; for a mother does not form the head without the members, nor the members without the head. Whoever, therefore, wishes to be a member of Jesus Christ, full of grace and truth, must be formed in Mary by means of the grace of Jesus Christ, which she possesses in its fullness, in order to communicate it fully to her children, the true members of Jesus Christ.[10]

Through Her the Holy Spirit Produces the Elect

13. (7) As the Holy Spirit has espoused Mary, and has produced in her, by her and from her, His masterpiece, Jesus Christ, the Word Incarnate, and has never repudiated His spouse, so He now continues to produce the elect, in her and by her, in a mysterious but real manner.

Mary Nourishes Souls and Gives Them Growth in God

14. (8) Mary has received a special office and power over our souls in order to nourish them and give them growth in God. St. Augustine even says that during their present life all the elect are hidden in Mary's

womb and that they are not truly born until the
Blessed Mother brings them forth to life eternal.
Consequently, just as the child draws all its nourishment from the mother, who gives it in proportion to the
child's weakness, in like manner do the elect draw all
their spiritual nourishment and strength from Mary.

Mary Dwells in the Elect

15. (9) It is to Mary that God the Father said: "My
daughter, let your dwelling be in Jacob," that is, in My
elect, prefigured by Jacob. It is to Mary that God the
Son said: "My dear Mother, in Israel is your inheritance," that is, in the elect. And it is to Mary that the
Holy Spirit said: "Take root, my faithful spouse, in My
elect." Whoever, then, is elect and predestinate has the
Blessed Virgin with him, dwelling in his soul,[11] and he
will allow her to plant there the roots of profound
humility, of ardent charity, and of every virtue.

Mary Forms Jesus in Us A Living Mold of God

16. St. Augustine calls Mary the living "mold of
God", and that indeed she is; for it was in her alone
that God was made a true man without losing any feature of the Godhead, and it is also in her alone that
man can be truly formed into God, in so far as that is
possible for human nature, by the grace of Jesus
Christ.

A sculptor has two ways of making a lifelike statue or figure: he may carve the figure out of some hard,
shapeless material, using for this purpose his professional skill and knowledge, his strength and the necessary instruments, or he may cast it in a mold. The
first manner is long and difficult, and subject to many
mishaps; a single blow of the hammer or the chisel,
awkwardly given, may spoil the whole work. The second is short, easy and smooth; it requires but little
work and slight expense, provided the mold be perfect
and made to reproduce the figure exactly; provided,

moreover, the material used offers no resistance to the hand of the artist.[12]

A Perfect Mold

17. Mary is the great mold of God, made by the Holy Spirit to form a true God-Man by the Hypostatic Union, and to form also a man-God by grace. In that mold none of the features of the Godhead is wanting. Whoever is cast in it, and allows himself to be molded, receives all the features of Jesus Christ, true God. The work is done gently, in a manner proportioned to human weakness, without much pain or labor; in a sure manner, free from all illusion, for where Mary is, the devil has never had, and never will have, access; finally, it is done in a holy and spotless manner, without a shadow of the least stain of sin.

Well Molten Souls

18. Oh, what a difference between a soul which has been formed in Christ by the ordinary ways of those, who, like the sculptor, trust in their own skill and ingenuity, and a soul, thoroughly docile, entirely detached and well molten, which, without trusting its own skill, casts itself into Mary, there to be molded by the Holy Spirit. How many stains and defects and illusions, how much darkness and how much human nature is there in the former, and oh, how pure, how heavenly and how Christ-like is the latter!

Paradise and World of God

19. There does not exist and never will exist a creature in whom God, either within or without Himself, is so highly exalted as He is in the most Blessed Virgin Mary, not excepting the saints or the cherubim or the highest seraphim in Paradise. Mary is the paradise of God and His unspeakable world, into which the Son of God has come to work His wonders, to watch over it and take His delight in it. God

has made a world for the wayfaring man, which is
that world in which we dwell; He has made one for
man in his glorified state, which is Heaven; and He
has made one for Himself, which He has called Mary.
It is a world unknown to most mortals here below and
incomprehensible even to the angels and blessed in
Heaven above, who, seeing God so highly exalted
above them all and so deeply hidden in Mary, His
world, are filled with admiration and unceasingly
exclaim: "Holy, Holy, Holy."

God Alone in Her

20. Happy, a thousand times happy, is the soul
here below to which the Holy Spirit reveals the Secret
of Mary in order that it may come to know her; to
which He opens the "Garden Enclosed" that it may
enter into it; to which He gives access to that
"Fountain Sealed," that it may draw from it and drink
deep draughts of the living waters of grace! That soul
will find God alone in His most loving creature. It will
find God infinitely holy and exalted, yet at the same
time adapting Himself to its own weakness. Since God
is present everywhere, He may be found everywhere,
even in hell, but nowhere do we creatures find Him
nearer to us and more adapted to our weakness than

in Mary, since it was for that end that He came and dwelt in her. Everywhere else He is the Bread of the strong, the Bread of the angels, but in Mary He is the Bread of children.[13]

No Hindrance to Our Union with God

21. Let us not imagine, then, as some do who are misled by erroneous teachings, that Mary, being a creature, is a hindrance to our union with the Creator. It is no longer Mary who lives, it is Jesus Christ, it is God alone Who lives in her. Her transformation into God surpasses that of St. Paul and of the other saints more than the heavens surpass the earth by their height. Mary is made for God alone, and far from ever detaining a soul in herself, she casts the soul upon God and unites it with Him so much the more perfectly as the soul is more perfectly united to her. Mary is the admirable echo of God. When we say, "Mary," she answers, "God." When, with St. Elizabeth, we call her, "Blessed," she glorifies God. If the falsely enlightened, whom the devil has so miserably illusioned, even in prayer, had known how to find Mary, and through her, to find Jesus, and through Jesus, God the Father, they would not have had such terrible falls. The saints tell us that when we have once found Mary, and through Mary, Jesus, and through Jesus, God the Father, we have found all good. He who says all, excepts nothing: all grace and all friendship with God, all safety from God's enemies, all truth to crush falsehoods, all facility to overcome difficulties in the way of salvation, all comfort and all joy amidst the bitterness of life.

She Imparts the Grace to Carry Crosses

22. This does not mean that he who has found Mary by a true devotion will be exempt from crosses and sufferings.[14] Far from it; he is more besieged by them than others are, because Mary, the Mother of the living, gives to all her children portions of the Tree of

Life, which is the Cross of Jesus. But along with their crosses she also imparts the grace to carry them patiently and even cheerfully; and thus it is that the crosses which she lays upon those who belong to her are rather steeped in sweetness than filled with bitterness. If for a while her children feel the bitterness of the cup which one must drink in order to be the friend of God, the consolation and joy which this good Mother sends after the trial encourage them exceedingly to carry still heavier and more painful crosses.

Conclusion

23. The difficulty, then, is how to really and truly find the most Blessed Virgin Mary in order to find all abundant grace. God, being the absolute Master, can confer directly by Himself that which He usually grants only through Mary. It would even be rash to deny that sometimes He does so. Nevertheless, St. Thomas teaches that in the order of grace, established by Divine Wisdom, God ordinarily communicates Himself to men only through Mary. Therefore, if we would go up to Him and be united with Him, we must use the same means He used to come down to us, to be made man and to impart His graces to us. That means is a true devotion to our Blessed Lady.

III. Our Sanctification by the Perfect Devotion to the Blessed Virgin or the Holy Slavery of Love: A Perfect Means

Devotions to Mary

24. There are several true devotions to Our Lady: here I do not speak of those that are false.

1. Devotion without Special Practices

25. The first consists in fulfilling our Christian duties, avoiding mortal sin, acting more out of love than fear, praying to Our Lady now and then, honoring her as the Mother of God, yet without having any special devotion to her.

2. Devotion with Special Practices

26. The second consists in entertaining for Our Lady more perfect feelings of esteem and love, of confidence and veneration. It leads us to join the Confraternities of the Holy Rosary and of the Scapular, to recite the five decades or the fifteen decades of the Rosary, to honor Mary's images and altars, to publish her praises and to enroll ourselves in her sodalities.[15] This devotion is good, holy, and praiseworthy if we keep ourselves free from sin; but it is not so perfect as the next, nor so efficient in severing our souls from creatures or in detaching us from ourselves, in order to be united with Jesus Christ.

3. The Perfect Devotion: The Holy Slavery Of Love

27. The third devotion to Our Lady, known and practiced by very few persons, is the one I am now about to disclose to you, predestinate soul.

A. Nature and Scope of the Holy Slavery of Love

Nature

28. *It consists in giving oneself entirely and as a slave to Mary, and to Jesus through Mary; and after that to do all that we do, through Mary, with Mary, in Mary and for Mary.*[16] I shall now explain these words.

Scope: Total Surrender

29. We should choose a special feast-day on which we give, consecrate, and sacrifice to Mary voluntarily, lovingly, and without constraint, entirely and without reserve: our body and soul; our exterior property, such as house, family and income; and also our interior and spiritual possessions; namely, our merits, graces, virtues, and satisfactions.[17]

It should be observed here, that by this devotion the soul sacrifices to Jesus, through Mary, all that it holds most dear, things of which even no religious Order would require the sacrifice; namely, the right to dispose of ourselves, of the value of our prayers and alms, of our mortifications and satisfactions. The soul leaves everything to be freely disposed of by Our Lady so that she may apply it all according to her own will for the greater glory of God, which she alone knows perfectly.

Surrender of the Value of Our Good Works

30. We leave to her disposal all the satisfactory and impetratory value of our good works, so that after we have made the sacrifice of them—although not by vow—we are no longer the masters of any good works we may do; but Our Lady may apply them, sometimes for the relief or the deliverance of a soul in Purgatory, sometimes for the conversion of a poor sinner, etc.[18]

31. By this devotion we also place our merits in the hands of Our Lady, but only that she may preserve, augment, and embellish them, because we cannot communicate to one another either the merits of sanctifying grace or those of glory. However, we give her all our prayers and good works inasmuch as they have an intercessory and satisfactory value, that she may distribute and apply them to whom  she pleases. If, after having thus consecrated ourselves to Our Lady, we desire to relieve a soul in Purgatory, to save a sinner, or to assist a friend by our prayers, our alms-giving, our mortifications, and sacrifices, we must humbly ask it of Our Lady, abiding, however, by her decision, which remains unknown to us; and we must be fully persuaded that the value of our actions, being dispensed by the same hand which God Himself makes use of to distribute to us His graces and gifts, cannot fail to be applied for His greater glory.

Three Kinds of Slavery

32. I have said that this devotion consists in giving ourselves to Mary as slaves.[19] But notice that there are three kinds of slavery. The first is the slavery of nature; in this sense all men, good and bad alike, are slaves of God. The second is the slavery of constraint; the devils and the damned are slaves of God in this second sense. The third is the slavery of love and of free will; and this is the one by which we must consecrate ourselves to God through Mary. It is the most perfect way for us human creatures to give ourselves to God our Creator.

Servant and Slave

33. Notice again, that there is a great difference between a servant and a slave. A servant claims wages for his services; a slave has a right to none. A servant is free to leave his master when he likes—he serves him only for a time; a slave belongs to his master for life and has no right to leave him. A servant does not give to his master the right of life and death over him; a slave gives himself up entirely, so that his master can put him to death without being molested by the law. It is easily seen, then, that he who is a slave by constraint is rigorously dependent on his master. Strictly speaking, a man must be dependent in that sense only on his Creator. Hence we do not find that kind of slavery among Christians, but only among pagans.

Happiness of the Slave of Love

34. But happy, and a thousand times happy, is the generous soul that consecrates himself entirely to Jesus through Mary as a slave of love after he has shaken off by Baptism the tyrannical slavery of the devil!

B. Excellence of the Holy Slavery of Love

I should require much supernatural light to describe perfectly the excellence of this practice. I shall content myself with these few remarks.

Imitation of the Trinity

35. (1) To give ourselves to Jesus through Mary is to imitate God the Father, Who has given us His Son only through Mary, and Who communicates to us His grace only through Mary. It is to imitate God the Son, Who has come to us only through Mary, and Who, "by giving us an example, that as He has done, so we do

also" (John xiii, 15), has urged us to go to Him by the same means by which He has come to us—that is, through Mary. It is to imitate the Holy Spirit, Who bestows His graces and gifts upon us only through Mary. "Is it not fitting," asks St. Bernard, "that grace should return to its Author by the same channel which conveyed it to us?"

It Honors Jesus

36. (2) To go to Jesus through Mary is truly to honor Jesus Christ, for it denotes that we do not esteem ourselves worthy of approaching His infinite holiness directly and by ourselves because of our sins; that we need Mary, His holy Mother, to be our advocate and Mediatrix with Him, our Mediator. It is to approach Jesus as our Mediator and Brother, and at the same time to humble ourselves before Him, as before our God and our Judge. In a word, it is to practice humility, which is always exceedingly pleasing to the heart of God.

It Purifies and Embellishes Our Good Works

37. (3) To consecrate ourselves thus to Jesus through Mary is to place in Mary's hands our good actions, which, although they may appear to us to be good, are often very imperfect and unworthy of the sight and the acceptance of God, before Whom even the stars are not pure. Ah! Let us pray, then, to our dear Mother and Queen, that, having received our poor present, she may purify it,

sanctify it, embellish it, and thus render it worthy of
God. All that our soul possesses is of less value before
God, the heavenly Householder, when it comes to win-
ning His friendship and favor, than a worm-eaten
apple presented to the king by a poor farmer in pay-
ment for the rent of his farm. But what would such a
farmer do if he were wise, and if he were well liked by
the queen? Would he not give his apple to the queen?
And would she not out of kindness to the poor man, as
also out of respect for the king, remove from the apple
all that is worm-eaten or spoiled, and then place it in
a gold dish and surround it with flowers? Would the
king refuse to accept the apple then? Or would he not
rather receive it with joy from the hands of the queen
who favors that poor man? "If you wish to present
something to God, no matter how small it may be,"
says St. Bernard, "place it in Mary's hands, if you do
not wish to be refused."

38. Great God! How insignificant everything that
we do really is! But let us place all in Mary's hands by
this devotion. When we have given ourselves to Mary
to the very utmost of our power, by despoiling ourselves completely in her honor, she will far outdo us in
generosity and will repay us a hundredfold. She will
communicate herself to us, with her merits and
virtues; she will place our presents on the golden
plate of her charity; she will clothe us, as Rebecca
clothed Jacob, with the beautiful garments of her
elder and only Son, Jesus Christ—that is, with His
merits, which she has at her disposal; and thus, after
we have despoiled ourselves of everything in her
honor, we shall be "clothed in double garments"; that
is, the garments, the ornaments, the perfumes, the
merits, and the virtues of Jesus and Mary clothe the
soul of their slave, who has despoiled himself and who
perseveres in his despoliation.[20]

Charity in the Highest Degree

39. (4) Moreover, to give ourselves thus to Our Lady is to practice charity towards our neighbor in the highest possible degree, because we give her all that we hold most dear, and let her dispose of it at her will in favor of the living and the dead.

It Increases the Grace of God in Us

40. (5) By this devotion we place our graces, merits and virtues in safety, for we make Mary the depository of them all, saying to her: "See, my dear Mother, here are the good works that I have been able to do through the grace of your dear Son; I am not able to keep them on account of my own weakness and inconstancy, and also because of the many wicked enemies who attack me day and night. Alas! One may see every day the cedars of Lebanon fall into the mire, and the eagles, which had raised themselves to the sun, become birds of night; and so do a thousand of the just fall on my left hand and ten thousand on my right. My most powerful princess, sustain me lest I fall; keep all my possessions for fear I may be robbed of them. All I have I entrust to you. I know well who you are, therefore I entrust myself entirely to you; you are faithful to God and to men; you will not allow anything to perish that I entrust to you; you are powerful and nothing can hurt you or rob you of anything you hold in your hands."[21]

"When you follow Mary, you will not go astray; when you pray to her, you will not despair; when you think of her, you will not go wrong; when she sustains you, you will not fall; when she protects you, you will not fear; when she leads you, you will not become tired; when she favors you, you will arrive safely."[22] And again: "She keeps her Son from striking us; she keeps the devil from hurting us; she keeps our virtues from escaping us; she keeps our merits from being destroyed; she keeps our graces from being lost." These are the words of St. Bernard. They express in substance all I have said. Were there but this one motive to incite in me a desire for this devotion— namely, that it is a sure means of keeping me in the grace of God and even of increasing that grace in me, my heart ought to burn with longing for it.

It Renders the Soul Free

41. (6) This devotion truly frees the soul with the liberty of the children of God. Since for love of Mary we reduce ourselves freely to slavery, she, out of gratitude, will dilate our hearts, intensify our love, and cause us to walk with giant steps in the way of God's commandments. She delivers the soul from weariness, sadness, and scruples. It was this devotion which Our Lord taught to Mother Agnes of Jesus,[23] as a sure means of delivering her from the severe sufferings and perplexities which troubled her. "Make yourself," He said, "My mother's slave." She did so, and in a moment her troubles ceased.

Obedience to the Counsels of the Church

42. To show that this devotion is rightfully authorized it would be necessary to mention the bulls of the Popes and the pastoral letters of the bishops speaking in its favor; the indulgences granted to it; the confraternities established in its honor; the examples of the many saints and illustrious persons who have practiced it. But all that I shall leave out.

C. Interior Practices of The Holy Slavery of Love: Its Guiding Formula

43. I have said that this devotion consists in doing all our actions, with Mary, in Mary, through Mary, and for Mary.

Scope of This Formula

44. It is not enough to have given ourselves once as slaves to Jesus through Mary, nor is it enough to renew that act of consecration every month or every week. That alone would not make it a permanent devotion, nor could it bring the soul to that degree of perfection to which it is capable of raising it. It is not very difficult to enroll ourselves in a confraternity, nor to practice this devotion in as far as it prescribes a few vocal prayers every day; but the great difficulty is to enter into its spirit. Now its spirit consists in this, that we be interiorly dependent on Mary; that we be slaves of Mary, and, through her, of Jesus. I have found many people who, with admirable zeal, have adopted the exterior practices of this holy slavery of Jesus and Mary, but I have found only a few who have accepted its interior spirit, and still fewer who have persevered in it.

Meaning and Explanation of This Formula Act *with* Mary

45. (1) The essential practice of this devotion is to do all our actions *with* Mary. This means that we must take Our Lady as the perfect model of all that we do.

46. Before undertaking anything we must renounce ourselves and our own views.[24] We must place ourselves as mere nothings before God, unable of ourselves to do anything that is supernaturally good or profitable to our salvation. We must have recourse to Our Lady, uniting ourselves to her and to her intentions, although they are not known to us; and through Mary, we must unite ourselves to the intentions of

Jesus Christ. In other words, we must place ourselves
as instruments in the hands of Mary that she may act
in us and do with us and for us whatever she pleases,
for the greater glory of her Son, and through the Son,
for the glory of the Father; so that the whole work of
our interior life and of our spiritual perfection is
accomplished only by dependence on Mary.

Act *in* Mary

47. (2) We must do all things in Mary;[25] that is to
say, we must become accustomed little by little to rec-
ollect ourselves interiorly and thus try to form within
us some idea or spiritual image of Mary.[26] She will be,
as it were, the oratory of our souls, in which we offer
up all our prayers to God, without fear of not being
heard; she will be to us a Tower of David, in which we
take refuge from all our enemies; a burning lamp to
enlighten our interior and to inflame us with divine
love; a sacred altar upon which we contemplate God
in Mary and with her. In short, Mary will be the only
means used by our souls in dealing with God; she will
be our universal refuge. If we pray, we will pray in
Mary; if we receive Jesus in Holy Communion, we will
place Him in Mary, so that He may take His delight in
her; if we do anything at all, we will act in Mary;
everywhere and in all things we will renounce ourselves.

Act *through* Mary

48. (3) We must never go to Our Lord except through Mary, through her intercession and her influence with Him. We must never be without Mary when we pray to Jesus.

Act *for* Mary

49. (4) Lastly, we must do all of our actions for Mary. This means that, as slaves of this august princess, we must work only for her, for her interests and her glory—making this the immediate end of all our actions—and for the glory of God, which must be their final end. In everything we do we must renounce our self-love, because very often self-love sets itself up in an imperceptible manner as the end of our actions. We should often repeat, from the bottom of our heart: "O my dear Mother! It is for you that I go here or there; for you, that I do this or that; for you, that I suffer this pain or wrong."

Practical Counsels Concerning the Spirit of the Holy Slavery

Not More Perfect to Go Straight to Jesus without Mary

50. Beware, predestinate soul, of believing that it is more perfect to go straight to Jesus, straight to God. Without Mary, your action and your intention will be of little value; but if you go to God through Mary, your work will be Mary's work, and consequently it will be sublime and most worthy of God.[27]

Not Necessary to Feel and Enjoy What You Say and Do

51. Moreover, do not try to feel and enjoy what you say and do, but say and do everything with that pure faith which Mary had on earth and which she

will communicate to you in due time. Poor little slave, leave to your Sovereign Queen the clear sight of God, the raptures, the joys, the satisfactions, and the riches of Heaven, and content yourself with pure faith, although you may be full of repugnance, distractions, weariness, and dryness, and say: "Amen, so be it," to whatever Mary, your Mother, does in Heaven. That is the best you can do for the time being.[28]

Not Necessary to Enjoy Immediately the Presence of Mary

52. Take great care also not to torment yourself, should you not enjoy immediately the sweet presence of the Blessed Virgin in your soul, for this is a grace not given to all; and even when God, out of His great mercy, has thus favored a soul, it is always very easy to lose this grace, unless by frequent recollection the soul remains alive to that interior presence of Mary. Should this misfortune befall you, return calmly to your Sovereign Queen and make amends to her.[29]

Wonderful Effects of This Interior Practice

53. Experience will teach you much more about this devotion than I can tell you; and if you remain faithful to the little I have taught you, you will find so many rich fruits of grace in this practice, that you will be surprised and filled with joy.

54. Let us set to work then, dear soul, and by the faithful practice of this devotion let us obtain the grace "that Mary's soul may be in us to glorify the Lord, that her spirit may be in us to rejoice in God," as St. Ambrose says. "Do not think that there was more glory and happiness in dwelling in Abraham's bosom, which was called Paradise, than in the bosom of Mary, in which God has placed His throne," as the learned Abbot Guerric says.

It Establishes Mary's Life in the Soul

55. This devotion, faithfully practiced, produces many happy effects in the soul. The most important of them all is that it establishes, even here below, Mary's life in the soul, so that it is no longer the soul that lives, but Mary living in it; for Mary's life becomes its life. And when, by an unspeakable yet real grace, the Blessed Virgin is Queen in a soul, what wonders she works there! She is the worker of great wonders, particularly in our souls, but she works them in secret, in a way unknown to the soul itself, for were it to know, it might destroy the beauty of her works.

Mary Causes Jesus to Live in That Soul

56. As Mary is the fruitful Virgin everywhere, she produces in the soul in which she dwells purity of heart and body, purity of intention and of purpose, and fruitfulness in good works. Do not think, dear soul, that Mary, the most fruitful of all pure creatures, who has brought forth God, remains idle in a faithful soul. She will cause Jesus Christ to live in that soul, and the soul to live in constant union with Jesus Christ. "My dear children, with whom I am in labor again until Christ is formed in you" (Gal. 4:19). If Jesus Christ is the fruit of Mary in each individual soul as well as in all souls in general, He is, however, her fruit and her masterpiece more particularly in a soul in which she dwells.

Mary Becomes Everything to That Soul

57. Finally, Mary becomes everything to the soul who is in the service of Jesus Christ. The mind will be enlightened by Mary's pure faith. The heart will be deepened by Mary's humility. It will be expanded and inflamed by Mary's charity; made clean by Mary's purity; noble and great by her motherly care. But why dwell any longer on this? Only experience can teach the wonders wrought by Mary, wonders so great that

neither the wise nor the proud, nor even many of the devout can believe them.

Special Function of the Holy Slavery in the Latter Times

Through Mary, Jesus Will Reign

58. As it is through Mary that God came into the world the first time, in a state of humiliation and annihilation, may we not say that it is through Mary also that He will come the second time, as the whole Church expects Him to come, to rule everywhere and to judge the living and the dead? Who knows how and when that will be accomplished? I do know that God, Whose thoughts are as far removed from ours as Heaven is distant from the earth, will come in a time and a manner that men expect the least, even those who are most learned and most versed in Holy Scripture, which is very obscure on this subject.

59. We ought also to believe that towards the end of time, and perhaps sooner than we think, God will raise up great men full of the Holy Spirit and imbued with the spirit of Mary; through whom this powerful Queen will work great wonders in the world, so as to destroy sin and to establish the kingdom of Jesus Christ, her Son, upon the ruins of the kingdom of this corrupt world; and these holy men will succeed by means of this devotion of which I do but give here the outline, and which my deficiency only impairs.

D. Exterior Practices of the Holy Slavery of Love

60. Besides the interior practice of this devotion, of which we have just spoken, there are also certain exterior practices, which we must neither omit nor neglect.

Consecration and Renewal

61. The first practice is to choose a special feast day on which to consecrate ourselves to Jesus through the Blessed Virgin Mary, whose slaves we make ourselves. On the same day we should receive Holy Communion for that intention, and spend the day in prayer. At least once a year on the same day, we should renew our act of consecration.

A Token of Our Slavery

62. The second practice is to pay to Our Lady, every year on that same day, some little tribute, as a token of our slavery and dependence; such has always been the homage paid by slaves to their masters. That tribute may consist of an act of mortification, an act of charity to the poor, a pilgrimage, or some prayers. Blessed Marino, we are told by his brother, St. Peter Damian, used the discipline on himself in public every year on the same day before the altar of Our Lady. Such zeal is not required, nor do we counsel it; but if we give but little to Mary, let us at least offer it with a humble and grateful heart.

Celebration of the Annunciation

63. The third practice is to celebrate every year, with special devotion, the feast of the Annunciation, which is the patronal feast of this devotion and which was established to honor and imitate the dependence in which the Eternal Word placed Himself on that day out of love for us.

Recitation of the Little Crown and the Magnificat

64. The fourth external practice is to say every day (not, however, under pain of sin, in case of omission) the *Little Crown of the Blessed Virgin*, which is composed of three *Our Fathers* and twelve *Hail Marys*; also often to recite the Magnificat (see prayer #2), which is the only hymn composed by Mary that we possess, to thank God for His graces in the past and to beg of Him fresh blessings for the present. Above all, we ought not to fail to say this hymn in thanksgiving after Holy Communion. The learned man Gerson tells us that Our Lady herself recited it after Communion.

IV. The Tree of Life: Its Culture and Its Growth or How to Make Mary Live and Reign in Our Souls

65. Have you understood with the help of the Holy Spirit, what I have tried to explain to you in the preceding pages? If so, be thankful to God, for it is a secret known and understood by only a few. If you have found the treasure hidden in the field of Mary, the precious pearl of the Gospel, sell all that you have in order to buy it. You must make the sacrifice of yourself to the Blessed Mother; you must disappear in her, so that you may find God alone.

If the Holy Spirit has planted in your soul the true Tree of Life, which is the devotion that I have just explained to you, you must do all that you can to cultivate it, in order that it may yield its fruit in due season. This devotion is like the mustard-seed of the Gospel, "which is the least indeed of all seeds, but when it is grown up, is greater than all herbs, and becomes a tree, in whose branches the birds of the air (i.e., the elect) come to dwell," and rest in its shade from the heat of the sun and hide there in safety from the beasts of prey.

66. This is the way, predestinate soul, to cultivate it:

No Human Support

67. (1) This Tree, once planted in a faithful heart, requires the open air and freedom from all human support. Being heavenly, it must be kept clear from any creatures that might prevent it from lifting itself to God in Whom its origin lies. Hence you must not rely on your own skill or your natural talents, on your own repute, or on the protection of men. You must have recourse to Mary and rely on her help alone.

Constant Concern of the Soul

68. (2) The one in whose soul this Tree is planted must, like a good gardener, constantly watch over it and tend it, for it is a Tree that has life, and is capable of yielding the fruit of life. Therefore, it must be cultivated and raised by the steady care and application of the soul; the soul that wants to become perfect will make this its chief aim and occupation.

Violence to Oneself

69. (3) Whatever is likely to choke the Tree, or, in the course of time, prevent its yielding its fruit, such as thorns and thistles, must be cut away and rooted out. This means that by mortification and by doing

violence to ourselves, we must suppress and renounce all useless pleasures and vain intercourse with creatures. In other words, we must crucify the flesh, keep recollected and mortify our senses.

No Self-Love

70. (4) You must also keep watch on insects, which might do harm to the Tree. These insects are self-love and love of comfort. They eat away the foliage of the Tree and destroy the fair hopes it gives of yielding fruit, for self-love is opposed to the love of Mary.

Horror of Sin

71. (5) You must not allow destructive animals to approach the Tree of Life. By these animals are meant all sins. They may kill the Tree of Life by their touch alone. Even their breath must be kept away from it, namely, venial sins, for they are most dangerous if committed without regret.

Fidelity to Religious Practices

72. (6) It is also necessary to water this heavenly Tree often with the fervor of piety in our religious practices, in our confessions and Communions, in all our prayers, both public and private; otherwise it will stop yielding fruit.

Peace in Trials

73. (7) Do not become alarmed when the Tree is moved and shaken by the wind, for it is necessary that the storms of temptation should threaten to uproot it, that snow and ice should cover it, so as, if possible, to destroy it. This means that this devotion will of necessity be attacked and contradicted, but provided we persevere in cultivating it in our souls, we need not fear.

Its Fruit: Our Lord

74. Predestinate soul, if you thus cultivate the Tree of Life, freshly planted in your soul by the Holy Spirit, I assure you that in a short time it will grow so tall that the birds of Heaven will come to dwell in it. It will be a good tree, yielding fruit of honor and grace in due season, namely, the sweet and adorable Jesus, Who always has been, and always will be, the only fruit of Mary.

Happy the soul, in which Mary, the Tree of Life, is planted; happier the soul in which she has acquired growth and bloom; still happier the soul in which she yields her fruit; but most happy of all the soul which relishes and preserves Mary's fruit until death, and forever and ever. Amen.

75. "He who holds (this), let him hold (it)."

God Alone!

Endnotes for The Secret of Mary

1. The holy slavery of Jesus in Mary was known, no doubt, before St. Louis de Montfort's time; yet he rightly calls this devotion *a secret*; first, because there lies in it, as in all things supernatural, a hidden treasure which grace alone can help us to find and utilize; secondly, because there are but few souls that enter into the spirit of this devotion and go beyond its exterior practices. Again, as no one had as yet thoroughly explained this devotion nor shaped it into a definite method of spiritual life, St. Louis de Montfort could say of a truth, "I have not been able to find this secret in any book old or new."

2. These words show how highly St. Louis de Montfort esteemed this devotion. As there are professional secrets committed only to men who know how to appreciate and exploit them, so this secret of sanctity must be entrusted only to those souls who are truly concerned with their own perfection; and following the recommendation of Our Lord not to profane holy things (Mat. 6:6), Montfort preserves this secret with a holy jealousy that denotes respect for divine things.

3. These words contain three important counsels: (1) This devotion must be practiced in the ordinary course of life as well as in the most important actions. (2) Only when we steadily persevere in it, and not merely try it for a few weeks, shall we be able to judge of its excellence and know its fruit. (3) It is necessary to remove all hindrances to this devotion (namely, sin and secret affection for that which is sinful).

4. See prayer #47 in this book.

5. See prayer #46 in this book.

6. Do not make light of this recommendation. It is an important one. If many persons do not become acquainted with the secret of this devotion, it is because they forget that in order to be allowed to enter this "Garden Enclosed," as Mary is called, they must beg the Holy Spirit, "who searches all things, yes, the deep things of God" (1 Cor. 2:10) to grant them that favor. [See The Tree of Life, (paragraph 65); also Prayer to Jesus, prayer #50].

7. Those who begin this devotion are here reminded of the recommendation of the masters of the spiritual life, namely, that the interior life must be their chief concern. They must be determined to obtain good results bought with the price of sacrifice. Compare these words with St. Louis de Montfort's advice on cultivating The Tree of Life, paragraphs 65-75.

8. This is characteristic of St. Louis de Montfort's devotion and makes it a special method of spiritual life.

9. The reasons given here to prove that Mary is the most perfect means for finding Jesus are a condensed treatise on Mariology. If the faithful meditate on these points, they will come to understand the function assigned to Our Lady, by virtue of her divine maternity, in the mystery of the Incarnation, and now in the whole Church.

10. Conclude from this, that we call Mary our Mother not because of mere feelings of piety and gratitude awakened in us by the conviction that she loves and protects us, but because *she* is our Mother in the spiritual order as truly as she is the Mother of Christ in the natural order. The spiritual motherhood of Mary, a consequence of her divine motherhood, is one of the truths on which the True Devotion of St. Louis de Montfort is founded.

11. The abiding of Mary in our souls may be explained in the following

manner: Her presence in us cannot be compared to that of God living in our souls by sanctifying grace and thus making us partakers of His divine life. Neither must we believe that Mary is bodily present in our souls. Some have wrongfully charged St. Louis de Montfort with inferring the omnipresence of Mary. But let us bear in mind Mary's privilege of being truly the Mother of God (which privilege is hers personally and exclusively). As a consequence of that privilege, Mary beholds our souls in a universal manner, and more excellently than the saints and angels do in their heavenly glory, and she is with us really, individually, and intimately. Thus, we are morally present to her and she is morally present to us, because by her prayers, her attention, and her influence she cooperates with the Holy Spirit in forming Jesus in our souls. By way of comparison, we might say, that Mary is present in our souls as the sun is present in a room by its light and warmth even though it is not there itself.

12. Therefore great docility is required on our part, if we would be "formed quickly, easily, and gently." This comparison of the mold explains very well the interior practice of this devotion. The devotion consists essentially in a single act which, under various forms and conditions, we apply to our whole lives, both interior and exterior. Such is the simplicity of St. Louis de Montfort's method.

13. This beautiful expression interprets the invitation of Divine Wisdom: "Come, eat the bread and drink the wine which I have mingled for you" (Prov. 9:5). It also accounts for the unexpected graces which this devotion draws upon those who persevere in its practice. Note that this method of spiritual formation is practically the same as the education given by a mother to her child. In ourselves, we experience the infirmities and the wants of infancy; in Mary we find the strong and never wearied love of a mother. All that we have to do is to abandon ourselves to Mary and to remain dependent on her in all things just like children.

14. St. Louis de Montfort has explained that his true devotion is an easy means of sanctification, yet he wishes to guard us against the common illusion that his method exempts us from spiritual labor and sufferings. He is himself a striking example of the manly education which Mary, the valiant woman, gives to her children, as well as of the love of Jesus crucified which she enkindles in their hearts.

15. All such devotions, remarks St. Louis de Montfort elsewhere, include but a limited number of devout practices and take up but a part of our daily life, while the one he proposes embraces our whole life and divests us of all things.

16. We must, therefore, note two things in this devotion: first, an *act* of total consecration to Jesus through Mary; and secondly, a *state* of being consecrated. That state consists in the permanent disposition of living and acting habitually in dependence on Mary; and it is called the spirit or the interior part of this consecration. This practice, although it embraces our entire life, appears so small and trifling at first glance, that St. Louis de Montfort has justly compared it to the mustard seed. But one comes to realize its vital energy and its wonderful effects when it has grown strong by persistent exercise.

17. These words show us the far-reaching effect of this consecration, which St. Louis de Montfort calls a perfect renewal of the baptismal vows, and, indeed, in making it we give ourselves anew to Jesus Christ, Our Lord, through the hands of Mary.

18. It may not be amiss to give here a short explanation of the Heroic Act of Charity, and to point out how it differs from this act of consecration. According to a definition of the Sacred Congregation of Indulgences (December 1885), the Heroic Act of Charity consists in this, that a member of the Church Militant offers to God for the souls in Purgatory, all the satisfactory works which he will perform during his lifetime and also all the suffrages which may accrue to him after his death. By the act of consecration to Jesus through Mary as taught by St. Louis de Montfort, we give to Our Lady not only the satisfactory works of our life, but all else, nothing excepted [see the Act of Consecration, prayer #49]. The use to be made of our good works and satisfactions is not determined by us, as it is in the Heroic Act, but it is left to Mary's intention and will. In his act of consecration, St. Louis de Montfort does not seem to comprise directly the suffrages which may accrue to us in Purgatory, but indirectly they are implied: "I leave to you...all that belongs to me...in time and in eternity." Neither the Heroic Act nor our act of consecration implies a vow, yet both may be made with a vow, if discretion and sound judgment are not lacking in making such a solemn promise to God.

19. These words show us the true nature of this consecration. By making it we place ourselves in a state in which we are owned by Jesus and Mary and are totally dependent on their will. Now that is the nature and the condition of a slave; but to remove the idea of there being any degradation or tyrannical violence in this noble servitude, St. Louis de Montfort explains that it is a voluntary slavery, full of honor and of love, giving us the liberty of the true children of God. There is then no reason for being scared or repelled by the words "slave" and "slavery." Consider the state, not the word which expresses the state of total, lasting, and disinterested subjection and dependence on the Master through the Mother. One may ask why not use other words? It is because there are none to express adequately this special state of consecration.

20. This charming comment on the words of St. Bernard will console and encourage certain souls who grow weary and sad when they become conscious of their unworthiness and their insufficiency. As St. Louis de Montfort loves to say, and his saying is very true, Mary will be "their supplement" with God.

21. These words ought to be considered by all who are concerned about their perseverance in grace and their interior perfection. Many there are who hesitate even to begin and many who draw back soon after starting, because they apprehend a possible failure or lack of perseverance.

22. St. Bernard, *Inter flores*, cap. 135, *de Maria Virgine*.

23. A Dominican nun who died in the odor of sanctity in the year 1634 at the convent of Langeac in Auvergne, France.

24. From these indications, however abstract, we may learn that the act of union with Mary, as understood by St. Louis de Montfort, requires two things in the work of our sanctification: (1) the removal of all obstacles (sin and its occasions) by renouncing ourselves, (2) the union of our wills with the will of God and of our actions with the impulse of divine grace. Without that self-renunciation in all things, our union with Mary would be very imperfect; our dependence on her would be an illusion (see paragraphs 69,70, and 71 The Tree of Life). Note also, that by telling us to renounce our own views and intentions, however good they be, in order to adopt those of Mary, Montfort counsels the practice of that which is most perfect.

25. *In* indicates an indwelling, an intimate union which produces unity. As St. Louis de Montfort expresses it, we must "enter into Mary's interior and stay there, adopting her views and feelings." Mary must become, as it were, the place and the atmosphere in which we live; her influence must penetrate us. As soon as this disposition of our souls has become habitual, we can say that we dwell in Mary, and having thus become like one moral person with her, we abide in her and she dwells in us, in the sense explained above (see endnote no. 8).

26. St. Theresa gives similar advice to beginners for keeping recollected and united with Our Lord when at prayer. She recommends the use of images, and in this she is of the same mind as St. Louis de Montfort, who had recourse to images and banners, to the erection of calvaries, and of other exterior displays which appeal to the senses and elevate the soul to God.

27. This does not mean that we may not approach Our Lord directly to speak to Him in prayer or contemplation; nor does it mean that in every action of ours we must think of Mary actually and distinctly; a virtual intention is sufficient. St. Louis de Montfort, indeed, says that our offering or act of consecration, if renewed but once a month or once a week (we might add, once a day), does not establish us in the spirit of this devotion, which is a state or a habit; yet he remarks that our interior look towards Mary, though it be but a general and hasty look, is sufficient to renew our offering.

28. This is useful advice to those who are but beginning and who might think that they do nothing good because they do not see or feel. St. Louis de Montfort reminds them of the truth that our union with God consists in an act of the will. In his True Devotion he says that that act may be either mental or expressed in words; it can be made in the twinkling of an eye. In his prayer to Mary (prayer #48 in this book), he makes us ask for detachment of the senses in our devotion.

29. This interior presence of Mary is a favor which St. Louis de Montfort enjoyed to an exceptional degree, as we may see by reading his life. He says: "It is a grace not given to all." Yet he exhorts us all to practice his true devotion, and promises to all without exception "that Mary's soul will be in them." It is true, he always insists upon the condition of perseverance in practicing this devotion. As there are, however, but few souls who remain faithful to its spirit even in a lower degree, we must say that this presence of Mary is not given to all.

77. The Responsibility of the Present Moment
by Jerome F. Coniker

See Days 38–40 on pages 195–227.

501

Appendix B
Total Consecration Resources & International Media and Training Centers

*enter more deeply into your
Total Consecration by living the
second dimension of Consecration:
"Consecration in Truth."*

Live the Faith!

*Learn the
Faith!*

*Share the
Faith!*

Preparation for
Total Consecration to Jesus
through Mary for Families

*According to St. Louis de Montfort,
with meditations by Pope John Paul II.*

This preparation manual will take your family through 40 days of readings, meditations and prayers. Each day you will be given a quote from St. Louis de Montfort. Prayers for the day are also suggested, along with the Family Rosary. You will read in the Holy Father's meditations how this de Montfort consecration changed his life, and will take a closer look at the spirituality and person of Pope John Paul II. This will truly help you and your family prepare for the great day of your Total Consecration to Jesus through Mary in union with St. Joseph.

Call for quantity discounts.

Also available, clear vinyl book cover, #707-1.

www.familyland.org
or call 1-800-77-FAMILY

40-Day Preparation for Total Consecration
Resource #155-186DK, 235 minutes

These eight presentations on DVD or CD guide you in your spiritual journey of entrusting your life to Jesus through Mary, as Pope John Paul II did.

Fr. Frederick Miller and Montfort Father Roger Charest share profound insights on the meaning of total consecration, the importance of grace in your daily conversion journey, and the role of merit in the spiritual life.

Francis Cardinal Arinze gives two talks on the relationship between consecration, reparation, and mission and how you can live out your consecration.

Includes the following presentations:

- *The Key To Understanding the Marian Consecration of St. Louis de Montfort*, with Fr. Miller (38 min.)
- *Spirit of the World* with Fr. Miller (22 min.)
- *Merit, Grace & the Slavery of Love* with Fr. Charest (24 min.)
- *Knowledge of Self* with Fr. Miller (24 min.)
- *Knowledge of Mary* with Fr. Miller (25 min.)
- *Knowledge of Jesus and the Total Consecration Prayer* with Fr. Miller (27 min.)
- *Reparation, Consecration and Mission* with Cardinal Arinze (37 min.)
- *Some Responsibilities of the Lay Faithful at the Present Moment* with Cardinal Arinze (47 min.)

Reparation, Consecration and Mission
This booklet by Francis Cardinal Arinze is a reflection on the reality of sin in the world, the consequences it brings, and the need for repentance and reparation through the Most Blessed Virgin Mary. Resource #336-48

Some Responsibilities of the Lay Faithful at the Present Moment
This booklet by Cardinal Arinze identifies the dimensions in which responsibility is to be lived every day: sacramental life, prayer and formation, family and community, work and evangelization. Resource #336-47

Be Not Afraid Family Hours®
Healing Through Consecration & The Priestly Prayer of Jesus (Jn. 17)

May be used in conjunction with this Preparation for Total Consecration book (resource #323-115).

Healing Through Consecration — Learn more about the Saint Louis de Montfort's consecration to Jesus through Mary with this series featuring Fr. Frederick Miller. Resource #133-450VK. Spanish Version: #133-B450VK.

The Priestly Prayer of Jesus (St. John Chapter 17) — Gives the essence of the second Dimension of Consecration: Consecration in Truth. Resource #133-740VK.

Be Not Afraid Family Hours blend faith formation and devotional prayer. The Family Hours present the teachings of Pope John Paul II, Mother Teresa, Cardinal Francis Arinze, and other outstanding teachers who discuss a particular theme which is developed during a nine-week period. Each Family Hour includes the Rosary, with meditations and dramatizations that bring the mysteries of the Rosary to life for the entire family.

The Family Hours may be used in homes or in parishes. In the church, families can worship in "spirit and truth" (cf. Jn. 4) in the Eucharistic Presence of Our Lord reserved in the Tabernacle, and experience the healing power of the sacrament of Penance.

Other Family Hour Series available:

The Immaculate Conception #133-361VK. Spanish Version: 133-B361VK.
The Holy Rosary #133-430VK. Spanish Version: #133-B430VK.
The Holy Spirit, Mary & the Virtue of Hope #133-600VK.
Mary, Life, and the Sacraments #133-550VK.
The Living Eucharist #133-390VK. Spanish Version: #133-B620VK.
Our Mission is Mercy #133-410VK. Spanish Version: #133-B410VK.
Saint Joseph #133-363VK. Spanish Version: #133-B363VK.
The Doctrine of Purgatory #133-530VK.

www.familyland.org
or call 1-800-77-FAMILY

Because of modern communications, some of the Church's best teachers can now reach the families of the world with the Truth that sets hearts free…

Partial List of Video Teaching Faculty:

Pope John
Paul II †

Francis Cardinal
Arinze*

Alfonso Cardinal
Lopez Trujillo*

Anthony Cardinal
Bevilacqua

Mario Luigi
Cardinal Ciappi*†

Edouard Cardinal
Gagnon*

Pio Cardinal
Laghi*

Adam Cardinal
Maida

John Cardinal
O'Connor†

Gaudencio
Cardinal
Rosales

Jose Cardinal
Sanchez*

Jaime Cardinal
Sin†

Edmund Cardinal
Szoka*

J. Francis
Cardinal
Stafford*

Jozef Cardinal
Tomko*

Archbishop
John Foley*

www.familyland.org
or call 1-800-77-FAMILY

Archbishop
Ramon
Arguelles

Bishop
Thomas
Daily

Bishop John
Magee

Bishop
Daniel
Conlon

Bishop
Socrates
Villegas

Fr. Pablo
Straub

Fr. Bernard
Geiger

Fr. Benedict
Groeschel

Fr. George
Kosicki

Fr. Frederick
Miller

Fr. Patrick
Peyton†

Fr. Frank
Pavone

Fr. Michael
Scanlan

Blessed
Teresa of
Calcutta†

Dr. Scott
Hahn

Giovanni Cardinal Cheli*
Christoph Cardinal Schonborn, O.P.
Archbishop Agostino Cacciavillan*
Archbishop Elden Curtiss
Bishop Roger Foys
Bishop Juan F. Torres
Bishop Peter Van Lierde †
Bishop Thomas Welsh
Monsignor Peter Elliott*
Msgr. John McCarthy
Msgr. Josefino Ramirez
Fr. Roger Charest, S.M.M.
Fr. Harold Cohen
Fr. Robert J. Dempsey*
Fr. Richard Drabik, M.I.C.
Fr. Thomas Dubay, S.M.
Fr. Gregory Finn, O.S.J.
Fr. Thomas Forrest

Fr. John H. Hampsch
Fr. John A. Hardon, S.J.†
Fr. Brian Harrison, S.T.L.
Fr. Adrian van Kaam, C.S.Sp., Ph.D.
Fr. M. Albert Krapiec, O.P.
Fr. S. Michalenko, M.I.C.
Fr. Bruce Nieli
Fr. Randall Paine
Fr. Burns Seeley, Ph.D.
Mother Immaculata, H.M.I.
Jeff Cavins
Jerry and Gwen Coniker
William Federer
John Haas, Ph.D.
Kimberly Hahn
Alice von Hildebrand
Susan Muto, Ph.D.
George Weigel, Ph.D.

Members of the Roman Curia – The Pope's Direct Staff   †Deceased

www.familyland.org
or call 1-800-77-FAMILY

Holy Family of Fatima Enthronement™
Resource #133-282VK

This program provides you with the
materials to enthrone the Holy Family in
your home, using the Holy Family of
Fatima portrait, which is centered on the
Sacred and Merciful Heart of Jesus.

- Holy Family of Fatima Enthronement
  video featuring Mother Teresa of Calcutta
  1-hour, VHS (call for availability on
  DVD).

- Dramatized Rosary video.
  Includes the Joyful, Luminous,
  Sorrowful, and Glorious Mysteries on
  2-hour VHS (call for availability on DVD)

- Family Consecration Prayer and Meditation
  Book

- Five Holy Family at Fatima Portraits—16" X
  20", full-color (four extra portraits so you can
  share this important enthronement with
  other families)

- Five Holy Family Enthronement
  Certificates

- Six Holy Family of Fatima Enthronement
  Ceremony Prayer Cards

Holy Family of Fatima Enthronement video only, Resource #133-281V

*To view these programs online or to download the portrait,
visit the "Family Consecration" section at*

www.familyland.org

Holy Family of Fatima Portrait

*The Holy Family is our model,
our inspiration and our strength.*

16 X 20 Unframed Portrait
#361-143

16 X 20 FRAMED Portrait
#361-148. The frame is
wooden (burnished gold)
with linen liner. Beautiful
and ready to hang.

The complete history and meaning of the
image is printed on the reverse side of
the portrait. (also see next page)

Dramatized Rosary Video

Pray-along video for the
entire family. Includes the
Joyful, Luminous, Sorrowful,
and Glorious mysteries, each
about 25 minutes long. Some
of the mysteries are in movie
format and others are accompanied by beautiful meditative pictures.

*Resource #115-378V, 2-hour Video
Call for availability on DVD*

www.familyland.org
or call 1-800-77-FAMILY

The Meaning of the Holy Family of Fatima Image and Interview with Sr. Lucia

This special portrait of the Holy Family depicts a vision that the three children of Fatima, Lucia, Francisco and Jacinta, saw during the "Miracle of the Sun" on October 13, 1917. Though this vision is explained in all of the major documentation of Fatima, not very many people are aware of it.

During the "Miracle of the Sun," the sun swirled in the sky and great shafts of color flooded the entire plateau of Fatima, Portugal. The sun then plummeted towards the Earth, and the over 70,000 people present thought it was the end of the world. At this same time, the children of Fatima saw the following vision, as described by Sr. Lucia:

When our Lady disappeared in the immense distance of the sky, next to the sun, we saw St. Joseph holding the child Jesus and Our Lady dressed in white with a blue mantle. St. Joseph and the child seemed to be blessing the world, making the sign of the cross (Letter from Sr. Lucia to her Bishop, December 8, 1941, Tuy, Spain).

Jerome Coniker, founder of the Apostolate for Family Consecration, with permission granted by Cardinal Ratzinger, personally visited Sister Lucia and asked for her blessing on this portrait of the Holy Family of Fatima, the work of the Apostolate for Family Consecration, Familyland® Television Network, and the special television production about the Fatima message.

During Sister Lucia's half-hour interview with Mr. Coniker, she spoke a lot about this beautiful portrait. **She said, "It's the best that any human being could do."** She also liked the symbolic additions that were made to the portrait. For instance, on the garment of St. Joseph is the reverse side of the Miraculous Medal (the cross going through the "M" and the two Hearts of Jesus and Mary, all encircled by 12 stars). This shows St. Joseph's love for the Hearts of Jesus and Mary and his protection over the Church, symbolized by the twelve stars which represent the twelve Apostles.

Sr. Lucia was happy to see our Lady holding the Rosary and the scapular in her left hand— summarizing the apparitions of our Lady at Fatima. The scapular is the sign of our consecration to Jesus through Mary and is an act of faith when worn with reverence.

The rosary-heart outlining the Holy Family shows that the Rosary is an integral part of the Fatima message. The family Rosary is the primary prayer that will protect the family, and becomes a window through which we can see, with eyes of faith, the interior life of the Holy Family and the principal mysteries of our Faith. Through the Holy Spirit's illumination and power of love—symbolized by the flames and dove above the heart-shaped Rosary—poured out through Mary, Mediatrix of all Grace, we are more and more able to live consecrated lives as adopted members of the Holy Family. This rosary-heart outline is also the logo of the Apostolate for Family Consecration.

Sr. Lucia noticed the image of the Sacred and Eucharistic Heart of Jesus with the flame of love and the cross above it, which depicts the Holy Eucharist and the Divine Mercy rays. The rays refer to the Divine Mercy apparition of Our Lord to St. Faustina, an apparition that our Holy Father, the Pope, has held up to the entire Church. The Fatima message is the formula for drawing down Divine Mercy. Once enough families follow this formula and are consecrated to Jesus through Mary in the truths of our Faith, and live these truths with great fervor, the era of peace promised by Our Lady of Fatima will be granted to the world.

The Immaculate Heart of Mary with the sword of sorrow going through her heart depicts our Lady of Sorrows and flame of love above it depicts devotion to her Immaculate Heart, which is also a prerequisite for world peace.

The portrait summarizes The Apostolate's prayer: *All for the Sacred and Eucharistic Heart of Jesus, all through the Sorrowful and Immaculate Heart of Mary, all in union with St. Joseph.*

At the end of the interview, Sr. Lucia clutched the picture in her arms while holding it against her chest and took the picture for her own room. She loved the Apostolate for Family Consecration's work and the Holy Family of Fatima portrait very much. She said she would pray for the members and work of the Apostolate for Family Consecration. The Apostolate was "conceived" in Fatima when the founding family lived there from 1971-1973, and "born" in America when it was founded in 1975.

Sr. Lucia holding the Holy Family of Fatima
portrait, given to her by Jerry.

See page 508 for the painting of The Holy Family of Fatima.

For a free download of the portrait, visit:
www.familyconsecration.org.

Other Marian Consecration Resources

God Alone, by St. Louis de Montfort

Unearthed 100 years after his death, this collection of writings of St. Louis de Montfort continues to exhibit a freshness and timelessness that seem to make them more sought after as time goes by. His Christo-centric Marian approach to the Father in the Holy Spirit continues to influence the lives of countless souls in search of authentic Christian life and spirituality. Includes such classics as *True Devotion to Mary*, *Secret of Mary*, *Secret of the Rosary*, *Love of Eternal Wisdom*, and *Friends of the Cross*, plus methods for Saying the Rosary, maxims and lessons of Divine Wisdom, St. Louis de Montfort's will, and more.
631 pp. Resource #520-28, hardcover.

True Devotion to the Blessed Virgin

Let she who formed Jesus in her womb form you into the likeness of her Son. This book is a classic on True Devotion. It holds the key to sanctity and salvation. Mary is the surest and simplest way of living our baptismal promises and of reaching Christ. Pope Pius XII said at St. Louis de Montfort's canonization, "The author distinguishes in a few precise words this authentic devotion from the false, and to some extent, superstitious devotion, which consists only in exterior practices and superficial sentiment. True devotion…aims at union with Jesus under the guidance of Mary." *198 pp.*
Resource #520-25, English, softcover.
Resource #520-25SP, Spanish, softcover.

Secret of Mary

Everybody loves a secret. But most people, including most Catholics don't understand one of the greatest secrets of all: Mary is the shortcut to Christ! This little, penetrating book, written by St. Louis de Montfort, is an abridged version of True Devotion to the Blessed Virgin.
96 pp. Resource #520-27

Secret of Mary Explained to Children

"Children, here is a secret that will help you to become saints. It is not, however, a new secret. For a long time grown-up people have known, practiced and liked it so much that they now want to tell it to you. Ordinarily when your mother or father says to you, 'That's a secret,' you do not ask anything more. Grown-up people have many, many secrets that they do not tell to children. But this book will tell you one of these great secrets."
67 pp. Resource #520-P1, softcover.

Jesus Living in Mary

A Handbook on the spirituality of St. Louis de Montfort. This book will guide you to a better understanding and help you live the spirituality. More than 1200 pages and over 100 photographs.
Resource #520-32.

Also available is a video explaining the life of St. Louis de Montfort.
Resource 520-JLMV, 107 min.

www.familyland.org
click on "Family Consecration"
or call 1-800-77-FAMILY

The Handbook of Indulgences: Norms and Grants
This book contains the norms for indulgences, three general types of indulgenced grants, and other types of indulgenced grants, including many prayers.
128 pages, Hard-cover, Resource #506-555-22

Particular Examen, by J.F. McElhone, C.S.C.
Deeply rooted in Scripture, tradition and the examples of the saints, this book will help you get rid of your faults and progress in holiness.
191 pages, hardbound, Resource #626-2

Brown Scapular Enrollment on Video
Explains how to become enrolled in the Brown Scapular. Any priest may enroll you.
Resource #133-216V, 30 minutes

> To order Brown Scapulars, contact:
> Aylesford Lay Carmelite and Scapular Center
> 8501 Bailey Road, Darien, IL 60561-8417   phone: (630) 969-5050

Miraculous Medal Video
Explains how to become invested in the Miraculous Medal. Any priest may invest you.
Resource #133-212V, 30 minutes

> To order Miraculous Medals, contact:
> Association of the Miraculous Medal   phone: (573) 547-8343

Navarre Bibles
Includes commentaries that explain the text and help you apply it to your daily life.

> New Testament (1-volume edition), *Resource #511-77*
> The Pentateuch, *Resource #511-81*
> Chronicles to Maccabees, *Resource #511-83*
> Joshua to Kings, *Resource #511-84*
> Major Prophets, *Resource #511-85*
> Minor Prophets, *Resource #511-86*
> The Psalms & Song of Songs, *Resource #511-82*
> Wisdom Books, *Resource #511-87*

Multimedia Resources Featuring
Francis Cardinal Arinze

Inside Vatican II Series

Roman Curia Cardinal Francis Arinze, Prefect of the Congregation for Divine Worship and the Discipline of the Sacraments, clears up the misconceptions about Vatican II and the Church.

• The truth about man	• Indulgences
• Grace and sin	• Reparation
• Mission of the Church	

These are some of the important topics covered in this series. Cardinal Arinze's down-to-earth commentaries on the documents of Vatican II enlighten you and give you the confidence to stand by the Truth of our faith and to share it with others.

- *Lumen Gentium* (Dogmatic Constitution on the Church) #1010-35, 12 tapes

- *Gaudium et Spes* (Pastoral Constitution on the Church in the Modern World) #1010-75, 8 tapes

- *Sacrosanctum concilium* (The Constitution on the Sacred Liturgy) #1010-110, 7 tapes

- *Inter mirifica* (Decree on Social Communications) #1010-134, 2 tapes

- *Dei Verbum* (Dogmatic Constitution on Divine Revelation) #1010-52, 5 tapes

- *Apostolicam actuositatem* (Decree on the Apostolate of the Laity) #126-3710, 4 tapes

- *Unitatis redintegratio* (Decree on Ecumenism) #1010-141, 2 tapes

- *Apostolic Constitution on the Revision of Indulgences* #1010-92, 3 tapes

On Papal and Vatican Documents
with Cardinal Arinze:

- *Ecclesia de Eucharistia*
  #1007-76, 10.5 program hours
- **Gospel of Life**, #115-237,
  6 one-hour programs
- **Splendor of Truth**, #115-197,
  8 one-hour programs

- **Letter to Families**, #115-208, 8 one-hour programs
- **Preparation for the Sacrament of Marriage**,
  #115-320, 3 one-hour programs
- **Letter to Women and Letter to Children**,
  #115-300, 3 one-hour programs
- **Crossing the Threshold of Hope**,
  #115-290, 5 one-hour programs
- **Lay Members of Christ's Faithful People**,
  #1017-8, 4 one-hour programs
- **On Reconciliation and Penance**,
  #126-3678, 4 one-hour programs
- *Redemptionis Sacramentum*,
  #1021-02, 6.5 program hours

Bible Study and Other Commentaries
with Cardinal Arinze

- **The Gospel of St. Matthew**
  #126-4025, 8 one-hour programs
- **The Gospel of St. John**
  #126-4101, 14 one-hour programs
- **Sacrament Preparation Program**
  #115-142, 15 one-hour programs
- **Alone With God: Summary of
  Our Faith**

  Discussion Peace of Heart Forum
  #126-3365, 4 one-hour programs

  Actual Reading of the Book
  #150-65AK, 4 one-hour programs

www.familyland.org or call 1-800-77-FAMILY

Total Consecration and Marian Peace of Heart Forums˚

On video or via Familyland˚ Television Network

These video programs bring spiritual books to life! *Peace of Heart Forums* focus on spiritual books and are ideal for prayer groups, cenacles, and study groups. These weekly forums can develop into strong support groups for individuals and families. They draw youth and adults deeper into their Faith to such a degree that they can transform their trials into stepping stones toward a life of union with God.

Fatima Today I — Video faculty: Fr. Robert Fox, Ricardo Montalban, Dr. Burns Seeley, Jerry Coniker. *4 hours. On audio and video. Resource #126-1687.*
Companion book: *Fatima Today*, by Fr. Robert J. Fox, Resource #517-29.

Immaculate Conception — Covers the sacred image of the Virgin Mary of Guadalupe. The supernatural origin of the image was scientifically demonstrated in the 1960s. Video faculty: Cardinal Mario Luigi Ciappi, O.P., Cardinal Silvio Oddi, Bishop John Van Lierde, O.S.A., Fr. Bernard Geiger, O.F.M. Conv., Mother Immaculata, H.M.C., Dr. Burns Seeley, and Jerry Coniker. *4 hours. Available on audio and video. Resource #126-1191.*
Companion book: *The Wonder of Guadalupe*, by Francis Johnston, Resource #510-085.

Theology of Total Consecration — Total Consecration according to St. Louis de Montfort. A review of the 33-day consecration to Jesus through Mary. Video faculty: Cardinal Francis Arinze, Fr. Dominic De Domenico, O.P., Fr. Bernard Geiger, O.F.M. Conv., Fr. Michael Scanlan, T.O.R., Dr. Burns Seeley, and Jerry Coniker. *6 hours. Available on audio and video. Resource #126-998.*
Companion books: *True Devotion to the Blessed Virgin*, by St. Louis de Montfort, Resource #520-25.
*Preparation For Total Consecration to Jesus through Mary for Families, Resource #323-115. (This Book)

Immaculate Conception and the Holy Spirit — A profound study of St. Maximilian Kolbe's basic discovery: Mary the Immaculata is the chief visible manifestation of the Holy Spirit's presence in the Church and the universal instrument of the Spirit's mission to unite all men to Christ our Savior. Video faculty: Cardinal Mario Luigi Ciappi, O.P., Msgr. Peter Elliott, Fr. Brian Harrison, O.S., Dr. Burns Seeley, and Jerry Coniker. *4 hours. Available on audio and video. Resource #126-1557*

Companion book: *Immaculate Conception and the Holy Spirit*, by Fr. H.M. Manteau-Bonamy, O.P., Resource #513-101-20.

Consecration in the Spirit of St. Vincent Pallotti — This series attempts to synthesize and to make contemporary the life and spirituality of St. Vincent Pallotti, whose ideas have been implemented only since the Second Vatican Council. Video faculty: Fr. Joseph Mungari, S.A.C., Fr. John Hardon, S.J., Dr. Burns Seeley, and Jerry Coniker. *4 hours. Available on audio and video. Resource #126-927.*

Companion book: *Yearning of a Soul*, by Fr. Flavin Bonifazi, S.A.C., Resource #503-SPO830.

Immaculate Heart of Mary: True Devotion — The purpose of this series is to present the Immaculate Heart of Mary in the Trinitarian and Christological light that illumines the authentic Christian life. Video faculty: Fr. Robert Fox, Dr. Burns Seeley, and Jerry Coniker. *4 hours. Available on audio and video. Resource #126-1638.*

Companion book: *Immaculate Heart of Mary: True Devotion*, by Fr. Robert J. Fox, Resource #502-32.

First Lady of the World — Video faculty: Cardinal Pio Laghi, Fr. Peter Lappin, S.D.B., Melissa Pierce, Dr. Burns Seeley, and Jerry Coniker. *4 hours. Available on audio and video. Resource #126-2034.*

Companion book: *First Lady of the World*, by Fr. Peter Lappin, S.D.B., Resource #527-091-6.

Other Topics: • Scripture • Papal Documents • Youth • Suffering • Purgatory • Liturgy • Theology • Philosophy • Catechetics • Lives and Writings of the Saints • Marriage and Family

**www.familyland.org or
call 1-800-77-FAMILY**

Forms
Minds.
Touches
Hearts.

Resource #380-139, 2-volume set, over 1300 pages

**Unites the family with the parish and school.
Can be used in school, parish, RCIA and the home.**

Provides a lifetime study guide on the truths of
our Catholic Faith for the entire family. This
unique catechism draws you into the:

• Catechism of the Catholic Church
• Sacred Scripture
• Vatican II documents
• Papal documents

*Found to be in conformity with the Catechism of the
Catholic Church by the Ad Hoc Committee to Oversee
the Use of the Catechism, USCCB.*

"THANK YOU for your courtesy in sending a copy
of 'The Apostolate's Family Catechism' published by
the Apostolate for Family Consecration...The cross-
references provided to the 'Catechism of Catholic
Church' will make it an especially helpful instrument
to parents and teachers. With prayerful best wishes
for the success of your vital Apostolate."

— **Joseph Cardinal Ratzinger**, Prefect of the Sacred
Congregation for the Doctrine of the Faith, now Pope Benedict XVI
(Prot. N. XII/91 C)

Sample page from the Family Catechism

Easy-to-Understand question and answer format makes it readable and accessible to all ages. Covers Creed, Sacraments, Prayer, and the Commandments.

Chapter 33 — The

Q. 121. Why is the Holy Spirit called the Soul of the Church?

The Holy Spirit is called the Soul of the Church because He animates it with His divine presence, giving supernatural life to all its parts.

Sacred Scripture

And I will pray the Father, and he will give you another Counselor, to be with you for ever, even the Spirit of truth, whom the world cannot receive, because it neither sees him nor knows him; you know him, for he dwells with you, and will be in you. *John 14:16-17*

Do you not know that you are God's temple and that God's Spirit dwells in you? *1 Corinthians 3:16*

Catechism of the Catholic Church

797 "What the soul is to the human body, the Holy Spirit is to the Body of Christ, which is the Church." "To this Spirit of Christ, as an invisible principle, is to be ascribed the fact that all the parts of the body are joined one with the other and with their exalted head; for the whole Spirit of Ch[...] is in the body, and the whole Spirit is in each of th[...] the temple of the living God"[...] "Indeed, [...]ntrusted.... In it is in her that com[...] the Holy Spirit, the pledge of [...] our ascent to God.... For where [...] there is the Church and every

Unique Theological Illustrations on almost every page captivate and teach children who are even still learning to read.

Splendor of Truth

No matter how many and great the obstacles put in his wa[...] and sin, the Spirit, who renews the face of the earth (cf. Ps 104[...] [...] fect accomplishment of the good. This renewa[...] beautiful, pleasing to God and in conform[...] gift of mercy, which offers liberation f[...] more." *(section 118)*

Quotes from Scripture and Church Documents provide a clear grasp of authentic Catholic teaching

Vatican Council II

In order that we might be unceasingly [...] with us his Spirit who, being one and th[...]

For commentaries on each question with Cardinal Arinze, Sr. John Vianney [...] [...]ndix E.

Sacred Scripture
Q. 121. Rom 8:9-17

Catechism of the Catholic Church
Q. 121. Paragraphs 692, **809**, 813.

Doctrine, Moral, Worship Exercises sharpen understanding and emphasize the behavioral implications of the faith.

...in the unity of the Father, the Son and the

Doctrine • Moral • Worship Exercise (see Appendix B for answer key)

1. Why is the Catholic Church called the Body of Christ? What is the role of the Holy Spirit in the Body of Christ?

2. As a member of the Body of Christ, in what specific ways do you strive to become a worthy member of the Body of Christ?

3. Each day, ask the Holy Spirit to help you and your family in your efforts to become holy, worthy members of the Body of Christ.

#P26_14-2

Chapter Summary Prayer

Come, O Creator Spirit blest, And in our souls take up Thy rest; Come with Thy grace and heavenly aid To fill the hearts which Thou hast made.

Great Paraclete, to Thee we cry, O highest gift of God most high! O font of life! O fire of love! And sweet anointing from above.

Thou in Thy sevenfold gifts art known, The finger of God's hand we own; The promise of the Father, Thou! Who dost the tongue with power endow.

Kindle our senses from above, And make our hearts o'erflow with love; With patience firm and virtue high The weakness of our flesh supply.

Far from us drive the foe we dread, And grant us Thy true peace instead; So shall we not, with Thee for guide, Turn from the path of life aside.

O may Thy grace on us bestow The Father and the Son to know, And Thee through endless times confessed Of both the eternal Spirit blest.

All glory while the ages run Be to the Father and the Son, Who rose from death; the same to Thee, O Holy Ghost, eternally. Amen.

Summary Prayers help develop a personal relationship with God and are perfect for dinnertime conversations to draw parents in and reinforce lessons learned.

Chapter 33 —

Family Wisdom Library.

See Appendix A for more references.

Q. 117. When did the Holy Spirit descend upon the Church?
Dei Verbum (Dogmatic Constitution on Divine Revelation), Vatican II, sect. 5, 8;
Lumen Gentium (Dogmatic Constitution on the Church), Vatican II, sect. 4, 5, 8, 48;
On the Holy Spirit in the Life of the Church and the World, John Paul II, sect. 25;
The Relationship Between Faith and Reason, John Paul II, sect. 44.

Q. 118. How does the Holy Spirit carry out Christ's work in the Church?
Dei Verbum (Dogmatic Constitution on Divine Revelation), Vatican II, sect. 5, 8;
Lumen Gentium (Dogmatic Constitution on the Church), Vatican II, sect. 4-9, 12, 48;
On Evangelization in the Modern World, Paul VI, sect. 75;
On the Holy Spirit in the Life of the Church and the World, John Paul II, sect. 67;
The Relationship Between Faith and Reason, John Paul II, sect. 44.

Q. 119. Where is God the Holy Spirit most present?
Dei Verbum (Dogmatic Constitution on Divine Revelation), Vatican II, sect. 5, 8;
Lumen Gentium (Dogmatic Constitution on the Church), Vatican II, sect. 4;
Catechesis in Our Time, John Paul II, sect. 24;
On Evangelization in the Modern World, Paul VI, sect. 75;
On the Holy Spirit in the Life of the Church and the World, John Paul II, sect. 25;
The Lay Members of Christ's Faithful People, John Paul II, sect. 18-20;
The Relationship Between Faith and Reason, John Paul II, sect. 44;
Splendor of Truth, John Paul II, sect. 103.

Q. 120. What does God the Holy Spirit accomplish for the Church?
Dei Verbum (Dogmatic Constitution on Divine Revelation), Vatican II, sect. 5, 8;
Lumen Gentium (Dogmatic Constitution on the Church), Vatican II, sect. 4-9, 12, 48;
On the Dignity and Vocation of Women, John Paul II, sect. 29;
On the Holy Spirit in the Life of the Church and the World, John Paul II, sect. 7, 25;
The Relationship Between Faith and Reason, John Paul II, sect. 44.

Q. 121. Why is the Holy Spirit called the Soul of the Church?
Dei Verbum (Dogmatic Constitution on Divine Revelation), Vatican II, sect. 5, 8;
Lumen Gentium (Dogmatic Constitution on the Church), Vatican II, sect. 4, 6-9, 48;
On Evangelization in the Modern World, Paul VI, sect. 75;
On the Holy Spirit in the Life of the Church and the World, John Paul II, sect. 25-26;
The Relationship Between Faith and Reason, John Paul II, sect. 44.

Q. 122. What is the task of the Holy Spirit in the Church?
Dei Verbum (Dogmatic Constitution on Divine Revelation), Vatican II, sect. 5, 8;
Lumen Gentium (Dogmatic Constitution on the Church), Vatican II, sect. 4-9, 12, 48;
On Evangelization in the Modern World, Paul VI, sect. 75;
On the Holy Spirit in the Life of the Church and the World, John Paul II, sect. 7, 25, 27;
The Lay Members of Christ's Faithful People, John Paul II, sect. 16-17;
The Relationship Between Faith and Reason, John Paul II, sect. 44;
Splendor of Truth, John Paul II, sect. 103, 118.

 Thought Provokers
Please see Appendix C for the answers.

Q. 117: When does God the Holy Spirit first dwell intimately in the lives of most Christians?
Q. 118: On the level of everyday living, how does God the Holy Spirit help us?
Q. 119: In a general sense, where can the Holy Spirit be found?
Q. 120: What is sanctifying grace?
Q. 121: As the "Soul of the Church," God the Holy Spirit gives it life. What does this mean?
Q. 122: How can individual Christians help the Holy Spirit in His work of purifying and renewing the Church?

Sample Illustrations from
The Apostolate's Family Catechism™

Includes hundreds of
theological illustrations

Family Catechism Commentaries™

Each series features one of the video faculty below explaining and expanding on the same questions found in *The Apostolate's Family Catechism* in an engaging, simple and thought provoking style that reaches all ages. Excellent for family, school, group, and parish-wide formation.

Francis Cardinal Arinze	Fr. Pablo Straub	Archbishop Ramon Arguelles
In English	In Spanish	In Tagalog

Family Catechism with Cardinal Arinze is available on CD or DVD.
Resource #115-93CK, 15-CD set
Resource #115-93DK, 7-DVD set

Family Catechism with Fr. Pablo Straub in Spanish is currently available on audio and video. Ask for availability on CD or DVD.
Resource #115-B368AK, 20 audio tapes
Resource #115-B368VK, 20 video tapes

Family Catechism with Archbishop Ramon Arguelles in Tagalog
contact our center in Asia: 632-871-4440 or email asia@familyland.org

"Totally Yours" Family Catechism Program™

Families learning the faith together through the creative use of the media.

Families come together weekly for an hour of formation and prayer using the "Family Catechism Commentaries" video series with Cardinal Arinze on DVD in English, Fr. Pablo Straub in Spanish, or Archbishop Arguelles in Tagalog (see preceding page). Then each day, families review at home the same questions in *The Apostolate's Family Catechism* book that were covered on the video.

As part of this program, families are also introduced to "consecration" through the "Message of Hope" video presentation and are encouraged to enthrone the Holy Family of Fatima in their home using the Holy Family of Fatima Enthronement Program. Once a year, they are encouraged to make or renew their Total Consecration to Jesus, through Mary, in union with St. Joseph, using the *Preparation for Total Consecration to Jesus, through Mary for Families* book, which was blessed by Pope John Paul II and includes his and St. Louis de Montfort's meditations.

**Visit www.familyconsecration.org
for more information**

Catechetical Program

Found to be in conformity with the *Catechism of the Catholic Church*

The "Consecration in Truth" program is a creative blending of multimedia technology (audio, visual and printed resources) and tried and proven interactive teaching methods to assist and unite parents, educators, and pastors in their sacred duties of teaching the Catholic faith to children and adults alike.

This theologically approved curriculum centers on Sacred Scripture, the documents of Vatican II, the *Catechism of the Catholic Church*, and classics of Catholic spirituality.

The Consecration in Truth Curriculum includes:

Textbook *(for all levels)*
The Apostolate's Family Catechism is a
Vatican-approved textbook. Each year,
students, teachers, and parents delve
deeper into the Faith! The Family
Catechism includes sections from or cross-
references with Sacred Scripture, Vatican II
documents, the *Catechism of the Catholic Church, Splendor
of Truth,* papal documents and other theological books.

Teaching Guides and corresponding "Teacher & Parent Prep" CDs

Teaching Guides for Levels 1-8, High
School and Adult RCIA, contain
lesson plans, optional activities, time-
coded video schedule, examination of
conscience, answer keys and more. The lessons
engage students in thought provoking discussions that
lead them to a deeper understanding of the Faith! The
Teacher & Parent Prep CDs are audio recordings of the
lesson plans and related references. They help busy teachers confidently prepare for each lesson and help parents
to really understand their Faith.

Student Workbooks

Each level has a corresponding Student Workbook. The
assignments in the workbooks guide students through
The Apostolate's Family Catechism, indicate which answers
or Scripture passages to memorize from the *By Heart
Catechism & Scripture Review* (Levels 1-8 only) and include
a resolution to practice throughout the week. Levels 1-4
also provide beautiful theological illustrations to color.

Apostolate's Family Catechism Commentaries
on DVD, Videotape, CD, and Audiotape
Roman Curia Cardinal Francis Arinze, Sr. John Vianney,
Bishop Ramon Arguelles and Bishop Socrates Villegas (in

Tagalog), and Fr. Pablo
Straub (in Spanish) present
the Faith with simple,
down-to-earth explanations
and stories as they review
the questions and answers
from *The Apostolate's Family
Catechism* book. The DVDs
or videotapes are normally

shown in the school or parish at the beginning of each lesson, and the parents are encouraged to use the corresponding CD/audiotapes in the home or car to reinforce what is
being taught in the classroom and to spark family discussions on the Faith.

By Heart Catechism and Scripture Review

The *By Heart Catechism and Scripture Review,*
for Levels 1– 8, is a condensed version of the
questions and answers in *The Apostolate's
Family Catechism.* This review book sums up
the fundamental teachings of the Catholic
Church in simple, easy-to-memorize language.
In fewer than 200 questions and answers, students in
levels 1-6 master the basics of the Catholic Faith. Levels
7 and 8 focus on short Scripture passages, giving students the Biblical basis for the key teachings of the
Catholic Church.

Heroes of Our Faith™ Stories

Heroes of Our Faith is a unique series of stories which depict saintly individuals or Bible
heroes speaking in the first person. These
partially fictional stories illustrate truths contained in the catechism by relating the life
experiences of saintly individuals in their
particular quest for holiness, encouraging and enlighten-
ing us in our own earthly pilgrimage so that we might
someday join the Communion of Saints in the Kingdom
of Heaven. *Francisco of Fatima* story is currently available.

Administrator, Teacher, and Parent Handbooks

The *Administrator Handbook* includes an overview of the catechetical program and guidelines for parents, faculty, and students. It covers topics such as parental participation, sacramental preparation, adult formation, faculty workshops, teacher evaluations, respect and reverence, liturgical life, discipline, and student evaluations.

The *Teacher Handbook* includes an overview of the materials and methods used in the classroom and suggestions on motivation, memorization, understanding, respect, reverence, discipline, prayer, and organization. Also included are essential components of the lesson plans, such as the Ten Steps to Mental Prayer, examinations of conscience for various levels, and basic prayers.

The *Parent Handbook* includes an overview of the discipline, prayer, materials and program methods which are described in the Administrator and Teacher Handbooks. The Thought Provoker section helps parents discuss each of the questions in *The Apostolate's Family Catechism* with their children.

The Consecration in Truth Catechetical Program uses a spiral learning method and multimedia approach. It unites the parents, school and parish.

www.familyland.org or call 1-800-77-FAMILY

Family Consecration
Prayer & Meditation Book
Divine Mercy Edition

The Preparation for Total Consecration to Jesus Through Mary for Families that you are now reading contains some of the prayers and meditations from this book. Get the complete edition today as a rich spiritual resource for your family.

It's both a "family consecration" prayer book and an in-depth meditation book which will help you to be "in tune" with the richness of God's Mercy every day.

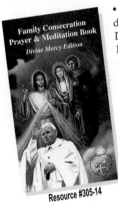

Resource #305-14

• A complete presentation of the five dimensions of the Divine Mercy Devotion: the Image, the Chaplet, the Novena (includes illustrated Stations of the Cross), the Feast Day (Mercy Sunday), and the Spreading of the Message

• Pope John Paul II's Encyclical on Divine Mercy — with Fr. George Kosicki's commentaries

• In-depth Examination of Conscience exercises

• Cardinal Arinze's spiritual classic for our times, *Alone with God*

• St. Louis de Montfort's *Friends of the Cross* treatise

• PLUS many other prayers, meditations, and commentaries that will bring down the mercy of God. Over 250 pictures and 650 pages!

www.familyland.org
or call 1-800-77-FAMILY

CHALLENGE AND CHANGE
The Foundation
by Fr. Peter Lappin, S.D.B.

The inspiring story of Jerry and Gwen Coniker from their childhood to the early years of their married life and their founding of the Apostolate for Family Consecration, an international lay movement focused on helping families get to heaven through consecration to the Holy Family and continuous formation in the truths of our Faith.

"I pray and hope that readers of the *Challenge and Change* may not only feel challenged, but may also be inspired to change to ever deeper commitment in sharing our Faith in Jesus Christ, the one Lord and Savior of all."

— Francis Cardinal Arinze

Resource #323-103

"This book clearly shows our Blessed Mother's hand in the life of a founder and his movement, the Apostolate for Family Consecration, which is focused on the Eucharistic and Marian spirituality of Pope John Paul II. It gives great hope for families in the modern world, and it is certainly focused on the triumph of the Immaculata."

— John Cardinal O'Connor

www.familyland.org
or call 1-800-77-FAMILY

Lay Ecclesial Evangelization Teams™

Transforming families, neighborhoods and parishes into God-centered communities through multimedia formation that galvanizes families to carry out spiritual and corporal works of mercy within their parish and neighborhood communities!

1. Parish/Neighborhood Core Formation and Resource Team

This Lay Ecclesial Team is the first team established in a parish or neighborhood area. It is the most basic unit of the Lay Ecclesial Team Evangelization System structure.

With the help of the pastor, up to 12 team couples (some team members may be single) are selected to make up this essential first team, which is usually led by a Disciple Member or Discernment Cooperator of the Apostolate for Family Consecration. Participants of the team can be Formation Cooperators, those who are active in other Church works but take part in Family Apostolate formation programs, or Evangelization Cooperators, those who initiate Family Apostolate programs, or Associate Cooperators, those who use Family Apostolate resources and are committed members of other Church-approved apostolates that have spiritual direction, norms for piety and established practices.

When possible, this team works closely with the parish priest to offer formation programs for parish committees, leaders and members of other parish-based organizations or movements without affecting their charisms. This includes training on how to use the Family Apostolate's theologically fail-safe multimedia and family-sensitive formation resources, especially *The Apostolate's Family Catechism*. This team would particularly focus on promoting the outreaches of Teams 4 & 5 and can also help manage the Parish Lending Library.

1a. Parish Library
supplies the multimedia
formation resources.
Usually coordinated by
Formation Resource Team

**2. Be Not Afraid Family
Hours** in homes and
parishes via FL-TV
Network, VHS, or DVD.
(Resource #120-317K)

3. Promotions — events,
outreaches, Familyland
Television Network
(Resource #120-412DVD)

4. Consecration
"Message of Hope,"
enthronement of the Holy
Family in the home and
daily Family Rosary
(Resource #133-282VK),
Total Consecration Program
(Resource 115-187DK & 323-115)

**5. Family-based, Parish,
and School Catechetics**
for families, religious
education in parishes and
schools, and adult/RCIA
programs (Introductory Kit,
Resource #380-135K, and Family
Catechism with Cardinal Arinze CDs,
Resource #115-680CK)

6. Eucharistic Devotions
Adoration, Forty Hours,
Benediction, First Friday
All-night Vigils, etc.
(Resource #1007-76CK, and
#150-100CK)

7. Teen Ministry
helping the elderly, right-
to-life outreach, whole-
some socials, etc.
(Gospel of Life Audio Set,
Resource #115-290AK)

8. Marriage Preparation and Enrichment
(Resource #126-198VK and 115-208AK)

9. Parish Retreats —
Includes First Saturday Days of Recollection (Resource #157-74V) and Divine Mercy Sunday Parish Missions (Resource 147-57VK)
Also visit familyland.org for new programming on FL-TV.

10. Single Parent Support Ministry — separate ministry for single parent women and men

11. Chemical Dependent Support Ministry

12. Helping the Poor or Jobless

13. Prison Ministry

14. Hospital and Home Visitation of the Sick and Elderly and Sacri-State Suffering Members
(Resource 120-305V & 126-1305VK or AK)

15. Boy Scouts Ministry

The Apostolate for Family Consecration's Lay Ecclesial Team Evangelization System™
Simultaneously Renewing the Family and Parish Community

 The Lay Ecclesial Team Evangelization System can serve your family, parish and neighborhood communities by helping you grow in the capacity to receive grace and to serve others.

The Lay Ecclesial Teams are groups of Lay People committed to serving the Family and Parish Community and other Church approved movements.

✔ **A dynamic family and parish evangelization system serving communities and parishes world-wide**
✔ **Using the media to spread the faith**
✔ **Frequent and fervent reception of the sacraments**
✔ **Respectful of and working in cooperation with Church hierarchy**

With the cooperation and support of the Bishop and pastor, most Lay Ecclesial Teams operate within the existing structure and outreaches of the parish and community, while providing multimedia resources for other movements in the Church.

The Apostolate for Family Consecration, because of its vast video library and multimedia resources, can serve the parish, organizations, and other movements in a special way so that everyone can truly learn the truth that will make them free and use that truth in their own unique way of serving the Church and saving souls. Spiritually nourished by the rich formation from expert teachers, the various parish committees/programs and movements will be empowered to bear more fruit for the Church.

www.familyland.org
or call 1-800-77-FAMILY

International Media and Training Centers of the Apostolate for Family Consecration

- USA— for Canada and the United States
- Mexico—for all of Latin America
- Philippines—for all of Asia
- Nigeria—for all of Africa

Lay Ecclesial Team in Belgium

- Podcast and Vodcast Media Team
- Family Formation for all of Europe

Holy Family Fests™

An opportunity for the entire family to experience Catholic community – to pray, work, and play together for seven days. Everyone learns how to use a parish evangelization program to draw families into Eucharistic worship. **Because Eucharistic worship "constitutes the soul of all Christian life,... the Eucharist becomes of itself the school of active love for neighbor."** *(Pope John Paul II, The Mystery and Worship of the Eucharist, 5,6)*

Tents and cabins...

with bunk beds...

...and a loft!

Eucharistic Adoration and Processions focus families on the center of our Faith.

St. John Bosco Swimming Pool & Boy Jesus Kiddie Pool

Pony rides

Scenic horse trail rides, tennis and basketball courts, waterslide and more

Vianney Chapel and Retreat Center

State-of-the-Art St. Joseph Auditorium *(seats 2100)*

Campfire Family Rosary followed by marshmallow roast

- No immodesty
- No foul language
- No excessive violence
- No disrespect for authority

www.familyland.org
or call 1-800-77-FAMILY

Marriage "Get-Away" Weekends

Get away with your spouse for three unforgettable days. You and your beloved will experience:

- insights from our Faith to live by
- the wisdom of others for inspiration
- strength from the Sacraments
- laughter to lift your heart
- a few tears of gratitude and healing
- the grace of God to send you forth with renewed commitment for Christ and one another
- plus valuable tips on parenting and spousal communication

Evangelization & Catechetical Workshops

Parents and parish and association leaders are trained to be part of Lay Ecclesial Teams, to bring about "the civilization of love" in the spirit of Pope John Paul II – an achievable goal if we plan and act now!

For more information call 1-800-77-FAMILY or visit www.familyland.org

The Apostolate's
Catholic Corps™

Women's Community

"I made a lifetime commitment to Christ as His bride, in the Catholic Corps. I believe that Our Lady, St. Joseph, and my love for my country have helped me and the other Catholic Corps members to lay down our lives for families, that they may know and achieve God's plan for their lives."
— Carolyn Stegmann

Living the hidden life of the Holy Family while helping to ignite the laity through the work and mission of the Family Apostolate

The Apostolate's

Catholic Corps™

Men's Community

"After discovering the Family Apostolate's focus of renewing the world and society through the consecration of families to Jesus through Mary, in union with St. Joseph and in the Truths of the Catholic Faith, I was hooked. I wanted to give my life totally to the service of helping families get to Heaven, for next to this, nothing else mattered. I thank God every day for the opportunity to serve Him just like Mary and Joseph did — hidden and faithfully, despite my many frailties and weaknesses. If I do my best, I'm convinced He'll do the rest!
— Dennis Brower

Living the hidden life of the Holy Family while helping to ignite the laity through the work and mission of the Family Apostolate

Praying or Suffering Sacri-State Cooperators

Mother Teresa of Calcutta with Jerry and Gwen Coniker.

In 1976, Mother Teresa of Calcutta joined the Apostolate for Family Consecration's Advisory Council and told Jerry and Gwen Coniker that the Family Apostolate would touch many more families if it gathered an army of suffering souls to support its active members.

Sacri-State Cooperators of the Apostolate for Family Consecration are those who offer up their prayers or physical sufferings to God, through Mary, for active members and for the Family Apostolate's mission of renewing families and parishes.

They are channels of spiritual power for The Family Apostolate's mission. They bear with love all of the crosses that God, in His infinite wisdom, chooses to send them. Sacri-State Cooperators are remembered in a special way in the Family Apostolate's daily prayers and are spiritually united with other associations.

To receive a Sacri-State application, write: The Family Apostolate, Bloomingdale, OH 43910-7903.

Sister John Vianney, S.S.N.D., the Family Apostolate's first Sacri-State Cooperator, suffered for over 40 years in bed, and yet taught the Faith to children from her bedside.

Appendix C

Spiritual Practices and Involvement in the Apostolate for Family Consecration®

Prayer

Formation   *Evangelization*

548

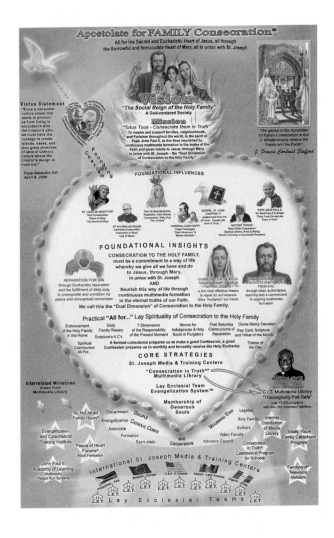

800 **Vision, Mission and Outreach Ministries**
as shown in the diagram on the previous page

800.1 The Apostolate for Family Consecration is an International Catholic Lay Movement founded by Jerry and Gwen Coniker in 1975 in response to God's inspiration and approved that same year by ecclesiastical authority in the Church.

800.2 **Our Vision: The Social Reign of the Holy Family within our families, neighborhoods, and parishes**

800.2.1 The ultimate vision of the Apostolate for Family Consecration is a Civilization of Love and Life and Truth, a society where neighborhoods are God-centered, where parishes are vibrant, where Catholic Culture abounds, and within which are consecrated families who love the Holy Eucharist, Our Lady, and the papacy: this is the complete social reign of the Holy Family within society! And this is a goal that we all long for and are striving to bring about.

800.2.2 Pope Benedict XVI made the following statement that perfectly describes the Founders' vision for the work and mission of the Apostolate for Family Consecration: "Since a consumer culture exists that wants to prevent us from living in accordance with the Creator's plan, we must have the courage to create islands, oases, and then great stretches of land of Catholic culture where the Creator's design is lived out."[1]

800.2.3 We envision a society made up of parishes and neighborhoods of families who deeply understand their Catholic Faith and are living lives consecrated to the Holy Family — to Jesus, through Mary, in union with St. Joseph. These families share common values, and support one another in the raising of their families in a Catholic culture. We call this

---

1. Benedict XVI, April 6, 2006.

Catholic cultural phenomenon "The Social Reign of the Holy Family."

800.3 Our Mission: "Totus Tuus" — "Consecrate Them in Truth" (John 17)

800.3.1 "You cannot have a mission unless you truly have and believe in a vision."[1]

800.3.2 We believe as Pope John Paul II did that Christ will conquer through Mary in union with St. Joseph. We believe that the most effective way to arrive at the social reign of the Holy Family is through the dual dimension of John Paul II's consecration: "Totus Tuus" (giving everything to Jesus through Mary according to the formation of St. Louis de Montfort, St. Maximilian Kolbe and John Paul II, all in union with St. Joseph), and "Consecrate Them in Truth" (John 17; consecrating our families in the Truth through continuous formation). This is truly the "Catechesis of the New Evangelization" that John Paul II said could renew the world — family by family, parish by parish, and diocese by diocese.

800.3.3 Through this total consecration, an ever growing spiritual army is being assembled by the Holy Family to bring society to God. It is truly a "Gideon's Army," where the consecrated few can be powerful instruments of atonement by giving their meager efforts to Mary so that she can increase their value and then present them to her Son. The great Message of Hope is that a consecrated few can offset the effects of the sins of many, and usher in a civilization of love and life!

800.3.4 Through God's grace, the Apostolate for Family Consecration has accumulated powerful multimedia tools and has forged strong human and spiritual alliances to amass a large and growing movement of consecrated souls. This will serve to support and

---

1. Cardinal Gaudencio Rosales, Archbishop of Manila, Philippines, and one of the Family Apostolate's key spiritual and theological advisors.

reinforce the hierarchy of our Church, which God has put into place to shepherd His people.

801 Definition of Terms

801.1 **Vision** — The ultimate "end goal" or "big picture" image of what it is that God has inspired our founders to achieve; the Founders' (Jerry and Gwen Coniker's) mental image of what the world could be.

801.1.1 The Vision, filtered through our Core Beliefs, Core Strategies, and founding Charism, is the driving force in the establishment of Outreach Ministries designed to achieve certain specific results which contribute toward the realization of our overall Vision.

801.1.2 The Vision along with the Charism and Spirituality of the Apostolate for Family Consecration are the unchanging patrimony of the founders and become fixed upon the death of the founders.

801.1.2.1 Canon 578: "The whole patrimony of an institute must be faithfully preserved by all. This patrimony is comprised of the intentions of the founders, of all that the competent ecclesiastical authority has approved concerning the nature, purpose, spirit and character of the institute, and of its sound traditions."

801.2 **Vision Statement** — The description of the future that our founders feel God has inspired them to work toward. In dictionary terms, it is "a mental image produced by the imagination". It involves seeing the optimal future for families, neighborhoods, the world, and vividly describing this vision.

801.2.1 A clear statement of our Vision is important in order to:

• bring focus and clarity to the desired future we are working towards.

- inspire our members to work towards this future.

- guide all of us in our decision-making as we reach for this future.

801.3 **Charism** — From the Greek "kair'is-uhm" meaning "gift". A Divine Spiritual Gift given by the Holy Spirit to individuals or groups for the good of the community.

801.3.1 Refers to the particular gifts, spirituality, intentions, and approach given by God to a Church approved organization through its founders to achieve its vision (see Canon 578).

801.3.2 An organization's Charism is not subject to change and becomes fixed with the death of the founder.

801.3.3 *Catechism of the Catholic Church* paragraphs on Charism:

> 798 The Holy Spirit is "the principle of every vital and truly saving action in each part of the Body." He works in many ways to build up the whole Body in charity: by God's Word "which is able to build you up"; by Baptism, through which he forms Christ's Body; by the sacraments, which give growth and healing to Christ's members; by "the grace of the apostles, which holds first place among his gifts"; by the virtues, which make us act according to what is good; finally, by the many special graces (called "charisms"), by which he makes the faithful "fit and ready to undertake various tasks and offices for the renewal and building up of the Church."

> 799 Whether extraordinary or simple and humble, charisms are graces of the Holy Spirit which directly or indirectly benefit the Church, ordered as they are to her building up, to the good of men, and to the needs of the world.

> 800 Charisms are to be accepted with gratitude by the person who receives them and by all members of the Church as well. They are a wonderfully rich grace for the apostolic vitality and for the holiness of the entire

Body of Christ, provided they really are genuine gifts of the Holy Spirit and are used in full conformity with authentic promptings of this same Spirit, that is, in keeping with charity, the true measure of all charisms.

801 It is in this sense that discernment of charisms is always necessary. No charism is exempt from being referred and submitted to the Church's shepherds. "Their office [is] not indeed to extinguish the Spirit, but to test all things and hold fast to what is good," so that all the diverse and complementary charisms work together "for the common good."

801.4 **Core Strategy** — A long range plan or approach believed to be the most effective means to achieve the organization's vision. Our Core Strategies are part of the founding charism and as such are not subject to change.

801.5 **Outreach Ministries** — a detailed, systematic initiative undertaken to achieve a specific goal or aspect of the Family Apostolate's vision. Although the nature and direction of these outreach ministries flow from our basic Core Beliefs and Core Strategies, they are subject to change with the opportunities, needs, and circumstances of the time and place.

801.6 **Spirituality** — A specific way of living some particular aspect of the Gospel which facilitates and nurtures growth in holiness. The ultimate end to which Catholic spirituality aspires is union with God, and we believe, like Pope John Paul II, that the most perfect way to Jesus is through Mary in union with St. Joseph—the Holy Family.

801.7 **Consecration to Jesus through Mary** — also known as "St. Louis de Montfort's Consecration formula to Mary," is the means by which one seeks to honor God through the Blessed Virgin by formally making an act of trust in Mary as Queen Mother, in her power as intercessor for us with King Jesus, and in the perfection of her will to bring all souls to her Son. One consciously and formally, with outward signs, places oneself under the mantle of her motherly protection.

801.7.1   The spiritually powerful aspect of this particular devotion is the reality that by offering our works and desires and sufferings to Mary to give to Jesus, she makes our offerings that much more beautiful and meritorious by multiplying them by her merits (see Cardinal Ciappi's letter on page 194).

802 A Brief History of the Apostolate for Family Consecration

802.1   Jerry and Gwen Coniker, parents of 13, and grandparents of 64 and counting, founded the Apostolate for Family Consecration in 1975 as a volunteer driven, media-based lay movement designed to help families to consecrate themselves to Jesus, through Mary, in union with St. Joseph (who perfectly lived this consecration). They wanted families to learn their Faith, live their Faith, and share their faith by transforming neighborhoods and parishes into God-centered communities—basically, to get their families to Heaven, to imitate the Holy Family and to bring as many others with them as possible.

802.2   As a young family, Jerry and Gwen experienced the difficulties of trying to raise their children in the midst of an unsupportive culture, including the schools, some key leaders and teachers in the churches, government, industry, and especially in the powerful media in all of its facets. As a result, they were inspired to help other families avoid this by creating a genuine Catholic culture in their neighborhood where families truly support one another as they strive to raise their children and live their Faith, where the peer pressure influence is toward God and not away from Him—a true Catholic Culture.

802.3   Over 30 years later this inspiration has matured into an international organization, focused on the priorities of Pope John Paul II, that offers a unique lay spirituality of consecration and provides the apostolic multimedia, theologically fail-safe resources, and organizational structure that has enabled families and parish communities the world over to grow in holiness and become active builders of the Civilization of Love and Life.

802.4 At this particular time, the Family Apostolate operates in the United States and Canada, the Philippines for Asia, Mexico for Latin America, Belgium for Europe, and Nigeria for Africa.

803 Outreach Ministries of the Apostolate for Family Consecration that support the Founders' Vision

803.1 The 24-hour *Familyland Television Network*, available through satellite and cable in the USA and all of Asia. In the USA we are also on Sky Angel Satellite through a dish-brand receiving system.

803.2 *Internet Distribution of the Consecration in Truth Multimedia Library*, which includes various podcasts (e.g., Cardinal Arinze Podcast, The Weekly Roman Observer Podcast, Challenge and Change Podcast and more). The vast library of over 500 teachers and 15,000 programs will be available for internet download at familyland.org in the future.

803.3 *Catholic Familyland and St. Joseph Media and Training Centers*, a place set apart in the United States, Mexico, the Philippines, and with plans on the way for Africa, where families come to experience Catholic community and learn how to evangelize other families; (renewal and training).

803.4 *Lay Ecclesial Team Evangelization System*, which consists of families and individuals who serve the local parish and neighborhood through the creative use of theologically fail-safe multimedia resources which inspire families to practice the spiritual and corporal works of mercy (apostolic involvement).

803.5 *Consecration in Truth Catechetical Program* for schools and parishes, designed to support parents in their responsibility to be the primary teachers of the Faith to their children, by uniting the parents with the teachers of the school and parish (a formal yet practical means to learning the faith).

803.6 *Totally Yours (Totus Tuus) Family Catechism Program.* Families come together weekly for an hour of formation and prayer using the "Family Catechism Commentaries" video series with Cardinal Arinze on DVD in English, Fr. Pablo Straub in Spanish, or Archbishop Arguelles in Tagalog, and then daily, review at home the same questions in *The Apostolate's Family Catechism* book that were covered on the video.

803.6.1 As part of this program, families are also introduced to "consecration" through the "Message of Hope" video presentation and are encouraged to enthrone the Holy Family of Fatima in their home using the Holy Family of Fatima Enthronement Program. (All available at: familyconsecration.org)

803.6.2 Once a year families are asked to make or renew their Total Consecration to Jesus through Mary in union with St. Joseph using the "Preparation for Total Consecration to Jesus, through Mary for Families" book, which was blessed by Pope John Paul II and includes his and St. Louis de Montfort's meditations. (visit familyconsecration.org for more information)

803.7 *Be Not Afraid Family Hours* on video, which was Blessed Mother Teresa's idea. Families gather in churches or homes to learn their faith and pray the Rosary. The Family Hours are designed to hold the attention of the entire family.

803.8 *Peace of Heart Forums* for continuous adult formation. Adults make a commitment to set aside time every day to prayerfully read a specific spiritual book. Then they come together to watch a video review with experts on the book they have been reading. Each gathering includes a discussion of what was read and just presented on video.

804 Overview of a Way of Life for Families in the Modern World — Our Spirituality

804.1   The Apostolate for Family Consecration consists of committed souls who work for the simultaneous renewal of the family and parish/neighborhood community using theologically fail-safe multimedia resources that feature some of the most credible teachers in the Church, like Blessed Teresa of Calcutta and Francis Cardinal Arinze, J. Francis Cardinal Stafford and Papal Theologian, Mario Luigi Cardinal Ciappi. The following is the "way of life in the modern world" of Family Apostolate Discernment Cooperators and Members.

804.2   If you are searching for your or your family's spiritual path in life and would like more information on how to use the multimedia resources of the Family Apostolate in your home, neighborhood, or parish, or become directly involved in the Apostolate for Family Consecration, email letshelp@familyland.org, and join in making the vision of the Family Apostolate become a reality throughout the world.

804.3   Reading these spiritual practices may seem overwhelming. However, if you were to write out all of the things you must do to drive a car, you would never try, but after a while it all becomes automatic. The same is true of these spiritual practices.

804.4   The habit of developing a prayer life takes the discipline of asking the Holy Family for the grace to set aside time for prayer and to pray throughout the day by talking to God and His Mother. Most of the recommended prayers and practices can be worked into your daily, weekly, and monthly routines. The reflective recitation of the daily prayers takes about 8 or 9 minutes a day (see 805.5.1 for the list of daily prayers); however, these vocal prayers should just be a part of your prayer life. You may want to use our "Prayers and Practices" CD, #160-760.

804.5   The recitation of the Rosary can be a great opportunity for meditation. It gives us a concrete plan for our lives based on the Mysteries of our Lord's life, death and glory. It should be used primarily as a means for meditating upon its Mysteries, Sacred Scripture, the virtues and gifts of the Holy Spirit, the words of the Our Father and Hail Mary prayers, or other dimensions of our Faith. (See 805.3.5.4 for how to say the Scriptural Rosary)

804.6   For rapid spiritual growth, make an appointment with God each day by setting aside one-half to one hour for quiet, reflective reading (including daily Scripture) and mental prayer. Sometimes this quiet time can be spent by just remaining in God's presence while you praise and thank Him for His Passion, goodness, and mercy. Mental prayer can also take place in the car or in transit.

804.7   To maintain a balanced perspective about the Church's gifts, try to include the daily themes specified in Section 805.9 during your mental prayer time with our Lord, His Mother, St. Joseph, the members of the Heavenly Court and the Holy Souls in Purgatory.

804.8   Please don't "speed read" the Scriptures or your spiritual books, instead, slowly read until the Holy Spirit moves you to pause and reflect on a certain Truth. Don't worry about completing all of your readings, but let them serve as a springboard into meditation, which will eventually allow God to draw you into contemplation in His due season.

804.9   The same principle can be used while listening to spiritual recordings while at home or in your "monastery on wheels" (your car). When you are listening and the Holy Spirit moves your spirit, pause the recording and talk to God or any member of the Holy

Family, your Guardian Angel or Heavenly Court about it. This is meditation.

804.10 The spirituality of the Apostolate for Family Consecration is a total consecration of our lives and our families to the Holy Family as we embrace our daily duties. We encourage our members to convert their entire day into an "All for" spiritual walk towards the highest levels of union with God that one could have. "All for" is a condensed version of the Apostolate's Motto and Spiritual Communion Prayer: All for the Sacred and Eucharistic Heart of Jesus, all through the Sorrowful and Immaculate Heart of Mary, all in union with St. Joseph. (#7c)

804.11 It also helps to ask often for the grace to be conscious of God's presence and of all He wants us to be conscious of, and for the grace to discern God's Will and let go of our own wills.

804.12 You can be certain that there is nothing more holy than doing God's Will throughout the entire day and night by faithfully responding to the grace of the present moment—in other words, trying to please our loving God by faithfully and lovingly fulfilling your responsibilities at each present moment.

804.12.1 Every time you need to make a big or little decision, respond to an encounter, etc., simply pause for a moment and say "All for." By this you are deepening your commitment to please God by doing His will; you are also entering into a spiritual communion with the Sacred and Eucharistic Heart of Jesus in order to ask for the grace to discern His Will at that moment under those circumstances, and for the grace to do it as perfectly and mercifully as you can. This is holiness. We strive to remember that we are always in God's presence, and we should always be seeking to know His providential Will and to do what most pleases Him and not ourselves. (See 805.2.1 for the definition of spiritual communion.)

804.12.2   "All for" is therefore a renewal of our consecration, offering everything all for the Sacred and Eucharistic Heart of Jesus, Who is the source of all grace, all through the Sorrowful and Immaculate Heart of Mary, who is the channel and multiplier of all grace, all in union with St. Joseph, who is the model for living the "All for" consecration to Jesus through Mary.

804.13   In order to better understand the Apostolate for Family Consecration's spirituality, frequently read sections 42a and 77 (FCPB or Days 35–40 of FCPB-TC). Also reflect on prayers 2a, 2d, 2f and 4 (FCPB).

804.14   **A Note of Caution**:

804.14.1   Once you have developed the habit of working prayer and quiet reflective spiritual reading or multimedia spiritual formation time into your daily life (adjusting your schedule to accommodate it), you should not become anxious when duties of state may prohibit completing some of your spiritual practices. God's Will for each present moment is the key.

804.14.2   Try to integrate these practices into your life in a fluid, non-coercive way.

804.14.3   God is our All. It is never His Will that we strain ourselves to the point of losing interior peace and going beyond the point of a healthy spiritual challenge in order to follow our schedule of spiritual practices.

804.14.4   We should, however, still make an appointment with God for our daily prayer time and strive to keep that appointment even more than we would

---

* FCPB = all Family Consecration Prayer and Meditation Books (includes *Preparation for Total Consecration to Jesus through Mary for Families*)
FCPB-DM = Divine Mercy Edition
FCPB-TC = Preparation for Total Consecration to Jesus through Mary for Families
FCPB-SJ = St. Joseph Edition

do with other important people and events (read *Appointment with God* by Fr. Michael Scanlan, book resource #384-1. Peace of Heart Forum on CD or DVD resource #172-203CK or DK).

804.15 Some Formulas to Keep You on Track:

804.15.1 **Scriptures 4 C's** of Confidence, Conscience, seed-Charity, and Constancy:

804.15.1.1 <u>Confidence/Trust</u>: Look to God as your source and totally trust in His providential care. Being overcome by fear and anxiety are offensive to God because by that we are in effect telling Him that we do not trust Him. If you look in the New Testament, you will notice that almost every cure only occurred when the person or his companions trusted in Jesus.

804.15.1.2 <u>Conscience</u>: Take time every day to pray and form your conscience through spiritual reading or listening to formation resources.

804.15.1.3 <u>Seed-Charity</u>: Charity is an action virtue, and by it we are truly planting a seed that will bear fruit in our lives. Our degree of charity will determine the amount of grace in our souls and our relationship with God for all eternity. One profound act of charity is sharing our Faith with others — evangelization.

804.15.1.4 <u>Constancy</u>: "God won't steer a parked car." He will not go against our free will. We must make continual acts of faith, hope and love and persevere in doing His Will even in times of severe trials, dryness and persecution. God will help us with His grace through our Lady. Frequently say the prayer, "My God, I believe, I adore, I hope and I love You, I ask pardon for all those who do not believe, do not adore, do not hope and do not love You." (FCPB #29b). We ask particularly, that you try to say this prayer during the consecration at Mass.

804.15.2 **The Responsibility of the Present Moment** — See section 77 in any *Family Consecration Prayer and Meditation Book* or Days 38–40 in the book *Preparation for Total Consecration to Jesus through Mary for Families.*

804.15.3 **Reparation and the Dual Dimension of Pope John Paul II's Consecration** — See section 42a in any *Family Consecration Prayer and Meditation Book* or Days 35–37 in the book *Preparation for Total Consecration to Jesus through Mary for Families.*

805 Daily Practices

For Discernment Cooperators and Members

Overview of Daily Practices

805.1 Daily Mass if your responsibilities permit

805.2 Acts of Spiritual Communion & offering the "All for" throughout the day in order to discern and do God's Will in every present moment

805.3 Family Rosary

805.4 Examination of Conscience Exercises (FCPB #53)

805.5 Family Apostolate Vocal Prayers, including the Chaplet of Divine Mercy and meditation on the theme of the day (see 805.9) and virtue & Scripture of the month (see 807.2)

805.6 Personal Prayer Time with Spiritual Reading and Multimedia Spiritual Formation

805.7 Norms for Indulgences—a way of life and daily heroic act of charity (see FCPB 45a and 45b)

805.8 Familyland Television Network viewing for spiritual formation of the entire family

805.1 Daily Mass

805.1.1 Attend daily Mass as often as your responsibilities permit. Sunday Mass is required by the Church.

805.1.2 It is suggested to pray the Act of Faith and Intercession (FCPB #29b) at the Consecration during Mass.

805.1.3   Pray the Apostolate's Act of Consecration (FCPB #4) after Mass or sometime during the day when possible. If for some reason you aren't able to pray the daily prayers, at least pray the Apostolate's Act of Consecration.

805.2 Acts of Spiritual Communion by praying the "All for"

805.2.1   What is a "spiritual communion"? "A great help or complement to sacramental Communion and a means of prolonging its influence is the practice which is called spiritual communion. It consists essentially in a fervent desire to receive the Eucharist and in giving God a loving embrace as if He had truly entered our hearts. This pious practice, blessed and encouraged by the Church, has a sanctifying efficacy and can be repeated frequently throughout the day. We can never sufficiently praise this excellent devotion, but even in this matter one must avoid carefully anything that is routine or mechanical, because this would diminish the merit of the act." (*The Theology of Christian Perfection*, by Antonio Royo Marin, O.P., and Jordan Aumann, O.P., page 302)

805.2.2   Spiritually unite your daily life to the Holy Sacrifice of the Mass, which is the source and center of our lives, by saying "All for the Sacred and Eucharistic Heart of Jesus, all through the Sorrowful and Immaculate Heart of Mary, all in union with St. Joseph," or simply "All for."

805.2.3   Draw closer to Jesus through frequent acts of spiritual communion (FCPB #11a and 7c) throughout the day and each time you say "All for." Keep in mind that you may also gain a partial indulgence for the Holy Souls in Purgatory each time you make an act of spiritual communion (see FCPB-TC #45b). Also, please pray for the petitions that have been sent in to the Apostolate for Family Consecration's St. Joseph Centers.

805.2.4 "All for" is a condensed version of the Apostolate's Motto and Spiritual Communion Prayer: All for the Sacred and Eucharistic Heart of Jesus, all through the Sorrowful and Immaculate Heart of Mary, all in union with St. Joseph. (FCPB #7c)

805.2.5 By this you are making a spiritual communion by asking for the EUCHARISTIC graces to discern and do God's providential Will in each decision, action, or response—to do His Will by fulfilling the responsibility of each present moment. We can be totally secure and confident that there is nothing holier than doing God's Will in each present moment because God has a providential plan for each moment of the day. Our Lord said that it is not those who say 'Lord, Lord' who will enter the Kingdom of God, but those who do the Will of His Father in Heaven (cf. Matthew 7:21).

805.2.6 The phrase "All for" should also be our common greeting and parting phrase for our members.

805.3 Daily Family Rosary

805.3.1 See prayer #6-7d with reflections on Scripture and the Mysteries.

805.3.2 Before beginning the Rosary, offer a few key petitions, including the intentions of Our Blessed Mother and those of the Family Apostolate's President, that the Family Apostolate will always retain the charism of its Founders and for the intentions of one's Sacri-state Cooperator(s).

805.3.3 Pray the Apostles' Creed and the one Our Father and three Hail Marys for the intentions of the

---

* FCPB = all Family Consecration Prayer and Meditation Books (includes *Preparation for Total Consecration to Jesus through Mary for Families*)

FCPB-DM = Divine Mercy Edition

FCPB-TC = Preparation for Total Consecration to Jesus through Mary for Families

FCPB-SJ = St. Joseph Edition

Holy Father, the Pope (this practice fulfills one of the requirements for gaining a plenary indulgence for the Holy Souls in Purgatory).

805.3.4   At the end of each decade, the Glory Be (#7a), the Fatima Rosary Prayer (#7b), and the Family Apostolate's Motto and Spiritual Communion Prayer (#7c) are then recited audibly.

805.3.5   End the Rosary by praying #8*, 9, one phrase of 10, 11a, and 11b (FCPB).

805.3.6   If you like, you can use one of the following methods to pray the family Rosary:

805.3.6.1   Traditional Rosary with Mysteries

805.3.6.2   Video: Use our Dramatized Rosary video (#115-378V) or Soul of the Rosary videos (#133-158VK) or other multimedia Rosary resources as issued by the Family Apostolate from time to time or that are part of our "Be Not Afraid Family Hours" or "First Saturday Cenacles"

805.3.6.3   FL-TV: the Rosary is aired every day on FL-TV

805.3.6.4   Scriptural Rosary:

805.3.6.4.1   For each decade, the leader announces the proper mystery for the day and everyone prays the Our Father audibly (#6b). Then the leader reads a short passage from Scripture while everyone else follows along in their Bibles. During the reading, family members may highlight or underline the words or phrases that inspire them. The leader announces the chapter and verses just read, as the family slowly prays the decade of Hail Marys (approximately three minutes) while meditating on the one or two verses or words which inspired them. With an older family or

---

* Prayer to St. Joseph—Pope Leo XIII had asked for a prayer to St. Joseph at the end of the Rosary)

community, the Hail Marys can be prayed silently while meditating on the Scripture just read. During this time, members ask Our Lady to help them draw the insights from Sacred Scripture that she wants them to live in their daily lives. The leader may repeat a word or short phrase within the decade of Hail Marys as they lead the decade of the Rosary.

805.3.6.4.2   At the end of the Scriptural Rosary, after the Act of Spiritual Communion (#11a) has been prayed (see 805.3.5), a commentary on the Scriptures may be read aloud from the Navarre Bible (Resource #511-77) with sufficient pause for reflection. At times, especially while traveling, the Bible on audio and the Family Apostolate's Scripture commentary series with Francis Cardinal Arinze and others may be used.

805.3.6.4.3   We recommend that you either follow the daily readings for the Mass or start with the Gospel of St. John. We like to start with the Gospel of St. John because he was representing the Church at the foot of the Cross and lived with Mary. This may take over a month to complete; then go to 2 or 3 of the Epistles (Letters), then the Gospel of St. Matthew, then 2 or 3 of the Epistles, then the Gospel of St. Mark, then 2 or 3 of the Epistles, and then the Gospel of St. Luke. You may want to alternate the Epistles with Psalms, Proverbs, Leviticus, Genesis, Daniel or some other book of the Old Testament; however, we encourage you to alternate with one of the Gospels every other time.

805.3.6.4.4   We recommend that every member of the family have the same translation of the Bible, preferably the Navarre Bible which includes commentaries on the Scriptures

(New Testament: resource #511-77, Pentateuch [first five Books of the Old Testament], resource #511-81, the Psalms, resource #511-82. See page 515 for other Navarre Bibles). Encourage your children to use a highlighter or underline key words or phrases. This will be their lifetime Bible that should be used daily for the rest of their lives.

805.4 Daily Examination of Conscience

805.4.1 Review #53a, 53h, 53i & 53m (FCPB) or another reflection from section 53 (FCPB) or read a section from the book entitled *Particular Examen* by Fr. James F. McElhone, C.S.C. (resource #626-2).

805.4.2 Write out a "key card" containing the virtues and Scripture verse which will help you overcome your primary faults. Examine your conscience at least once a day using your "key card" and part of section 53 (FCPB) or the Particular Examen book. Try to reflect on part of 1 Corinthians 13 (FCPB #2i).

805.4.3 During your morning and evening prayer time and other times during the day, visualize yourself practicing the virtues that are the exact opposite of your faults. (See FCPB #53b and #53L) and ask our Blessed Mother for the grace needed.

805.5 Daily Family Apostolate Vocal Prayers

Develop the habit of saying the following daily prayers. They can be found in any Family Consecration Prayer and Meditation book, unless otherwise noted.

805.5.1 Key Prayers: #2a, 2b, 2c (3 times daily before meals if possible), 2d, 2e, 2f, 2g, 2h, 2i, one phrase of 10, 11a, 49 (on First Saturdays). Optional prayers are 2j (previously 40c) and Blessed Teresa of Calcutta's prayer 11b. The prayers are also available on CD #160-760, FL-TV or www.familyland.org.

805.5.2 Family Apostolate's Act of Consecration (#4 FCPB). It is recommended that you pray this after

Mass, but if that's not possible then some other time during the day.

805.5.3   Chaplet of Divine Mercy (#20f). Pray the Chaplet daily while reflecting on one or more of the Stations of the Cross (#59). In our busy schedules, one can simply pause for a moment at 3 p.m., or as close to the Hour of Mercy as possible, and think about Our Lord's Passion, reverently ask for His Mercy and say, "Jesus I trust in You," and if possible the "Eternal Father" prayer (FCPB #20f).

805.6 Daily Spiritual Reading and/or Spiritual Multimedia Formation

805.6.1   We recommend that you spend at least 30 minutes each day in quiet meditative prayer and spiritual reading or formation, which should also include some Scripture.

805.6.2   We recommend praying the prayer "The Holy Spirit: Secret to Sanctity and Happiness" by Cardinal Mercier (FCPB #46e) as you begin your quiet reflective "listening time".

805.6.3   A Family Apostolate Formation Assistant/ Guardian Angel, who is familiar with the teachings of the Bible, Vatican II, and Pope John Paul II on the role of the laity, can assist you in selecting your daily meditative spiritual reading. Don't try to read everything at once. Always leave time for quiet mental prayer, for "listening time".

805.6.4   The daily spiritual readings can include:

805.6.4.1   Sacred Scripture (we recommend reading the Navarre Bible Commentaries),

---

* FCPB = all Family Consecration Prayer and Meditation Books (includes *Preparation for Total Consecration to Jesus through Mary for Families*)

FCPB-DM = Divine Mercy Edition

FCPB-TC = Preparation for Total Consecration to Jesus through Mary for Families

FCPB-SJ = St. Joseph Edition

805.6.4.2   In Conversation with God reflections on the daily Mass readings,

805.6.4.3   One of the *Family Consecration Prayer and Meditation Books,*

805.6.4.4   Peace of Heart Forum book.

805.6.5   Other recommended readings include:

805.6.5.1   *The Apostolate's Family Catechism,*

805.6.5.2   Family Apostolate Covenant,

805.6.5.3   Vatican II and papal documents,

805.6.5.4   *Abandonment to Divine Providence*, by Fr. Jean-Pierre de Caussade,

805.6.5.5   Spiritual works by Saint Josemaria Escriva, Pope John Paul II, Francis Cardinal Arinze, and Family Apostolate Founders, Jerry and Gwen Coniker,

805.6.5.6   Marian consecration readings or multimedia formation, preferably from the works of St. Louis de Montfort, St. Maximilian Kolbe, Pope John Paul II, or Francis Cardinal Arinze,

805.6.5.7   Spiritual works and prayers from the daily themes listed in section 805.9, to help you focus your prayers and thoughts,

805.6.5.8   The works of St. Thomas Aquinas, St. Francis de Sales, St. Francis of Assisi, St. Dominic, St. Ignatius, St. Augustine, the Fathers and Doctors of the Church and other patrons of the Apostolate for Family Consecration (see FCPB #40).

805.7   Daily Indulgences

805.7.1   It is very important to refer to sections 45a (FCPB) and 45b (FCPB-TC) for the norms and grants for indulgences. Members should seek to gain a plenary indulgence and many partial indulgences every day for the Holy Souls in Purgatory. The norms for partial indulgences complement our daily lives and those for plenary indulgences complement our devotional lives.

805.7.2   One powerful source of intercession for our families and work is our petitioning the Holy Souls in Purgatory to pray that our families and the Cooperators, Members and families of the Family Apostolate do God's Will. The prayers of gratitude from the Church Suffering in Purgatory who have been helped or can be helped by our indulgences, plus those of the Church Triumphant in Heaven, can be a powerful force for us who are still in the Church Militant on earth.

805.7.3   Ask Our Lady to apply your indulgences to the Holy Souls of your loved ones and others in Purgatory (FCPB #45a), but keep in mind, that we have entrusted everything to her through our consecration, so we realize that it is her right to make use of our indulgences as she knows best. They are now hers to do with as she wills.

805.8   **Viewing of Familyland Television Network**

805.8.1   The shows on FL-TV can be pre-recorded.

805.8.2   Recommended programs are:

805.8.2.1   Family Apostolate programs that feature Cardinal Francis Arinze (many of these are on Pope John Paul II's writings),

805.8.2.2   Programs on the teachings of Pope John Paul II,

805.8.2.3   *Challenge and Change* (focused on the Family Apostolate's spirituality),

805.8.2.4   *Weekly Roman Observer* (review of Pope's weekly newspaper),

---

* FCPB = all Family Consecration Prayer and Meditation Books (includes
    Preparation for Total Consecration to Jesus through Mary for Families)
FCPB-DM = Divine Mercy Edition
FCPB-TC = Preparation for Total Consecration to Jesus through Mary
    for Families
FCPB-SJ = St. Joseph Edition

805.8.2.5 *Spiritual Response to September 11th,*

805.8.2.6 *Destiny in the Balance* (a monthly evangelization update).

805.9 Daily Themes and Optional Theme Prayers

We encourage families to develop the habit of thinking about the themes for each day throughout the day. We have developed these themes because they help us enter into the riches of the Catholic Church and keep the fundamentals of our faith at the forefront of our lives.

805.9.1 Sunday

Theme: Gratitude, the Resurrection and the Church

Recommended Theme Prayer: Litany of Thanksgiving, #34 (FCPB)

805.9.1.1 Pray for the Holy Father, the Pope; bishops; priests; all consecrated celibates; and leaders in the Family Apostolate.

805.9.1.2 Thank the Holy Trinity for blessings received, and ask for the grace to do God's Will.

805.9.1.3 Reflect on the meaning of the Resurrection of Jesus from the dead.

805.9.1.4 Read part of Pope Paul VI's proclamation on the Apostles' Creed (FCPB-DM #70) or Holy Trinity Prayer in the Spirit of Fatima #21 (FCPB) or read from the Pope's newspaper L'Osservatore Romano or any papal document or any appropriate resource.

805.9.2 Monday

Theme: The Holy Spirit & the Last Things

Recommended Theme Prayer: Veni Creator, #46 (FCPB) and pray for the Holy Souls in Purgatory.

805.9.2.1 Pray to the Holy Spirit for the gifts of charity, apostolic zeal, and wisdom.

805.9.2.2 Pray for the Holy Souls in Purgatory and invoke them to intercede for the work of the

Apostolate for Family Consecration and its families.

805.9.2.3   Reflect on the Norms for Indulgences 45a (FCPB) and 45b (FCPB-TC), which is a way of life.

805.9.2.4   Reflect on the Last Things [eternity]: Death, Judgment, Purgatory, Heaven, and Hell.

805.9.2.5   Read part of Pope John Paul II's encyclical on the Holy Spirit, or part of #45 (FCPB-JS), or #46e (FCPB) or any appropriate resource.

805.9.2.6   Apostolate chaplains are asked to offer the votive Mass for deceased relatives, friends, and benefactors of the Family Apostolate, or to offer the Mass of the Holy Spirit if the liturgical calendar permits.

805.9.3   **Tuesday**

Theme: The Church Triumphant

Recommended Theme Prayer: Litany of the Patrons of The Apostolate for Family Consecration, #40 (FCPB)

805.9.3.1   Pray to and invoke the angels and saints to intercede for all families, cooperators and members of the Apostolate for Family Consecration and for their work.

805.9.3.2   Reflect on the lives of the saints.

805.9.3.3   Read from Pope John Paul II's teaching on the angels (FCPB-JS #36) or any appropriate resource.

805.9.3.4   Apostolate chaplains are asked to offer the votive Mass of the Angels or Saints or for

---

* FCPB = all Family Consecration Prayer and Meditation Books (includes
    Preparation for Total Consecration to Jesus through Mary for Families)
FCPB-DM = Divine Mercy Edition
FCPB-TC = Preparation for Total Consecration to Jesus through Mary
    for Families
FCPB-SJ = St. Joseph Edition

vocations in the Apostolate for Family Consecration, if the liturgical calendar permits.

805.9.4 **Wednesday**

Theme: St. Joseph

Recommended Theme Prayer: Act of Consecration to St. Joseph, #14 (FCPB)

805.9.4.1 Pray the "Seven Sorrows and Joys of St. Joseph Chaplet" (FCPB #14a) in place of the Rosary.

805.9.4.2 Reflect on the life of St. Joseph and his faithfulness to his commitments.

805.9.4.3 Ask St. Joseph to protect the Family Apostolate, to help you keep your commitments, and to protect and inspire couples to draw on the graces of the Sacrament of Matrimony.

805.9.4.4 Read something about St. Joseph or part of Pope John Paul II's Apostolic Letter on St. Joseph, Guardian of the Redeemer (FCPB-JS #66), or read part of Familiaris Consortio or section 77 (FCPB or Days 38-40 of FCPB-TC), or any appropriate resource.

805.9.4.5 Apostolate chaplains are asked to offer the votive Mass in honor of St. Joseph, if the liturgical calendar permits.

805.9.5 **Thursday**

Theme: The Holy Trinity & the Eucharist

Recommended Theme Prayer: Holy Trinity Prayer in the Spirit of Fatima, #21 (FCPB)

805.9.5.1 Pray for an increased devotion to the Holy Eucharist, and call down the Precious Blood of Jesus upon the work, families, cooperators and members of the Family Apostolate and upon the suffering members of your family and members and families of the Apostolate.

805.9.5.2 Reflect on the great gift God has given us of Himself in the Most Holy Eucharist.

805.9.5.3 Read something about the Holy Eucharist or part of Pope John Paul II's letter on the Eucharist (FCPB-DM #69), Ecclesia de Eucharistia, or the Vatican II Constitution on the Sacred Liturgy. Also pray #11a (FCPB) or any appropriate resource.

805.9.5.4 Apostolate chaplains are asked to offer the votive Mass of the Holy Eucharist; the Precious Blood; or Jesus Christ, Eternal High Priest, if the liturgical calendar permits.

805.9.6 **Friday**

Theme: Reparation and the Sacred Heart

Recommended Theme Prayer: Act of Reparation to the Sacred Heart of Jesus in the Spirit of Blessed Teresa of Calcutta, #22 (FCPB)

805.9.6.1 Make reparation to the Sacred Heart of Jesus and pray in a special way for the intentions at the foot of the altars in the Apostolate for Family Consecration's St. Joseph Centers throughout the world and for increased First Friday devotions.

805.9.6.2 Pray the "Mercy of God, Way of the Cross" (FCPB #59) on First Fridays and all Fridays of Lent. (encouraged)

805.9.6.3 Reflect on God's infinite mercy and the "All for" formula for drawing it down upon us all.

---

* FCPB = all Family Consecration Prayer and Meditation Books (includes *Preparation for Total Consecration to Jesus through Mary for Families*)

FCPB-DM = Divine Mercy Edition

FCPB-TC = Preparation for Total Consecration to Jesus through Mary for Families

FCPB-SJ = St. Joseph Edition

805.9.6.4 Read part of Friends of the Cross #67a (FCPB-DM) or Pope John Paul II's encyclical on Divine Mercy (FCPB-DM #102) or any appropriate resource.

805.9.6.5 Apostolate chaplains are asked to offer the votive Mass of the Sacred Heart or of the Divine Mercy, if the liturgical calendar permits.

805.9.7 **Saturdays**

Theme: Our Blessed Mother

Recommended Theme Prayer: The Magnificat, Luke 1:46-55, #2 (FCPB)

805.9.7.1 Honor Our Lady and pray for increased devotion to her Immaculate Heart and the spreading of the daily family Rosary, consecration, and the First Saturday Day of Recollection and Communion of Reparation devotion.

805.9.7.2 Reflect on the spiritual motherhood of Mary.

805.9.7.3 Read something about Our Lady, particularly from Pope John Paul II's encyclical Mother of the Redeemer, his Marian prayers or document summaries at the end of most of his writings, or his Marian reflections in the book "Preparation for Total Consecration to Jesus through Mary for Families (#323-115), one of St. Louis de Montfort's works (FCPB-TC #48, 49, 50, or 67), the prayer by St. Maximilian Kolbe (FCPB #50b) or any of his works, part of #42a (FCPB or Days 35-37 of FCPB-TC), or any appropriate resource.

805.9.7.4 Apostolate chaplains are asked to offer a votive Mass in honor of one of Mary's titles if the liturgical calendar permits.

805.9.7.5 Note: See First Saturday Reparation Promise (FCPB-TC #33).

805.9.8 **Occasionally**

Read and reflect on the following:

> 805.9.8.1 Part of Pope Paul VI's January 1, 1967, statement on reparation (FCPB-DM #42).
>
> 805.9.8.2 #42a (FCPB or Days 35–37 of FCPB-TC).
>
> 805.9.8.3 the 17th chapter of St. John's Gospel (FCPB #50f).

806 Weekly Practices
For Discernment Cooperators and Members

806.1 **Formation Meeting.** Attendance at a Peace of Heart Forum (see pages 518–519)or a "Be Not Afraid Family Hour" (see pages 504-506) or an approved formation program on one's own. These programs air regularly on FL-TV.

806.2 **Lay Ecclesial Team Meeting.** Attendance at Lay Ecclesial Team meetings, which often includes the above formation meeting, with evangelization strategy and accomplishment reports.

806.3 **Other Evangelization Outreach** or work for Family Apostolate centers.

806.4 **Canticle of the Lord's Day** in honor of the Holy Family (FCPB-TC #34c). We recommend that families or Lay Ecclesial Teams have the Lord's Day Meal before the evening meal on Saturdays when possible. This could be done weekly or once a month. (optional)

---

* FCPB = all Family Consecration Prayer and Meditation Books (includes
   Preparation for Total Consecration to Jesus through Mary for Families)
FCPB-DM = Divine Mercy Edition
FCPB-TC = Preparation for Total Consecration to Jesus through Mary
   for Families
FCPB-SJ = St. Joseph Edition

807 **Monthly Practices**
For Discernment Cooperators and Members

807.1 **Confession** twice a month when possible. Frequent Confession gives us the grace to see and overcome our faults. We also encourage this practice so that members have an opportunity to gain a plenary indulgence each day for the Holy Souls in Purgatory.

807.2 **Scripture and Virtue of the Month**

807.2.1 Meditate on and live the virtue and Scripture of the month. The Scriptures may be periodically updated on familyland.org.

807.2.2 St. Alphonsus Ligouri suggests focusing on the following virtues for each month, which the Apostolate for Family Consecration has adopted:

Month	Virtue	Scripture (or visit familyland.org for current Scripture of the Month)
January	*Mortification*	Matthew 16:24-25
February	*Recollection*	Matthew 14:23
March	*Deepening Prayer Life*	Luke 11: 1-4
April	*Self-Denial*	2 Timothy 1:7-8
May	*Faith*	Hebrews 11:1-3
June	*Hope*	Romans 15:13
July	*Love of God*	1 John 4:16, 20-21
August	*Love of Neighbor*	John 13:34-35
September	*Poverty*	2 Corinthians 8:9
October	*Chastity*	Romans 12:1-2
November	*Obedience*	Matthew 7:21
December	*Humility*	Matthew 11:29

807.3 **First Fridays**

807.3.1 Mass and Stations of the Cross (FCPB #59) if possible.

807.4 **First Saturdays**

807.4.1 Make reparation for the sins that offend the Immaculate Heart of Mary by receiving Holy

Communion, watching a First Saturday Cenacle on video or praying the Rosary with 15 minutes of meditation on one or more of its Mysteries, and going to Confession within a reasonable period of time. All of this is to be offered in reparation for the sins that offend the Immaculate Heart of Mary.

807.4.2   If possible, attend a morning or day of recollection with formation and prayer.

807.4.3   Try to renew your total consecration with prayer #49b or 50b (FCPB).

808   Yearly Practices/Events/Retreats
For Discernment Cooperators and Members

808.1   **Celebrate the Feast of Divine Mercy** on the Second Sunday after Easter (FCPB-DM #20e).

808.2   **Annual Total Consecration Renewal** using this book. Begin on February 20 (the Memorial of Blesseds Jacinta and Francisco of Fatima), renew on March 25 (the Solemnity of the Annunciation) and complete on the 40th Day, March 31. If this is your first consecration, start as soon as possible — see page 10 for the "Daily Exercises and Schedule of Readings" chart for the closest starting date.

808.3   **Attendance at the following Family Apostolate Events:**

808.3.1   Silent Retreat for Discernment Cooperators (encouraged) and Members (required).

808.3.2   Marriage Get-away Weekends (encouraged).

808.3.3   Holy Family Fests with Evangelization and Catechetical training workshops and conferral of the Brown Scapular (required for Discernment Cooperators and Members).

808.3.4   Totus Tuus "Consecrate Them in Truth" Family Conferences (encouraged).

838 Generous Souls Serving or Being Served by the Apostolate for Family Consecration

As mentioned above, within the Apostolate for Family Consecration there exists a generous collaboration of souls within various memberships and cooperator levels that help further its mission or are served by it. These generous souls fall into two categories within the Family Apostolate: (1) Cooperators and (2) Members. The sections below define and explain these two categories and the benefits.

839 Benefits for Cooperators and Members and their Families

Members and Cooperators of the Apostolate for Family Consecration become part of a vibrant community that is continually consecrated in the Truth through theologically fail-safe multimedia resources and are part of an international movement for family sanctification. Cooperators and Members of the Apostolate for Family Consecration share in:

839.1 all the Masses, prayers and good works of the Apostolate for Family Consecration.

839.2 all the collective graces and merits derived from the many spiritual alliances made by the Family Apostolate with other powerful spiritual communities.

839.3 the special indulgences of belonging to the Archconfraternity of Our Lady of Guadalupe and the St. Louis de Montfort's Association of Mary, Queen of All Hearts (after the act of total consecration is made), both of which have authorized branches at Catholic Familyland in Bloomingdale, Ohio, USA.

839.4 the Sabbatine Privilege—this has been extended to all the members and benefactors of the Apostolate for Family Consecration who fulfill the conditions listed in section #41b (FCPB-TC).

840 Cooperators in the Apostolate for Family Consecration

840.1   A Cooperator is a broad category of involvement in the Family Apostolate. Cooperators are not members, but may include those who:

- are discerning an exclusive commitment as a member of the Apostolate for Family Consecration OR

- volunteer to serve a Lay Ecclesial Team, outreach or at a Family Apostolate St. Joseph Media and Training Center AND/OR

- donate to the work and mission of the Apostolate for Family Consecration AND/OR

- who promote or benefit from the vision and mission programs of the Apostolate for Family Consecration and in some cases, may belong to another religion.

840.2   **Types of Cooperator involvement in the Apostolate for Family Consecration:**

840.2.1   **Discernment Cooperator.** Fully practicing Catholic discerning (striving for) membership as a Disciple, Mourning Star or Catholic Corps Member.

- Makes the act of Total Consecration to Jesus through Mary in union with St. Joseph.

- Discerns whether they want to make the Apostolate for Family Consecration their principal apostolic work

- Throughout their discernment process, they give their lives to the Church through the Apostolate for Family Consecration and make private vows of poverty, chastity and obedience according to their state in life and respective Covenant.

- Regularly participates in the Apostolate for Family Consecration's multimedia formation and helps the work in various ways.

- Studies the Dual Dimension of Consecration — Totus Tuus, giving everything to Jesus through Mary in union with St. Joseph, and "Consecrate them in Truth" (John 17) — and strives to apply this in their daily lives. (See sections 42a and 77 [Days 35–40 of this book]).

- Is open to learning more about membership in the Apostolate for Family Consecration and strives to pray its daily prayers and to live its spiritual practices as presented in Sections 805, 806, 807, 808, and also presented on CD#160-760.

- Attends an annual Holy Family Fest, other events with their family and a yearly silent retreat when possible

840.2.2 **Formation Cooperator**. Regularly uses the Apostolate for Family Consecration's multimedia formation resources by their self or within a group. They may participate in the Apostolate's Lay Ecclesial Team's formation or outreach program, such as formation with The Apostolate's Family Catechism.

840.2.3 **Evangelization Cooperator**. Is a practicing Catholic and is actively evangelizing by regularly initiating and implementing the Apostolate for Family Consecration's formation and evangelization programs in homes, churches and schools. Evangelization Cooperators strive to live a basic sacramental and prayer life of at least Sunday Mass, monthly confession, and daily personal prayer. They receive evangelization training from the Apostolate for Family Consecration

840.2.4 **Associate Cooperator**. Is a practicing Catholic and is a committed member of another Church approved society with specific in-depth formation, prayers, practices and spiritual direction which requires an exclusive association, and, because of their exclusive commitment in another association, will not be able to go any deeper into a spiritual relationship with the Apostolate for Family Consecration. Associate Cooperators participate in an Apostolate's Lay Ecclesial Team's formation or outreach program.

840.2.5 **Sacri-state Cooperator**. Blessed Mother Teresa of Calcutta's Idea. Includes those offering their physical suffering (Suffering Sacri-state Cooperator), those offering their sacrifices involved with caring for the physically suffering (Simon Caretaker Sacri-state Cooperator), and those who offer prayers and their daily duties (Oblate Sacri-state Cooperator) — all for a particular Cooperator, Member, or team or the general work and mission of the Apostolate for Family Consecration. The Oblate Sacri-state Cooperator can be a contemplative community, an individual, a child praying for our work and mission, or a priest who offers some of his available Masses for the work and mission of the Apostolate for Family Consecration. Sacri-state Cooperators enjoy all the spiritual benefits of membership and strive to daily pray the Family Apostolate's Morning Offering prayer (FCPB #2a).

840.2.6 **Advisory Council, Author and Video Faculty Cooperators**. Advisory Council, Author and Video Faculty Cooperators are those prominent individuals who publicly endorse the work and mission of the Apostolate for Family Consecration and/or are open to giving advice or counsel in their areas of expertise when asked, such as writing for the Family Apostolate or teaching through the Family Apostolate's multimedia programs. Their service is at the very heart of the Family Apostolate's work to consecrate families in the Truth.

840.2.7 **Legatee Cooperator**. Is of any faith and benefits from the Family Apostolate's various multimedia resources, including its CD, Podcast, radio or Familyland® television network and programs or who has attended Family Apostolate functions.

Legatee Cooperators may also volunteer their apostolic services or financially support the work of the Apostolate for Family Consecration.

840.2.8 **Holy Family Cooperator**. Makes their Total Consecration to Jesus through Mary and registers it through the Family Apostolate.

850 Membership in the Apostolate for Family Consecration

850.1 Membership includes Catholics at different commitment levels (First Degree, Second Degree and Life) who meet the requirements of the particular category of involvement. The main apostolic endeavors are carried out through Familyland/St. Joseph Media and Training Centers by Disciple, Catholic Corps and Mourning Star Members.

850.2 All First Degree, Second Degree, and Life Members of the Apostolate for Family Consecration:

- Are fully practicing Catholics who uphold all of the teachings of the Catholic Church,

- Have a deep devotion to the Real Presence of Our Lord in the Most Holy Eucharist, and a love for the Blessed Virgin Mary and St. Joseph.

- Have an uncompromising loyalty to the Vicar of Christ, the Pope, and are faithful to the Teaching Magisterium of the Catholic Church.

- Are committed to the vision and mission of the Apostolate for Family Consecration.

- Regularly attend or make use of Family Apostolate multimedia formation programs.

- If possible, promote events at Familyland/St. Joseph Centers and watch Familyland® Television Network.

- Do not promote or associate themselves with any unapproved apparitions or movements.

- Are encouraged to tithe (Malachi 3:9-11) to the diocese, parish, the Apostolate for Family Consecration or other Church-related works.

- Make private vows of poverty, chastity and obedience according to their state in life, these statutes and their respective covenants.

- Exercise a charitable respect for the Office of the Bishop and the role of the priest.

- Follow all the policies and procedures of the Apostolate for Family Consecration.

- Follow all spiritual practices, including daily prayers, as explained in their respective covenants.

- Hold up the work of the Apostolate for Family Consecration as their primary apostolic work in the simultaneous renewal of the family and parish/neighborhood communities in their efforts to work for the Social Reign of the Holy Family—a Catholic culture.

850.3 **Types of Membership in the Apostolate for Family Consecration**

850.3.1 **Disciple Members.** Those of any degree who have made a commitment to enter into the formation of the Apostolate for Family Consecration and devote themselves to work in the Apostolate for Family Consecration or to assist the Lay Ecclesial Teams or Family Apostolate St. Joseph Media and Training Centers. They follow the prayers and spirituality of the Apostolate for Family Consecration according their covenant and policies and procedures of their particular commitment level.

850.3.2 **Mourning Star Member.** Those who are widows and widowers at different commitment levels who have also made a private vow of perpetual celibacy according to the norms of these statutes and the covenant and policies and procedures of their category of membership and to devote their principal energies to the work and mission of the Apostolate for Family Consecration. They follow the prayers and spirituality of the Apostolate for Family Consecration according to their covenant and policies and procedures of their particular commitment level.

850.3.3 **Catholic Corps Members.** The Catholic Corps form two divisions: Catholic Corps Women and Catholic Corps Men. They are single men and women who live a consecration of life separately at various levels of commitment in service to the Church through the work and mission of the Apostolate for Family Consecration according to the norms of their respective covenants and the policies and procedures of their category of membership. Some Catholic Corps Men members may be ordained priests for service as chaplains for the Apostolate for Family Consecration..

850.3.3.1 Catholic Corps Intercessor Members. Some Catholic Corps Members may become Catholic Corps Intercessor Members for a period of time or indefinitely when mutually discerned by the individual and the Local Coordinating Committee with confirmation from the Global Coordinating Committee when possible or if not possible, from the next higher level of authority. The Intercessors would spend most of their day in prayer and contemplation for the vision and mission of the Apostolate for Family Consecration. The rest of their day would be spent in assigned work for the St. Joseph Media and Training Center to which they are assigned.

860 Action Points

860.1 Pray for the success of our work, the safety of our members, and that we may be faithful witnesses of God's love to the world and be loyal to our founding charism.

860.2 Consecrate your family by visiting familyconsecration.org and begin the journey toward consecration.

860.3 Bring your family and invite other families, your bishop, and your parish priest, to Catholic Familyland for our 7-day Holy Family fests, where they can meet other families striving to live their Faith, and learn more about our evangelization resources that make it easy for them to bring the fullness of the Faith to others.

860.4 If possible, subscribe to Familyland Television Network and bring a steady flow of Catholic Formation and wholesome family entertainment into your home 24 hours a day, 7 days a week.

860.5 Ask about Lay Ecclesial Teams in your area.

860.6 Support the Apostolate for Family Consecration financially by becoming a Familyland Partner and participating in a monthly giving plan.

For more information,
visit www.familyland.org or contact:

USA and Canada
Catholic Familyland
3375 County Road 36, Bloomingdale OH 43910
1-800-77-FAMILY or 740-765-5500   usa@familyland.org

Asia
St. Joseph Media and Training Center
P.O. Box 0026, Las Piñas City, PHILIPPINES
(632) 871-4440   Fax: (632) 875-3506   asia@familyland.org

Latin America
St. Joseph Media and Training Center
Municipio de Atlautla, Estado de Mexico, C.P. 56970, MEXICO
52-59-7976-7093   Fax: 52-59-7976-3316   latinoamerica@familyland.org

Africa
africa@familyland.org

Europe
europe@familyland.org   www.familylandeurope.com

Apostolate for Family Consecration's Video Faculty, Authors, and Advisory Council

Administration

Jerome F. Coniker*** ****
President, Co-Founder with Gwen Coniker†, Consultor, Pontifical Council for the Family
Robert A. Coniker**
Exec. Vice-President
James F. Kocisko**
VP Engineering
Theresa M. Schmitz ** ***
VP Operations
Rev. Kevin S. Barrett*** ****
Int'l Chaplain
Carolyn E. Stegmann**
Treasurer
Montserrat Friedrich*** ****
Secretary

Theological Auditor

Fr. Bernard Geiger, O.F.M. Conv. *** ****
Dr. Regis Martin, S.T.D. **
Franciscan University of Steubenville

Primary Theological & Spiritual Advisors

Francis Cardinal Arinze* *** ****
Mario Luigi Cardinal Ciappi, O.P.†* ****
John J. Cardinal O'Connor†**
Gaudencio B. Cardinal Rosales (Philippines)**
Jaime Cardinal Sin (Philippines) † **
J. Francis Cardinal Stafford* ****
Alfonso Cardinal Lopez Trujillo* **
Archbishop Ramon C. Arguelles (Philippines)****
Archbishop Valerian Okeke (Nigeria) **
Bishop Roger J. Foys**
Bishop John J. Magee (Ireland)* ****
Bishop Juan F. Torres Oliver **
Bishop Martin Igwe Uzoukwu**** (Nigeria)
Bishop Jose de Jesus Martinez Zepeda** (Mexico)
Rev. Msgr. Juan Espona Jimenez** ***
Rev. Msgr. Paul A. Lenz**

Rev. Msgr. Josefino Ramirez**** (Philippines)
Fr. Roger Charest, S.M.M.****
Fr. Michael Scanlan, T.O.R.****
Fr. Sebastian, M.C. (Italy) ****
Fr. Timothy M. Sparks, O.P.† ****
Fr. Pablo Straub, C.Ss.R****
Blessed Teresa of Calcutta†****

Video Faculty and Advisory Council Members of the Roman Curia

William Cardinal Baum**
Agostino Cardinal Cacciavillan* **
Giovanni Cardinal Cheli* **
Georges Marie Martin Cardinal Cottier, O.P. *
Jorge A. Cardinal Medina Estevéz*
Edouard Cardinal Gagnon, P.S.S.* ****
Darío Cardinal Castrillón Hoyos* **
Pio Cardinal Laghi* ****
Renato Cardinal Martino* **
Augustine Cardinal Mayer, O.S.B. * **
Silvio Cardinal Oddi†* *
Eduardo Cardinal Pironio† *
Paul Cardinal Poupard * **
Giovanni Cardinal Battista Re*
Agnelo Cardinal Rossi†*
Opilio Cardinal Rossi†*
Jose Cardinal Sanchez* **
Sergio Cardinal Sebastiani* **
Crescenzio Cardinal Sepe* **
Edmund Cardinal Szoka* ****
Jozef Cardinal Tomko* **
Archbishop Paul J. Cordes* **
Archbishop Michael L. Fitzgerald, M.Afr.* **
Archbishop John P. Foley* ****
Archbishop Gabriel Montalvo*
Archbishop Pietro Sambi*
Archbishop Robert Sarah*
Archbishop Stanislaw Rylko*
Bishop Peter Canisius J. Van Lierde†* ****
Rev. Federico Lombardi, S.J. * **

* = Roman Curia, Pope's direct staff ** = Video Faculty *** = Have written for our work
**** = Featured on multiple video programs † = Deceased

Video Faculty and International Episcopal Advisory Council Members and/or Fire of Mercy Co-Chairmen

Anthony Cardinal Bevilacqua****
John Joseph Cardinal Carberry†
Norberto Cardinal Rivera Carrera** (Mexico)
Terence Cardinal Cooke†
Godfried Cardinal Danneels (Belgium)
Francis Cardinal George, O.M.I.
Stephen Cardinal Fumio Hamao* **
Claudio Cardinal Hummes (Brazil)
William Cardinal Keeler
Adam Cardinal Maida**
Jose Cardinal Saraiva Martins, C.M.F.*
Humberto Cardinal Medeiros†
Nicolas Cardinal de Jesus Lopez Rodriguez (Dominican Republic)
Christoph Cardinal Schonborn (Austria) **
Adrianus Cardinal Simonis (Holland)
Christian Cardinal Tumi (Cameroon)
Ricardo Cardinal Vidal (Philippines) **
Archbishop Raymond L. Burke
Archbishop Fernando Capalla** (Philippines)
Archbishop Charles Chaput, O.F.M. Cap.
Archbishop Elden F. Curtiss**
Archbishop Timothy M. Dolan
Archbishop John F. Donoghue**
Archbishop Patrick F. Flores
Archbishop Harry J. Flynn
Archbishop Barry James Hickey** (Australia)
Archbishop Murilo S.R. Krieger, SCI (Brazil)
Archbishop Angel N. Lagdameo** (Philippines)
Archbishop Diarmuid Martin (Ireland)**
Archbishop John J. Myers**
Archbishop Edwin F. O'Brien (Military Archdiocese of the United States)
Archbishop Simeon Pereira (Pakistan)
Archbishop Orlando Quevedo** (Philippines)
Archbishop Gabriel V. Reyes (Philippines)
Archbishop Oscar Rodriguez, S.D.B. (Honduras)
Bishop Paul Andreotti, O.P. (Pakistan)† **

Bishop Samuel J. Aquila
Bishop Abelardo Alvaredo A. (Mexico)
Bishop José Luis Astigarraga (Peru)
Bishop Ayo-Maria Atoyebi, O.P. (Nigeria)**
Bishop Warren L. Boudreaux†**
Bishop Fabian W. Bruskewitz
Bishop Leo Brust†**
Bishop Luis Artemio Flores Calzada** (Mexico)
Bishop Ignatius A. Catanello**
Bishop R. Daniel Conlon**
Bishop Thomas V. Daily**
Bishop William L. D'Mello (India)**
Bishop Everard de Jong (Holland)
Bishop Norbert M. Dorsey, C.P.
Bishop Joseph A. Galante
Bishop Hector Gutierrez Pabon (Columbia)
Bishop Antonius Hurkmans (Holland)
Bishop José Mariá Hernandez Gonzales (Mexico)
Bishop John Joseph (Pakistan)†**
Bishop J.B. Kakubi (Uganda) **
Bishop Joseph J. Madera** (Military Archdiocese)
Bishop Jesse Mercado (Philippines)
Bishop Bernard Martin Ngaviliau, C.S.Sp. (E. Africa)
Bishop Isidro Sala Ribera (Peru)
Bishop Lawrence J. Riley†
Bishop Dennis M. Schnurr
Bishop Augustine M. Shao, C.S.Sp. (Tanzania)
Bishop James S. Sullivan
Bishop Thomas J. Welsh****
Bishop Frans Wiertz (Holland)
Bishop Donald W. Wuerl****
Bishop John W. Yanta

Advisory Council Members and Video Faculty

Abbot Edmund McCaffrey, O.S.B. **
Rev. Msgr. Robert J. Dempsey* **
Rev. Msgr. Francesco Di Felice* **
Rev. Msgr. Peter Elliott* *** ****
Rev. Msgr. William P. Fay (USCCB)
Rev. Msgr. P. Luciano Guerra (Portugal)**
Rev. Msgr. John McCarthy, J.C.D., S.T.D. ****
Rev. Msgr. Ugo Moretto
Rev. Msgr. Eugene Pack†**

Rev. Msgr. Alphonse S. Popek†**
Rev. Msgr. Michael J. Wrenn**
Fr. Henri Bechard, S.J.†****
Fr. Alfred Boeddeker†****
Fr. Timothy Byerley****
Fr. Raniero Cantalamessa, O.F.M., C.A.P.
   (Papal Preacher)* **
Fr. Messias Dias Coelho (Portugal)****
Fr. Gabriel Calvo**
Fr. Harold Cohen, S.J.† ****
Fr. Dominic De Domenico, O.P.****
Fr. William Dorney†****
Fr. Thomas F. Egan, S.J.****
Fr. Francis Filas, S.J.† **
Fr. Luis Barrera Flores
Fr. Tom Forrest, C.Ss.R.****
Fr. Lambert Greenan, O.P.* ****
Fr. Benedict Groeshel, C.F.R. **
Fr. John Hardon, S.J.†**** ****
Fr. Brian Harrison, S.T.L.****
Fr. Richard M. Hogan, Ph.D.****
Fr. M. Albert Krapiec, O.P. (Poland)****
Fr. Maynard Kolodziej, O.F.M.****
Fr. George Kosicki, C.S.B.*** ****
Fr. Alfred J. Kunz†****
Fr. Peter Lappin, S.D.B.†**** ****
Fr. Francis Larkin†**
Fr. John LeVoir***
Fr. Lawrence Lovasik, S.V.D.†*** ****
Fr. Martin J. McDermott, S.J.
Fr. Seraphim Michalenko, M.I.C.****
Fr. Thomas Morrison, O.P.***
Fr. Joseph Mungari, S.A.C.****
Fr. Bruce Nieli, C.F.R**
Fr. Francis Novak, C.Ss.R.****
Fr. Randall Paine****
Fr. Frank Pavone****
Fr. Gabriel Pausback, O.Carm†** ***
Fr. Howard Rafferty, O.Carm†**
Fr. Charles F. Shelby, C.M.**
Fr. Stanley Smolenski****
Fr. Andrej Szostek, M.I.C. (Poland)**
Fr. Edmundo Ortega Tirado (Mexico)
Fr. Werenfried van Straaten†
Sr. Concetta, F.S.P.
Mother M. Dolorosa, H.P.B.
Mother M. Immaculata, H.M.I.*** ****
Sr. John Vianney, S.S.N.D.†****

Lic. Emilio Burillo Azcarraga (Mexico)
Lic. Carlos Abascal (Mexico)
Mrs. Patricia Balskus†***
Dr. Warren Carroll, Ph.D.**
Dr. N.M. Camardese, M.D.*** ****
Mr. Raymond E. Cross**
Ambassador Howard Dee (Philippines)**
Ambassador Henrietta DeVilla**
   (Philippines)
Dr. Richard DeGraff**
Hon. Jeremiah Denton**
Manual and Marilyn Dubon
Dr. Richard Dumont*** ****
Dr. Damien Fedoryka***
Mr. Frank Flick†
Mr. Dale Francis†***
Kimberly Hahn**
Dr. Scott Hahn****
John† and Eleanor Hand**
Mr. Frederick W. Hill**
Mr. Carl Karcher**
Mr. August Mauge†
Allen & Marlene McCauley**
Mr. Frank J. Milligan, Jr.† **
Mr. Thomas Monaghan**
Dr. Anthony N. Paruta****
Dr. Wanda Poltawska**
Dr. Herbert Ratner, M.D.† **
Mr. Anthony F. Sansone, Sr.
Mr. Charles F. Scholl
Her Imperial Highness Duchess Maria**
   Vladimirovna (Russia)
Dr. Alice von Hildebrand****
Dr. Joaquin Navarro-Valls* **
Dr. Charles Wahlig†****
Dr.† and Mrs. Paul Whelan****

[Partial List]

Appendix D

Tribute to
Gwen Cecilia Coniker

September 27, 1939 — June 15, 2002

Wife

Mother   *Co-Founder*

Gwen Cecilia Coniker

September 27, 1939 – June 15, 2002

Wife, Mother of 13, Grandmother of 64 and counting,
Co-founder of the Apostolate for Family Consecration.

Family-maker
Home-maker
Peace-maker

Gwen's Way of Life

Holiness and happiness are fruits of joyfully fulfilling
the responsibility of each present moment…All for
the Sacred and Eucharist Heart of Jesus,
all through the Sorrowful and Immaculate Heart
of Mary, all in union with St. Joseph.

See #2j in Appendix A for the
Prayer for Gwen and Family Unity.

"All for the Holy Family"
as lived by Gwen Coniker

Each moment of the day carries a responsibility, which manifests God's will for us. When we are in the state of grace and fulfill the responsibility of each present moment to please God, sanctifying grace increases in us. We become more pleasing to Him, a stronger instrument to repair for sin, and advance true peace and justice in families and in the world. We can develop the habit of consulting God more frequently throughout the day by praying "**All for You O Holy Family**" (or just **"All for"**) before every encounter, decision, or action. We can do this with the intention of making a spiritual communion and asking for the Eucharistic grace to discern His will moment by moment, and the strength to do it in times of peace or conflict. It is then that we experience a sense of security, joy, and God's peace, no matter what the outer storm looks like and knowing that we are doing what God asks of us, which is truly uniting every act with the Holy Sacrifice of the Mass while abandoning ourselves to God's providence.

(To better understand how to grow in grace, see paragraphs 460 and 1996-2029 in the *Catechism of the Catholic Church*. For more on doing God's will, see Mt. 21:23, Jn. 4:34, and Jn. 6:38. Also read *Abandonment to Divine Providence* by Jean-Pierre de Caussade and section 42a in our *Family Consecration Prayer and Meditation Book* or in Days 35 to 37 in this prayer book.)

Gwen Coniker is an outstanding model for wives, mothers, grandmothers and evangelists striving to live with great love the responsibility of the present moment, as asked for by Vatican II (Cf. "Dogmatic Constitution on the Church"*[Lumen Gentium]*, Section 34). Some of her greatest virtues were gratitude and a willingness to listen. She had a true mother's heart that was filled with forgiveness, gratitude and disinterested selfless love. She would say, "Charity is always first."

See #2j in Appendix A for the
Prayer for Gwen and Family Unity.

Biographical Sketch

Gwen Cecilia (Billings) Coniker was born in Chicago on September 27, 1939. She met her future husband, Jerry, when she was 14 years old, while they were both attending St. Gregory High School. They were married on the Feast of the Assumption, August 15,

Gwen holding her 13th baby, Mary

1959, and consecrated their marriage to Jesus through Mary at Our Lady's side altar. Jerry was 20 years old and Gwen was 19. They had no idea then what Our Lady would call them to do.

Seeing the decline in Christian values in society, Jerry and Gwen soon became deeply involved in the right-to-life and family values movement. Gwen loved children and always said she would like to have a dozen. "There's nothing like a baby!" she would say. Her first child, Maureen Therese, was born on June 22, 1960. Then followed Kathy Lynne, Laurie Ann, Margaret Rose, Sharon Marie, Michael John, and Robert Anthony.

The direction of the Conikers' lives was drastically changed on April 28, 1971 (Feast of St. Louis de Montfort), when they made their consecration to Jesus through Mary according to the formula of St. Louis de Montfort. This is the same consecration that changed the life of Karol Wojtyla, Pope John Paul II. His papal motto is "Totus Tuus, Mater Ecclesiae" (Totally yours, Mother of the Church). After making this consecration, Jerry and Gwen were convinced more than ever that the battle to end abortion and save the family was primarily a spiritual one, so they decided to devote their lives to serving God full-time.

On May 13th, 1971 (Feast of Our Lady of Fatima), the Conikers sold their home and later, their business. On September 8th (Our Lady's birthday), they moved their family to Fatima, Portugal. Their third son, Joseph Vincent, was born in Portugal. During their 2-year stay in Portugal, Our Lady prepared them for their work in the Church. They returned to the United States in June of 1973 to work with Rev. Bernard Geiger, OFM. CONV., who was the superior of his Franciscan community and local

August 15, 1959

June 12, 2002

The Coniker Family during the founding years (1970's)
of the Apostolate for Family Consecration

*director of St. Maximilian Kolbe's "Knights of the Immaculata."
Soon after, Gwen gave birth to her ninth child, James Francis —
the first of four caesarean births. Maria Ann was born a year later
on September 4th.*

*During the Holy Year of 1975, on the Feast of the Sacred
Heart, Jerry and Gwen founded the Apostolate for Family
Consecration in Kenosha, Wisconsin. When Gwen became preg-
nant with her eleventh child, she adamantly refused to abort her
baby, despite the doctor's sincere warnings that she would not sur-
vive the birth. However, Theresa Marie, a healthy baby girl, was
born just after Christmas in 1975. A year later, Gwen miscarried
their twelfth child, Angelica. On October 23, 1977, Gwen gave
birth to their thirteenth child, Mary Elizabeth.*

*Jerry and Gwen were married for almost 43 years, and their
love for each other grew every day. They had the joy of watching
their family grow, first with their 13 children, then 11 faithful
spouses and 64 grandchildren (and still counting!), who through
the grace of God are all in the Faith.*

*Their love for God and each other blossomed as the
Apostolate for Family Consecration grew into an international
movement for families. It has five key interrelated family min-
istries that serve the vision — Familyland® TV Network, Catholic
Familyland training and media centers in the USA, Mexico,
Philippines, Europe and Nigeria, Consecration in Truth
Catechetics, Peace of Heart Forums, and Lay Ecclesial Teams*

(with cooperators and members on five continents).

Gwen had a kindred–spirit friendship with both Pope John Paul II and Mother Teresa. From 1984–2002, Gwen was privileged to have nine papal encounters. Pope John Paul II read her soul as he looked deeply into her eyes. On April 29, 1999, the Holy Father appointed Jerry and Gwen to be members of his Pontifical Council for the Family, which advises the papacy on family matters in the world. The Coniker family represented the theme – "Children, the Springtime of Hope for Family and Society" at the Jubilee Year 2000 celebration at St. Peter's Square with the Pope before hundreds of thousands of people. On October 7, 2001, Jerry and Gwen received the Pro Ecclesia et Pontifice Award from Pope John Paul II through Bishop Gilbert Sheldon of Steubenville, and were later received into the Pontifical order of the Knights of St. Michael of the Wing by the crown prince of Portugal. Thus Gwen was named "Lady Guenevere."

On November 2, 2001, Gwen was diagnosed with cirrhosis of the liver and was told that she had less than a year to live. This disease was contracted by a blood transfusion during one or more of her caesarean births in the mid 1970's. She peacefully accepted her sickness and physical sufferings. **She repeatedly said she had no regrets.** She loved Jerry and all her children and she loved life. On May 13, 2002, she left the Cleveland Clinic, which had also diagnosed her with cancer. She spent her last days in pain and peaceful acceptance as she prepared her family for her death. At 5:30 a.m. on Saturday, June 15, 2002, after the Anointing of the Sick by Fr. Geiger, the Conikers' spiritual director, she passed away in the arms of her loving husband at their home at Catholic Familyland . She was 62 years old. It is no coincidence that she died on June 15th, which was the Solemnity of the Sacred Heart in 1917 – the same year that Our Lady appeared to the three

Shepherd Children at Fatima, Portugal. The Apostolate for Family Consecration celebrates its founding on this moveable feast.

Gwen was laid to rest on June 22, 2002, the 42nd birthday of her first child, Maureen. Her body lies in the crypt of The Apostolate's St. John Vianney Oratory Chapel at Catholic Familyland, Bloomingdale, Ohio, behind the altar of our Blessed Mother. The altar contains a relic of St. Louis de Montfort and a copy of the original handwritten manuscript of his famous work, "True Devotion to Mary" — a spirituality that formed her life and the life of Pope John Paul II. A "Tomb of the Unborn Child" commemorating millions of aborted babies has been erected near Gwen's crypt, as a testimony to a mother who was willing to sacrifice her life for her children. She died the way she lived — never complaining and always caring.

Gwen said it all in the closing paragraph of her letter to her family on June 10, 2002: **"My prayerful wish is that each one of my children will raise their family close to God and find God's will for their life. All my grandchildren, I love you. —Mom"**

+
LDM   28 May 2005

Dear Jerry Coniker,

    Thank you for all you are doing for families to help them live in God and to bring the love of God to all they encounter. As Gwen said, each one is special, special to God and a special reflection of His love. I am sure she is helping you now from heaven, and that our Mother is helping you too.

    You are in our prayers, Jerry. Please pray for us too, especially at Holy Mass when we are united as one family around the altar of Jesus' sacrifice.

        God bless you,

        M. Nirmala

    Sr. M. Nirmala, M.C.

Superior General of Blessed Mother Teresa of Calcutta's
Missionaries of Charity

When I Said 'I Do'

When I said I do, I had no clue
what I'd be doing,
The mystery, how it would be,
or what the future would bring.

REFRAIN
Now looking back through all the years,
Smiling still after so many tears,
I know the prize was worth the price,
The joy is greater than the sacrifice.

God's love would give, time and again,
new life for us to welcome in,
The babies laughed, the children played,
they grew up strong and good just like I'd prayed.

[REFRAIN]

Now my life has proved, my words were true,
my commitment kept no matter what we went through.
Some have regrets, for their own choice,
but as for me, I only rejoice!

[REFRAIN & VERSE ONE]

What I have now is a family,
Something that will last for eternity.

O what has become of me? In giving all <u>I am set free</u>.

I said "I do" to you; if I could do it again,
it's the only thing I'd do.

The above song written and composed by the celibate Catholic Corps Women's Community of the Apostolate for Family Consecration in honor of their beloved co-founder, Mrs. Coniker ("Mama C"), who lived and breathed the virtue of charity and whose motto was "love is patient, love is kind, love never ends." For this song, ask for audiotape #198-659A. For more videos and audios on the life of Gwen, ask for "A Tribute to Gwen Coniker: Wife, Mother, Co-founder," (#164-486V), "Gwen Coniker: A Mother Giving to the Lord with No Regrets,"(#164-563), "A Tribute to Gwen Coniker" (#155-168), "To My Greatest Treasure, My Family" (#155-170), "Love and Peace Forever" (#155-171), and "Gwen's Funeral Mass" (#107-128). For a booklet on Gwen, ask for "Gwen's Way of Living" (#328-61).   www.familyland.org

Please be loyal to the following benefactors who have made it possible to print this prayer book.

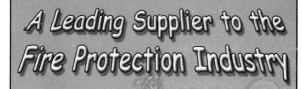

602

Illustration Index

Subject Index

Letter from Mother Teresa of Calcutta
*who gave us the key for achieving our vision
through our mission and outreach programs*

MISSIONARIES OF CHARITY

JMJ.

23/3/92

Dear Jerry and Gwen Coniker,
Thank you for your
kind letter and prayers
for me. I am well thank God
It will be a real gift of
God if the adoration of
the Bl. Sacrament could
fully penetrate family life
The holy hour as family
prayer in our Society has
been the greatest gift of God.
"Be Not afraid" Our Lord will
always be with you
Bring prayer as much as
possible into the family life
Consecration to the Sacred
Heart and Rosary family - Very
pleasing to the Heart of Jesus
Keep praying for our Society, our
Poor + me.
God bless you
M Teresa

Mother Teresa and the Coniker family at The Apostolate's center in 1981

Mother Teresa and Gwen Coniker (mother of 13) in 1988

620

Letter from Pope John Paul II
read by his Ambassador,
Archbishop Cacciavillan, at the
Family Apostolate's annual
Totus Tuus Conference™.

I have learned with pleasure that on October 22-24, the Apostolate for Family Consecration will sponsor a Conference in Pittsburgh on the theme "Consecrate Them in Truth." I would ask you kindly to convey to all associated with this worthy initiative my greetings and the assurance of my closeness in prayer.

Since the Conference aims to support and implement the message of the recent World Youth Day, I renew the invitation which I made in Denver: "I ask you to have the **courage to commit yourselves to the truth**. Have the **courage to believe the Good News about Life** which Jesus teaches in the Gospel. Open your minds and hearts to the beauty of all that God has made and to his special, personal love for each one of you" (Vigil, August 14, 1993, No.4).

It is my hope that the Conference will inspire many Christian families to become ever more authentic "domestic Churches," in which the word of God is received with joy, bears fruit in lives of holiness and love, and shines forth with new brilliance as a beacon of hope for all to see. The faith-filled witness of Christian families is an essential element in the new evangelization to which the Holy Spirit is calling the Church in our time.

I am pleased that the Conference will seek to develop effective means of passing on to families and parishes the rich deposit of the Church's faith as presented in the *Catechism of the Catholic Church*. Because "family catechesis precedes, accompanies and enriches all other forms of catechesis" (Catechesi Tradendae, 68), **I encourage the Apostolate for Family Consecration in its efforts to promote an effective catechesis in homes and parishes.**

With these sentiments, I commend the work of the Conference to the intercession of Mary, Mother of the Church. To the organizers, speakers and participants I cordially impart my Apostolic Blessing, which I willingly extend to all the members of their families.

From the Vatican, October 10, 1993

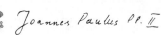

Joannes Paulus PP. II